MISIA

MISIA

THE LIFE OF MISIA SERT

BY ARTHUR GOLD
AND ROBERT FIZDALE

VINTAGE BOOKS • A DIVISION OF RANDOM HOUSE, INC. • NEW YORK

FIRST VINTAGE BOOKS EDITION,
DECEMBER 1992

Copyright © 1980 by Arthur Gold and Robert Fizdale

All picture and photographic credits, as well as other pertinent information about the illustrations, appear on pages ix-x. Other acknowledgments appear on pages xi-xii and on page 320.

Library of Congress Cataloging-in-Publication Data
Gold, Arthur.
Misia: the life of Misia Sert / Arthur Gold, Robert Fizdale. — 1st Vintage Books ed.
p.   cm.
Originally published: New York: Knopf, 1980.
Includes bibliographical references and index.
ISBN 0-679-74186-0 (pbk.)
1. Sert, Misia, 1872-1950.   2. Poles—France—Paris—Biography.
3. Paris (France)—Biography.   4. Arts—France—Paris—History.
I. Fizdale, Robert.   II. Title.
[DC705.S47G65   1992]
944′.36081′092—dc20
[B]   91-51189
CIP

Manufactured in the United States of America
10   9   8   7   6   5   4   3   2   1

TO FIVE EXTRAORDINARY WOMEN:

EUGENIA DELAROVA DOLL,
ROSE FIZDALE,
DENISE MAYER,
CHRISTOPHE DE MENIL,
AND
ANNETTE VAILLANT

Contents

Illustrations

All unacknowledged photographs in this section were taken by Alfred Natanson at Villeneuve-sur-Yonne; from the archives of Annette Vaillant.

Cyprien Godebski (Paul Uldace Collection) / Misia, age two (Boris Kochno Collection) / Misia's stepsister, Misia, and her brothers (Uldace Collection) / Misia and Thadée Natanson / Misia / Thadée and Misia / Le Relais / Misia in costume / Misia in front of Le Relais / Misia in the garden / Cipa Godebski, Vallotton, Vuillard, Stéphane Natanson, Marthe Mellot, Thadée, and Misia / The fan Mallarmé inscribed to Misia (Uldace Collection) / Drawing of Mallarmé by Misia (photograph by Anne de Brunhoff) / At Le Relais after Mallarmé's funeral / Bonnard / Vallotton / Vuillard / Thadée, Vallotton, Romain Coolus, and Cipa / Misia and Henri de Toulouse-Lautrec / Colette (Uldace Collection) / Renoir (Uldace Collection) / Misia by Toulouse-Lautrec (Uldace Collection).

COLOR PLATES FOLLOWING PAGE 114

Madame Thadée Natanson au Théâtre (gouache on cardboard, detail. Metropolitan Museum of Art. Gift of anonymous donors, subject to a life estate of the donors) / *Misia au Piano* (oil on canvas. Private collection, Switzerland)† / *Madame Misia Natanson au Piano* (oil on cardboard. Museum of Fine Arts, Berne, Donation of Hilde Thannhauser) / *A Table Chez M. et Mme. Natanson* (Vuillard, Misia, Vallotton, and Thadée; oil, gouache, and pastel on board. John A. and Audrey Jones Beck Collection, Museum of Fine Arts, Houston) / *Misia Natanson* (oil on board. Private collection, New York) * / *La Musique* (Misia at the piano, surrounded by her niece Mimi, nephew Jean, and sister-in-law Ida Godebska; distemper on canvas. Musée du Petit Palais, Paris. Photo: Bulloz)† / *Misia et Thadée Natanson* (oil on paper mounted on canvas. Museum of Modern Art, New York, Gift of Nate B. and Frances Spingold)† / *La Revue Blanche* (color poster. Herbert Schimmel Collection, New York) / *Dans le Jardin* (oil on canvas. Private collection, on loan to the Kimbell Art Museum, Fort Worth; photograph by Bob Wharton)† / *Misia et Vallotton* (oil on cardboard. Private collection, New York)† / *Misia et Thadée Natanson* (Oil. Musées Royaux des Beaux-Arts de Belgique)† / *Misia* (oil on canvas. The Tel Aviv Museum, Gift of Dr. Herman Lorber, New York) * / *Portrait de Misia* (oil on canvas. Reproduced courtesy of the Trustees, The National Gallery, London) * / *Misia aux Roses* (oil on canvas, Mrs. James Stewart Hooker Collection, Palm Beach) * / *Misia à son Bureau* (tempera on cardboard. Private collection, Paris) * / *Misa sur un Canapé* (oil on canvas. Chrysler Museum, Norfolk, Virginia) * / *Les Tasses Noires* (oil on canvas. Private collection, Paris).†

FOLLOWING PAGE 242

On the deck of the *Aimée* (Paul Uldace Collection) / Alfred Edwards (Uldace Collection) / Misia during World War I (Uldace Collection) / Geneviève Lantelme (Gold and Fizdale Collection) / Sert and Misia with the daughters of Alexandre Benois (photograph by Igor Stravinsky, 1914; Vera Stravinsky Collection) / José-Maria Sert (Uldace Collection) / The Sert apartment (Uldace Collection) / A Sert mural from Kent House / Marie Laurencin's drawing of Misia (Uldace Collection) / Misia's passport photograph (Jenny Bradley Collection) / *Misia Godebska de Profil* (charcoal on cardboard. The Louvre, courtesy Musées Nationaux, Paris) * / *Le Ronde Célèbre* (pen and india ink. Private collection, New York) / Cocteau's drawing of Sert, Massine, Misia, and Diaghilev (photograph by Anne de Brunhoff) * / Roussy Mdivani and Serge Lifar (Bobsy Goodspeed Chapman Collection) / Leonide Massine (Uldace Collection) / Misia and Diaghilev (Uldace Collection) / The Lido (Count Henri de Beaumont Collection) / Chanel and Misia (Lilian Grumbach Collection) / Chanel (photograph by Horst) / Jean Cocteau (photograph by Man Ray) / Erik Satie (Private Collection, New York) / Marcel Proust (Private collection, New York / Igor Stravinsky (Vera Stravinsky Collection) / Diaghilev's funeral (Vera Stravinsky Collection) / Misia with Mimi (photograph by André Ostier).

* S.P.A.D.E.M., Paris. 1979.
† © 1992 ARS, N.Y./SPADEM, Paris

Authors' Note

WE ARE EXTREMELY GRATEFUL TO Marie-Louise Ristelhueber and Paul Uldace for permission to quote from the writings of Misia and Boulos. Special thanks are due to the following people for their invaluable help: Jenny Bradley, François Daulte, Denise Mayer, Annette Vaillant, and Liliane Ziegel.

We should also like to thank Lady Ia Abdy, the late Juliette Achard, M. and Mme. Georges Auric, George Balanchine, Carl Paul Barbier, Comte Henri de Beaumont, Anka Begley, the late Fira Benenson (Countess Ilinska), Diane Benvenuti, Bettina Bergery, Antoinette Bernstein, Pierre Bertin, Aiméry Blacque-Belair, Thierry Bodin, Marie-Claude de Brunhoff, Richard Buckle, Gilbert Cahen-Salvador, Jean Cahen-Salvador, Comte Alexandre de Castéja, Contessa Cesare Celani, Bobsy Goodspeed Chapman, François Chapon, Doda Conrad, Douglas Cooper, Robert Craft, Count Joseph Czapski, Alexandra Danilova, Lucia Davidova, Alice Delamar, Edouard Dermit, Anton Dolin, Parmenia Migel Ekstrom, Prince Jean Faucigny-Lucinge, Jacques Février, Roy Fisher, Pierre Georgel, Comte Hubert de Givenchy, Jean Godebski, the late Maurice Goudeket, the late Lydia Gregory, George Gruber, Lilian Grumbach, Baron Nicolas de Guinsburg, the late Anthony Harwood, Horst, Jean Hugo, Mme. Henry Kapferer, Boris Kochno, Ewa Kossak, Joseph Lafosse-Satie, Serge Lifar, Contessa Marina Lulling-Volpi, Leïla Mabilleau, Suzanne Mante-Proust, Igor Markevitch, the late Léonide Massine, the late Darius Milhaud, Madeleine Milhaud, Hervé Mille, the late Paul Morand, Jan Mycinski, the late Nicolas Nabokov, Raymond Nacenta, Renée Claudel Nantet, Vicomte Charles de Noailles, André Ostier, Gaston Palewski, Simone Porché, Jacques Porel, René Radiguet, Vittorio Rieti, Liouba Roland-Pallu, Antoine Salomon, Jacques Salomon, Henri Sauguet, Hélène Schopfer-Fol, José Luis Sert, Flora Solomon, Vera Stravinsky, the late Mme. Léopold Survage, Germaine Tailleferre, Charles Terrasse, François Valéry, Agathe Valéry-Rouart, the late Duca Fulco di Verdura, Diana Vreeland, and Jean Wiener.

For reproducing photographs, paintings, and documents we thank the following photographers: Anne de Brunhoff, Larry Bercow, J. E. Bulloz, and J.-L. Charmet. Special thanks to Horst and to André Ostier for permission to reprint their photographs of Misia.

For help with research we thank Dominique Paulvé and Nancy Rosen; for valuable editorial assistance, Mary Barnett, Martha Kaplan, and Neal T. Jones. Special thanks to our editor, Robert Gottlieb, for invaluable advice and understanding.

We thank the following institutions: in Paris, the Bibliothèque de l'Arsenal, the Bibliothèque Nationale, the Bibliothèque Littéraire Jacques Doucet de l'Université de Paris, the Bibliothèque Polonaise; in New York, the Museum of Modern Art and its Department of Film, the Metropolitan Museum (Library), the New York Public Library (Library of the Performing Arts), the Spanish Institute, and the Stravinsky-Diaghilev Foundation. Special thanks to Trapezoid, Inc., for permission to publish the letters of Igor Stravinsky, and to the Juilliard School for encouragement and support. Other publishers and individuals to whom our appreciation goes are listed on page 320.

We owe an enormous debt of gratitude to Francis Steegmuller and to his publishers, Little, Brown (Boston) and Macmillan (London), for permission to quote, from his biography of Cocteau, his translations of the following passages: Cocteau's statement about *Parade* on page 183, the letter from Satie to Cocteau on page 186, the two letters on page 187, the letters from Cocteau and from Satie to Valentine Gross on page 189, the letters from Cocteau and Satie on pages 190, 191, 192, and 193, and the last four sentences of the letter from Cocteau to Misia on page 196. We also thank Random House for permission to quote C. K. Scott Moncrieff's translations of excerpts from Marcel Proust's *Remembrance of Things Past*. In all other cases translations from the French are our own.

MISIA

Prologue

à *Misia Sert*

LA VALSE

Poème chorégraphique pour Orchestre

Des nuées tourbillonnantes laissent entrevoir, par éclaircies, des couples de valseurs. Elles se dissipent peu à peu: on distingue une immense salle peuplée d'une foule tournoyante. . . .

To *Misia Sert*

LA VALSE

Choreographic Poem for Orchestra

Eddying clouds give glimpses, through rifts, of waltzing couples. The clouds gradually scatter, and an immense hall can be seen, filled with a whirling crowd. . . .

—MAURICE RAVEL

In the year 1880, a young girl looks down from the balcony of Madame Maurice's boarding school on the avenue Niel in Paris. With her rounded arms resting on the iron railing, her dark eyes and radiant complexion framed by chestnut-colored curls, she is the essence of the pensive Renoir child.

An organ-grinder appears, trundling his instrument down the quiet street. He sees the girl, stops, assumes the organ-grinder's inimitable wide-legged stance, and serenades her with a popular tune. The girl listens with rapt attention, then disappears into the house. A moment later she returns and tosses a trinket to her musician friend. He catches it neatly in mid-air. It is a little gold pig, the child's most treasured possession. The swarthy musician removes his hat, looks up at the girl intently, and slowly makes his way down the street.

An ardent glance, the thrillingly dissonant wheeze of a mechanical organ, an impulsive, extravagant gesture, and Misia's career as a patron of the arts begins.

The child, grown up, became not only a patron of the arts but a muse, an inspiration to artists. A glittering portrait of her appeared many years later in Marcel Proust's *Remembrance of Things Past.* In an evocation of those magical years when Paris saw the "prodigious flowering of the Ballets Russes, revealing one after another, Bakst, Nijinsky, Benois, the genius of Stravinsky," Proust described Misia, transforming her into the "Princess Yourbeletieff, the youthful sponsor of all these new great men," who appeared in her box at the ballet "bearing on her head an immense, quivering aigrette, unknown to the women of Paris, which they all sought to copy. One might have supposed," he added, "that this marvellous creature had been imported in their innumerable baggage, and as their most priceless treasure, by the Russian dancers." In characteristic fashion Proust made Misia a princess. Although not a princess—in her three marriages she was simply Madame Thadée Natanson, Madame Alfred Edwards, and Madame José-Maria Sert—her charm was so captivating and her temperament so commanding that, like royalty, she was known to the world by a single name —Misia.

Few characters in Proust escape his malice. In the same way that Odilon Redon, at one time Misia's country neighbor, adds to a flower painting of mysterious beyondness an acid touch of green that gives it surprising potency, Proust, in a moment of double vision, saw Misia as two characters. He portrayed her as Princess Yourbeletieff, whom he finds as dazzling and seductive as the Ballets Russes itself, but he also used her as one of the models for Madame Verdurin, that unpleasant *arriviste* whom he acidly refers to as the "boss." When he goes on to describe how Madame Verdurin rose to her unique position in Parisian society through a combination of good luck and canny maneuvering, he is in a way tracing Misia's own career.

Proust was by no means the first man of genius who responded to the "marvellous creature" born Marie Godebska. When she was a child, her dark-eyed vitality and pianistic gifts delighted both Liszt and Fauré. As a young bride she was the friend and model of Vuillard, Bonnard, Toulouse-Lautrec, and Renoir. Each of them painted her many times. Later, as Diaghilev's closest Parisian friend, she sat enthroned at his side, the *éminence rose* of the Ballets Russes.

To know Misia was a card of admission to Diaghilev's circle, for she was one of the few women whose opinion he valued and whose advice he sought. In the first season of the Ballets Russes, young Jean Cocteau, eager to be a part of the troupe, ambitious to create stories for the Diaghilev ballets and hopeful that Misia would use her influence on his behalf, became her protégé. He was a protégé whom she alternately helped and hindered, coddled and tormented. Cocteau was to make Misia the heroine of his First World War novel, *Thomas l'Imposteur*. No one has described better than he Misia's unique charm, her insouciance, her *sans-gêne*. Like Proust, he chose to think of her as a noblewoman:

The Princesse de Bormes was Polish. Poland is the country of pianists. She played with life the way a virtuoso plays the piano. Like a virtuoso, she was able to create great effects as easily with mediocre as with the most beautiful music. Her duty was pleasure. It was thus that this excellent woman could say, "I don't like the poor. I hate the sick." It is hardly astonishing that these words were considered scandalous.

She wanted to be amused and she knew how to be. She had understood, unlike most women in her set, that pleasure is not to be found in things themselves but in the way you take them. This attitude demands robust health. Over forty, she had sparkling eyes in the face of a young girl, eyes that boredom could deaden in a second. Therefore she avoided boredom and enjoyed a good laugh, which other women avoided because it causes wrinkles. Her health, her gusto for life, and the singularity of her clothes, her manner, and the way she walked gave her an extraordinary reputation.

Actually she was purity and nobility itself. It was exactly this that confused people for whom nobility and purity were sacred objects whose usage was sacrilege. For the princess did use them, made them supple, and gave them a new luster. She molded virtue to her uses the way elegance molds a new suit that is too stiff, and beauty of soul was so natural to her that no one noticed she had it.

After the Second World War, Misia, in her late seventies, unhappy, addicted to drugs, and almost blind, dictated her memoirs to the devoted friend and companion of her last years, Boulos Ristelhueber. Although we have found the memoirs to be generally accurate, many of those friends of Misia's who shared their recollections with us spoke of her book as a "tissue of lies." Certainly much is omitted, episodes are romanticized, outlines are blurred. It was as though the files of her memory had been carelessly scattered about. The past whispered to her, but only indistinctly. Sadly enough, in her attempts to recapture the past, morphine did not work as well for Misia as the madeleine did for Proust. But after all, what she chose to remember is her essential poetic truth.

Like many attractive women, Misia lied about her age. She changed the birth date in her passport from 1872 to 1882—clumsily scratching an eight over the seven—to make herself ten years younger. And so Misia, whom Erik Satie called a magician, made the years disappear with a flick of her pen. It was the one lie that was swallowed by everyone, chroniclers and friends alike. They accepted without question her statement that she had married as soon as she reached the then "legal age of fifteen years and three months," although her first marriage certificate plainly states that she was twenty-one. Nor did anyone question her when she telescoped the four years of indecision before her second marriage into a whirlwind courtship that took no time at all.

Unlike her contemporaries across the Channel, the Bloomsbury group, whose reactions to every social issue, every artistic current—even every shared cup of tea and each moment of constipation—were recorded in conflicting versions in their journals and discussed in their witty and sometimes anguished letters, Misia kept no journal and wrote few letters. She allowed many of the thousands of letters she received to disappear, just as she allowed the drawings that Toulouse-Lautrec made at her dining table to be swept away with the crumbs. Therefore this story will be as unofficial as Misia herself. Sometimes we shall be looking at Misia, and sometimes we shall be looking over her shoulder at the things she saw and the people she knew, at those she wrote about and those who wrote about her.

Misia rarely spoke of the past. She lived for the moment and made an art of it. Her salon was an informal theatre that changed its casts and its meanings with the changes in her life. The young diplomat Paul Morand in his *Journal d'un Attaché d'Ambassade* describes a visit he made to Proust— Proust in bed in a room so cold that Morand had to keep his fur-lined coat on. Proust spoke of Misia as a "historical monument." Morand adds, "In fact, Misia is a monument brought from a distant country to Paris, like the obelisk, and placed at the center of French taste, just as the Needle of Luxor is at the center of the Champs-Elysées."

PART ONE

Misia

Overleaf, Misia Godebska, c. 1890

. . . these Russian ladies whom Prometheus must have fashioned from one of the blocks of ice he had found on the Caucasus, and one of the rays of sunlight he had stolen from Jupiter . . . these ladies endowed with a fineness of sensibility and an intuition far above the average, which they owe to their double inheritance as Asiatics and Europeans, to their cosmopolitan curiosity, and their indolent habits . . . these strange creatures who speak every language, hunt the bear, live off sweets, and laugh in the face of every man who cannot master them . . . these females with voices at once musical and hoarse, superstitious and skeptical, fawning and fierce, who bear the indelible mark of the country of their origin, who defy all analysis, and every attempt to imitate them.

—ALEXANDRE DUMAS *fils*,
translated by Gerard Hopkins

The Godebskis are an ancient Polish family. Their coat of arms—crossed pine branches, which evoke the dark and endless Polish forests—was given to a warrior ancestor in 1004. Through the centuries they were soldiers and jurists, court chamberlains and government officials. Then in the eighteenth and nineteenth centuries, writers and artists began to flower on the branches of the family tree. Misia's great-grandfather Cyprien, a legionnaire in Napoleon's army, was a well-known poet. Her grandfather François Xavier was an impassioned patriot. Like many others involved in the struggle for Polish independence, he emigrated to France, where the Godebski family has lived ever since. A theatre man, François Xavier wrote light comedies, vaudeville sketches, ballet and opera librettos. As a Rossini patter song might put it, the French translation of the Italian libretto of Rossini's opera *The Turk in Italy* was written by this Pole in France.

Misia's father, the sculptor Cyprien Godebski, was born in France at Méry-sur-Cher in 1835. Curiously enough, there were no great sculptors in the middle of the nineteenth century except for Rodin. But what extraordinary men there were in the other arts! Degas, Monet, Manet, Pissarro, Renoir, Verlaine, Mallarmé, Ibsen, and Tolstoy all were born within ten years of Godebski's birth. Their works had an originality and a force that carried into the twentieth century and so were part of Misia's world. Misia's father, on the other hand, was one of those gifted but academic artists whose work showed more industry than inspiration, more métier than meaning. To channel the emotions of his viewers Godebski gave his pieces such delirious titles as *Brute Force Strangling Genius* and *Poland, the Awakening*. Visitors to the Paris Salon of 1864, where *Poland, the Awakening* was shown, were undoubtedly moved by the melodramatic aspects of sculpture which seems mock-heroic to us now. The opaline light of Paris filtered down through the glass roofs of the exhibition rooms on statues that aroused the powerful emotions so fashionable at the time—hope and despair, exaltation and dejection. Such grand concepts as tyranny, patriotism, and liberty were, titillatingly enough in that overclothed age, symbolized by the naked bodies of muscular men and rotund women, a forest of writhing, wildly gesticulating figures, their eyes rolling heavenward. With his good looks and his slavic charm, Cyprien Godebski was a master at arranging commissions for public monuments. Back and forth he travelled: from France to Poland, from Austria to Belgium, from Russia to Italy, where, in his grandiose aspiration to the Michelangesque, he bought a marble quarry in Carrara.

What energy nineteenth-century artists had! Cyprien Godebski must have worked as relentlessly as Balzac, if not with the same splendid results. Yet how curious is the fate of the Cypriens of the world. They think deep thoughts. They lead fascinating lives. They meet everyone they care to know. Their faith in their talent is confirmed by the rewards they receive. They are sought after, praised, and well paid. But when they die, they leave little of lasting interest. Yet Godebski's works are scattered everywhere. Sailors who have maneuvered their way through the treacherous waters of the Pointe du Raz in Brittany are welcomed by a monument rising from the sea like the Statue of Liberty. They see the Virgin, the Holy Child, and a poor shipwrecked sailor with arms outstretched whom the stormy waters seem to have cast at their feet. Godebski statues also gaze down at those other adventurers at the mercy of chance, the gamblers at the casino in Monte Carlo. In Warsaw there is Cyprien's sensitive bust of the great Polish poet Adam Mickiewicz, and in Lima, Peru, his monumental statue of the revolutionary leader General San Martín. In Paris he worked on the restoration of the Louvre, which also bought some of his sculptures. These statues are now peacefully at rest in the basement, along with other forgotten works of art.*

As a young man Godebski was romantically handsome, with strong, regular features and long hair swept back à la Liszt. A fashionable success, he had that air of confident sexuality which elicited respect from men and was often fatal to women. With the self-assurance of the nineteenth-century egotist, he gravitated naturally to center-stage, a place he occupied with engaging ease. He earned a great deal of money, led the good life, had an unerring eye for the main chance and a gift for falling in love with rich women. Equally at home with artists and aristocrats, he was happiest at the luxuriant crossroads where their two worlds meet. Godebski knew everyone. Dumas *fils*, Théophile Gautier, and Alphonse Daudet were his friends, as were Franz Liszt, Gabriel Fauré, and Gioacchino Rossini (whose bust won Godebski an honorable mention at the 1866 Paris Salon). They and their friends were his world—the world of haute bohème. A fascinating storyteller, in later years Cyprien was to amuse his children with tales and gossip about his celebrated friends.

Godebski shared his contemporaries' attitudes toward women. Conversation about sex was for men only, and a good deal of chest-thumping exaggeration went with it. Dumas *père* boasted that if he were alone in a room with five women and a play to write, at the end of an hour he would have written all five acts and had all five women. Gautier prided himself on being able to solve complicated mathematical problems while making love. Gustave Flaubert had casually lit and smoked a cigar while having sex with a whore. Real women, he said, were no more to him than a couch on which lay the woman of his dreams. But sex of course was not their only diversion. They enjoyed drink, food (Daudet's wife and Dumas *père* each wrote a cookbook), and the social pleasures of salon and café. There they practised that other art, conversation—conversation that was mordant, daring, and endlessly brilliant.

Speaking of his seventeen children, Gautier said, "It's curious; I don't

* Recently at La Foire à la Ferraille et au Jambon, the fair of old iron and country hams at La Villette on the outskirts of Paris, we found a handsome, larger than life bas-relief of a French countess, a skillfully wrought lace shawl covering her shoulders. Elaborately framed and signed Godebski, it was leaning against an old commode among the bric-a-brac. The price was impressive.

think of myself as a father at all. I'm kind to my children. I love them, but not as my children. They are there beside me, they are my branches, that is all." From the indifferent way in which he brought up his children, Godebski himself might have spoken these words.

Misia's maternal grandfather, Adrien-François Servais, was one of the most celebrated cellists of his time. The son of a poor church musician, who gave him his first lessons, Servais was born and died in the town of Halle near Brussels. When he was a student, fortune appeared in the form of a patron, the Marquis de Sayve, and the boy was on his way. But marquis or no marquis, three times a week he walked all the way to Brussels, his cello on his back, in order to study at the Royal Conversatory of Music. In less than a year he won first prize. By the time he was thirty he had given concerts in every corner of Europe and composed many works for the cello. Some of them, such as the *Grand Fantasy on Motifs from Rossini's Opera The Barber of Seville* and the *Souvenir de Spa*, are still performed.

Servais' playing was admired everywhere, but nowhere with greater enthusiasm than in Russia. In St. Petersburg he met Sophie Féguine, the pretty young daughter of a prosperous, music-loving Jewish family that had been converted to Christianity. By now Servais was considered the most brilliant cellist in the world. Honors were heaped on him: he was made cellist to the King of Belgium and to the Emperor of Austria. Proudly wearing the poppy-red ribbon of the Order of Leopold, he married Mademoiselle Féguine in 1842. He was thirty-five, she twenty-two. In Halle they built a vast villa in the Italian style and settled down to a life of music, family, and friends. They produced three daughters, Sophie, Marie, and Augusta, and two sons, Franz and Joseph. Franz became a composer and conductor, Joseph a cellist like his father.

The Servaises entertained in a manner almost unimaginable today. The house brimmed over with friends and relatives, many of whom lingered on for months at a time. Among them were Franz Liszt and Hector Berlioz, the pianist Anton Rubinstein, the violinist Henri Vieuxtemps—who together with Servais composed a *Duo for Violin and Violoncello*—and the conductors

Hans Richter, Hans von Bülow, and Charles Lamoureux. One of the guests who made a more lasting impression than most was Cyprien Godebski. Invited to decorate the villa, he fell in love with the eldest daughter. And so it was that on January 23, 1865, two distinguished artistic families were united when the thirty-year-old sculptor Cyprien Quentin Godebski married the cellist's twenty-two-year-old daughter, Eugénie Sophie Léopoldine Servais.*

A wonderful life was predicted for the bride and groom. It seemed only natural for them to live with her parents, as Cyprien's work often took him away, and the Servaises were delighted to keep their daughter at home. Sophie's father died a year after the wedding, but new life came to the house in the next few years with the births of Sophie's two sons, Franz and Ernest. Then in 1871 Cyprien was invited to Russia to make sculptural decorations for Princess Yusupov's summer palace at Tsarskoë Selo near St. Petersburg. As this meant a long separation, Sophie was thankful to be in her mother's house, especially when after a few months she found that she was pregnant once again.

Godebski had left for Russia armed with letters of introduction to Tsar Alexander and to his mother-in-law's family. The Féguines welcomed their new relation with open arms, unfortunately only too open in the case of his aunt by marriage, his mother-in-law's attractive young sister Olga. In no time they were lovers and soon Olga too was pregnant. Cyprien of course did not refer to this somewhat incestuous state of affairs in the letters he wrote his wife. How she looked forward to them! One day, opening the eagerly awaited envelope with its Imperial Russian stamp, Sophie found a mysterious scrawl denouncing Cyprien. Through her tears she read that her husband and her aunt were lovers and that they too were expecting a child. Her daughter Misia later wrote about this dramatic episode in her memoirs:

> Her decision was made in an instant, and the same evening, after having kissed her two little boys good-bye, she left to travel the three thousand kilometers which separated her from the man she adored. She was more than eight months pregnant.
>
> God knows by what miracle Sophie Godebska managed, in the

---

* Sophie's youngest sister, Augusta, later married the celebrated Wagnerian tenor Ernest van Dyck.

glacial Russian winter, to reach the end of her journey, an isolated house buried in snow!

She climbed the flight of steps leading to the house, but before ringing the bell she leaned against the doorway to catch her breath. The sound of laughter, laughter which she recognized, came to her through the closed door. After the superhuman effort which love alone had given her the strength to perform, she was overcome by an immeasurable weariness, an agonizing feeling of despair. Her hand hesitated.

The following day her husband, notified of her presence, arrived just in time to see her die as she was giving birth to me. The drama of my birth left a deep mark on my destiny.

It left a deep mark on Misia's grandmother as well. Sophie Servais reproached herself bitterly; if only she had forbidden her daughter to go to Russia, surely she would still be alive. It was incredible that her son-in-law and her own sister had behaved so monstrously. Grief over her daughter's death and shame at the family scandal intensified the feelings of the warm-hearted Russian woman for the granddaughter she had not yet seen. To her father, however, Misia was just a helpless bundle of linen, an unwanted burden. In his egotistical way he gave his mistress the responsibility for taking care of Misia as well as of their illegitimate child, then went about his work. And so it was Misia who became the intruder in this peculiar domestic situation. A perverse pattern was set that persisted throughout her life. Attracted to virile, artistic men with an overpowering presence and a suggestion of the monstrous, Misia was apt to feel that she loved them most when they, like her father, abandoned her for another woman.

Misia, born in St. Petersburg on March 30, 1872, was christened Marie Sophie Olga Zenaïde Godebska. Her first photographs were taken before she was two years old. With a kitten's curiosity she stares out at what must have seemed a man with a black box for a head, his arm reaching out to squeeze the bulb of a magic machine: a Magritte before the fact. Mounted on gray cardboard with the legend "St. Petersburg" in flowing gold script, the sepia photographs of the beguiling little girl speak of a comfortable nineteenth-century childhood.

What person who spent even his earliest years in St. Petersburg is not filled with nostalgic love for its half-remembered images: images as intangibly real as icy landscapes traced by a child's fingernail on a frosty window pane? The endless star-shaped flakes of snow, sometimes soft and silent, sometimes lifted like confetti by sudden gusts of wind, fell on little Misia. Wrapped up like a woolly cocoon, she was led by her mittened hand through streets lined with pastel palaces, thoroughfares where troikas scudded by, where smart one-horse sleds were driven by gentlemen in furs, where coachmen slapped their arms briskly across their chests, their steamy breath visible in the falling snow. And when the weather turned warm and nurses paraded their charges in English prams in the Summer Park, did the infant Misia look unblinkingly, the way infants will, at a child called Serge Diaghilev being perambulated in the opposite direction? Serge was born in Perm in the same year and the same month as Misia—in fact, only eleven days earlier. Did he already have his air of speculative amusement? And did each already possess the love of beauty and the passion for intrigue that drew them together when they were formally introduced thirty-six years later in Paris?

Cyprien Godebski did not allow his equivocal family situation to interfere with his thriving career. Certainly he lost no time hovering over the two cradles. Appointed professor at the Academy of Fine Arts for two years, he did sculpture-portraits of Tsar Alexander II, the Imperial Family, and the great men in government. He even did busts of Bach and Beethoven for good measure. Tireless in work as in love, he travelled far and wide. In Sebastopol he made a memorial monument to the soldiers killed in the Crimean War. And in Warsaw he made a romantic conquest—of Matylda Natanson, the widow of a prosperous Jewish banker. She too was a sculptor and a gifted pianist as well. It was not long before Cyprien took her off to Italy, where they were married. She brought as her dowry her fortune, her intelligence, and her two attractive but unfortunate children: an epileptic son, Isaac, and a consumptive daughter named Claire. The Godebski salon, elegantly run in the French style, quickly became the talk of Warsaw; Matylda's friends, the great actress Helena Modjeska and Henryk Sienkiewicz (author of *Quo Vadis?*) were two of its most brilliant attractions.

Now that Cyprien was settled in Poland, it was arranged for Misia to live in Belgium with her grandmother and her brothers. For the next few years the motherless girl was surrounded by love. Misia adored the small, pretty woman covered with jewels who fussed over her and dressed her in beautiful clothes. And everything about her grandmother's luxurious Victorian villa intrigued the child. There were so many rooms to explore—rooms filled with ornate furniture and the delicious smell of wax. It was a house of music; the massive pianos that stood everywhere were rarely silent. Beethoven, Liszt, and above all the avant-garde Wagner were the household gods. Solemn and attentive, Misia would stand in a corner transfixed, listening to the music. One day she climbed up onto a piano stool. Her feet dangling in the air, she astonished everyone by beginning to play in the inexplicable way of child prodigies. She could make out her notes before she could read or write.

What joy it gave her grandmother to see Misia, so pretty and clever, show musical talent as well! It seemed to Sophie Servais that her husband's musical gifts had been reborn in their little granddaughter. Grandmother would take her into the vast, high-ceilinged salon decorated with allegorical figures and, pointing to St. Cecilia at the organ and King David with his harp, would tell her stirring tales of those legendary musicians. Legendary, too, were the stories about her grandfather. She would be handed the crown of golden laurel leaves, so heavy the child could barely lift it, one of many gifts given him by admiring ladies. And when she was taken to church, there in the church square stood the statue her father had made of the grandfather she had never known.* As Grandfather had been cellist to King Leopold, the fragrant, elegant lady for whom Misia did her best curtsey when she came to drink white coffee with Grandmother was Queen Marie-Henriette.

Sophie Servais was hospitality itself and entertained at Halle as though she were living on a great Russian estate. If there was anything she enjoyed more than listening to her celebrated guests play the piano, it was feeding them. Hours were spent planning the menus for the endless succession of elaborate meals. Misia would steal into the larger of the two dining rooms, the one with Chinese pictures, where the sumptuous, lace-covered table, heavy

---

* Even today pilgrims who visit the fourteenth-century church of St. Martin often assume that the statue represents the saint and devoutly kiss the stone foot of Adrien-François Servais as he holds his marble cello.

with crystal and silver, was set for sixty. Her dark eyes shone with wonder
at the sight of hundreds of Bohemian wine glasses answering the flickering
gaslight with fiery glints. A life of worldly privilege—and Misia was never
to know any other—meant innumerable servants. There were servants pounding away washing sheets, servants making and unmaking the beds, servants
pressing everything in sight, even the shoelaces—servants starching clothes,
sewing, mending, carrying coal, wood, and water, emptying chamber pots,
waxing floors, sweeping, grooming horses, tending gardens, announcing
guests, being pinched by them in dark corners, seeing them off in their
carriages, polishing glass and silver, baking brioches and bread, cakes and
pâtés for the incredibly copious meals. Country houses were independent
little kingdoms, and Misia was the princess of the Servais realm.

Shivering with fear and delight, Misia would hold tight to her brothers'
hands when they took her down to explore the enormous vaulted cellars of
the house. There they would see huge tubs of butter, casks of wine, hundreds
of jars of preserves, hams from the Ardennes, and great rounds of cheese.
When Ernest and Franz lifted their candles, the bloody sides of beef hanging
from heavy hooks in the ceiling cast frightening shadows on the thick stone
walls and filled Misia with fairy-tale horror. But when they emerged into the
sunshine she was proud of having been brave. Still, what a relief it was
when they climbed into their wicker dogcart and rode laughing through the
solemn, golden countryside.

Franz Liszt made a great impression when he came to stay with the
family. Misia remembered his face "covered with warts and framed with
long hair" and a lady with him dressed as a man. Liszt was a friend not only
of the Servaises' but of her father as well. *Le Monde Illustré* published a
highly charged engraving of the two artists in Godebski's studio, with Cyprien
hammering and chiselling away while Liszt, seated at the piano, his head
thrown back, is scanning the upper reaches of the atelier in search, no doubt,
of inspiration. No woman who sat on Liszt's knee—and there were many—
seems ever to have forgotten the experience. Misia was no exception.
Enthroned on the mighty lap, the child prodigy played Beethoven for him
and her grandmother's other guests. Everyone was wreathed in music-loving
smiles. "Ah, if only I could play like that," said the most brilliant pianist
of his day and, old charmer that he was, promptly predicted a great future
for her.

In Halle, Misia discovered the heady delights of melodrama and gossip.

The villa was filled with whispers and assignations, all to the strains of Wagner's latest opera. Misia never forgot the night that the consumptive Polish pianist Zarembski, wearing a billowing white silk shirt and a black velvet waistcoat, staggered into the dimly lit music room, played a few measures of Chopin's Funeral March, collapsed on the keyboard, and died. Going up to bed each night. Misia passed her Uncle Franz standing in the shadows of his room, the Stradivarius his father had given him held to his ear. Like the ghost of Paganini, he was listening to otherworldly sounds only he could hear. There were rumors about Franz that the child did not understand. It was said that this Hoffmannesque figure was the illegitimate son of Liszt, a distinction claimed by an improbably large number of musicians. When her uncle died, Misia was told that he had accidentally shot himself while cleaning his gun after a day of hunting with the Prince de Caraman-Chimay. Later she learned the truth: Franz had committed suicide when his love affair with the wife of the director of the Royal Conservatory of Music had been indiscreetly revealed by her talkative grandmother.

There was another tragic suicide in the family. One of Grandmother's Russian relatives, the beautiful young Julia Féguine, had come to Halle on a visit. Dumas *fils* met her there, fell in love, and swept her off to Paris. Despite her thick Russian accent—or perhaps because of it—he was able to persuade the Comédie Française to present her in the title role of Musset's *Barberine*, a play set in Hungary. She became the mistress of the Duc de Morny who took her with him when he was appointed ambassador to Russia. There, alas, society refused to receive her. When she returned to France she shot herself. Misia, who thrived on the excitement of personal drama, later claimed that Julia committed suicide because she discovered that her lover was engaged to be married: "When he came to see her, she was in her bath. She seized a revolver from her dressing table and ordered him not to move one step nearer and to swear that the news of his marriage was false; otherwise she would kill herself on the spot. As the duke only shrugged his shoulders, she shot herself point-blank. She was not yet twenty." Pure Sardou! It was the kind of lurid story Misia liked. But for the child these gothic tales were only deliciously frightening overtones to her happy life at Halle.

Unfortunately the Victorian idyll could not last forever. When Misia was eight, her father and stepmother moved from Warsaw to Paris, where they bought a house with Matylda's money. Soon they sent for Misia and her brothers. When the children arrived, excited and fearful, at the Gare du Nord, Cyprien picked Misia up, gave her an affectionate kiss, and studied her intently for a few moments. Then he put her down and hardly gave her another thought. Off in a hansom cab went Cyprien and his children, rolling across the bustling Seine and up the endless rue de Vaugirard to the house where Misia was to make a new life. The imposing, richly dressed woman who kissed her coldly and announced that she was her new mother frightened her. It was clear from the beginning that stepmother and stepdaughter would never get along. Used to her own submissive children, Matylda Godebska found the independent, spoiled little girl too much for her. For the first time in her life the high-spirited child had reason to be unhappy. Ernest, too, was unhappy. Both children missed their brother Franz, when he was sent to boarding school. Precociously nostalgic, they spoke longingly of their grandmother, their uncles, and the mother Misia had never known. To their new mother they presented a united front of sullen rebellion. Matylda reacted with impatient resentment—but she was not altogether heartless. Impressed by the exceptional musicality of Cyprien's children, she arranged for them to have piano lessons. These lessons gave Misia some of the happiest moments of that miserable first winter in Paris. Her only other pleasure was her ready-made half-brother Cipa, three years younger than she.

Oddly enough, Misia felt most at home when Matylda took her to visit her first husband's brother, Adam Natanson. A rich Polish-Jewish banker, Natanson had moved to Paris with his Russian wife and their sons, Alexandre, Thadée, and Alfred. Misia loved their apartment on the Place St. Michel overlooking the Seine. The slavic accents, the cozy samovar, the steaming tea in glasses with silver holders reminded her of her Russian grandmother. Above all, the friendly playfulness of the Natanson boys made her feel at home.

One day as punishment for some mischief, Ernest was locked up in his stepsister Claire's room. Playing with a gold watch that he found on her dressing table, he dropped and broke it. In a panic he threw it into the toilet, hoping against hope that it would not be missed. But of course it was, and in the good nineteenth-century way the boy was made to swear his innocence on a crucifix and on his dead mother's photograph. Flinging himself at his mother's picture, he covered it with kisses. Finally, half dead with terror, he confessed his guilt. Looking on, Misia knew that she must leave the hateful house; somehow she must get back to her grandmother. Running down the dark street with a few pennies in her pocket, she was soon caught, dragged home, and flogged. At a time when well-brought-up little girls were not even meant to look out of the window and certainly never allowed on the streets alone, Misia's attempted escape shocked Madame Godebska deeply. In her agitation she decided that Cyprien's children were beyond control and shipped Ernest and Misia off to strict boarding schools— Misia to the school of Mademoiselle Maurice in the avenue Niel. There the runaway was confined to her room for six months. It was not surprising that she hated school. To her relief, after the interminable winter she was sent back to Halle. It was the first in a series of shuntings back and forth, so often the fate of stepchildren. The only person she regretted leaving behind was Cipa. Born with one arm and leg shorter than the other, Cipa was showered with the love that Matylda denied her stepchildren. As he was younger than Misia, he was the baby, the pet, the child everyone in the family loved.

At Halle there were more guests, more food, and more Wagner than ever. Nowhere were the rites of the Wagner cult observed with more solemnity than in the Servais household. It was in fact largely owing to Uncle Franz's efforts that Wagner's operas were performed in Brussels. The great conductor Hans von Bülow, a frequent guest, spent hours playing *Parsifal* on the Servais piano. In spite of the fact that his wife Cosima (one of Liszt's few authentic illegitimate children) had left him to live with Wagner, he was still the loyal champion of the Master's music. Misia, then and later, remained dry-eyed while her uncle and his friends were moved to tears by Wagner's feverishly erotic chromaticisms. Nevertheless, the atmosphere of affluent bohemianism in the Servais circle, the life of elegance and personal anarchy led by past masters of both, had enormous appeal for Misia. When imprisoned at school or at her stepmother's she dreamt of High Bohemia as the land of freedom and happiness. And it was in that fabled land that her talents, her charm, and her high spirits would be most appreciated.

At the end of the summer of 1881 Misia was sent to Ghent to live with her mother's beautiful sister Marie and her husband, Raymond de Coster, a rich industrialist. Clearly Cyprien and Matylda were not eager to have the difficult girl with them. Besides, Aunt Marie, who had no children of her own, had grown fond of her troubled, temperamental niece and decided to adopt her. And so Misia settled into yet another home. But once again romantic tragedy intervened, this time as a sad story of provincial life. One day Misia's aunt boarded a horse-drawn tram and, looking into the eyes of the handsome conductor, felt an urgent, irresistible longing for him. She had never been in love with her stodgy husband, but to find herself attracted to a mere tram conductor, so much her social inferior, was unthinkable. Despite herself she invented excuses to take the tram so that she could be near him and perhaps even touch his hand when she paid her fare. Then one day, feeling desperately ashamed, she went to her room, closed the shutters, curled up in bed, and slowly starved herself to death.

Like all the family dramas of Misia's childhood, the story was clothed in sinister detail. She was told that when her aunt died, her legs stiffened, curled under her, and had to be broken in order to fit into the coffin. It was a bloodcurdling echo of Misia's mother's death. Now the death of her mother's sister left her homeless and unwanted once again. Sent back to Paris, she was enrolled in the school of the Convent of the Sacred Heart in the boulevard des Invalides.* There she was to remain for eight years.

From the moment Misia entered the convent school in 1882 her only thought was escape, but the long, monotonous days turned into years. The pretty dress she arrived in was taken from her. Sadly she put on the drab school uniform. The girls slept in an unheated dormitory patrolled by a nun who circulated among the narrow, uncomfortable beds to make certain that the students were not whispering or showing their affection for one another in any way. In winter they were awakened while it was still dark. Shivering with cold and half asleep, they were marched to seven o'clock mass, a sleepy celebration of candles, bells, and incense. At the end of the mysterious incantations they were taught to kneel and kiss the ground. Soon the other girls showed Misia how to trick the nuns by kissing her own hand instead. After all, they said, her body, like the earth, was only dust.

There were schoolgirl crushes on favorite teachers and conjecture about

* Now the Rodin Museum.

why the pretty younger nuns had chosen a life without men. These speculations were relieved by uncontrollable fits of laughter in the deportment class, where the dancing master, a tiny old gentleman, played waltzes and quadrilles on his miniature violin. The giggling girls were shown the complex art of the court curtsey—six steps forward and four steps back, with a plunge at the fourth step—and the even more complicated art of saying *bonjour* and *au revoir* with varying inflections. (To add *monsieur* after *bonjour* was a subtle indication that one was speaking to an inferior.) Cyprien asked that Misia be given a bath every week. While this seemed a bizarre idea to the nuns, they grudgingly agreed and Misia, along with the daughters of other hygienically minded eccentrics, was allowed to bathe weekly—though always in her petticoat for modesty's sake.

Too impatient to be a scholar, yet too intelligent to enjoy the shoddy education and too spoiled to submit to authority, Misia found the Sacred Heart a finishing school she could hardly wait to finish.

Once a month she was given permission to visit her family. The Godebskis had moved to an imposing house with adjoining studio in the newly fashionable rue de Prony near the Parc Monceau, a house that Cyprien, in a grand gesture, had built with Matylda's money. It was an elaborate mansion, its relatively simple exterior decorated with Godebski's gold mosaic medallions of Shakespeare, Dante, Michelangelo, and da Vinci. The interior was gloomy but grand: trompe-l'oeil ceilings painted with billowing curtains held back by golden ropes, Louis XVIII tapestries, gold and blue velvets, red damasks, all lit by hissing bronze gas lamps shaped like dragons. Magnificent Boulle cabinets flanked a huge fireplace studded with Luca della Robbia plaques. And a life-sized statue of Joan of Arc surrounded by potted palms rose resplendent from a circular tufted-satin pouffe.

Misia found it somewhat oppressive. But she loved to play "ballerina" on the monumental staircase that led to her stepmother's Chinese boudoir. And when her pet pony wandered from the garden into the dining room, Misia fed it lumps of sugar. Most of all she was taken by the charming conservatory, the ideal setting, she thought, for the grown-up love stories she read in secret. Around the walls of the *grand salon* ran a pompous inscription in gothic lettering: "Love nature more than art. Art more than glory. Art is the means. Nature is the principle." In this room the Godebskis received their friends with a hospitality that rivalled the Servaises'. It was a worldly, even official, bohemia. In their circle were the Alphonse Daudets, whose sons Léon and Lucien Misia was to know well, the brilliant Belgian artist Félicien Rops (whose erotic engravings illustrated the writings of Verlaine, Baudelaire, and the Goncourts), the publisher Georges Charpentier and his wife, whom Renoir painted, and the composer Gabriel Fauré. Of course they invited all their Polish friends. It was a cosmopolitan yet deeply Polish atmosphere that Misia found when she went home.

The Monceau district had recently been transformed from a tough wasteland of peddlers and cheap street fairs to a place where rich Poles and fashionable artists built their town houses and their sumptuous studios. It was logical for Cyprien, who was both a rich Pole and a fashionable artist, to settle there and just as logical for him to make a monument for the Polish National School nearby. After all, his father had been one of the founders of this school for Polish boys, and Cyprien, as Paris' leading Polish sculptor, was one of the school's illustrious alumni. The monument was inscribed *L'Emigration Polonaise à la France Hospitalière*. Indeed, Polish émigrés had reason to be grateful for France's hospitality. Many of them succeeded brilliantly in their adopted country, particularly in music and the theatre. The glorious voices of the de Reszke brothers and Marcella Sembrich resounded at the Opéra and the Théâtre des Italiens. Paris was filled with Polish pianists, both men and women. Little wonder that Misia dreamt of becoming a piano virtuoso.

Although the Monceau district was the center of "Little Poland," the grandest of the Polish aristocrats lived elsewhere. Misia's godmother Countess Zamoïska had settled near the Etoile, as did the Poniatowskis. Both families were descended from the kings of Poland. The leader of the colony, Prince Czartoryski, lived on the Ile St. Louis in the magnificent Hôtel Lambert, where Misia's grandfather Godebski had heard Chopin play. Misia too was taken by her family to the Hôtel Lambert for the traditional Christmas and Easter celebrations. Toasts were drunk *à la polonaise*—a single glass passed from hand to hand as a symbol of enmities forgiven. (Toasts of reconciliation were certainly advisable at least twice a year to keep the quarrelsome colony together.) At Easter a preciously guarded ceremony was performed at the Polish National School: the most distinguished Poles in Paris waited on table for the young students' Easter lunch, a gesture of humility rare among these nobles. A full-throated performance of the national anthem ended the afternoon, stirring Misia to the depths of her Polish being. She was even more exhilarated when, dressed in national costume, they all went to the Kriegelstein Ballroom to dance the intricate steps of the Varsoviana and the Cracoviana. Even the quarrelsome girl was happy when her father and stepmother, nodding approval, whispered to their friends, "*Elle danse comme une vraie Polonaise.*"

Realizing that Misia was on her way to becoming a real pianist, the Godebskis had arranged for one of the nuns to take her to Gabriel Fauré's studio for lessons every Thursday. As the years went on she applied herself brilliantly, pouring all her passionate feelings into her music. After playing Mozart, Beethoven, and Schubert for Fauré, she had the joy of listening to him play the same pieces to her with the profound insight that only a great composer-pianist can bring to music. Then he would perform his own works with their half-lights and velvet shadows. The weekly meetings between the gentle composer and the gifted girl who was so much in need of affection changed her profoundly. Fauré gave Misia a precious, lasting gift, a love and understanding of music that were to be an unequivocal pleasure for life.

Distinctly more equivocal were the pleasures introduced into the Godebski circle by Dr. Samuel-Jean Pozzi, man-about-town and inseparable friend of Napoleon's niece, the Princesse Mathilde. Invitations to watch the worldly surgeon perform his revolutionary gynecological operations were much sought after by his society friends. Dr. Pozzi organized a secret society called the League of the Rose, whose members met at the Godebskis and, following Pozzi's rules, played a kind of orgiastic truth game. Misia was aware that the grown-ups were not just playing doctor, for the players were not only made to answer questions about their sexual preferences but to act them out as well. These games gave the young adolescent a good deal to think about through the long days at the Sacred Heart.

At the same time the precocious half-child, half-woman was lavishing her affection on the only creature she was allowed to fondle: Rose, a life-sized doll who could say *maman* and *papa* in a voice that went straight to her heart. Rose had been a gift from her godmother, who had lost a daughter Misia's age, and Misia was childishly attached to it. One day she found the doll had disappeared. Her stepmother, thinking Misia ridiculously old for dolls, had given it away. Misia was heartbroken—but Rose was not the last submissive creature she was to love and mourn.

When Misia and Cipa were allowed to join their parents in the dining room, sumptuously lined in cordovan leather, they were all ears. Children, of course, were meant to be silent at table, but there was nothing to prevent them from listening to the cultivated conversation seasoned with racy gossip at which their parents' guests were so adept. While Edmond de Goncourt and his brother Jules were analyzing the doings and sayings of the Godebskis' friends, Misia and her brother were also comparing notes and conjecturing about what they had overheard. It was a special, a very Parisian education.

One night when Misia was fifteen, she was awakened by one of the nuns, told to dress quickly, hurried into a carriage, and taken home. She was led through a crowd of hushed visitors and up the stairs into her stepmother's dimly lit boudoir. There to her horror lay the dead body of Matylda Godebska. Sobbing with grief, Misia's father dragged her to the bed and forced her to kiss the cold cheek of the corpse. Misia never forgot her terror, or the comforting embrace of the veiled lady who was watching over the body with her father. The stranger was her father's mistress Catherine, the Marquise de Ganville.

Although Misia had not been aware of it, Matylda had been seriously ill for some time and Cyprien had been consoling himself with the marquise. A curious reference to a chance meeting between Alphonse Daudet and Matylda Godebska a year before her death, at a time when both were suffering from painful illnesses, is recorded in the Goncourt Journal of May 31, 1886. Daudet, who was planning to write about suffering, felt that he could make a "beautiful and cruel page of this: At an evening at the Charpentiers, suffering unbearable pain, [Daudet] went to walk it off in the corridor, where he met . . . la Godebska . . . making horrible grimaces, but hiding them under smiles as soon as she saw him."

Matylda was hardly in her grave when Cyprien, following his motto "Nature is the principle," married Madame de Ganville and moved into her house. In her will Matylda had left the house near the Parc Monceau to her two Natanson children. To Misia she left three hundred thousand francs, to be hers when she married, and some splendid solitaire diamonds which were promptly appropriated by the new Madame Godebska. The legacy would seem to indicate that Matylda was more devoted to Misia than Misia to her.

To her surprise, Misia found that her new stepmother was kindness itself. She responded by falling in love with her, but alas, the Godebskis soon moved to Brussels, taking the boys with them. Misia was not to see them for more than two years. A flood of passionate letters reached the tenderhearted marquise from the lonely school girl until they were intercepted by one of the nuns, who found them alarmingly ecstatic. "Only God can be loved in that way, my child," said the nun who seemed to know a surprising amount about affairs of the heart. "If you go on loving like this, love will kill you." And so even this innocent love was denied her.

Her years at the Sacred Heart gave Misia next to nothing of formal education, but neglect taught her independence, and loneliness taught her courage. And nature had given her something even more important than beauty: a radiance that everyone who met her found irresistible. Under her well-marked eyebrows, her large, expressive dark eyes missed no opportunity for appraisal, irony, or wit. Strong and well-fleshed, with a small, supple waist and magnificent legs tapering down to pretty feet, she moved as lightly, as precisely, as a not quite domesticated cat. In fact, Misia had become a seductive armful, too grown up to be locked away in a convent school. Two more years went by however before her father sent for her. How she looked forward to being with her new stepmother! But when she arrived in Brussels in 1890, she found that her father had worked his domestic magic once again: the tender marquise had become an alcoholic. At breakfast while everyone else dipped bread into café au lait, Catherine dipped hers into a cup of chartreuse. After violent scenes Ernest had been sent to a military school. Cipa too was now a stepchild neglected by his father and mistreated by his stepmother. In desperation Misia decided once again to run away from home. In a peculiar repetition of the drama with her first stepmother, her decision hinged on a jewel. This time it was a ring given her by the marquise that Misia accidentally let slip down the drain while washing her hands.

> The disaster was discovered at dinner. In her anger my stepmother said such horrible things that, my nerves out of control, I threw my plate at her head and fled.
>
> Hiding in the conservatory a little later, I overheard from the adjoining salon a conversation which revealed that I would be sent to a reform school. My head was on fire. Everything became strangely confused in my brain. One idea remained clear: to escape, to leave this house, where I felt only hatred, by any means possible—and never to return.

It was at this point in her memoirs that Misia chose to eliminate six years from her life. Certainly she was not at all the runaway child she claimed to be, but an attractive young woman of eighteen. Planning her escape carefully, she managed to borrow a considerable sum of money from one of her father's friends, packed a small suitcase, and slipped out of the troubled house at midnight. The dark streets terrified her, but the thought of being caught terrified her even more. By the next day she had made her way to Antwerp, where she boarded a ship for England. As she stood leaning on the ship's rail, watching the Belgian coast recede, she knew she was leaving her unhappy childhood behind.

In London, Misia, happy in her new freedom, settled down in a boarding house in Mayfair. At last she was doing whatever she pleased whenever she pleased—wandering the streets of Victorian London, looking at the smart shop windows, boldly returning the admiring glances of passers-by, playing the piano as much as she liked, buying her own clothes, and living completely on her own—or so she always claimed.

There is another, more romantic version of her stay in London, however. The great actress Réjane, who later became Misia's intimate friend, told her son Jacques Porel that Misia had run off with the Belgian artist Félicien Rops. Rops, whom Misia had often met at her father's house, was forty years older than she and at the height of his career. A satanist, he captured in his unique work what J. K. Huysmans described as "the supernatural essence of depravity, the heaven—and hell—which lies beyond all EVIL." Misia must have been awed and attracted by the handsome father figure, and certainly he must have been struck by Misia's looks. Her erect carriage, her physical abundance, her high breasts, snub nose, and sensuous face were the embodiment of the fantastic women in his erotic drawings. Did Misia's attraction to the older man lead to a prolonged sexual escapade? Could part of the charm of giving herself to her father's friend have been that she was no longer excluded from Dr. Pozzi's adult games? Did Misia leave London as the knowing pupil of one of Europe's most sophisticated eroticists, or was she the independent but virginal young lady she claimed to be? When Misia told Réjane she had been Rops's mistress, was it true, or was it simply a sexual fantasy about the virile, perverse older man? These are things we may never know. In any case, when she returned to Paris after several months, she was alone.

In Paris, Misia optimistically spent the last of her dwindling funds on a small apartment near the avenue de Clichy. Rarely had she enjoyed anything as much as doing it up. Everything was bought at Dufayel's department store on the seductive new installment plan: bamboo furniture, silver-threaded curtains, and her special pride and joy, a multi-colored lantern equipped with the latest novelty, "electric gas." "I couldn't come home," Misia said, "without immediately climbing up on a chair to kiss my lantern." The flat was all exuberantly pink and blue.

The first person she called on was Fauré. Solid bourgeois that he was, he begged his rebellious pupil to go back to her family. But Misia's freedom meant too much to her. Determined to be on her own, she timidly asked him to find pupils for her. When she went to see her father, who was living in Paris again, she was greeted with tragic news: her brother Ernest had been killed in Tonkin in the Indochinese war on the very day she had run away. But even before the news of Ernest's death had reached the Godebskis, her stepmother Catherine had put on mourning—for Misia. To the melodramatic marquise Misia's scandalous disappearance was worse than death.

With the death of Misia's first stepmother, Matylda Natanson Godebska, Misia had more or less lost sight of the Natanson boys; but now one day she ran into their father, Adam Natanson. Half shyly, half proudly, she told him that she was living alone and earning a living by giving piano lessons. More middle-class than Cyprien Godebski, he was deeply shocked. It was unheard of for a girl of good family to be earning money, and out of the question for her to be living alone. He felt it immoral that Misia, whom he had known since her childhood, was allowed to do both. In his fatherly way he arranged a meeting with the Godebskis to discuss her future. At the heated family council, Misia bluntly refused to go back to living with her father and step-mother. And she would burn down the convent, she swore, when they suggested she go back there. Finally a compromise was reached: Misia could continue her teaching and her lessons with Fauré on the condition that she give up the apartment and move to a well-chaperoned *pension*.

When Monsieur Natanson told the story to his sons, Thadée was intrigued to hear that Misia was behaving so differently from the other well-brought-up girls he knew. A few months later he happened to meet her at a party to which she had been taken by Suzanne Avril, a young actress who lived in her *pension*. Thadée was taken aback. His younger brother's playmate, whom he remembered as a girl in hair ribbons, had become a husky-voiced, flirtatious beauty. Her catlike head was set on a strong neck, her chestnut hair was piled up like a brioche, her torso's slender curve melted into swelling hips. Gone were the restraints of her childhood. She was now a poised young woman with a teasing half-smile and a disconcerting way of blurting out what was on her mind: rough truths in a beguiling frame of wit. And she asked such personal questions! One eyebrow raised in a circumflex, Thadée screwed his monocle into place, took a closer look—and fell in love.

Thadée and Misia began to meet often. Four years older than she, Thadée was a large, lumbering young man, sensitive, intellectual, and filled with ambition. Misia found his enthusiasm infectious and his extravagant disregard for practical detail admirable. His affectionate teasing touched her in a strangely moving way. Usually so conscious of the faults of others, Misia did not seem to mind the fact that he was slightly pretentious, somewhat conceited, and distinctly overdressed. And Thadée had never met a girl with such ebullience, such blazing temperament. She was no longer "caged up at her father's house, a beautiful panther, imperious and bloodthirsty," as the writer Eugène Morand remembered her. Purring under Thadée's attentions, the panther drew in her claws and was all laughter and charm.

Volubly excited, he told Misia that he and his brothers had started a new magazine called *La Revue Blanche* and that once a week he went to Liège to see to its printing. When Misia said she always spent summers in Belgium with her grandmother, they felt that particular delight in coincidence which seems magical to people who are attracted to one another. Impulsively she invited him to visit her whenever he came to Belgium. With each of his visits that summer of 1891, their feelings for one another grew. He read her his art criticism and the installments of his novel, *Pour l'Ombre*, as they appeared in the new review. He shared his aspirations with her and spoke eloquently about his gods Verlaine and Mallarmé, whom he had met and whose poetry he worshipped. The nineteen-year-old Misia, though not an intellectual, responded with instinctive sensitivity. She seemed to know more through osmosis than most people learn from books.

Before long Thadée asked Misia's father for her hand in marriage. Cyprien gave his blessing and Misia was happy to accept. She did not feel passionate love for Thadée, but she had an immense need to be loved. She admired him, she was altogether at ease with him, and best of all, they amused one another endlessly. In a sense they were both outcasts. Misia had liberated herself from her family in a scandalous way. And in a city pervaded by that most unchristian of prejudices, anti-Semitism—the Dreyfus case was soon to explode—Thadée was at best grudgingly accepted as a rich Jew, but if he stepped out of line, scorned as a dirty one.* The new life Thadée was offering Misia was another step to freedom: marriage would be a final release from her parents' oppressive supervision and their suffocating disapproval. It was not unlike an arranged marriage—except that Misia herself had arranged it. The wedding would take place at her grandmother's new house in Ixelles, near Brussels. They were busy, happy days as Misia went from Belgium to France and back again. Engaged, she became even more engaging. Uncle Franz's friends began to sit up and take notice. While Franz played *Parsifal* and his own opera, *L'Apollonide*, Misia was being initiated by his friend Henry van de Velde to the decadent thrills of J. K. Huysmans' *Là-bas*, the symbolist mysteries of Maurice Maeterlinck, and the involuted novelty of his own Art Nouveau designs. To keep up with her erudite fiancé, Misia read day and night. There were festivities as well, fittings and parties and even a royal ball where she danced with the Belgian Crown Prince: "It was because of the Queen's friendship for my grandmother that I was invited to a court ball," she wrote in her memoirs. "A pale blue tulle ballgown with a wide moiré sash had been made for me. When I saw myself in the enormous mirror in the entrance to the palace, I was bowled over by the apparition. And when I realized that it was really I, I rushed to the looking glass and kissed my reflection passionately, to the astonishment of an army of gaping footmen."

* An entry in the Goncourt Journal five years later gives a picture not only of the quick rise of the Natansons and the *Revue Blanche* but of anti-Semitism in the literary world: "We were speaking today of N . . . [Natanson], where *le Tout-Paris* goes to dinner. . . . At a certain moment, when the theatre was the only branch of literature where one could make money, the only Jewish writers were playwrights: for example, Dennery and Halévy. . . . But now the young generation of Jews has understood the all-powerful weight of criticism and the kind of blackmail that critics can exert on theatres and publishers and has founded the *Revue Blanche*, which is a real nest of 'Yids.' One can well imagine that with the help of their elders, who provide the money for almost all newspapers, they will control French literature within twenty-five years" (January 26, 1896).

In 1892, the year before her marriage, Misia began to take her place in the grown-up Parisian world. There was the excitement of her first public concert: an evening in honor of the poet-composer-singer Maurice Rollinat, a founder, along with Rodolphe Salis, of the legendary artists' café, the Chat Noir. Handsome and dissolute, he must have been heady company for Misia. In the February issue of the *Revue Blanche*, Lucien Mühlfeld wrote:

> The Rollinat concert at the Théâtre d'Application was a truly important musical and literary event. Rollinat is generally known as a poet, above all as a poet of the macabre. Listeners on Sunday were surprised and charmed to become acquainted with a Rollinat new to them, an exquisite poet, a delicate singer by nature, a strange and powerful musician. Perhaps he lacks a little formal training . . . but Gounod's remark, "He's a madman of genius!" proves that Sunday's public was right to acclaim his astonishing songs, which made a most profound impression on everyone. It was a treat to hear Yvette Guilbert in *The Idiot* and *The Funeral Procession*. The Mounets made us shudder. Worms charmed us; Coquelin made us weep! ! ! Lugné-Poë, Mlles. Dufrene, Mellot and Rose Syma struggled valiantly to keep up with their elders. . . .
>
> The three waltzes of Rollinat which served as an overture to the second part of the concert were executed by a very young lady, Mlle. Godebska, with a feeling and a personality altogether rare. We are told that Mlle. Godebska is the granddaughter of the great Servais. She certainly takes after her grandfather, and we predict for her the future of a great artist.*

* Rollinat's poems were declaimed by four of the greatest actors of the Comédie-Française: the brothers Paul Mounet and Jean Mounet-Sully, Worms, and Coquelin *cadet*, who had been Henry James's classmate at school in Boulogne.

In the younger group two were to become close to Misia and Thadée: Lugné-Poë— who was a student of both Worms and Coquelin *cadet* at the Conservatoire—and Marthe Mellot, the gifted actress who was to marry Thadée's brother, Alfred. Yvette Guilbert was, of course, Yvette Guilbert.

Misia was overjoyed with the glowing account of her playing and Thadée, in love, lost no opportunity to give equal pleasure to other members of her family. Uncle Franz received praise for his opera *L'Apollonide*, and Misia's father must have felt he was gaining a good son-in-law indeed when he read in the May issue of the *Revue Blanche* the account of his evening of *tableaux vivants* called "Poems of Love." The description makes one think of Alma-Tadema paintings brought to life:

> In the forest, calm in the gathering dusk, a voice is heard, sometimes fierce and manly, sometimes softly melodious and feminine; the voice of the Poet who speaks. He speaks of Love past, exalts Lovers and the Beloved: David, Catullus, Venus; Judith or Mary Magdalen. . . . The forest grows darker and yet lights up as if with an interior vision, an evocation of antique loves. And at the same time, while we are lulled by music, the long amorous procession passes before our dazzled eyes, from Eve to Cleopatra, from Daphnis to Des Grieux.
>
> These living pictures, harmonious in line, ravishing in color, artistically conceived and staged, we owe to the talent of the sculptor Cyprien Godebski. . . .
>
> We particularly want to thank Mlle. Mellot, who moved us deeply and whom the public will remember.
>
> These evenings of pure art and of dreams are only too rare.

Fauré was bitterly disappointed when he heard of Misia's engagement. They had worked hard together and he was certain that she could have a brilliant career as a pianist. With tears in his eyes he begged her to give up all thoughts of marriage. But Misia, determined to escape her family and an uncertain future, was less enthusiastic about the joys of living alone than she had been. Besides, Thadée's world was a fascinating one; his circle of young painters, writers, actors, and musicians was a milieu in which she felt happy and at home. Even before their marriage she was at ease with artists like Stéphane Mallarmé:

18 March 1893

Dear Monsieur Mallarmé,

I just this instant had a note from Madame Normand, who has a very bad cold and will not be able to receive on Sunday. So here I am with another idea. After the concert, would you like to come to dinner with some friends, without any fuss? Wouldn't Geneviève [Mallarmé's daughter] come too?

We missed you very much yesterday. All the more reason you cannot refuse me for Sunday. Please give my warmest greetings to Madame Mallarmé and to Geneviève, and believe me,

> your friend completely
> Misia

A few days later Misia learned that her grandmother was very ill. Sadly she returned to Belgium, where she remained until the wedding. But again there were slavic shadows. Like a ghost from the past, Grandmother's sister Olga (her father's mistress of twenty years ago) arrived from Russia to say her good-byes and beg her sister's forgiveness. A strange presentiment made Misia, from whom the whole story had been carefully concealed, refuse to meet her great-aunt. Only now, on the eve of her marriage, was she told the dramatic circumstances of her birth and of her mother's death. The deepest shadow of all was cast by the death of Misia's grandmother two weeks before the wedding. To Misia's surprise Uncle Coster gave her an impressive sum of money as a dowry, and in the first of a lifelong series of extravagant gestures, she spent it all on a trousseau. And so, in Ixelles on April 25, 1893, the twenty-one-year-old Marie Sophie Olga Zenaïde Godebska became the wife of the twenty-five-year-old Thadée Natanson. The first cycle of Misia's life had been completed. The next day the young couple left for Paris.

PART TWO

Madame Natanson

Overleaf, Misia Natanson, c. 1897

The Natansons took a flat in the rue St. Florentin just off the Place de la Concorde, which was as noisy and difficult to cross then as it is now. Cabs and double-decker omnibuses drawn by huge Percheron horses came at one from all directions. "Lions," those dandies who prided themselves on the elegance of their footmen and horses, rattled by in their carriages, pleased with the noisy clatter of their wooden wheels. (Rubber tires were only for the aged and the ailing.) Cavalry in magnificent uniform cantered by in one direction while regiments of soldiers marched by in the other. Top-hatted gentlemen riding off to the bridle paths of the Bois de Boulogne greeted elegantly dressed ladies clinging to their parasols on their way to the rue de la Paix. Schoolchildren in smocks exchanged solemn handshakes as they threaded a path through the maze to play in the Tuileries. Herds of goats and mares were led across the Place, stopping to be milked on request. There were flower sellers, cocoa, ice cream, and water vendors, peddlers with trees of little French flags on long poles. There were women sweeping the streets with witches' brooms, and wretched women between horse traces dragging heavy carts. The Place de la Concorde was the center, the heart of Paris.

Pungent odors rose everywhere. The surrounding streets, paved in wood, gave off a forest scent. The smells of horse dung, leather, urine, and coffee mixed unashamedly with fashionable perfumes—Chypre d'Atkinson, Fougère Royale, and Héliotrope—while from the gardens came the country smells of flowers, trees, and earth. Like the mixture of perfume and dung, Paris was a world of unquestioning privilege for the rich and, for the most part, resigned misery for the poor. Yet even for the poor there was the feeling that it was a unique privilege to be a Parisian. For throughout most of Misia's life Paris was the most exuberant, most cultivated, most stimulating city in the world. But even then a disquieting symbol of change loomed above the city: that new, that incredibly lofty metal stabile piercing the sky, the Eiffel tower.

The pleasure of having her own apartment, the shared intimacies with an adoring husband gave Misia added assurance. But something was lacking. Although Thadée was deeply in love with her, their marriage was more cozy than carnal. It was a very different time from the licentious eighteenth century, or our own twentieth century with its solemn belief that men's organs are respectable pillars of society and women's, deep caves of desire. Husbands were meant to be sexually aroused by their wives, but wives were expected to yield reluctantly. Though a great flirt, Misia never claimed to be a sexual athlete; that was for the ladies of the demimonde. Still, she took it for granted that not only was her husband in love with her, but so, more or less, were all his friends. It was the thing, to be in love with Misia.

For the French, who find exoticism appealing, Misia was always *la Polonaise*. Though she had never lived in Poland, there was a suggestion of the Slav in her rolled r's and the inflections of her musical voice. More slavic still was her gift for immediate intimacy, a quality foreign to the French but one which they find disarming in foreigners. She had tremendous *allure* in the French meaning of the word—a sense of how to carry herself with style. The way she moved, quickly, as if sailing before the wind, was a provocative combination of the knowing and the innocent. A mistress of feminine guile, Misia knew how to lean on a parasol, handle a fan, show her rounded arms and breasts to advantage as she adjusted her hat and veil. Her friends called her *"snobinette,"* not because of her extravagant clothes but rather for her above-it-all air. Yet beneath the good manners of the well-brought-up convent girl were the free and easy ways of the bohemian. Tart and tender at once, observant and curious, she listened attentively and responded with enthusiasm, candor, and an independence of judgment startling in one so young. Her speech was salted with irony and peppered with four-letter words, which on her lips somehow escaped vulgarity. She was a rough-and-ready princess.

And she was a born iconoclast, a highly valued commodity on the Parisian intellectual market. It was in her nature to lay down the law, quickly and with authority. As the wife of a rising young editor, Misia was toadied to, fawned over, and flattered by writers and artists who hoped to be included in his magazine. It was her first taste of power, a weapon she used with skill and enthusiasm. She fought generously for the artists whose work she loved. As for the others, she shrugged them off, muttering *"C'est la barbe."* And her shrug of boredom carried weight. But Misia was not a Valkyrie prowling the forest of art with bludgeon and shield. Her position, combined with her unique personal style, her seductive charm, and her almost physical need to be constantly surrounded by people, was to make her the magnetic center, the feminine touchstone for one of the most gifted circles of artists Paris has ever known.

The Natansons knew everyone in intellectual and artistic Paris. Most of their friends were in their twenties or early thirties; many of them contributors to the *Revue Blanche*. Not only did Thadée write articles in praise of the young, little-known artists he admired, and show their work in the offices of the magazine, but he and his family often proved to be their best customers. Thadée even convinced his brother Alexandre and his cousin Paul Desmarais to commission large decorative panels from Edouard Vuillard. Misia and Thadée were touched by Vuillard's growing affection for them, "an affection doubly moving from a person so infinitely reserved and shy," Thadée wrote, adding, "Of all the reasons to love Vuillard, the sweetest was the conviction he gave that he loved you." Compared with those bantam cocks, their writer friends Romain Coolus and Tristan Bernard, Vuillard was a serene yet ardent presence in their midst.

The Belle Epoque could not have been a more beautiful time for those who were privileged—and Misia and Thadée truly were. Young and attractive, they had plenty of money and time to enjoy it. They lived for pleasure and—greatest privilege of all—their deepest pleasure lay in their enjoyment of art. With an unerring eye for what was best in new art, they were among the few who were able to read the paintings of their contemporaries in much the way we read them today. And they responded to the new in music, literature, and the theatre with insights that reached most people only many years later. With the excitement of explorers, they discovered that new art was speaking to them and describing their emotions. Though not artists themselves, they felt art as artists do.

Unlike many painters who, indifferent to their surroundings, live with a few reproductions of masterpieces tacked up in their studios and their own canvasses turned to the wall, the Natansons lived in style. Misia had a genius for decoration. She created interiors which looked like Vuillard paintings—and Vuillard could hardly wait to paint Misia's flat and Misia in it. In his *Salon with the Three Lamps*, one of his many paintings of the Natansons, color and pattern are everywhere—patterned papers on the walls and on the picture frames, patterns in the Spanish shawl on Misia's piano, patterned carpets on the floors—all bathed in the golden light of gas lamps with ruffled silk shades. With Thadée's bentwood rocking chair as the calligraphic center of the salon, Vuillard evokes a magic stillness, an atmosphere of domesticity and artistic pursuits combined: Thadée reading aloud, their friend Romain Coolus listening pensively, Misia bent over her sewing. Thadée's reading has filled the salon with a quiet peace. But in *Misia au Piano*, a more subjective vision of the same interior, Misia's playing has set the room ablaze. *The Salon with the Three Lamps* is a nocturne; *Misia au Piano*, a rhapsody, vibrant with kaleidoscopic color. The walls of the salon are now, like Vuillard's imagination, stretched out, quivering with the glow of emotion.

The Natansons had fallen under the spell of their artist friends. Acquisitive for pleasure, they eagerly bought Vuillards, Bonnards, and Roussels. As the painters were quite unknown there was no thought of their works as valuable objects; and certainly no thought of future gain. It was all high spirits, and fun. Fifteen years later, in 1908, Thadée fell into financial difficulties and sold some of his paintings at auction. The sale included seven Roussels, nineteen Bonnards, and twenty-seven Vuillards, as well as works by Cézanne, Delacroix, Daumier, Guys, Marquet, Redon, Seurat, and Vallotton.

Still later, when Misia commissioned Bonnard to paint a frieze for a new apartment, she found the long, straight edges of his canvas monotonous and cut them into scalloped shapes. By that time Bonnard was recognized as a great painter, and her friends were scandalized. The same friends, Misia recalled, had laughed and said, "Are you sure they're not hanging upside down?" when she and Thadée had bought Bonnards in 1893 and 1894. Now when they reproached her for her lack of respect, she replied, "I don't respect art; I love it." It was very like Misia, and the kind of answer her artist friends understood. At the end of his life, whenever he made one of his infrequent trips to Paris, Bonnard would come to sit quietly in a corner of Misia's salon in a tender, adoring silence.

The first years of the Natansons' marriage were everything Misia had hoped for. She and Thadée together went over the manuscripts of the works he was publishing, and there were hours every day when she practiced the piano diligently. In spite of the fact that they belonged to the comfortable middle class, middle-class conventions played a rather small part in their lives. There was no carriage with restless horses waiting at three o'clock to take Misia on a round of formal calls. In proper circles each hostess had her weekly reception day, but Misia, with engaging informality, held open house every day of the week. Thadée brought so many of his collaborators home from the *Revue Blanche* that Misia christened their apartment "the annex."

There never seemed to be time enough to do all the things they wanted to do. No *vernissage* or opening night seemed complete without the young couple, and of course Misia never missed a concert. Misia as spectator is the subject of several Toulouse-Lautrec pictures. In a poster commissioned by an American firm, Ault and Wiborg, "Makers of Fine Printing and Lithographic Inks," Misia and Dr. Tapié de Céleyran, Lautrec's cousin, are seen from the front, seated in what looks like a box at the circus. In the splendid gouache *Madame Thadée Natanson au Théâtre*, Misia is shown from the back, her body leaning forward in rapt concentration. And in *Les Grands Concerts*, a drawing of a rehearsal of Ambroise Thomas' opera *Françoise de Rimini*, we see only her hat, a broad-brimmed boater whose feathers curl upward with such panache that it could belong to no one but Misia. Bicycling, the latest rage, was another of Lautrec's subjects. Misia loved the sport, and the tough world of bicycle racing fascinated her. Tristan Bernard (called Tristan not for Wagner's hero but for a horse on which he had bet and won) took the Natansons to the Vélodrome Buffalo. Seated on wooden benches, they would watch mesmerized as the racers rode round and round the tub-shaped course while rough sporting types yelled raucous encouragement. It was at the Vélodrome that Lautrec immortalized Bernard, its director: Bernard, a stocky young man in knickerbockers and bowler hat, proudly surveying his bicycle kingdom.

They all went to café-concerts to hear the Montmartre singers in their daring songs. At the Scala and later at the Moulin Rouge the insinuating Yvette Guilbert bewitched them with her refreshing cynicisms and naughty *double-entendres*. Deafened by the shrill brass band, they strained to hear the stories Lautrec told them. Lautrec, whose mordant line indelibly traced Guilbert's bird-like neck and long black gloves, amused them by repeating her perverse little confession: her gloves were copied from a strict teacher on whom she had had a schoolgirl crush. Overcome by the mingled odor of rice powder, perspiration, tobacco, and beer, his friends listened spellbound as he pointed out the pimps, named the predatory whores strolling arm in arm, and described in lurid detail Miss Rigolette's liaison with La Môme Fromage.

Lautrec and the Natansons, along with Bonnard, Vuillard, and Tristan Bernard, would go to Rodolphe Salis' Chat Noir. Salis, a mathematician and painter, said, "God created the world, Napoleon founded the Legion of Honor, and I invented Montmartre." He dressed his waiters as members of the Académie Française, his headwaiter in the Swiss uniform of a Papal guard, and his cabaret in the style of Louis XIII. Poems were declaimed, and performances were given of *les ombres chinoises*, the Chinese shadow theatre, forerunner of the moving picture. There too, Aristide Bruant sang in his black felt hat and flowing red scarf. Did he really exist or did Lautrec invent him? Most interesting of all to Misia were those evenings when Vincent Hyspa sang to Erik Satie's accompaniment, while Claude Debussy, aloof and enigmatic, sat quietly listening in a corner.

Not all their pleasures were so lofty. They enjoyed the earthy, very Belle Epoque performances of the *Pétomane*, the world's most accomplished farter, who could play tunes simply by breaking wind. His poster proudly announced:

EVERY NIGHT FROM EIGHT TO NINE

Le Pétomane
The only performer
who doesn't pay composers' royalties.

There were private entertainments that were equally diverting. Pierre Louÿs (whom Valéry called Debussy's literary conscience) wrote about them in the June 1894 issue of the *Revue Blanche:*

Two new troupes of marionettes have made their debuts in Paris. The performances never last more than one night, but these ephemeral appearances are great events. The sets, costumes, and direction are carefully worked out for months in advance . . . the acting is rehearsed and the lighting is set, for the shorter an existence is, the more exquisite and perfect it must be.

Such was the life of Mme. Judith Gautier's marionettes. They were modelled in clay by skillful hands. Mme. Gautier, who is a poet, is also a sculptor and painter. . . . When the small Tanagra figures were created, she herself brought them to life and painted their costumes in shades of green and blue. The puppets had chosen to perform *The Valkyrie.* . . . Everything was perfection and those who saw it will never forget Sieglinde's passionate warning gesture as she listened to the "Narrative" at Hunding's table. . . .

A very select audience watched these little marvels: M. and Mme. Thadée Natanson, M. and Mlles. de Hérédia, Henri de Régnier, Robert de Montesquiou with his riding crop, and Ferdinand Hérold, another director of marionettes.

The latter are classic marionettes, made of wood and cardboard, their arms manipulated by invisible strings. *Paphnutius* by Hroswitha was the text they chose for their only performance, and M. Hérold was instructed by them to translate the drama of the pious abbess from Latin into precise, harmonious French. Out of deference he asked them which painters should be entrusted with the decor. They replied, "Paul Ranson, Edouard Vuillard, K.-X. Roussel, and his brother Alfonse Hérold." Everything was carried out according to their wishes and they were recalled over and over again by MM. Stéphane Mallarmé, Paul Valéry, Claude Debussy, and fifty other excellent judges. *Paphnutius*, which is a masterpiece, waited eight hundred years for its premiere, a fine example of patience for overly eager young writers.

Along with the general public, Misia and Thadée made a cult of Sarah Bernhardt. The divine Sarah, like many great actresses, had a weakness for juicy roles in second-rate plays. Theatrical fare, then as now, was generally bombast or banality. But since the Natansons were interested in theatre as literature, it was the genius of Ibsen that made a profound impression on them. The playwright's harsh psychological insights and social truths struck serious theatre-goers with the force of revelation. Many European intellectuals studied Norwegian in order to read him in the original. Ibsen's plays, like a clear, sharp wind from the north, created a new moral climate which attracted the young poets and painters. In 1893, the year of the Natansons' marriage, Thadée's school friend Lugné-Poë opened his Théâtre de l'Oeuvre with the first performance in France of *Rosmersholm*, following it with *An Enemy of the People*. Vuillard and Bonnard helped design the decor for Lugné's productions, and Vuillard illustrated many of the program covers. It was truly an artists' theatre.

As a kind of delayed honeymoon, early in the summer of 1894, Misia and Thadée made a pilgrimage to Norway with Lugné-Poë to meet Ibsen and see his plays performed by Norwegian actors. Lugné, who had added *The Master Builder* to his theatre's repertory, was anxious to discuss questions of staging with the playwright. The Natansons, of course, were eager to meet the king of Scandinavian drama. Misia, young and clear-sighted, did not miss a trick. Nor did the English actor Richard Le Gallienne, who later described Ibsen's daily entrance at the Grand Hotel in Christiania:

> The large café was crowded, but we found a good table on the aisle, not far from the door. We had not long to wait, for punctually on the stroke of one, there, entering the doorway, was the dour and bristling presence known to all the world in caricature. . . . The great ruff of white whisker, ferociously standing out all round his sallow, bilious face as if dangerously charged with electricity, the immaculate silk hat, the white tie, the frock-coat martinet's figure dressed from top to toe in old-fashioned black broadcloth, at once funereal and professional, the carefully folded umbrella—all was there, apparitionally before me; a forbidding, disgruntled, tight-lipped presence . . . straight as a ramrod; there he was, as I hinted, with a touch of grim dandyism about him, but with no touch of human kindness about his parchment skin or fierce badger eyes. . . .
>
> As he entered and proceeded . . . to the table reserved in perpetuity for him, . . . a thing new and delightful—to me a mere Anglo-Saxon— suddenly happened. As one man, the whole café was on its feet in an attitude of salute, and a stranger . . . said to me in a loud but reverent aside: "That is our poet, Henrik Ibsen." All remained standing till he had taken his seat, as in the presence of a king.

Misia, less reverent, remembered other details about the great man. On being introduced to Ibsen, she was puzzled to see him remove his top hat and, staring into its depths with grim concentration, fluff up his famous side-whiskers and carefully comb his leonine mane of hair. After a moment, she realized to her amusement that the vain old man had a mirror concealed in the crown of his hat. Wandering the dreary streets of Christiania the next day, Misia was taken aback to see photographs of Ibsen for sale in shop windows. At their next meeting she asked Ibsen's interpreter if she might have an autographed picture of the master. She would have to pay for it, she was told. Apparently Ibsen's share in the sale of his photographs was one of his favorite sources of income. It occurred to Misia that the steely look in those "fierce badger eyes" expressed not only moral indignation but good old-fashioned stinginess as well.

That evening Thadée distinguished himself at a banquet in Ibsen's honor. Even the grumpy playwright, who disliked banquets and speeches, smiled when Thadée compared him to the midnight sun, and there were bravos from the gloomy Norsemen for his subtle appreciation of their national treasure. The next morning Ibsen, coming to take them to a rehearsal of *The Master Builder*, presented Misia with his photograph, signed, framed—and free of charge. What a picture they must have made that evening, when the forbidding playwright gave his arm to the radiant young woman and led her to the center box for a performance of *A Doll's House*. Just before the curtain rose, a stout soprano strode into the spotlight, waved the French flag in honor of the visitors from Paris, and burst into the *Marseillaise*. The gesture seemed charmingly provincial to the sophisticated young Parisians, but a few minutes later they were deeply immersed in the play, profoundly moved by its revolutionary idea of a married woman's right to her own identity. Nora had behaved courageously, Misia thought. But, she felt with a certain complacency, she herself had been even more courageous. She had escaped from stifling authority and established her own identity before marriage. Like Madeleine in Maupassant's *Bel Ami*, Misia had resolved that the man she married must consider her an equal, not an inferior, and in Thadée she had found that man.

Misia considered Ibsen pompous, but she was taken with the simple modesty of Edvard Grieg. And besides, he spoke French! Ibsen's musical collaborator invited them to a rehearsal of *Peer Gynt*, where Misia wept at the scene of Aase's death. Afterward the composer asked her to play the incidental music with him. Grieg's *Peer Gynt Suite* was being performed in every parlor in Europe, and Misia knew it well. All the same, she felt transported when she found herself seated on a bench with Norway's leading composer, playing "In the Hall of the Mountain King" and "Anitra's Dance."

It was an idyllically romantic trip. Leaving Lugné-Poë behind to work with Ibsen, the Natansons made an excursion to the emerald-green lake of Telemarken. As a Shakespearean finale they crossed to Elsinore in Denmark, where Misia, seeing herself as Ophelia, scattered violets on the terrace of Hamlet's castle. Her last memory of the trip was of stretching out and falling asleep on Thadée's shoulder as their small sailboat, returning to Norway, followed the shimmering track of the moon.

After their Scandinavian interlude Misia and Thadée returned to their apartment in the rue St. Florentin. More friends than ever gathered at the "annex," and Thadée's brothers came round constantly. The Natanson brothers, as is often the case with children of émigrés, had arrived at varying stages in the transition from foreign to French. They were sometimes facetiously called Alexander the Great, Thadée the Proud, and Alfred the Good. The oldest—nervous, pale-eyed Alexandre, a successful lawyer and businessman—had the stately manner of a Polish gentleman. Alfred (Fred to his friends), being the youngest, was totally French. A gifted writer, sensitive, easy, full of laughter, he was the most appealing, the spoiled darling of the family. The middle son, Thadée, ostentatious and extravagant, had a slight suggestion of the foreigner. If he was proud, he had good reasons: his charming wife, his talented friends, and above all, the position he had achieved with the *Revue Blanche*.

The Natanson boys had been educated at the Lycée Condorcet, a school which produced a remarkable number of celebrated men. Among the students with whom Thadée formed lasting friendships were many who became contributors to the *Revue*: Lugné-Poë; the writers Marcel Proust, Romain Coolus, Pierre Veber, and Léon Blum, the future premier of France; and the painters Ker-Xavier Roussel, Maurice Denis, and Edouard Vuillard. According to Pierre Veber, "Thadée Natanson and Charles Leclercq were always pointed out at school for their elegance and their extravagance. It was in the Passage du Havre that the '*jeunesse dorée*' would meet before going back to class. Leclercq and Natanson raised hell with the girls in the arcade. They impressed us tremendously because they wore monocles, which made them seem infinitely our superiors." These gilded youths of the Lycée Condorcet were astonishingly erudite and blessed with a gift for passionate involvement in all that was new and most interesting. For Thadée, of course, the *Revue Blanche* was to become the center of his life—and of Misia's too therefore. As her education had been rather sketchy, living with the *Revue Blanche* gave Misia a cultivation she might otherwise have lacked. For her the *Revue* was a pipeline to poetry, *belles lettres*, aesthetics, world politics, science, law, philosophy, religion—even sports and travel. She never became an intellectual, but, unhampered by that sometimes onerous responsibility, she absorbed essences and meanings with the adroitness of the intuitive and the understanding of the intelligent. And she was very hard to fool. The *Revue Blanche* had been in existence for only a few years. It was founded in 1889, when Thadée's younger brother Alfred, then a boy of seventeen, spent the summer in the Belgian resort town of Spa. There he made friends with a group of cultivated French and Belgian students. The terrace of the Belle-Vue Café resounded with their animated discussions of painting, literature, and the theatre. With the courage of youth, the *jeunes hommes en fleur* decided to launch a literary review even though hundreds already existed. What to call it? There were *La Revue Bleue* and *La Revue Rose*, so they chose the name *La Revue Blanche*. White, they had learned in science class, was the sum of all colors, and their magazine would be not a partisan review but an eclectic one, open to all shades of opinion. Perhaps too the erudite young men were thinking of Mallarmé's evocative reveries about the mysteries of *la page blanche*, the blank white page which confronts the poet. Before Thadée's engagement to Misia, the review was published in Belgium; then in 1891, with the financial help of his father and brother Alexandre, it was moved to Paris. By 1893, the year Thadée and Misia married, it came into its own—as did they.

The *Revue Blanche* soon became a periodical of international scope and lasting interest. Its tone was worldly but never weary. Parisian lightness, charm, and wit shone through its pages, yet it treated important subjects with serious insight. The first Right Bank review, it had a quality of elegant dandyism which set it apart. Accusations of social snobbery and political anarchism only added sheen to the success of the young publication. Its hospitality to neo-Parnassians, Symbolists, and Decadents inspired Mallarmé to call it *"l'amicale, à tous prête Revue Blanche"*—the friendly *Revue Blanche*, open to all. It is an absorbing social, literary, and artistic encyclopedia of 1889 to 1903, the fourteen years of its existence. And it makes as lively reading today as it did when it was first published.

In the *Revue Blanche* Thadée and his colleagues examined topics which are still vital today: population control, woman's place in society, socialism, and the plight of the worker. They anticipated the current interest in Buddhism and Eastern thought, and they had a flair for presenting relatively unknown artists, both French and foreign, who are still considered important and influential. All the foreign work published in the review was appearing in French for the first time. The list of writers is dazzling: the Russians Tolstoy, Chekhov, Turgenev, Gorky, and Bakunin; the Scandinavians Ibsen, Strindberg, Bjoernson, and Knut Hamsun; the British Jane Austen, Rudyard Kipling, Robert Louis Stevenson, and Oscar Wilde; the American Mark Twain; the Italian Futurist Marinetti. The French, of course, were richly represented from Saint-Simon to Jarry, from Stendhal to Gide, Zola to Péguy, Mallarmé to Proust, Verlaine to Kostrowitsky (who signed his name Apollinaire for the first time in the *Revue Blanche*). Thadée contributed astute art criticism; Claude Debussy, under the pseudonym Monsieur Croche, was one of the review's music critics; and Léon Blum wrote on literature, theatre, and sports.

In every magazine there is a nucleus of house writers. Some of the *Revue Blanche* regulars who were popular then have faded with time, although Jules Renard, Claude Anet, Tristan Bernard, Octave Mirbeau, Romain Coolus, Henri de Régnier, and Léon Blum can still be read with pleasure. Very *fin de siècle*, Blum was refined and arrogant. A lover of smart paradox and esoteric discussion, he seemed little interested in politics and even less in the misery of the working class. No one could have foretold that one day he would be the premier of France, the coalition leader of liberals, Socialists, and Communists united under him in the Popular Front.

Most of these young men were often at the Natansons'. Coolly elegant, splendidly dressed, they carried themselves with the slight condescension expressed by that favorite word of the Symbolists, *hautain*. Their entrances at Misia's, the graceful but ironic deference with which they kissed her hand, their cutting witticisms, and their parting shots were all as elaborately planned as their carefully turned prose.

It was said that the young Marcel Proust was eager to visit the Natansons but that his parents disapproved. Perhaps they thought Misia and Thadée too racy for their son, not realizing that the temptations he was apt to encounter in the *Revue Blanche* set were not the ones that would lead him astray. Despite the fact that Proust was considered a fawning young man, too taken by duchesses and the drawing rooms of the Faubourg, Thadée recognized his talent and published some of his earliest pieces. One was "Friendship," a short lyric sketch that describes the sweet torment of being alone in bed and dreaming of love: a fourteen-line presage of the miraculously luxuriant revery to come.

Among the older writers, Paul Verlaine was revered by the *Revue Blanche* circle. One evening Gustave Kahn, often regarded as the inventor of the prose poem, arranged for some of the group to meet Verlaine at a café in Montmartre. Kahn wrote an account of the soirée for the review:

> The battered poet received his young admirers with gracious condescension. We came as though to a mystic shrine . . . to the poet who seems sanctified by suffering. Verlaine spoke and then read some passionate verses, saying, "For I, too, have had my infatuations . . . and here are some words of love and farewell to a fiancée I had long ago."
>
> We begged him to recite from memory poems we wanted to hear which he had not brought with him. He did so with an effort, stopping sometimes, till one of us completed the unfinished phrase. Sometimes with a large, slow gesture he brought his hands to his temples. His gestures had a sublime majesty. He gave us some unpublished poems.
>
> The scene was a narrow room opening onto a silent street. The walls were covered with obscene Japanese prints. In the next room, amidst the noise of the drinkers, someone was playing popular waltzes on the piano.

Two poems that Verlaine had given them were printed on the page opposite Kahn's article.

Another café frequented by Verlaine and the *Revue Blanche* writers was not far from the review's offices. Misia liked to spend an hour or two there listening to the guitarist in the back room. Years later she wrote:

> It was there that I struck up a friendship with Paul Verlaine. Usually between benders, and always sad, he would come in the early evening, sit down with me, drink, read me beautiful poems, and weep.
>
> One felt the unconquerable, the tragic youthfulness of his heart. Somewhere behind that immense forehead lived a soul which knew the uttermost bounds of purity. This drunken bum zigzagging across the Latin Quarter, this luminous beggar dragging his feet in the mud was conscious only of the sky. The horror of being ugly, of being ugly every day, without respite, every minute, even when his heart was dazzled by love for another being, had gradually taught him a profound

humility. The blows of life? He had brushed them all aside. They did not prevent him from coming back to sit at a sticky marble café table, order an absinthe and a dreadful little pen, scratchy and squeaky, one of those pens born to be dipped into the inkwells of the poor . . . His were simple words, transformed into treasures. . . .

It was my tender memory of this little café which made me go to see him in the hospital when I heard he was seriously ill. I shall never forget that poor ravaged face, the long shaky hand he could barely lift to take mine and the light in his feverish eyes that tried desperately to express what his lips no longer had the strength to say. . . . Two days later Verlaine died. His funeral procession, and Debussy's, were the only ones I ever followed on foot.

Misia's admiration for the great poet seems natural in retrospect, but Verlaine was not appreciated with such understanding by everyone. In 1895 Edmond de Goncourt wrote spitefully, "Who, after all, are the three idols of today's youth? They are Baudelaire, Villiers de l'Isle-Adam, and Verlaine: three men of talent, admittedly; but a sadistic bohemian, an alcoholic, and a murderous pederast."

In the summer of 1893 the *Revue Blanche*, youthfully flexing its muscles, had announced, "From now on we are going to be better and stronger," adding that each issue would contain an original print. The first artists chosen were Vuillard, Bonnard, Roussel, Denis, and Ranson. In the years to come there were illustrations by Manet and Monet, Corot, Pissarro, Renoir, Sisley, Puvis de Chavannes, Johann Jongkind, and Félix Vallotton. Even the writers Verlaine and Jules Laforgue drew amusing sketches for the review, and a superbly witty *Revue Blanche* poster by Toulouse-Lautrec was pasted up on the walls of Paris. Still in his twenties, Lautrec adored Misia, whom he playfully called "L'Alouette' (the Lark), a tribute to her swift grace. The poster, later used as a cover for the magazine, shows Misia dressed in a splendid ice-skating costume: a long blue coat dotted with red, a gray fur cape and muff, and a hat with feathers like plumes of green smoke spiralling into the air. With his genius for *mise-en-page*, Lautrec stops the image just below the knee, eliminating the skates but keeping the skater's forward-leaning stance, the push toward the spectator.

Of the painters published by the *Revue Blanche*, the ones who became intimate friends of the Natansons were Lautrec, Vuillard, Bonnard, Vallotton,

Cyprien Godebski,
Misia's father,
St. Petersburg, Russia

Misia, age two, in St. Petersburg

Misia's stepsister, Claire, Misia,
and her brothers Franz and Ernest, St. Petersburg

Misia and Thadée Natanson
Opposite, Misia

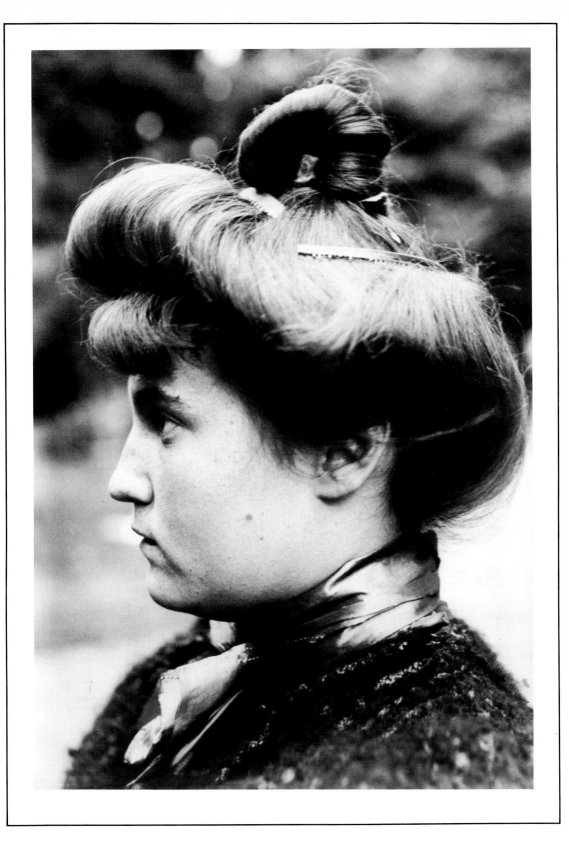

Thadée and Misia
Left, Le Relais,
the Natansons' house
at Villeneuve-sur-Yonne
Right, Misia in costume

Misia in front of Le Relais
Opposite, Misia in the garden

Standing, Cipa Godebski, Misia's half-brother; *on the lawn*, Felix Vallotton,
Edouard Vuillard, Stéphane Natanson, Marthe Mellot, Thadée, and Misia

Top left, the fan Mallarmé inscribed with a quatrain to Misia
Opposite, drawing of Mallarmé by Misia.
Above, At Le Relais after Stéphane Mallarmé's funeral:
Pierre Bonnard, Cipa, his wife, Ida,
Thadée, Misia, and Auguste Renoir

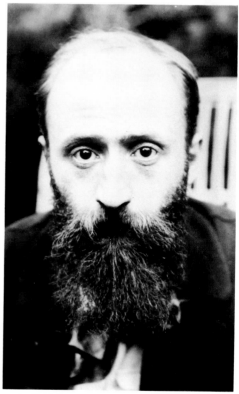

Clockwise from left,
Bonnard, Vallotton,
and Vuillard

Thadée, Vallotton, Romain Coolus, and Cipa, playing checkers

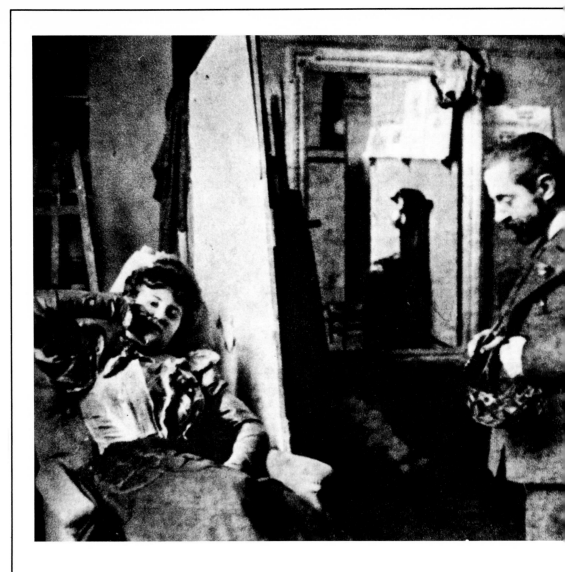

Misia and Henri de Toulouse-Lautrec

Colette

Renoir

Misia by Toulouse-Lautrec,
sketch for a poster for *La Revue Blanche*

and Roussel. Theirs was a rare integrity, which the Natansons cherished. Octave Mirbeau, one of the review's editors, wrote that these artists

> . . . were among those who attract, instantly and passionately, the atten-
> tion of serious-minded men whose constant desire is to enrich their
> intellectual domain. To be their friend was both joyous and profitable.
> . . . They opened up a spiritual world which . . . was in some way
> closed and obscure. And they added to the taste for enjoying life,
> reasons that were more valid, sounder, and loftier. . . . And in this way,
> without making a fuss, without impatience or bitterness, quietly,
> joyously, by their beautiful example, in art and in life, little by little
> they inscribed in the history of our painting, already so beautiful, one
> of the most beautiful, most significant, most moving chapters.

This glowing appreciation of the *Revue Blanche* painters by one of its writers is complemented by a somewhat less reverent view of the writers by one of its painters, Pierre Bonnard. In his playful drawing *Les Bureaux de la Revue Blanche*, he shows Mirbeau and Régnier in serious discussion, Alexandre haranguing Thadée, Félix Fénéon, one of the review's most influential editors, entering a doorway, and Jules Renard scribbling at a desk. On the wall at the left hangs a portrait of Misia, a seductive feminine presence. The *Revue Blanche* offices were used as a place of business, an art gallery, and a clubroom combined. The artists and writers met there regularly, then were swept off by Thadée to join Misia at the "annex." There the Natansons received the distant Gide, who did not like Misia, and the charming Valéry, who did. Most important to the Natansons were the visits of the Symbolist poet Stéphane Mallarmé. For them he was the soul of the *Revue Blanche* and the writer they valued above all others. Since music was Misia's first love, naturally musicians were invited as well. Fauré would appear with his young pupil, Maurice Ravel, small as a jockey and just as elegant. The ironic and fastidious Debussy, who had had his first great success in 1892 with his *Prélude à l'Après-midi d'un Faune*, brought his young wife, to whom Misia was devoted. One of the review's other music critics, Henri Gauthier-Villars, who married in the same year as the Natansons, brought his young wife too. The uproariously amusing Gauthier-Villars signed his newspaper articles "The Journal of an Usherette" and his novels "Willy." For the *Revue Blanche* he wrote several articles on Wagner, among them "Bayreuth and Homosexuality." At least, one assumes he wrote them, for it was an open secret that he had a stable of anonymous writers who produced his novels.* He even locked his wife in her room and forced her to compose novels that he unscrupulously signed "Willy." Since his wife was Colette, the world has reason to be grateful for his outlandish behavior. The couple made a singular impression on Misia: "The ravishing Colette, with her triangular face and wasp waist so tightly pinched in that she had the silhouette of a schoolgirl, and her husband Willy, whom we called 'the professor' and whose stories were so crude I was not sure I understood them completely."

Editing the prestigious *Revue* required sure taste, passionate involvement, and ruthless weeding out of mediocrity. For Thadée and for Misia—whom many people considered the passport to Thadée—it meant wielding power, giving and withholding favors: in a word, manipulation, a dangerous game that suited their somewhat devious natures. Theirs was a god-like position, one that they assumed with proprietary pleasure.

In 1894 Alexandre Natanson commissioned Vuillard to create nine large decorative panels for the dining room of his luxurious new house, at 60 avenue du Bois de Boulogne (now avenue Foch). Vuillard chose to paint women and children in the open air, a subject which in the eighteenth century Fragonard had treated in a magically idealized way. But Vuillard, who felt that a wall decoration should not impose itself, recorded everyday scenes—women gossiping on park benches and children playing among the trees—with an intimacy, a modesty, and an affectionate wit that have a magic of their own: one which makes the viewer long to be transported back to the Paris of the nineties. One feels he made these panels at a time when his "only guide," as he wrote to Maurice Denis, "was instinct, pleasure, and satisfaction."

* In 1898, when Gauthier-Villars refused to sign a document written by the *Revue Blanche* editors protesting Dreyfus' imprisonment, Pierre Veber, one of Willy's anonymous writers, said, "It's the first time he's refused to sign anything written by someone else."

To show off the paintings and their sumptuous new home, Alexandre and his wife gave a party for three hundred friends which became the talk of Paris. The housewarming took place in the exceptionally cold winter of 1895, when the snow, Jules Renard wrote, "was swirling around like a Loie Fuller." In an inspired moment Alexandre asked Toulouse-Lautrec to stage the party and design the invitations. The guests were invited to the *Bar des Natansons* and told, in English, that there would be "American and other drinks" and that "Mr. and Mrs. Natanson will be very pleased of your company at 8 h. ½." (The next day *Le Figaro* maliciously predicted that the invitations to the Natansons' next party would be in Hebrew.) The barmen for the gala evening were the 4½-foot-tall Lautrec (who, Madame Tristan Bernard said, was so short that to look down at him made her dizzy) and the 6½-foot painter Maxime Dethomas. Both were dressed in white barmen's suits. To complete his costume, Lautrec wore a waistcoat made from the American flag, and shaved his head.

Inspired by this ludicrous sight, Romain Coolus wrote:

> *Ah! Je comprends que l'on jalouse*
> *En barman ton profil grec*
> *Extraordinaire Toulouse*
> *Lautrec!* *

Above the immense bar was a sign in English: "Don't speak to the Man at the Wheel." Lautrec invented monstrous cocktails in layers of bright green, red, and yellow liqueurs. Paul Leclercq described the great colorist running amok at the bar:

> Lautrec's imagination was inexhaustible. After a series of drinks which had to be taken in one gulp, there followed a gamut of pink cocktails, undreamt-of concoctions which had to be sipped slowly through a straw. . . . He also compounded substantial cocktails of sardines in gin or port: he would set these aflame in a long silver dish, and before long they would be scorching the throats of the unwary. . . .

* *I understand that one envies the views*
Of your—the barman's—profile Greek
Extraordinary Toulouse
Lautreek!

There were also prairie oysters, their palatability unimproved by cayenne pepper.

As barman, Lautrec combined the roles of an impeccable gentleman's gentleman and a mad inventor. Before long his victims were clinging to the bar with one hand while clutching their drinks with the other. Jules Renard was wickedly amused by the sight of Madame Vallette (the novelist Rachilde) with her boyish haircut, ink-black eyebrows, flaming red dress, and heavy amber beads, waltzing in a corner with her rather domesticated husband, the editor of the *Mercure de France*. Holding on to each other's shoulders, they were almost the only people dancing to the deafening music of the orchestra.

Catulle Mendès and Ernest La Jeunesse roared incoherently at each other about the comparative virtues of French and German wine. The writers present swarmed all over Prince André Poniatowski, pretender to the Polish throne, who had never been so *tutoyé*-d in his life. And little wonder; Prince Charming, as Mallarmé fondly called him, had just married a California heiress and was looking for contributors to a projected American *Revue Blanche*. Amidst the drunken crowd Mallarmé alone maintained his Symbolist *regard hautain*. He and his daughter Geneviève watched the rowdy goings-on with graceful detachment.

The Rumanian Prince Bibesco was there, as were André Gide, Pierre Louÿs, and the actor Lucien Guitry. The air was thick with smoke and reeked of alcohol. Vuillard and Bonnard arrived late, having spent the day in the country. Exhausted and hungry, they could not cope with Lautrec's dizzying concoctions. Soon they could barely stand and had to be pushed— or rather, half carried—to one of the rooms which Lautrec had wisely arranged as an emergency ward.

Chambermaids and English governesses acted as nurses for the growing number of casualties. In no time all horizontal surfaces were occupied. Alfred Jarry and Félix Fénéon were among the first to succumb. Thadée never forgot "the gesture of smiling if unsteady politeness with which Fénéon arose, not without difficulty, in order to give his place to Bonnard and Vuillard. They did not even recognize him. Vuillard was barely conscious, his face as red as his beard, and Bonnard, dead drunk, fell stiffly into bed. Both were snoring soundly before Fénéon could leave the room, clinging to the arm of his chambermaid-nurse more out of caution than gallantry." At dawn Lautrec proudly announced that he had served two thousand drinks. He left the party fiendishly delighted that he had succeeded in getting everyone else drunk while he, for once in his life, remained completely sober.

❖

Misia and Thadée spent the summers of 1894 and 1895 visiting his family in Normandy and making short trips to Brittany. In a letter to Mallarmé, Thadée evokes the atmosphere of a seaside resort in the nineties:

Etretat-les-Mauves [1894]

. . . The pretty excursion with which we ended our trip had its unhappy moments. Beautiful bicycle rides, another beach with very beautiful rocks, a country fair swarming with noisy Bretons and pigs leading one another about, a jewel of a church called Folgoat. . . .

But at the end of the trip Misia caught a severe chill. A provincial pedant dared speak of inflammation of the lungs. He wanted to keep us there at least ten days and did not even catch the irony of his patient asking if he didn't have enough to keep him busy for the moment. We escaped—but only after three days. . . .

Here we work feverishly at doing nothing. A strict schedule divides our time: bicycling, tennis, rides in the carriage, playing cards, beach gossip, and meals. There's not an instant to waste on a book or a thought. We barely speak, and when we do it's about gambling or sports. We are in a daze and drown our boredom and all memory in a wave of distractions . . . which take the place of sea-bathing and seem more important.

Only a few tiny tots and two or three famous, elaborately dressed bathing beauties put in a conspicuous appearance, jump onto the pebbled beach, dive into the water, or shake themselves dry, to the joy of the well-dressed women who come to see the show. Kodaks of all models swallow with a little dry click the latest fashions to be admired.

Misia is frightfully bored—I less—I gamble. All the same I yearn, as she does, for Valvins. Nothing can make us forget it; we are just a little worried about the site. I rejoice at the thought of seeing, with you, the changing colors of the forest. . . .

The site in question, in the village of Valvins near Fontainebleau, contained a house called La Grangette and the Natansons were thinking of buying it. Valvins was not new to them, for Misia's father owned a grand villa there, and Mallarmé spent the summers in a small house on the Seine just a few steps from La Grangette. The Natansons did not hesitate for long and were soon happily settled in. A vine-covered house with a charmingly irregular façade, La Grangette still stands among tall trees a stone's throw from the river. It was comfortable, cluttered, and a bit shabby; that was part of its charm. Above the small, cozy ground-floor rooms was a large loft, rather like a granary, sheltered by a low, timbered ceiling. Here Misia installed her piano and Thadée's writing desk. Through the open dormer windows the pungent river smells rose from the water, and there at the river's edge Misia could see the pale green willows swaying and trembling in the breeze.

It was a magical time in Misia's life. As a married woman with her own country house, she was free to indulge in the youthful pleasures, the undisciplined intimacies she so much enjoyed: the easygoing life of an artist among artists. In the family tradition she filled her house to overflowing, and very soon La Grangette became the summer annex of the *Revue Blanche*: "But by now I had done some sorting out and invited, above all, those chosen by my heart. Vuillard and Bonnard installed themselves *chez moi* once and for all, and Toulouse-Lautrec came regularly from Saturday to Tuesday. He liked to bring along his cousin Tapié de Céleyran."* Misia's three young artists could not have been more different. Vuillard, with his questioning charm and melancholy smile, passionate beneath his laconicism, was Misia's confidant from the start. Bonnard, untroubled detachment itself, always affectionate and helpful, sparkled with satirical wit and laughter. Lautrec, of course, was a law unto himself, irreverent, foulmouthed, dictatorial. Although he bullied his cousin Tapié constantly, he

---

* The present owner of La Grangette, a Parisian doctor, uncovered a drawing by Lautrec scratched into the plaster chimneypiece over the sitting-room fireplace: a portrait of Tapié de Céleyran looking rather like a nineteenth-century Don Quixote in top hat and frock coat.

was all teasing tenderness with Vuillard, Bonnard, and the Natansons—his response to their sympathetic understanding.

It was a fine arrangement for everyone. Misia was surrounded, just as she liked to be. And certainly Vuillard and Bonnard had no objection to the friendly crowding. After all, in 1891 they had shared a studio with Maurice Denis and Lugné-Poë in which they painted away while groups of actors declaimed Ibsen and Bjoernson in the mesmeric chant Lugné favored. The struggling young painters, the boyish Bonnard in his bicycle knickerbockers and metal pince-nez, and the shy, red-bearded Vuillard, found it delightful to have friends who put them up for the summer, posed for them, bought their paintings, and enthusiastically found other buyers as well. The painters painted everything in sight: La Grangette, the garden, Mallarmé's house, the Seine dotted with boats. They painted Misia's brother Cipa, they painted Thadée, they painted one another, but most of all they painted Misia: Misia sewing, Misia walking in the fields, Misia at the piano. She was their country muse. The weeks sped by with picnics and parties, amateur theatricals and parlor games, bicycling, sailing on the river, and tremendous amounts of food, music, talk, and laughter.

Once Misia, Lautrec, and Romain Coolus stretched the short carriage trip from Paris to Valvins into a hilarious week. Dawdling over the elaborate lunches ordered by the gourmet Lautrec—he even travelled with a nutmeg grater to season his pre-lunch port—they took in the sights, and at Lautrec's urging sampled vast quantities of wine at each roadside café. Coolus was Lautrec's brothel and bar companion. Hoarse-voiced, with a cracked laugh, he was almost as short as the painter and just as explosive. Lautrec called him Co, Coco, and when he felt especially expansive, Colette. Alone with the two men, Misia flirted with both. Lautrec knew she was not serious; Coolus was not quite certain. When Misia had first met Lautrec, she had found the dwarf-like painter monstrous. His swollen lips, bulbous nose, oversized head, and enormous hands, together with the horribly painful way he dragged himself along with a cane, all made her want to look the other way. Nor did his drunkenness help. But by now she had forgotten her feelings of revulsion and was under the spell of the little man, so cruelly observant, so riotously gay, so magnificently talented.

Together the two men put on a real show. Lautrec talked with non-stop enthusiasm about a friend's adventures in Togoland, about who had the best phaeton in Paris, about Degas, whom he admired more than anyone.

Had they been to see Loie Fuller? He must show them his lithograph of her. *L'Américaine* was miraculous as she danced under changing electric lights waving long poles of swirling chiffon in the air. What? They had not gone to the latest sensational trial! They must not miss Dr. Péan's aluminum operating table, which went up and down at the touch of a button. When probing inside his patient's stomachs, Lautrec said, Dr. Péan looked as if he were searching his pockets for money, and he was so strong he could extract a molar with his fingers. What would they like him to cook when they reached Valvins? A *gigot de sept heures*? Calves' liver with prunes? Stewed squirrel? Leeks in red wine? And for dessert, what about chocolate mayonnaise, or those phallic cookies called convent serpents, or *pets de nonne*, pastries as light and delicate as a nun's fart? When Lautrec stopped talking long enough to breathe, he would make Misia and little Coolus jump by suddenly firing his pistol into the air.

The country near Fontainebleau was filled with friends. Besides the Mallarmés there were the Bourges,* the Redons, the Mirbeaus, and the Poniatowskis—all constantly in and out of each other's houses. When Octave Mirbeau's wife, a socially ambitious actress, invited the poet Alfred Jarry to lunch, he bicycled over from his decrepit river shack dressed in an undershirt and a pair of Madame Vallette's elegant velvet-laced slippers "dirty enough to frighten anyone," Misia remembered. "When Madame Mirbeau gazed with refined distress at his shoes, their large bows covered with mud, he said, 'Don't worry, Madame, I have another pair, much dirtier.' Roast beef was served for lunch. Ignoring the slices, Jarry grabbed the bone. There was a deadly silence, dominated by a wrathful look from the mistress of the house, a weird wink from the father of *Ubu*, and a stifled roar of laughter from the guests."

Friends arriving from Paris by train were met by the Natansons in their carriage, the intrepid Misia at the reins. Sometimes in sunny weather Misia would bicycle over to fetch them and lead them back along the forest paths to La Grangette. From the windows of her rustic studio, so touchingly depicted in Vuillard's *Room Under the Eaves*, Misia could see the bridge spanning the river and Mallarmé's trim little yawl bobbing up and down. Often, turning from the piano, she would watch the poet sailing on the pewter-colored Seine in the calm splendor of early evening. "There, I have

* Elémir Bourges, an unjustly neglected novelist much admired by Henry James.

a completely different impression of myself," Mallarmé wrote to Verlaine. "My only passion is sailing on the river—the river which I honor, for entire days are swallowed up in its watery abyss without leaving even a shadow of remorse. There I am a simple traveller in my mahogany yawls, or the passionate sailor proud of his fleet." With his wife and daughter Geneviève, Mallarmé lived on the second floor of a modest house between the Natansons and the bridge. The rooms were sparsely but exquisitely furnished. One well-chosen piece of furniture, Mallarmé felt, was enough to evoke a feeling of great luxury. A desk, a four-poster bed hung with red *toile de Jouy*, a Persian rug on the red-tiled floor, a painting by Berthe Morisot on the white-washed wall, and a magnificent view of the tranquil Seine made a home for which Mallarmé deserted Paris more and more. Surely it is Misia whom Mallarmé's biographer, Henri Mondor, is describing when he writes:

Among the faithful in Valvins there is a very young woman whom Mallarmé sometimes takes sailing. He explains marvellous things to her. He names the constellations, dreams of beautiful words arranged in patterns like the stars. For him, each word brings forth a world of images which he reveals to his young friend. She understands, discovers a superior truth, returns intoxicated by the Master. "What did he say?"—She no longer knows.

She believes. She is like the blind girl in the Andersen fairy tale who holds in her closed hand a bit of the dust of the touchstone of the Wise Men; when she opens her hand before the book in which are written the great mysteries of the world, a dazzling light falls on the page and all becomes clear. . . . Far from the sorcerer, the apprentice no longer understands.

In exchange for Mallarmé's stories, Misia, pouting with concentration, would play Beethoven and Schubert to him. From the dimly lit room with its shadowy rafters the poet would gaze at the river flowing past to the sea. Then, lighting his pipe, he would sink into a revery, "a man," in his words, "accustomed to the Dream." Never had Misia known such a sensitive listener.

While the phrase of music was born, breathed, took shape, grew steady in that silence whose singular quality emanated from his presence, we were united by a fragile, emotional communion so close that the rhythm of his thought rose to my lips.

> *... Et dans le soir, tu m'es en riant apparue*
> *Et j'ai cru voir la fée au chapeau de clarté*
> *Qui jadis sur mes beaux sommeils d'enfant gâté*
> *Passait, laissant toujours de ses mains mal fermées*
> *Neiger de blancs bouquets d'étoiles parfumées.*

> *... And in the evening you appeared to me, laughing*
> *And I thought I saw the fairy with the cap of knowledge*
> *Who once passed through my beautiful dreams of a spoiled child*
> *Letting fall like snow from her half-closed hands*
> *White bouquets of perfumed stars.*

These lines from Mallarmé's *Apparition*, which she whispered to herself as she played, seemed to Misia to be "words carved into a thousand precious stones whose facets suddenly dazzled me, blinded me so wondrously, that my eyes filled with tears. Exhausted, I felt the music fade away and die under my fingers." Mallarmé would give the ladies he particularly admired Japanese paper fans on which he had written haiku-like poems. Each New Year's Day Misia received a *pâté de foie gras* and a fan. The only one that survives has these charming lines about Misia's tempestuous playing:

Aile que du papier reploie	*Unfolding wing of paper*
Bats toute si t'initia	*Flutter fully, if not long ago*
Naguère a l'orage et la joie	*You were initiated by Misia*
De son piano Misia.	*To the storm and the joy of her piano.*

For a short while Mallarmé had taught at the Lycée Condorcet, where he was admired by a few of the more perceptive students, among them Thadée and Vuillard, but sadly misunderstood by the others. Indeed, the hermetic quality of his writing put many people off. Even when he was elected "Prince of Poets" by his fellow writers, there were those who felt that his poetry was too obscure, that it was all mystification and double-talk. Jules Renard said in his philistine way that Mallarmé was impossible to translate—even into French. But the younger poets venerated him as a man of great nobility. The aura that Mallarmé radiated of both spiritual and physical grace was charmingly described by Manet when he called him "half priest, half dancer." As a special friend of Mallarmé's, Misia was among the few women ever to be invited to one of his famous Tuesday evenings. Short, with smiling blue eyes, the pointed ears of a faun, and a moustache which flowed into his pointed graying beard, Mallarmé would stand in front of a porcelain stove in his dining room and smoke continually. In Symbolist fashion he said that he liked to have a cloud of smoke between himself and the crowd. Rising on his heels, he spoke in an even, muted voice, like a man "attentively listening to the wandering course of his own thoughts," the writer Ernest Raynaud said. "He expressed himself clearly and precisely, without the complicated convolutions of his poetry, using very simple words to which the timbre of his voice gave a new lustre—the most ordinary details became transfigured. As Moréas said, he could make an actress's tights into a subject worthy of Plato."

But the Mallarmé that Misia knew best was not the high priest of poetry receiving his disciples in the holy temple, or the tortured poet struggling to write what he called "The Book"—the one perfect poem—or the genius who saw words in a new way. For her he was an enchanting friend, relaxed and at home in the country, amused to be with intelligent and gifted young people. He was the man who, when he earned a little money, bought an English carriage and a circus pony to pull it. The pony, dreaming of his days in the ring and the dizzy exaltation of the waltz, was bored by the straight forest paths. Whenever they came to a clearing, Mallarmé would give him his head, and the animal, reminded of his former triumphs, would gallop tirelessly in perfect circles. Then, with the poet acting as trainer, the pony would fetch Geneviève's handkerchief, uncover a watch hidden in the sand, and nod at the guest who had drunk most heavily at lunch. Among the pony's ardent admirers were three young ladies, the sisters Paule and Jeannie Gobillard and their cousin Julie Manet. Julie, the daughter of Berthe Morisot and the niece of Edouard Manet, had lost her parents when very young, and Mallarmé and Renoir were her guardians.

In her perceptive journal, the seventeen-year-old Julie often spoke of the Natansons:

September 18, 1896

Mme. Natanson, charming in a light blue dress with a high waist, a very pretty white low-cut square collar, and short sleeves. She wore a necklace on her lovely rounded white neck. She played Beethoven's C minor symphony in an extraordinary fashion, sad, noble, grave, suggesting all the instruments of the orchestra. She has a beautiful broad powerful way of playing, not at all French.

Three days later Julie, her cousin Jeannie (who was to marry Paul Valéry), the Mallarmé family, and the Bourges again spent the evening at the Natansons'. Julie, a fine pianist herself, wrote: "Mme Natanson played charming Handel dances, among others the passacaglia, which she tore into with as much lift as if she were bowing it." (Little wonder that Thadée called Misia the "piano tamer," and Mallarmé described her playing as stormy.) When the summer drew to an end, Mallarmé wrote to his wife and daughter, who had returned to the comforts of Paris, "Everyone is gone except the Natansons and me. The country has reverted to its natural inhabitants." His letters often spoke of Misia and the beautiful clothes she wore—and he was an authority, for he had once written and published a fashion magazine. Every evening, dressed in a long cape and wooden *sabots*, a lantern in one hand and a bottle of wine in the other, Mallarmé walked along the muddy path to the Natansons' for one of Misia's copious meals. Entering La Grangette he would remove his *sabots* to reveal exquisite black stockings (he was vain about his small feet, Thadée said). He would tell stories to make Misia laugh and then, shaking with laughter himself, would say, *"Qu'elle est gentille!"* But she was not always nice—far from it. One night after dinner, while listening to him read a poem, Misia, not always up to such loftiness, suddenly interrupted him, pretending to be ill. Sadly Mallarmé left. Misia was deeply ashamed when the poet reappeared a few minutes later with some pills for *la malade imaginaire*. Geneviève, however, had told Misia to tease her father often so that he would not lose the habit of being teased. On Sunday evening, November 8, Mallarmé wrote his family that his last letter must have reached them while he was listening to Misia play Beethoven's Eighth Symphony. He had been to lunch at the Natansons that afternoon. "What truly kind people, what kind friends they are. They even understand that they must not over-feed me."

In December 1896 the Natansons and their friends were caught up in a historic theatrical storm. The storm center was *Ubu Roi*, a play for which Bonnard had created the decor with the help of Vuillard, Lautrec, Sérusier, and Ranson. The painters boyishly pitched in to help Lugné-Poë with the direction, and Claude Terrasse, Bonnard's brother-in-law, provided the music. The play was written by Alfred Jarry, whose works the *Revue Blanche* had begun to publish in March of that year. The *répétition générale*, the dress rehearsal, which in Paris is more important than the official opening night, was Misia's initiation to the feverish excitement of a Parisian theatrical scandal. All in all, December 9 was a memorable day for the theatre-goers of Paris. It began at noon in the Grand Hotel, where a banquet for five hundred people was given for Sarah Bernhardt. The great actress' entrance was theatricality itself. There was a hushed silence when she appeared at the top of the curved staircase leading down into the banquet room. She wore a magnificent gold-embroidered white dress adorned with chinchilla, English lace, and a long train. Leaning on the banister, her radiant face transfigured, she descended in an incomparable series of poses that brought the guests to their feet in admiration. She looked, Jules Renard said, as if she were standing still while the staircase revolved around her. Bravos rang out as five hundred glasses were raised to the divine Sarah. After lunch the guests followed her to the Théâtre de la Renaissance to applaud her in scenes from *Phèdre* and *Rome Sauvée* and to listen to sonnets composed in her honor. (Only that morning in *Le Figaro* Sarah had modestly pronounced herself "the faithful priestess of poetry.") Everyone was overwhelmed with emotion, and her son Maurice wept in his loge.

That evening, many of the same theatre-goers—Thadée and Misia among them—attended the dress rehearsal of *Ubu Roi*. While some felt they were going from the sublime to the ridiculous, history suggests that it was perhaps Sarah's matinee that was slightly ridiculous and that Jarry's evening had its share of the sublime. When the house lights went down,* the short, twenty-three-year-old Jarry appeared in front of the curtain. He was heavily made up, with hair blackened and plastered down, and dressed in the baggy suit of a clown. Seated at a table covered in rough burlap, he hammered out the prologue in a metallic sing-song, ending, "Now for the action. It takes

---

* Lugné-Poë was the first director in Paris to stage plays in a darkened theatre, although Wagner's operas had already been performed that way in Bayreuth. The Parisians objected violently; they felt that they were missing half of the spectacle because they could not see each other.

place in Poland—that is—nowhere." The curtains parted on a hilly land-scape. On one side flurries of snow fell on a canopied bed complete with chamber pot; on the other a giant boa constrictor twisted itself around a palm tree. The decor was completed by a skeleton hanging from a scaffold, a window with owls perched on it, and an outsize fireplace that opened in the center for the performers' entrances and exits. An actor hung up a sign read-ing, "The House of Monsieur and Madame Ubu," and the play began. With the golden voice of Bernhardt as Phèdre still ringing in their ears—*Oui, Prince, je languis, je brûle pour Thésée* (Yes, prince, I languish, I burn for Theseus)—the audience was startled by Père Ubu's first word, "Shee-it!" (*mer-dre*) and Mère Ubu's, "Oh! that's nice, Pa, you're a big bastard." These novel opening lines were received with laughter, but as the play con-tinued, following its own aggressively obscene logic, an uproar arose in the audience.

"Don't you see Jarry's making damn fools of us!" Georges Courteline shouted while Harry Bauer, an illegitimate son of Dumas *père*, cheered at the top of his lungs. Jean de Tinan took both sides, applauding and booing simultaneously. Colette roared with laughter and Willy, turning to the audience, shouted, "On with the show!" One woman applauded violently while screaming, "You old bastard!" at the conservative critic Francisque Sarcey. Rachilde, who admired Jarry, tried unsuccessfully to stop the booing and whistling. Fernand Gregh's shout to the audience, "You wouldn't even understand Shakespeare!" was answered from the balcony, "You've never read Shakespeare yourself, you idiot!" It was the voice of Gregh's brother. The actor playing Père Ubu improvised a frantic jig that brought the audience under control for a moment or two. To silence the crowd, Lugné-Poë turned the house lights up. But when they were turned down again, the spectators made so much noise that it was impossible to hear the actors. Above the din someone screamed, *"Lugné-Pot-de-chambre!"* It was the wildest theatrical scandal Paris was to know between Victor Hugo's *Hernani* in 1830 and Stravinsky's *Le Sacre du Printemps* in 1913. And there is no denying that during the riotous evening of December 9, 1896, Jarry became one of the heroes of twentieth-century art.

There was so much talk about the first performance of *Ubu Roi* that, just as in the case of *Le Sacre*, many who had not been present claimed that they had. The word "Ubu" entered the language. People "Ubu-ized," imitating Jarry's trenchantly obscene locutions. Bonnard named his basset hound

Ubu. And even Mallarmé, who did not like Jarry—possibly finding his homosexual hooliganism unsavory—wrote him that he had created a haunting character and christened his cats Monsieur and Madame Ubu. Jarry became a constant and brilliant contributor to the *Revue Blanche*, which was to be his main source of income. In fact, the review's demise four years before his own left him destitute. He tried to destroy himself with the same violent originality with which he attacked bourgeois society. Rachilde said he began each day with two bottles of wine, drank three glasses of absinthe before lunch, and continued on the same exalted level all day. Apollinaire added, perhaps apocryphally, that Jarry soothed his stomach by taking a large glass—half vinegar, half absinthe, seasoned with a drop of ink—each night before falling into bed. As he lay dying at the age of thirty-four, the last request of this nose-thumbing Pulcinello was for a toothpick.

The following spring the Natansons decided that, much as they loved La Grangette, it was too small for their ever-expanding house party. Looking for a larger house, they scoured the countryside in one of the first motor cars bought in France. The proud owners were photographed in the high, brass-fitted automobile: Misia at the wheel in a "duster," Thadée at her side. On one of their excursions they discovered Le Relais, a large, handsome posting house at Villeneuve on the banks of the Yonne, with the date 1807 carved into its stone façade. The house was set in a spacious garden shaded by ancient elms leading down to a gentle curve in the river. Misia, who always had mixed feelings about her father, did not mind leaving him behind in Valvins. In any case, he and Cipa came frequently with their families to stay at Le Relais. La Grangette did not disappear from her life, however, for Cipa took it over and kept it in the family for years. Misia's only regret was losing Mallarmé as a neighbor. In an affectionate letter Thadée consulted him about having a boat built and insisted that he come to see them. Villeneuve was extremely pleasant, he wrote, "if not the marvel that Valvins remains in our memory. . . . The little Yonne does not have the majesty of your Seine. . . . The upholsterer is busily hammering away . . . and Misia's piano is pouting in silence. . . ."

Summer life continued even more pleasantly than at Valvins. Apollinaire came to see them and Vallotton visited a good deal. Pale-eyed and reserved, he had become an indispensable member of the household. Jules Renard described him as a man with "a sweet, simple, distinguished air, straight hair neatly parted, restrained gestures, not very complicated theories, but with an indefinable egotism in everything he said." Thadée's brother Fred brought his charming wife, the actress Marthe Mellot, who was to play Ophelia to Bernhardt's Hamlet. Coolus and Roussel appeared often. And as before, Vuillard, Bonnard, and Lautrec were constant visitors. A record of the Natansons' country life exists in their friends' paintings, drawings, and photographs. The Kodak had captivated them all. Fred would round them up for group pictures, taking everyone and everything in sight: the front of the house with Misia standing at the door, Lautrec and Coolus seated beside her, Thadée leaning out of a window above. There are photographs of the friends playing *boules*, lolling on the grass, and sitting on the garden furniture that Lautrec had had made for them in Albi; of Marthe Mellot at the lunch table; of Misia with a parasol, strolling on the lawn. Everything is grace, relaxation, peace.

Vuillard would wander about, then suddenly say in his quiet way, "One second, please," and his subjects would freeze till released by the click of his accordion-pleated camera. His photographs of Misia and her friends served as sketches for paintings that have the intimacy of a snapshot— a moment informally captured for all time. What a pity Vuillard never pointed his Kodak at Lautrec, squatting beside Misia, playfully tickling the soles of her bare feet with a brush as he painted imaginary landscapes on them. But at least there is a photograph of him, chasing butterflies with his little cane as he shouted, "Tally-ho! Tally-ho!" Just as he had at Valvins, Lautrec spent the days boating and swimming in the river. He liked to have his picture taken and, mugging for the camera, seemed to feel an aggressive pleasure in having his deformed body photographed in the nude. Poor Lautrec was trying unsuccessfully to curb his drinking habit. Only a few months earlier at the Natansons' in Paris, he had been hopelessly drunk at dinner and upset them by making lewd advances to their maid.

Fortunately, drinking did not keep Lautrec from his work. At Villeneuve he began a painting of Coolus in the manner of El Greco and one of Misia at the piano that he planned to name after Beethoven's *Ruins of Athens*. It was a piece his mother had played, and in his childishly insistent way he begged Misia to repeat it again and again as he painted her. "Ah, the pretty ruins, the beautiful ruins, let's have the ruins again, Misia," he would say. Swept up in his frenzied enthusiasm, she would play it ten times over while he sang along in a voice which set the dogs to howling. When Yvette Guilbert had asked him why he made the women in his paintings so ugly, Lautrec replied, "Because they are." Just as Guilbert had complained that he'd made her neck too long, Misia teased Lautrec by saying that he'd made her neck too short, her eyes too small, and her chin too heavy. Lautrec took his playful revenge. At dinner one night he drew Misia as the madam of a brothel presiding over her clients. (Lautrec was an authority on the subject of brothels. When Yvette Guilbert asked him where he lived, he casually gave the address of a well-known whorehouse. Asked how he could stay in such a place, the eccentric aristocrat replied, "My God, would you rather I entertained such riff-raff at home?") Misia, careless as a butterfly and more than a little annoyed, tossed Lautrec's caricature into the waste-basket. But Lautrec persisted. He painted *A Table chez M. et Mme. Natanson*, with Misia, stout and blowzy, thirty years added to her age, her hair dyed a poisonous red. Her jowl jutting forward, her elbows firmly planted on a table, she seems ill-tempered but in control of the situation. As her "clients": Vuillard looking cross, Vallotton cool and aloof, and Thadée facing her, his expression invisible to the spectator. Lautrec had more endearing ways of returning the Natansons' hospitality. After giving a lunch party for them in Paris, with each dish at a different restaurant and special wines from his mother's cellar, he decided to end the meal with a surprise. Without telling his guests where he was taking them, he led them up three steep flights of stairs to the apartment of the bassoonist Desiré Dihau.* Eyes shining in admiration, Lautrec pointed at Degas' painting, *Dihau Playing in the Orchestra at the Opera*, and said, "There you are—that's your dessert."

It was becoming apparent, however, that Lautrec should be sent to a clinic. Gray, haggard, and sick, he would come home, sometimes badly beaten up, after his nocturnal wanderings. He was burning himself out, but his friends could not reason with him. In March 1899 they arranged for him to be kidnapped by two male nurses and taken to a clinic in Neuilly, the Folie-Saint-James in the avenue de Madrid. Misia visited him daily at what it amused him to call "Madrid-les-Bains," as though it were a fashionable spa. His nickname for Misia had always been "L'Alouette"; now, however, he greeted her as "La Colombe de l'Arche," hoping that she, like the dove of the ark, had come to signal the end of disaster. In fact Lautrec was

---

* Dihau was a composer of popular songs as well. One of them, "La Sagesse," was published with a picture of Misia by Lautrec on the cover.

released a short time afterward, but his improvement was only temporary. Two years later, in September 1901, he lay dying in the family château at Albi. Misia wept when she heard that his eccentric father, Count Alphonse, sat at his bedside and pegged at the flies that settled on the inert body of his dying son with a slingshot made of the elastic from his shoes, while the invalid muttered, "Will you always be such a silly bugger?" She remembered how Lautrec had startled them with a pistol shot from his room at Le Relais and how relieved they had been to find him sitting cross-legged on his bed shooting at a spider spinning a web. And, funny but sad, she recalled Lautrec, in yellow oilskins, conscientiously having a drink in every dark little café in Villeneuve "to open the hunting season."

That first summer of 1897 at Villeneuve, Vuillard painted two extraordinary portraits: one of Lautrec in his yellow oilskins, the other of Misia seated, an expression of tender solicitude on her face. The latter is as much a portrayal of Vuillard's feelings for Misia as it is of Misia herself. For the twenty-nine-year-old painter had fallen in love with the wife of his friend Thadée. One evening as the Natansons were about to leave for a trip to Normandy, Vuillard asked Misia to join him for a last walk along the river. Fifty years later she wrote:

> We started out at twilight. Solemn and dreamy, Vuillard led me along the river through the tall, silvery birches. I think we did not speak. He advanced slowly in the yellowing grass and I unconsciously respected his silence. Night was falling rapidly, and to go back we took a short cut through a beet field. Our silhouettes, side by side, were still shadows against the pale sky. The ground became rough under our feet. I caught my heel on a root and almost fell. Vuillard stopped short to help me regain my balance. Suddenly our eyes met. In the growing darkness I could see only the gleam of his sad eyes. He burst into sobs. It was the most beautiful declaration of love any man ever made to me.

When Vuillard died in 1940, his will stated that his personal papers were not to be opened for fifty years. But a moving glimpse of his feelings for

Misia is revealed in his letters to Vallotton. Although he never actually names her, it is clear that his hopeless love for Misia was making him unhappy. In the letters he wrote to Vallotton, Vuillard confided—in words as elusively subtle as the strokes of his painting—the hopelessness of his situation.

> July 20, 1897
> Villeneuve-sur-Yonne

My dear friend,

I cling to you in order not to eat my heart out any longer. Confusing problems are killing me. Your stay here remains with me like a memory of paradise; since then it has been abominably stormy; everything is going badly. I work relentlessly to keep up my morale, which is rather low. . . . However, I must not continue in this vein. . . . Yesterday at table Thadée read us your letter, which cheered us all up. Everyone here loves you.

Lautrec is here and is beginning to calm down, though not without difficulty. But one must not despair; he has good moments and is really very attached to Thadée and his wife. We have received Fred's first snapshots. Your photo is superb. We plan to go to Valvins tomorrow. Perhaps it will do us all good. There are really bad moments to conjure away. It seems to me that it would be cowardly to leave; otherwise I would escape at once or go and be desperate somewhere else. I shall write you later, I hope in a better mood. Don't pay too much attention to what I tell you, but it would be an act of charity if you would do me the favor of writing to me,

> Your,
> Vuillard

Vallotton's answer may be among Vuillard's sealed papers. Judging by the letter that Vuillard wrote him two weeks later from Paris, Vallotton too was going through a sentimental crisis.

> 342 rue St. Honoré
> August 5, 1897

My dear friend,

Your letter reached me only yesterday—wrong address. It makes me sad; however, I trust that this is the bitterest moment of a period in

your life which is as nightmarish as mine was when I wrote you last.
. . . In my lowest moment I came to the conclusion that anything I
could say would be useless. I shall suffer, that's all, but it's fate. And it
seems that we are made for this little game of ups and downs, since we
are able to endure it for thirty or forty years. . . . Besides, I don't want
to burden you.

I spoke a bit to Thadée, who expects you as soon as he returns—i.e.,
next Tuesday or Wednesday. He's not writing you now, as he's busy
running after trains and his wife. He is going with Misia to Houlgate;
we left Villeneuve together yesterday morning, and I shall go back
with them without hesitation as soon as they return. I have only had
time to see Roussel, who has done three or four pastels in which there
are delicious things. He too is thinking of spending a few days at
Villeneuve. Bonnard, whom I see tomorrow, leaves with me. Also Fred,
Marthe, Coolus, and Alex are expected around the fifteenth. Perhaps
Lautrec . . .

Vallotton must have been taken aback to learn that Vuillard had decided
to return to the Relais. But Misia and Thadée, somewhat perversely, perhaps,
insisted on keeping their friend with them to see the situation through.

From Villeneuve, Vallotton received a letter written jointly by Vuillard
and Misia in which one can see the cruelly playful tone that Misia used to
jolly Vuillard out of his emotional impasse:

October 23, 1897

Yes, my dear friend, I have been here for two weeks, unhappy to see
the time fly by so quickly when the weather is so beautiful and we are
so comfortable. There is painting, of course, to spoil things, but the
kindness of Misia and Thadée repairs the damage. . . . Misia will tell
you her news herself. She is very happy with their plan to go to Italy,
but what she will not tell you is that she is always a charming and good
woman. She is sporting the violent colors that delight you as much as
they do me. Perhaps you will come back soon? . . .

E. Vuillard

Vuillard is acting as my husband, as you can see, my dear Vallo, but
naturally he is not behaving well. Thadée left this morning for Paris

to get things started for our trip to Italy. We leave in about ten days and I am mad with joy. I am beside myself, especially at the thought of Venice and the gondolas. Yes, Vallo, I have become sentimental and romantic since you last saw me. I dream of serenades, of rope ladders, of gondolas and palaces! What will all these dreams lead to? . . . You know we are not leaving here for at least a week. Come quickly and spend a few days. The weather is marvellous and you will find the intimacy you were crying for this summer. There are just the four of us, Vuillard and Chietrop [a scatological pun on Cipa's name]. The latter is very busy—we are worried that he will get meningitis if he does not take care of himself. All the same, he has managed to find the time to send you his regards. I send you, *mon petit Vallo*, heaps of affectionate greetings from Thadée and from us.

> Your friend,
> Misia

The address [that of the Vallotton family's chocolate factory in Lausanne] on your envelope makes me dream, dear friend. My little stomach would be so happy with a few little chocolates! And come out soon.

VUILLARD TO VALLOTTON

> 96 rue des Batignolles
> November 7, 1897

My dear friend,

. . . You know what my character is; I stayed with Thadée and Misia as long as I could because I was as happy there as I am capable of being. So they didn't have to insist in order to keep me with them, and even to take me as far as Dijon. . . . After all, we must live where best we can and in the company of those with whom we breathe most easily. There is nothing abnormal or illogical in that. If you are upset, take the train soon. We owe each other a great deal, but basically we have so much good will that our friendship cannot be useless, in spite of all the egotistical feelings which we seem to think are necessary. My heart is full and I can't express myself clearly. It would be easier to chat with you. I hope it will be soon.

I have painted several pictures at Villeneuve that I shall try to sell. My train of thought is the same as when you last saw me. I am still trying to understand what a picture is, to paint, and to make that my life. It is not easy, but still it is necessary to think about it all first.

Misia has asked me to tell you what pleasure your chocolates gave her. She was packing and could not write you immediately; she will do it en route. You know her—she loves you very much and asked me to tell you so. What a good and kind woman! It is true that we shall miss her very much. I have rediscovered the Thadée I missed. As for Cipa, I'll tell you some preposterous stories. He is becoming more and more epic. . . . I do not know what's been happening here. I've just arrived and am resting by writing to you.

> Your friend,
> E. Vuillard

That summer the elegant and worldly novelist Claude Anet, a boyhood friend of Thadée's, used the money he had won in a tennis tournament to commission some panels from Vuillard. In these masterpieces of decorative art Vuillard captured the evanescent atmosphere at Villeneuve. Summer fills the canvas, but no shadow darkens the garden or the people in it. It is a world in which man and nature are one. Is that a woman or a butterfly passing? Nothing leaps to the eye; everything inhabits the canvas as though the paint had magically soaked in from behind. Myriad shades of muted green, ochre and red, white and black cover the figures, clouds, benches, and trees, making the canvas shimmer with an inner splendor, a quiet peace. The paintings are a lyric sublimation of Vuillard's love for Misia. In them we see the friends strolling about or reading in the garden. In one panel Bonnard is seen with his mistress Marthe, glancing at an illustrated paper; in another Misia in a flowing white dress, her feet lost in the long grass, is seated in one of the chairs given her by Lautrec. She dreams midsummer dreams, a smile of sibylline contentment on her lips. It is the summer of her youth. With these paintings Vuillard had come to terms with the situation. Almost apologetically he wrote to Vallotton that he was in a better mood:

One thing is certain: everything is going as well as possible, and I don't know why. I believe we have more inner resources than we think on gloomy winter days, because we have such an ability to forget and to dissipate. (I mean dissipate in the sense of letting our troubles disappear). The positive pleasures of beautiful summer weather and a few slight differences in our surroundings are enough to cure us of our ridiculous ambitions. . . . I have room left to add a moral. The best way to prepare for the future is really to enjoy the present. I leave you from the heights of my wisdom, knowing that you will not make fun of me.

Perhaps the act of painting the panels had done more for Vuillard than he realized. He was able to continue seeing Misia and Thadée with a certain equanimity. Not long after, Vallotton introduced him to Monsieur and Madame Jos Hessel, cousins of the picture dealer Bernheim. With them Vuillard was to repeat, more or less, the pattern of his relations with the Natansons—though some say that he was more successful with Madame Hessel than with Misia. In any case, Misia and Vuillard met less and less as time went by. Many years later when they had almost lost sight of one another, Misia sent Vuillard a Beethoven recording with a message saying that he would always be her closest friend. Touched, the white-haired bachelor wrote Misia about his regrets, his bitterness, his continuing struggle to come to terms with life, and his enduring affection for her:

I have always been very shy with you, but the certainty, the confidence in a perfect understanding between us, relieved me of all constraint, and this understanding lost nothing in being always unexpressed. Now that we have not seen each other for so long, I often ask myself with bitterness if it is still the same.

Your card answered my question. Oh, no! I did not find your thought ridiculous; I saw in it only your affection. Through you I shall owe yet another joy to old Beethoven, a melancholy joy like all that comes from him. But he also evokes such a feeling of health and sanity, just like you, Misia, who have such a large share of both. Good old Bonnard has explained it all so well to me. But everyone sees things in his own way, and that is the way Bonnard likes to see people. He is very prudent; it's the only way to keep out of trouble.

I envy him and really wish that we could all think of one another in his way. Sometimes I manage to, but not often enough—only when the weather is radiantly beautiful, as it is now in this corner of Normandy where I find calm and a little feeling of live-and-let-live. But too often I torment myself. I would not, however, have believed that I myself could become a torment to my friends. I wish—as much as the word has meaning—I wish I knew you to be full of life and at peace. If you were here I would not speak, but I am as confident as I was in the old days that you would understand me very well.

In 1898, when the countryside around Villeneuve was glorious with the first promise of autumn, Misia and Thadée learned of Mallarmé's death. With almost no warning he had died on the ninth of September. It was an irreparable loss. Only two years earlier, Misia had walked with Mallarmé along the boulevard St. Michel in what began as a small procession following Verlaine's funeral. As they went along, such a crowd of students, friends, the rowdy, and the curious joined the procession that by the time they reached the cemetery on the edge of Paris an hour later, there were thousands of people in the cortege. And now Misia and Thadée were making their way from Villeneuve to Valvins where, unbelieving, they found themselves in Mallarmé's modest room, looking for the last time at the poet with whom they had spent so many happy days. A small group of friends, many still in country clothes and bicycling costumes, had managed to reach Valvins in time for the funeral. The young poet Paul Valéry, who, if anyone, was to inherit the mantle of Mallarmé, was among the first to arrive. Rodin appeared, and Renoir, bringing Julie Manet with him.

JULIE MANET'S JOURNAL: SUNDAY, SEPTEMBER 11, 1898

We arrive at Valvins about two o'clock. How painful it is to go down the road along the banks of the Seine toward that little spot. I cannot bear to think that he whom we weep for is no longer there. The boat looks lonely—his boat which he loved so much. It reminds me of the first promenade I made in it with *maman* and *papa*, who asked Monsieur Mallarmé if he had ever written anything about his boat. "No," he replied, looking at his sail, "I am leaving that great page blank."

My heart feels heavy as I enter the little garden, go up the stairs, and see the two unhappy women. How sorry I feel for them. How to console them? One can only weep with them. Ah, poor Geneviève, what a life she has. It's painful to see this charming interior without

Monsieur Mallarmé, and to see his coffin there instead of listening to him talking in the garden under the chestnut tree which Geneviève planted when she was small. It's horrible! . . .

The writers and the peasants, to whom Monsieur Mallarmé was so kind, gathered together in great numbers in the garden to join the heartbreaking funeral procession. There was sadness graven on every face.

The ceremony at the church of Samoreau [the village nearest Valvins] was very simple and good. The cemetery borders the Seine and looks toward the forest that Monsieur Mallarmé loved so much. He is buried next to his son, whom he lost early. Trembling with emotion, Roujon said a few words in the name of the old friends. . . . He spoke very simply about Mallarmé's character, making us feel all its sweetness. He brought tears to our eyes when he described how, when one went to him in the difficult moments of life, he held out a helping hand, half lowering his eyelids over his great child-like eyes.

What a discreet and accurate likeness, just the way Monsieur Mallarmé would have liked it to be. Then Paul Valéry spoke for the young; but he was so overcome that he could not go on. Sobbing, we left the cemetery with Geneviève.

Still, this is perhaps the least horrible part—the day when all your friends come to embrace you and weep with you. What is terrible is to see life take up its course again as if no one had disappeared, and the period in which we lived with the person we mourn recedes little by little. How gloomy it is this evening with everyone gone, alone with the two women. From now on they will be without the man for whom they existed. . . .

After the funeral Misia and Thadée asked their friends to come back to Villeneuve with them. Sadly they all left: Renoir, Lautrec, Vuillard, Vallotton, Bonnard, Claude Terrasse, Vollard, Mirbeau, Coolus, Bourges, Maurice Maeterlinck, and Georgette Leblanc. At dinner that night, unnerved by the tensions of the day, everyone was suddenly overcome by hysterical fits of laughter. Misia, the first to recover, was angry and ashamed. Renoir, who loved Mallarmé and was closer to him in age than the others, reassured her gently, saying, "Don't upset yourself, Misia; one doesn't bury Mallarmé every day."

PART THREE
Madame Edwards

Overleaf, Misia Edwards on the *Aimée,* c. 1905

And what excuse is more convenient from our point of view than the one which gives the impression that we are yielding to force?

—CHODERLOS DE LACLOS

What is it a woman really wants?

—SIGMUND FREUD
[after fifty years of practice]

For Misia the first year of the twentieth century meant many things. Practically at her door was the 1900 Exposition, extending from the Place de la Concorde past the splendid new Pont Alexandre III to the Eiffel Tower. It was Paris' delirious celebration of itself. The Exposition was officially proclaimed the synthesis of the spirit of the century, representing the grandeur, the grace, and the beauty which reflect the genius of France. Paris swarmed with exotic visitors from all over the world. Overnight a fantastic city within a city appeared: mosques and minarets, Arab towns, Swiss villages, wooden houses from Sweden, gypsy cabarets from Hungary, even a reproduction of San Marco in Venice. There were belly dancers to see and mines to visit. The fashionable thing to do was to watch the dancers at the Thé de Ceylan while sipping iced tea, the latest novelty. A seemingly endless moving sidewalk provided a panoramic view of the Exposition and the opportunity, as Courteline pointed out, to show one's backside to thirteen thousand, eight hundred and eighty-seven people. The river and the pavilions along it sparkled with brilliant colored lights. Electricity was king. Misia boarded the model Trans-Siberian Railway and before she could take in the luxury of the wagon-salon, decorated in plush, onyx, crystal, and marble, she was being whisked off to the country of her birth. A painted landscape of Russia unfolded outside the train window while she munched on *zakuski* and drank tea served by a *moujik* in a belted blouse. A panorama of barren steppes, wide rivers with pine-covered islands, gold mines, and Mongol tombs rolled past her. Suddenly the Russian peasant disappeared and *hop-la!* a Chinese boy in blue silk popped up, serving jasmine tea in china cups. "Peking. Everyone off!" Leaving the train, Misia found herself miraculously transported to the gates of the Forbidden City, pagoda roofs and all.

At Vuillard's urging, Misia went to see Sada Yacco, the Japanese actress-dancer. Vuillard had written that the elegance, the costumes, the comic and tragic effects, in short, the perfection of the Japanese theatre, was as great as that of Japanese art. (Among Sada Yacco's admirers were three visitors from England: Sir Henry Irving and Ellen Terry, accompanied by Lord Alfred Douglas, on his way to the Transvaal to volunteer in the Boer War.) At the Exposition, French submarines "sank" the enemy fleet in mock naval battles staged on an artificial lake—a display of military strength that alarmed Thadée and his pacifist friends. Nineteen hundred was also the year of Charpentier's *Louise* and Debussy's *Nocturnes*. Monet's *Water Lilies* and Rodin's *The Kiss* were shown. Sixteen new rooms were opened at the Louvre. Oscar Wilde died at the Hôtel d'Alsace, where he had lived under an assumed name after his release from prison. Everyone was reading Tolstoy's *Resurrection*, and raw beef blood was recommended as the new cure for tuberculosis.

While Misia's hopes of becoming a professional pianist had faded, her friends were enjoying popular success: Tristan Bernard and Claude Terrasse with their operetta *La Petite Femme de Loth* (*Lot's Little Woman*), Jules Renard with the dramatization of his *Poil de Carotte*, and Octave Mirbeau with *The Diary of a Chambermaid*. When two women writers tried to join the Society of Men of Letters, Mirbeau, his moustache bristling, summed up the prevalent Belle Epoque view of women: "Woman is not a brain, she is a sex, and that is much better. She has only one role in this world, to make love, that is, to perpetuate the race. She is not good for anything but love and motherhood. Some women, rare exceptions, have been able to give, either in art or literature, the illusion that they are creative. But they are either abnormal or simply reflections of men. I prefer what are called prostitutes because they at least are in harmony with the Universe." Despite Mirbeau's forbidding words, certain women refused to confine their activities to making love and bearing children. Misia's women friends were as active in other fields as her men friends, often with greater success. Colette's *Claudine à l'Ecole*, "corrupt, depraved, knowing a thousand things she should not have been aware of," was praised by Rachilde as "the most extraordinary creation that could blossom under the pen of a beginner." Rachilde was not as kind to the notorious beauty Liane de Pougy, who also produced a novel that year. "Why," wrote Rachilde, "does a powerful and beautiful lady of easy virtue want to become a mediocre writer?"

One of the stars of the Paris theatre, Misia's friend Réjane, played Madame Sans-Gêne and brought to the role a new realistic style of acting. (Additional glory was hers when her little carriage, its roof festooned with fresh cherries, won first prize at the Bois de Boulogne flower festival.) Sarah Bernhardt created one of her greatest roles, Edmond Rostand's *L'Aiglon*. "Offstage," observed Léon Daudet, "Madame Bernhardt is most natural and unaffected; absolutely simple, without the least pose of any kind, not even that of simplicity." Bernhardt could hardly be accused of simplicity when she received visitors dressed as Napoleon's son, sword in hand, leading her pet panther on a leash. For weeks before the opening, the dedicated actress wore the stiff and glittering uniform designed for her by the young Paul Poiret so that she would feel at ease in it. Her dedication was rewarded; she played *l'Aiglon* two hundred and thirty-six times to ecstatic audiences.

France was still deeply involved in the Dreyfus affair, that bitter struggle between civil liberty and authoritarian government. While the unfortunate, colorless victim, Captain Alfred Dreyfus, rotted in prison, his prophet and protector Emile Zola became the hero of the hour with his thundering *"J'Accuse."* The country was split in two. Even such apolitical men as Mallarmé and Renoir found it difficult to avoid the subject, as Julie Manet had noted in her journal:

We put on costumes to receive Monsieur Mallarmé and Monsieur Renoir, who did not have the carnival spirit and started in all over again on the eternal discussion of the Dreyfus case. . . . Perhaps they are interesting, but really, we have had enough of this affair. . . . We have nothing to say on the subject. It must have been grotesque, the two men having a serious talk—with Monsieur Renoir very excited— and three people in bizarre costumes sitting and listening without opening their mouths. I could not help thinking that the party in Asnières would have been more amusing. [March 17, 1898]

Misia too could not help feeling that dressing up and going to parties was more amusing than listening to interminable arguments about social issues. The tight-lipped righteousness and jockeying for position among her zealous liberal friends brought out the cynic in her. Was it necessary, she wondered, to consume sumptuous dinners at the Léon Blums' before discussing the

Rights of Man? Did no one else find it strange that the guests in the Zolas' vast, lugubrious dining room stuffed themselves on woodcocks stewed in champagne and kangaroo steaks while discussing Free Bread for the Poor? The Dreyfus affair kindled in Thadée a fiery dedication to liberal ideas, but his growing obsession with politics bored Misia. As that social phenomenon, the idealistic capitalist, Thadée was full of grandiose plans to improve the conditions of the working class while making a fortune for himself. He had begun to lose interest in the *Revue Blanche*; besides, it was becoming a serious drain on the family pocket. Only the unprecedented success of Henryk Sienkiewicz's novel *Quo Vadis?*,* a *Revue Blanche* publication, kept the magazine afloat. "Quo vadis?" was a question Misia might well have asked Thadée, as she watched him turn from artistic pursuits to money-making schemes. "Unfortunately," Misia wryly observed, "Thadée had discovered that he was a financial genius." In fact, with his energy and enthusiasm he was to make and lose several fortunes. Among other projects he had been dabbling with the development of tram lines in Toulon. And he had taken Misia to Cannes, where he planned to build a hydroelectric plant on his father's large property on La Croix des Gardes. Although Misia loved what money could buy, she was bored by how it was made. But how she enjoyed spending it! Having nothing to do, she diverted herself by building a villa in Cannes and decorating it in a new open-air Mediterranean style.

Against the festive background of the Paris Exposition, Thadée's new social awareness, and the general political unrest, a personal drama began which was to change Misia's life. For her the crucial event of 1900 was her meeting with Alfred Edwards.

A man of mystery, Alfred Edwards was the talk of Paris. People said that he was Dutch, English, French; it was even whispered that he was Levantine, as if that were synonymous with evil. Some said his father was dentist to

---

* The novel's popularity was so widespread that in 1906 Mikhail Fokine created *Eunice* a ballet based on *Quo Vadis?* at the Maryinsky Theatre in St. Petersburg. The young Polish dancer Vaslav Nijinsky had a small role, and Anna Pavlova made a great impression in *The Dance of the Seven Veils*. However, her tights daringly painted to look like bare feet, met with severe official disapproval.

the Turkish sultan and had made a fortune selling false teeth; others, that his millions came from the opium trade. Actually his father, Charles Edwards, was English and had been physician to the Fuad Pasha in Cairo. His mother, Emilie Caporal, born in France at Montauban, was probably of Near-Eastern origin. Edwards himself was born in Constantinople on June 10, 1856. When Doctor Edwards died, he left his son a substantial inheritance. Alfred invested it brilliantly, expanding it into a vast fortune. He bought railroad bonds and real estate. He bought the Théâtre de Paris and its adjoining casino. He bought *Le Matin*, and when he sold it eleven years later he had turned it into the newspaper with the largest circulation in Europe. Then, riding the wave of humanitarianism, he published a sensational penny tabloid, *Le Petit Sou*, on which he gladly lost a fortune for the pleasure of ruining his wife's brother-in-law, Pierre Waldeck-Rousseau, Président du Conseil. Gross and imposing, Edwards was a violent man. There was a story that once on the grand staircase of the Paris Opéra he caned a man who was trying to collect a debt. Edwards was said to be so strong that he had twisted brass andirons with his bare hands in a scene with one of his many mistresses. He was known to be a coprophiliac—a man erotically obsessed with excrement. Monumentally vulgar, he knew how to use his crudeness to throw his enemies off balance. Renard's journal records what must certainly be one of the least graceful introductions in Parisian society: "Capus admires Edwards, who greets a woman in the following way: 'Hello, you old whore!' And, turning to Capus, 'Meet my mother.' "

Curiously enough, Misia did not know Edwards, although Thadée had often pointed him out at the theatre. As Lugné-Poë said, "No theatrical event was considered a success unless both the Natansons and the Edwardses were present. Everyone bowed to the Natansons in their stage box as if they were royalty. Madame Alexandre Natanson was always in front with Misia, sibylline, other-worldly, and radiant. Then everyone bowed to the adventurer Edwards and his guests in the box opposite the Natansons." It was in Edwards' Théâtre de Paris that he and Misia met at last. The occasion was a benefit for the League of the Rights of Man, an organization dedicated to the belief that the masses were entitled to free culture as well as free bread. As Thadée was unable to come, Mirbeau had asked Misia to join him in Edwards' box. While Misia was observing the conspicuous absence of the "masses" in the sea of sables and diamonds around her, Edwards was observing Misia. At twenty-eight she was at the height of her sumptuous beauty. The opulent curve of her body, her radiant complexion, her nonchalant elegance, her provocative wit, her perverse little smile—everything about her intrigued him. From the moment he bent to kiss her hand, Edwards had eyes for no one else. But even Misia, a flirt who took her conquests for granted, was disconcerted by his frankly sexual appraisal. Tall, heavy, asthmatic, his good looks running to fat, Edwards fingered the topazes he always carried in his pocket and made Misia squirm with a relentless stream of gallantries. Finding Edwards rather disgusting, Misia's first impulse was to leave. But good *Parisienne* that she was, she felt she must not ruin the evening. She would be polite for a few hours, then never see him again. But Edwards was used to having his own way. He invited her to dine with such relentless insistence that the next evening she found herself with Thadée in the Edwardses' grand apartment.

There Misia met a different *Tout-Paris* from the one she knew: a theatrical, racy set of high-powered journalists and actresses, of demimondaines and celebrities, of coarse stories and coarser laughter. The stories were no more vulgar and no less witty than the ones Toulouse-Lautrec and Coolus told, yet there was a difference in tone, a professional toughness that Misia found disagreeable. The other-worldly muse was out of her element. Edwards' protégé Alfred Capus, who boasted that since he'd been married, he'd never "set foot in another woman," was there, as were Dr. Robin and his mistress Liane de Pougy. Looking admiringly at the celebrated cocotte, Misia could see why Henri Meilhac, co-author of the libretto for the Offenbach operetta *La Vie Parisienne*, had paid eighty thousand francs for the privilege of seeing her naked. But Misia blushed when she heard that her friend Jean Lorrain had received an envelope with a flea enclosed and a note saying, "Killed on the cunt of Liane de Pougy." Misia often used obscenities herself with no loss of elegance or charm, but this time she was shocked. At dinner Madame Edwards' brother, the explorer Jean-Baptiste Charcot, spoke of the supplies he was laying in for an Arctic expedition. Everyone except Misia roared with laughter at the interminable jokes about the perversions the sailors would perform with the artificial rubber woman, the one indispensable object they were taking aboard the *Pourquoi Pas?* Misia felt stupid, offended, bored, and upset. On the way home she swore that she would never see any of them again.

Thadée found Misia's holier-than-thou attitude childish and irritating. He needed financial backing, and Edwards might provide it if they played their cards right. What a stroke of luck that Edwards was so taken with her! Just this once, why couldn't she put her charm to good use? It wouldn't hurt her to invite him to dinner. After all, it was a wife's duty to help her husband, and in the end they both would benefit. Misia flatly refused to have Edwards in their apartment. Finally, after endless bickering, she agreed to entertain him in a restaurant if she could cushion herself with a group of friends. Misia arrived at the restaurant rather late and found Edwards waiting for her at the entrance. He was leaning on his cane, the jewels gleaming in his vast shirtfront. "Let's chuck all these bores," he said, "and go off for dinner, just the two of us." Pretending she had not heard, Misia slipped past him with an uneasy little laugh.

A few weeks later Thadée left for the south of France to see to his tramways and his hydroelectric plant. No sooner was he gone than Edwards began to bombard Misia with flowers and telephone calls. Although she could not help feeling flattered, she ordered the servants to tell Monsieur Edwards that Madame was not at home, that Madame was out of town, that Madame had joined Charcot at the North Pole—anything to avoid seeing him again. One day Misia was strolling up the boulevard Haussmann and looking at antiques while her chauffeur followed in the car. Glancing into a shop window to adjust her feathered hat, she was startled when a man in a black suit grasped her arm and shouted, "At last! I've got you! Now I'll never let you go." It was Edwards. Explaining that her husband had just returned from his trip, Misia escaped to her car. But as fate would have it (or was Edwards following her?) the next afternoon she met him again in the Place Vendôme. This time he had laid his plans more carefully. When Misia mumbled incoherently that Thadée was waiting for her, Edwards said, "But it's precisely Natanson whom I want to see." Tight-lipped, Misia motioned him to her car and ordered the driver to take them home.

In the Natansons' apartment the two men disappeared into Thadée's study, where they remained closeted for an ominously long time. When Edwards finally left, Thadée was beside himself with enthusiasm. Their fortune was made! Edwards had offered him the directorship of huge coal mines in Hungary! He would be leaving for Koloschvar immediately. Thadée began to build castles in the air—complete with up-to-date housing for the miners. He hadn't wanted to trouble Misia with his problems, but things were going very badly. The *Revue Blanche* could not last much longer; his family was tired of sinking money into it. Besides, he had borrowed a tremendous amount for his business projects, and he did not know how he could repay it. He saw now that he would never be a real writer, and the idea of spending the rest of his life reviewing other people's work bored him. In any case, Misia was wrong about Edwards; he was not as bad as she thought—a diamond in the rough, really. With his help they could make millions.

Misia did not share his enthusiasm. It was a Machiavellian plot, she said. Couldn't he see that Edwards was in love with her and would do anything to separate them? The mines were a pipe dream, a mirage, a trick to get Thadée out of Paris so that Edwards would be free to pursue her. Thadée laughed condescendingly. Misia was ridiculous—she always imagined that everyone was in love with her. This had nothing to do with love; Edwards was a financial genius; it was the chance of a lifetime. Nothing Misia said could discourage Thadée. A few weeks later he left for Koloschvar with a thousand optimistic plans. Misia found it impossible to understand why her husband, who had accomplished miracles with the *Revue Blanche*, wanted to bury himself in a town in Hungary that no one had ever heard of.

Her fears were well founded. The moment Thadée left, she was submerged by invitations from Edwards. Feeling more intrigued than she cared to admit, Misia told herself that her husband had, after all, begged her to cultivate this man. She began to see Edwards more and more often through the long months of Thadée's absence. But she felt guilty, for she knew that she was playing a dangerous game and that the financier's infatuation was becoming an obsession. One evening at the Edwardses', Misia was surprised to find herself dining alone with Edwards, his wife, and his brother-in-law Charcot. There was tension in the air. To lighten it Misia told amusing stories of her honeymoon trip to Norway. Suddenly Edwards turned pale and left the room. Dinner ended in a constrained silence. As they rose from the table, Madame Edwards and her brother each took Misia by the arm and began to harangue her. Edwards was very ill, they said. His asthma had been dangerously aggravated by Misia's coquettish behavior. He spent the nights gasping for breath. How could she be so heartless as to speak of her honeymoon to Alfred, knowing how sensitive and jealous he was? Her indifference was driving him mad. He was threatening divorce in order to marry her. There was only one solution: she must save Madame Edwards' marriage by becoming Alfred's mistress. Misia burst into tears, gathered up her cloak, and fled.

In a panic she decided that the only way to escape the Edwardses was to join Thadée in Hungary. As she boarded the Orient Express, she felt that the trip would at least bring some relief from the tensions of Paris. But just before the train reached Vienna there was a knock on the door of her compartment. There stood Edwards. "We must have a quiet talk," he said. As if hypnotized, Misia followed him off the train at Vienna. From the hotel she sent telegrams to Thadée and Vuillard begging them to come at once. Over dinner Edwards told her that he was deeply disappointed in Thadée. The Koloschvar appointment had been a wonderful opportunity, but Thadée had bungled affairs so badly that he was in debt for millions. Creditors were hounding him. Catastrophe was imminent. But Misia was not to worry; Edwards was there to straighten everything out. He was their friend, and he loved Misia. He wanted her more than he had ever wanted anything in his life. It was quite simple, he said. All she had to do was divorce Thadée and marry him, and he would rescue them from bankruptcy. That neither she, nor Thadée, nor Madame Edwards wanted a divorce was brushed aside. And more important, he added, he could make her happier than she had ever dreamt of being. Didn't she realize that her life with Thadée was mediocre—that she was meant for a life of splendor? He would cover her with diamonds and emeralds, chinchilla and sables. He had a château and a yacht. He could see that she was a woman of imagination; it would give him pleasure to gratify her most bizarre caprice. Misia was frightened, dazzled—and tempted.

As soon as Vuillard received Misia's wire, he hurried to Vienna, but Thadée did not have the heart to come. He telephoned to say that it was impossible to leave Koloschvar. "I am a lost man," he told her; "I beg you, arrange everything." It was inconceivable that her husband, her own Thadée, was pushing her into Edwards' arms. "Arrange everything!" Could Thadée be so naïve as to imagine Edwards arranging anything without demanding everything in return? At Vuillard's suggestion she asked Edwards for a month alone to think things over quietly. Edwards agreed. He would return to Paris, and she could go to Basel with Vuillard. But there was one condition: she was not to see Thadée. From Basel, on September 29, 1900, Vuillard wrote Vallotton: "I found Misia rather better, above all, more resigned, finding it almost charming to lead a cloistered life, which, obviously, is the most novel thing that could happen to her." Ignoring her promise to Edwards, Misia wired Thadée to join her in Switzerland. She hoped to hear that the situation was not as black as Edwards had painted it. But when Thadée arrived he confessed that it was worse: he had lost everything. Furthermore, he had persuaded Fred, Cipa, and even some of their friends to invest heavily in the mines, and their money was gone too. He felt that no one but Edwards could help them. Edwards helped them by continuing

Thadée's salary—which forced him to return to Hungary. There the unhappy man consoled himself by writing passionate love letters to Misia. Reluctantly she faced the fact that Thadée's "arrange everything" was his way of suggesting that she become Edward's mistress. And so his "I have never loved you so much" in every letter failed to move her. Yet perhaps living with Edwards, as her husband seemed to be urging her to do, was the worldly solution. If discreetly handled, certainly it would be more civilized than the scandal of two divorces. But there was a new complication: Edwards had found sweeping Misia off her feet an irritatingly slow process and now decided that nothing short of marriage would satisfy him.

Misia felt everything slipping from under her. In a sense she had married for protection, but now Thadée, like a helpless child, expected her to protect him. It was a role she was not prepared to play. Seduced by the thought that as Madame Edwards she would be one of the richest women in Paris, she began to feel the troubling, the almost sexual stir of worldly ambition. She who loved powerful men began to see Thadée as a helpless knight in tarnished armor, unable to protect her from the dragon. She began to imagine that if she married the dragon, she would no longer need protection. Thadée, she felt, was a child, Edwards a man. His fortune, his authority, even the fact that he was sixteen years older than she, seemed more and more attractive. She felt what Benjamin Constant described as the "agitation which strongly resembles love." In thinking about Thadée it now seemed to her that affection rather than love had led her into marriage with her childhood friend. And besides, as Misia later wrote, "Had I ever caught in Thadée's glance that fire of devouring passion which burned in Edwards' eyes?"

Five years were to pass before Misia's dilemma was resolved. Hers was a painful decision, caught as she was between a husband she was fond of but no longer respected, and a lover she respected but did not love. In a sense she was choosing a career. She would have an uncertain position with Thadée, who was now nothing but an employee, a commanding position with Edwards, whose millions made him one of the kings of Paris. The world would think her cynical and avaricious should she marry Edwards, a non-entity were she to remain with Thadée. She would cheapen herself if she married for money. But she would be forced to live on the cheap if she continued as Madame Natanson. There were stormy separations and hopeless reunions with Thadée. One of their last meetings was in the railway station in Basel. Once again Misia was seeing him off to Koloschvar. Although Thadée tried to behave as if it were just another parting, Misia sensed that these were in effect their last moments together as man and wife. As they spoke quietly, Misia felt there was really nothing she could reproach him with. Even in the fiasco he had made of their lives, he had been motivated by his ideals and had worked hard to improve the miserable life of the miners. He approached social problems with the same fervor and sensitivity that he had brought to the *Revue Blanche*. Was it his fault that the qualities which succeeded so well in the world of art had failed so miserably in the world of business?

Walking up and down the station platform, Thadée talked about the League of the Rights of Man. In his imploring eyes there was an unexpressed question. While he spoke, Misia thought of summer evenings in Valvins, evenings when she had played the piano for Mallarmé, and Thadée had watched them both with deep tenderness. She remembered, too, golden afternoons in the garden at Villeneuve when she had been surrounded by laughing friends, and thought of the beauty of those friendships. It was such a short time ago; yet Mallarmé was gone, Lautrec was gone, and although Thadée did not seem to realize it, in a few moments he too would be gone from her life forever. As he boarded the train, Misia, for whom jewels were tangible symbols of love, impulsively took off the pendant with two large emeralds that she always wore. Tearing it in half, she kept one stone and gave the other to Thadée. The train slowly pulled out of the station, the smoke vanished, and heavy sobs rose to her throat. Her innocence was gone: she had chosen to be expelled from a certain paradise and was about to taste the fruits of worldly knowledge. She must let Edwards know at once that he had won.

A most curious footnote to this chapter in Misia's life is Thadée's own statement on the subject, a play called *Le Foyer*. Written in collaboration with Octave Mirbeau, it was a melodrama in the style of 1900 with daring social overtones—Sardou with Ibsen sauce. *Le Foyer* was first performed by the Comédie Française on December 7, 1908, three years after Misia's

marriage to Edwards. The "stormy, violent, revolutionary play," as one critic
described it, created such a scandal that it was closed almost immediately.
Le Foyer is a home for orphan girls run by a sadistic lesbian. She fondles
her favorites but punishes the others so enthusiastically that she is responsible for two melodramatic deaths: one child is killed by over-zealous flagella-
tion, another is locked in a closet and forgotten. The honorary director of
the orphanage, a distinguished senator and member of the Académie (the
character is unmistakably Thadée), is so corrupt that he offers to overlook
the woman's crimes if she will conceal the fact that he stole the Foyer's funds.

The public-spirited were so shocked by this picture of corruption in
high places that Jules Claretie, director of the Comédie Française, discon-
tinued the performances and demanded revisions from Natanson and
Mirbeau. The playwrights refused and sued for breach of contract. The
audience at the trial was even more brilliant than the crowd at opening night.
Thadée and Mirbeau won the suit, the Comédie Française was ordered to
resume production, and Claretie resigned in protest. The resulting publicity
made *Le Foyer* more of a *succès de scandale* than ever. (It was produced in
Turin, then in Berlin, where it was directed by Max Reinhardt, and again in
Paris in a 1938 revival.) For those in the know, the real scandal was that
the play exposed the notorious trio, Misia, Edwards, and Thadée himself.
Astonishingly, Thadée did not tell the story as his family and friends saw it.
To them he was the hero, Misia and Edwards the villains; but although
Le Foyer portrays all three characters as corrupt, it exonerates Misia completely. Baron Courtin (the Thadée character) has embezzled funds to
cover his financial losses. He is in a desperate situation, threatened with
scandal, exposure, and imprisonment. He begs Baroness Courtin (Misia) to
save him by "arranging everything" with her ex-lover Biron (Edwards), who
hopes to marry her. When she refuses, there is a violent scene in which
Thadée almost strikes her and then, appalled at his own behavior, falls
sobbing to the sofa. Misia reluctantly goes to Edwards to try to "arrange"
things. The character based on Misia is a frivolous, fascinating woman,
with more than a hint of perversity, who is surrounded by men in love with
her: her husband, ex-lover, and the very young lover who is currently enjoying her favors. The last scene takes place in Biron's house, where Baroness
Courtin has come to ask for money to save her husband.

MISIA (Baroness Courtin): Help us out of the goodness of your
   heart. Give us the money and then never see us again.

EDWARDS (Biron): Impossible!

MISIA: You don't know the joy of helping someone you love, of sacrificing your own pleasure.

EDWARDS: My own pleasure is enough for me.

[*Misia offers to make sacrifices: if Edwards helps them, they will give up their luxurious life and go off to a small town to live simply, working side by side.*]

EDWARDS: You are mad. It won't work. You need a life in which you can indulge all your caprices to the hilt, as you used to say. Tomorrow you will again be the delicious woman who dared to say there is no ecstasy she would scorn.

MISIA: I was that woman?

[*Edwards tempts her by saying they can all go to Venice on his yacht, the* Argo. *She can choose the guests—as many or as few as she would like. She can be alone with him, or they can take her husband and her young lover along. Or if she prefers, she can invite the beautiful young girls who had joined them on past cruises, the girls she loved to watch dancing naked in the moonlight.*]

MISIA: Why do you always excite my worst instincts?

Thadée enters and realizes that his wife has indeed "arranged everything" when Edwards announces triumphantly, "We are off on an Adriatic cruise." The curtain falls as Edwards leads Misia offstage, Thadée following. "Venice, Venice, Venice!" they all cry as they depart for the city the real Misia loved more than any other.

But it was not to Venice that they went in real life. Instead, at the end of 1903, Edwards carried Misia off to Spain. What a relief, she felt, to be with a man who was strong enough to make the decisions. Moved by the violence of his love, Misia went through the requisite motions. She was his mistress and would become his wife, but though he now owned her, something intangible eluded him. The economics of desire—the ratio between his supply of money and his demand for love—were not functioning smoothly. He could buy anything except Misia's love. Wandering the streets of Madrid one day, she admired a fan in a shop window. Edwards bought it for her instantly —but he could not stop there. "Never," Misia recalled, "could I have imagined that so many precious fans existed: fans of lace, tortoiseshell, gold, lacquer, ivory, and delicately painted seventeenth- and eighteenth-century fans. . . . Soon I had a real collection. . . . When I tired of these endless fan-hunting expeditions, Edwards went out alone, after carefully locking the door of my room. . . . I spent whole days locked up. He was as jealous as a wild animal, and I should not have been surprised to hear him roaring outside my door. Of whom could he be jealous in a city where I did not know a soul?"

But all the fans and jewels Edwards gave her were not enough to prevent Misia from having second thoughts. Unlike her ecstatic first trip to Venice with Thadée, her lonely stay in Madrid left her wondering if she was not making a great mistake. It was not surprising that she fell ill. Troubled and homesick, she wrote to her friends in Paris. Shortly after the New Year she received an answer from Bonnard.

January 4 [1904]

Dear Misia,

Your letter moved me as I read into your heart, between the lines. I too think of you often—not without concern, I admit, even though I don't feel it's my place to judge what your new life has brought you in the way of joy or sorrow. I sense that the emptiness you left in our hearts must have its echo in your own.

And then to be sick in a foreign country is enough to demoralize someone even more gallant than you. I hope to have better news of you soon. I should be happy to know that you've come to the south of France, nearer to us. It's quite likely that I shall go there too in about a month. But as my life is very complicated, I'm never certain of my plans. In any case, a change of scene is always a good idea for someone who takes things as personally and as hard as you do. . . .

The story of your portrait in a Spanish costume is most amusing, and the artist must think himself very lucky to have you for a model—a model who has never yet been painted by anyone worthy of her. (I speak for myself, with no false modesty.) But it's marvellous of you to take an interest in painting in the midst of your worries, as one needs peace of mind to attach any great importance to those grown-up children's games. Since it's the time of year for good wishes, I wish you, my dear Misia, every possible joy that could brighten your life, a life that is so uncertain for the moment. You must believe (as Capus says) that everything works out in the end; only later does one realize that this was the way things had to be. Believe in my most profound friendship.

Your
Bonnard

While the ailing odalisque waited behind locked doors, Edwards, never a man to waste time, was playing a game of high finance with the Spanish government. In going through his father's papers, he had come across an old deed of purchase to some marshlands at Santander on the Basque coast. His father had bought the worthless tract to use for duck-hunting. When Edwards inspected the property, he found that the marshes had been drained and extensive docks were under construction for what was to be the largest port on the Atlantic coast. Here was a chance to make another fortune. When he confronted the authorities in Madrid with his ownership of what was now an extremely valuable site, they offered to buy him out. Edwards coolly refused. It was his land; no one had asked his permission to build on it; he did not want their money. All he asked was that they remove the docks immediately and turn his property back into wetlands so that he could go hunting. That was why he had come to Spain. Madrid laughed—but not for long. In the end Edwards condescended to accept a huge sum and a percentage of the port's revenues. Pleased with his afternoon's work, he stopped on his way to the hotel and bought Misia another fan.

Misia had left for Spain the respectable wife of an intellectual editor; she returned to Paris the notorious mistress of a newspaper tycoon. Extravagantly dressed and even more extravagantly jewelled, she lived with Edwards in his Château des Tourelles at Corbeil. In town he bought a large apartment at 244 rue de Rivoli overlooking the Tuileries. While it was being done up, he took rooms for her on the ground floor of the Hôtel du Rhin in the Place Vendôme, a suite she was to keep as a pied-à-terre for years. In a city nourished on scandal, the Misia-Thadée-Edwards story was the most delicious dish of the season. Though Misia preferred to think of herself as a heroine who had saved her husband by allowing him to sell her to a monster, not everyone shared her point of view. Some of her friends— and, naturally, the Natanson family—saw Thadée as the innocent victim in a vicious situation, heartlessly manipulated by his wife. They were convinced that Misia had been Edwards' mistress from the beginning, that she had played the two men against each other, and that she had chosen Edwards for his money. Her cheerful announcement that she loved her new chinchilla cape so much that she slept in it seemed to bear out this theory. Undoubtedly the truth was that both Misia and Thadée were at fault, but that both were also victims. Each had swallowed the bait of wealth and power Edwards had dangled before them.

Of course Edwards and Misia came in for their share of Parisian ridicule. It had been amusing when Mallarmé and Thadée teasingly called her the piano tamer for her stormy playing of *la polonaise de Chopin*. Now Misia squirmed, knowing that everyone was laughing at them when, repeating Lucien Guitry's *mot*, they called Edwards *le chopin de la Polonaise*. (*Un chopin*, an easy mark; *la Polonaise*, the Polish woman—Misia.) Misia was not in love with Edwards; she had not been in love with Thadée; she had, in fact, never been in love at all. In her own words she had exchanged "a charming, subtle, and erudite playmate" for a man who made of her "the most spoilt little girl in the world." Gratified, if not fulfilled, by Edwards' obsessive passion, Misia later liked to say that though Alfred was a great lover, she found herself planning the next day's menus while he was making love to her.

Most women of her class who had lovers avoided the scandal of divorce. But Misia was indifferent to bourgeois standards, and she ignored stuffy opinion with a *je-m'en-fiche* shrug. Naturally she felt disapproval from all sides, but with her instinctive sense of privilege she did as she pleased. Without bothering to wait for a divorce, she had left her husband and was living as conspicuously as possible with her lover. After all, she felt, she was not the first woman to have behaved irregularly. There was no change within her. The emphasis had merely shifted to suit the new chapter in her life. No longer a private person, Misia had become a public figure. She had moved from the poets' theatre to the theatre of the boulevards, from Mallarmé to Henry Bernstein. And then—and then—there was all that money! For Edwards had given her carte blanche; that had been part of their agreement. She could have anything she wanted, as long as what she wanted was extravagant and original. She was a visible symbol of Edwards' wealth.

But Edwards, like many millionaires, had moments of comic economy. One day at the Automobile Club he lost three hundred thousand francs gambling. Feeling poor, he decided to walk home in a driving rain and arrived covered with mud. When Misia said, "You really might have taken a cab in such filthy weather," he replied with unexpected bitterness, "One can see that money costs you nothing." Yet the next morning jewellers appeared as usual, and more precious stones were bought and set for the jewel-sated Misia. She had always adored diamonds and emeralds, but now she carelessly stuffed them into drawers and announced that she preferred to wear feathers and lace around her neck. It was precisely this perverse nonchalance that Edwards found irresistible. Baudelaire's definition of a dandy is a perfect portrait of the new Misia. "The dandy regards neither love nor money as an end in itself. He leaves those gross passions to more ordinary mortals, and unlimited credit is wealth enough for him. Dandyism is not, as many seem to think, an exaggerated love of fine clothes and material comfort. These things, to the perfect dandy, are mere symbols of his own spiritual aristocracy. Dandyism is primarily a desire to be individually original, but always within the limits of polite social convention. It is the love of startling others and of never being startled oneself."

Bonnard's magnificent portrait of Misia painted during those years is a deeply felt metaphor of her as the embodiment of worldly elegance. Only the eighteenth century, Bonnard must have felt, could evoke the spirit of Misia's luxurious new life. He painted her seated in a Louis XVI armchair, dressed in a pink and white ball gown as luminous as pearls. Her expression is grave as she seems to search the darkest imaginings of a hidden heart: a sibyl in modern dress. How different was Jules Renard's sour note in his journal: "She no longer knows how to dress except expensively." Renard added that Edwards, in love, is making "futile attempts to be pleasant." Perhaps in self-justification, Misia was beginning to think that Edwards was not the monster he was generally thought to be. His "attempts to be pleasant" pleased her, if no one else. She began to discover humor and kindness in her imposing lover. Always outspoken, she could match his obscenities with a disarming bluntness of her own. Soon she found the key to his complicated nature and felt at ease with his corsair-like restlessness. For Edwards was a successful pirate for whom business was swashbuckling adventure—rapacious and exciting. His desire to humiliate men and be humiliated by women made him both violent and suspicious. If bribery and display were behind his generosity, his generosity was nonetheless regal. Edwards was a warlord of the fourth estate.

Once Misia was an unwilling witness to her lover's brutal dealings. When Gaston Calmette took over the editorship of *Le Figaro* from Edwards' friend Perivier, Edwards decided to get rid of him. On the sly, he managed to buy the major part of the newspaper's shares from Calmette's father-in-law. Then, one evening he invited the gentle, cultivated Calmette to dine. Moving to the salon after dinner, Edwards announced in his deadly cool way that he was going to replace him as editor of *Le Figaro*. How could he dare to make such a statement? Calmette asked. Surely he was joking. Edwards explained that as he now had a controlling interest in the paper, he could do exactly as he pleased, and it pleased him to fire Calmette. Suddenly to Misia's embarrassment Calmette sank to his knees and, crawling the length of the salon, dragged himself to her chair. His hands clasped in supplication, he begged her to intervene. Had she been told of such a scene, Misia would have shuddered and found it unimaginable. But there was poor Calmette grovelling at her feet. Furious with Edwards for forcing her to sit by and watch Calmette's humiliation, she pleaded with him to change his mind. Perhaps to impress her, he agreed. In gratitude Calmette covered Misia's hands with kisses.

Finally Madame Charcot-Edwards came to the bitter realization that her marriage had not been saved when Misia agreed to become Edwards' mistress. As for Misia, by now she was more than willing to marry the millionaire who paid so handsomely for the privilege of worshipping her. In a country where divorce by mutual consent was difficult to obtain, Edwards, for whom bribery was a way of life, was able to "arrange everything." Both couples were divorced in 1904, the Natansons in February, the Edwardses in July. Seven months later, on February 24, 1905, Misia and Alfred were married at the town hall in Batignolles. Misia's new position encouraged something in her nature for which she already had a penchant—fashionable idleness. Boredom was its natural companion. Art and society became a feast at which Misia, the connoisseur, delicately picked and chose. She now had the poise and authority of the very rich. Added to her charm was the fascination that women of great position exercise on the imagination. Her friends watched with curiosity to see how she would behave in her new role. Her apartment told the story: gone were the cozy Vuillard-like cretonnes of her former life. Vast seventeenth-century tapestries, Venetian chandeliers, and Louis XVI furniture filled the awesome spaces. There were footmen to greet her guests and butlers deferentially waiting at table.

Beneath the grandeur, however, Misia was still a bohemian. She felt like a prisoner behind the high walls of Edwards' château and refused to live there. In her belittling way she said that it was idiotic to live in a château unless it had been in the family for generations. Why not summer on his yacht? No sooner had Edwards agreed than she perversely changed her mind. Wouldn't a houseboat be more amusing? Besides, the yacht, the *Dame Jeanne*, was named for his former wife. Edwards, who liked Misia to keep him hopping, obediently ordered a boat built for her in Amsterdam. He named it *The Beloved, L'Aimée*, a charming phonetic pun on her new initials, M.E. Of all her caprices it was the *Aimée* that gave Misia the greatest pleasure. Spacious—a hundred and twenty feet long—it was ideal for floating house parties. It had a large dining room, a sitting room, and seven luxurious cabins with long windows all around that extended almost down to the water line. There was antique furniture everywhere, a mirrored dressing room with white lacquered panels, and best of all, a salon with bay windows, where Misia's grand piano was rarely silent. Shaded with pink and white awnings, the deck was like a summer verandah with wicker furniture and great tubs of geraniums. A smart captain and a crew of five provided care and comfort. As Misia said,

I loved my boat so much that even after our return to Paris I often went to live in it for weeks at a time. During the winter it was moored at the quai des Orfèvres. It was a joy for me to know that I had several homes to choose from, according to my mood (besides the apartment in the rue de Rivoli, I had kept the ground-floor apartment which we had in the Hôtel du Rhin). That was probably the period when my life was overflowing with everything a woman could desire. There was really nothing left to wish for. And yet I remember sitting languidly in my rocking chair in the bow of the *Aimée* one Sunday morning. Sadly I watched the sun caressing the waters of the Seine. . . . and said to myself, "Oh God, oh God! Will my life always be so unhappy and so dull?"

If Misia had once dreamt of being a concert pianist, those dreams had ended. She had chosen another path. And if she had dreamt of being a woman who lived for love, she knew now that this too had escaped her. For the moment she found refuge and comfort in the pleasures of art and the protection of artists. There lay her love, her enduring reality.

The Edwardses' first trip on the *Aimée* was to Trouville in the spring of 1905. The guests—Réjane, Marthe Letellier (a mistress of Edward VII), the opera singer Lucienne Bréval, the cartoonist Sem, the painter Jean-Louis Forain, and the explorer Jacques Faure—provided beauty, talent, scabrous wit, daring, and a dash of scandal. It was a mixture that Misia concocted with Parisian ease. When they arrived, Misia invited Enrico Caruso on board. He had often joined her for a glass of champagne in the mirrored room behind her box at the Paris Opéra.* Day after day, with Misia at the piano, Caruso filled the salon of the *Aimée* with shatteringly beautiful sounds. Feeling that she was about to drown in the sentimental sea of "Marecchiare" and "Santa Lucia," Misia told the famous tenor that she could not bear to hear one more Neapolitan song. Stupefied, Caruso puffed himself up as only tenors can and spluttered, "No, that's really too much! It's the first time anyone's ever asked me to stop. Me, the great Caruso! Kings have begged me on their knees to open my mouth, and you, you tell me to shut it!" Then with a defiant look, Caruso raised his glorious voice in "O Sole Mio."

---

* From Misia's memoirs: "At that time I had one of those ravishing loges at the Opéra situated on the stage itself. They were removed after the 1914–1918 war . . . a great loss, for nothing was prettier or more decorative than those small, red-velvet balconies hanging right and left over the stage, so that women with aigrettes in their hair casually leaned over the spectacle. These boxes were entered through a kind of small salon. . . . The performers and friends would come for a drink . . . during the intermissions. It was also a refuge from boredom: if the performance was bad, one could retire there for a quiet chat.

Réjane's children, Germaine and Jacques Porel, were spending the summer at her house in Hennequeville nearby. When the Edwardses invited them to lunch on board, young Jacques, a handsome boy of twelve, instantly fell in love with Misia. Taking her aside, he ardently announced that she had the most ravishing body of any woman he had ever seen and asked if there was a cabin where he could consummate his passion after lunch. Misia tactfully suggested that they wait for a more propitious moment. The moment never came but Misia invited Jacques and his sister to sail back to Paris with her while their mother remained in Normandy to prepare her roles for the following season. In his memoirs, *Fils de Réjane*, Jacques Porel describes Edwards aboard the *Aimée* opening a trunk and running his fingers through the topazes which filled it. He looked like someone out of the *Arabian Nights*, except that he was dressed in a blazer and a yachting cap comically small for his large head. Misia seemed to the boy a worthy wife for this oriental potentate. For she treated all the luxurious objects that Edwards heaped on her as toys of no importance which she might toss to the nearest person as soon as she tired of them. The precocious love the boy felt for Misia was serious; only very slowly, he recalled, did it turn from passion into a deep friendship that lasted for forty-five years.

Young Jacques shared a cabin with the sardonic, immaculately dressed Sem and Jacques Faure, who was later to be eaten by a lion in Africa. Germaine shared a cabin with Marthe Letellier, whom Porel described:

> The morning spectacle was to go up on deck to look at Marthe, who, upon getting out of bed, would come up for fresh air and dazzle us with her vivid beauty. The Parisian nymph in a *robe de chambre*, her voluminous hair hanging down to her shoulders, would scream at the surprise appearances of the Nordic giant Jacques Faure, followed by the two little jockeys, Sem and myself. On the foredeck not far from Misia and Alfred, the masters of the boat, a cot had been put up for Lucienne Bréval, a dark, good-natured *femme fatale* who had joined the cruise at the last minute. . . .
>
> This "impressionist" promenade lasted a week. "Réjano," Marthe said to me, "go fetch a shawl from my cabin." . . . I hastened to serve the famous beauty. One day we were painfully steaming upstream against a strong current when Marthe let her shawl fall into the water and said, "A kiss for the man who gets it back for me." She laughed, seeing the determination on my face. "No, not you, Réjano, you're too

small." In an instant Jacques Faure had undressed except for his under-
shorts and, impulsively risking his life, jumped into the Seine. . . .
Very soon we saw his ash-blond hair disappearing in the direction of
the sea. We had to stop, put the motor in reverse, and go after him. I
can still see him, exhausted but delighted with himself, climbing aboard
with his trophy in his hand. I have forgotten the kiss.

When we reached Paris we dropped anchor at the Pont Neuf. Some
friends came to lunch on the boat: Forain and his wife, accompanied by a silent, bearded Spaniard with a large hat whom I was
seeing for the first time—José-Maria Sert.

Soon after their return to Paris the Edwardses set out again on a more
ambitious cruise. This time they invited the painters Bonnard and Pierre
Laprade (both of whom made paintings of Misia on board), the young
composer Maurice Ravel, and Cipa and Ida Godebski. Ravel had met the
Godebskis the year before at Edwards' Casino de Paris, where a curious
number devised by his father was being rehearsed. As early as 1868 Josef
Ravel had built an automobile that he proudly drove around the streets of
Neuilly, to the terror of his neighbors. Now he had perfected a new invention that could execute a death-defying stunt with clockwork precision. A
driver in padded leather appeared in an automobile at the top of a perilously
high curved ramp. At breathtaking speed he hurtled down—up—and off the
ramp; the car somersaulted, hung suspended in the air for a moment, then
landed neatly on its four wheels. Like the dissonances in his son's music, it
was a daring jolt, neatly resolved. Then the driver stepped out, smiling and
bowing to the applause of the four people present in the vast hippodrome.
They were the inventor Josef Ravel, his twenty-nine-year-old son Maurice,
unrecognizable in retrospect with curling black moustaches and beard, Cipa
Godebski, and his blond Polish wife Ida, wearing a stylishly trailing dress
of heavy knitted silk. For the Godebskis and Ravel, this meeting was the
beginning of a life-long friendship. The composer was to make Cipa, Ida,
and their children Mimi and Jean his foster family.

In later years, whenever Ravel came to Paris from his house in Montfort-
l'Amaury, he always stayed in a hotel opposite the Godebskis' apartment in
order to be near them. Their quarters were modest, but the Godebskis' salon
rivalled, some thought surpassed, Misia's in quality. For while Misia offered
a lively grab bag—writers, artists and popular singers, *femmes fatales* and
gypsy fortune tellers, the snobbish Boni de Castellane, the shrill Robert de

Montesquiou, and the enchanting Réjane—the Godebski salon was more austerely artistic. Then and in the years to come, the writers Valéry, Gide, Larbaud, Joseph Conrad, and Arnold Bennett; the painters Vuillard and Bonnard; the publisher Gallimard and the art dealer Vollard; the composers Satie and Milhaud, Poulenc and Stravinsky—all would climb the stairs for some tea and good talk. The pianist Ricardo Viñes would play the latest Debussy and Granados, and Ravel would improvise for hours in a kind of trance that had the precision and incoherence of dreams.

Ravel had been trying to win the Prix de Rome since 1901. When the jury of 1905 refused even to accept his application, Misia was so incensed that she persuaded Edwards to publicize the affair in *Le Matin*. Ravel was, after all, the most gifted young composer in France even though the conservative jury, drawn from the dustiest faculty members of the Conservatoire, found his music too advanced. Other newspapers took up the issue, and Ravel's public identity was established. Misia's scheme worked so well that the director of the Conservatoire was forced to resign, and a forward-looking era began with Fauré—Ravel and Misia's teacher—as the new director. Since Ravel had been barred from the competition, it was as a consolation prize that the Edwardses invited him to join them on an early-summer cruise through the rivers and canals of Germany and the Low Countries. For Ravel, the trip was everything Misia had hoped it would be. "The joy of this day, old boy! And it's just the beginning. The nightmare of recent days is forgotten," he wrote to the composer Maurice Delage. His letters trace the course of the *Aimée*:

Le Chesne
June 7, 1905

The Ardennes. We have gone through twenty-nine locks, one after the other in one rainy morning. . . . Wrapped in my raincoat, I watched the park-like meadows slipping past us. . . . It made me think of a French garden, of the beautiful ships of the eighteenth century, and also of some illustrations in the novels of Jules Verne.

June 11, 1905

We are arriving at Liège. . . . Splendid and unusual factories, especially one that looks like a kind of romantic cast-iron cathedral. . . . Red smoke and tongues of flame shoot up from it.

After the Edwardses and their guests stopped at Liège for two days to visit a provincial version of the Paris Exposition, Ravel continued: "We saw Senegalese villages, Russian seacoast villages, merry-go-rounds, etc. . . . Magnificent sunshine. . . . We are happy to be alive." Obviously he was coping nicely with the Prix de Rome disaster. He wrote another friend: "At the moment I am recovering on a fabulous trip. Every day I offer thanks to the gentlemen of the Institute." On July 5 he wrote Delage from Germany: "This is nothing like the Rhine as I had imagined it, tragic and legendary. There are no nixies, gnomes, or Valkyries. . . . no Hugo, Wagner, or Gustave Doré." Even more than the "revelation" of Franz Hals in Haarlem, or the Rembrandts, Cranachs, and Velasquezes in Frankfurt, Ravel was impressed by the industrial town of Haum on the Rhine:

> A gigantic foundry in which 24,000 men labor day and night. As night fell, we disembarked to go to the factories. How can I describe to you these castles of flowing metal, these fiery cathedrals, the wonderful symphony . . . of whistles, of frightful hammer blows that envelops us? Over all, a red, gloomy, burning sky.
>
> A thunderstorm broke over us. We turned homeward thoroughly soaked, each of us variously affected by it. Ida wanted to weep from fear, I from joy. How musical this all is! I have the firm intention of putting it to use.

Ravel had joined the cruise at Soissons as he had had to stay in Paris to finish his *Introduction and Allegro for Harp, String Quartet, Flute, and Clarinet*. Written in eight days, it was almost lost to posterity when he left it at the shirtmaker's in his hurry to catch up with the *Aimée*. Fortunately the manuscript was found, and Ravel duly inscribed it "to Madame Alfred Edwards, née Godebska." The composer's dedications of the piano *Sonatine*, the song *Le Cygne*, and the piano duet *Mother Goose* show his devotion to the Godebski clan. The palpitating, perfectly proportioned *Sonatine* is dedicated to Cipa and Ida Godebski, and *Le Cygne* to Misia. It was in the year after the cruise that Ravel decided to set Jules Renard's bestiary, *Histoires Naturelles*, to music. In his words, "the clear, direct language and deep hidden poetry" of Renard's prose poems were perfectly suited to the new kind of declamatory vocal line he was inspired to compose. Renard, however, was not interested. In his journal of November 19, 1906, he drily recorded the arrival of an emissary: "Thadée Natanson says to me:

'There's someone who wants to set some of your *Histoires Naturelles* to music. He's highly thought of as a musician, so avant-garde that for him Debussy is already an old bore.' " Thadée's peurile salesmanship did not convince Renard. He was not pleased; he was not touched; no, he had no message for Ravel. Above all, he had no desire to hear the music. On January 12, 1907, Ravel went to see Renard to persuade him to come to the first performance that evening. Renard, who felt that Toulouse-Lautrec's witty illustrations had in no way enhanced the deluxe edition of his poems, suspiciously asked what Ravel thought his music could add. Ravel's explanation of his new aesthetic was not enough to tempt Renard, who found the dandified composer "too dark, rich, and elegant." Renard sent his wife and daughter to the concert, but he himself stayed at home.

Perhaps it was just as well. In spite of the singer Jane Bathori's sensitive interpretation, Ravel's novel idea that melodies should imitate the inflections of ordinary speech did not go down well with the conservative French public. Misia, however, knew a masterpiece when she heard one. She must have admired the Lisztian rippling, the watery sounds that accompanied the tale of the swan who hungers after fleecy clouds reflected in the pond, who plunges his beak as if to eat them and then draws back his neck like a graceful woman pulling her arm from a sleeve, who exhausts himself pursuing these mirages. Will he starve to death, victim of this illusion? And Misia must have savored Ravel's quiet, staccato chords that drily match the irony of Renard's closing words: "What am I saying? Each time he dives, he probes the nourishing mud with his beak and brings up a worm. He grows fat as a goose." But did it occur to her that *Le Cygne* might be Ravel's malicious portrait of Misia: Misia, whose gliding walk and graceful gestures were as sinuous as a swan's; Misia, who pursued the cloud-like mirage of art comfortably sustained by the nourishing mud of Edwards' money? In any case, she must have been pleased that *"mon petit Ravel,"* as she always called him, had dedicated the extraordinary new song to her.

Mother Goose (Ma Mère l'Oye) was dedicated to Misia's niece and nephew in 1908 when Mimi was nine and Jean was seven. It was written at La Grangette, where Ravel often came to stay with the Godebskis. In some tender recollections Mimi, whom Ravel called his "little bride," wrote that she loved Ravel because he told her wonderful stories—some of which provided "programs" for the music. "I would settle down on his lap, and tirelessly he would begin again, 'Once upon a time . . .' It was Beauty and the

Beast and The Ugly Empress of the Pagodas, and above all, the adventures of a little mouse he invented for me. I laughed a great deal at this last story; then I felt remorseful, as I had to admit it was very sad." Mimi went on to say that each Christmas Ravel brought her and Jean "piles of presents. He had a taste for the marvellous and the magical; the ingenious inventions and toys of the stands on the boulevards at New Year's amused him as much as us. He loved the rococo and the baroque, and a certain kind of bad taste enchanted him."

Both Misia and Ravel adored the Godebski children. Misia, who said she was "violently put off by newborn babies and everything to do with childbirth," happened to be present in 1899 at Mimi's birth. "She was born with the sunrise and looked so pretty that I've never forgotten it. When the midwife showed me the infant, I was astonished by her beauty." The infant turned into a lovely child, as Arnold Bennett confirms in his description of a visit to La Grangette on September 29, 1908. "To the Godebski's for tea. . . . Ida Godebska playing Borodin, and the rest of us at the wide open window with the landscape of Verlaine behind a mist of rain; and the regular noise of the rain on tens of thousands of leaves. . . . Mimi, damp, came scurrying in dishevelled from the forest with whole bags of mushrooms. . . . The perfectly exquisite attitudes and gestures of Mimi playing with the dog."

Ravel had hoped that Mimi and Jean would give the first public performance of *Ma Mère l'Oye*. The children worked hard, goaded by Ida and Misia, but after weeks of struggling they could not master its difficulties. For though they were musical, neither was the child prodigy their aunt had been. Misia was extravagantly disappointed; Misia-like, she was already over-ambitious for the children, who were as charming as they were attractive. But their gifts lay elsewhere; Jean was a talented painter, Mimi a writer. At seventeen she wrote *Daphénéo*, a poem that Satie used as the text for one of his most captivating songs. Since the Godebskis were called *les God* by their friends, the song's words were credited to "M. God," Satie's playful pseudonym for his young collaborator.

Ravel's music enchanted Misia, but Debussy's moved her profoundly. In 1902 Pierre Louÿs had invited some friends to his apartment to hear *Pelléas et Mélisande*. As was often the case Misia was the only woman present. She recalled that as Debussy began to play on the upright piano, singing all the roles,

. . . a footman dressed in a white jacket passed cocktails. . . . They were made of a series of yellow, green, and red liqueurs floating in separate layers in the glasses. I swallowed several, stretched out on a Récamier chaise longue, lost in admiration for a life-size Japanese doll that was facing me. I listened distractedly to Maeterlinck's words. Only Debussy's playing moved me. In my mind, dazed by all the colors of the cocktails, Mélisande became the Japanese doll and I invented a long story totally unrelated to the miracle occurring in the room.

I turned crimson when Debussy said to me at the end: "Well?" I prayed he might mistake my complete stupidity for emotion. It was only several months later, when *Pelléas* was given at the Opéra-Comique, that I succumbed to its spell. I went to a rehearsal there in a very bad mood . . . with no desire to listen to music. Léon Blum had told me it was a work of genius, and this irritated me greatly. Would I have to force myself to admire it?

Suddenly, when *"Voilà ce qu'il écrit à son frère Pelléas"* began, my nerves vibrated like violin strings, too tightly stretched, and I understood that a great miracle was taking place. It was my first love. When I left the theatre the sun was setting. (It was spring.) I walked a few yards along the boulevard and arrived at the *Revue Blanche* office in a state of collapse. . . .

I did not see Debussy till the next day at the dress rehearsal. The audience was very rowdy. They made fun of it. . . . Once again Debussy said to me: "Well?" But this time I burst into sobs and we embraced. . . . For two years I had to go back to see *Pelléas* each time it was performed. And I (who made such fun of the fervent Bayreuth admirers eternally repeating the same phrase of Wagner) could sit at the piano and pick out the beloved harmonies of my *Pelléas* forty or fifty times in succession.

Misia, torn as she was at that time between Edwards and Thadée, must have identified with the other-worldly, the *"Ne me touchez pas"* Mélisande. The unearthly music underlining the mesmeric chant, the untouchable heroine loved and desired by two men, were designed to reach Misia's innermost ambiguities, her sensual, hothouse dreams of passion without physical consummation.

Among the friends from the Valvins days, Renoir was one of the few who felt closer to Misia as Madame Edwards than as Madame Natanson. Her snub nose, almond-shaped eyes, pouting lips, the fresh flush of her skin, her exuberant health, all made her an ideal model for the great painter. Pale, sickly women were not for him. As he said, "You'd have to pay me to sleep with *la Dame aux Camélias*." Above all, Misia's high, firm breasts invited his —or at least, his brushes'—caressing touch. Women's breasts were as much Renoir's subject as social realism was Zola's. One day Hortense Schneider, the adored singer of Offenbach operettas, entertained Renoir, his brother Edmond, and Zola in her dressing room. The talk turned to the aesthetics of painting. For Renoir, who once said that art "must be indescribable and it must be inimitable. . . . If they could explain a picture, it wouldn't be art," the discussion was a bore. Impatiently interrupting the conversation, he turned to La Schneider and said, "That's all fascinating, but let's talk about more serious things. How's your bosom these days?" "What a question!" she answered with a dazzling smile as she opened her bodice to prove that her breasts were more splendid than ever.

One of Misia's few regrets in later years was that she had not done the same. During the sittings for the many portraits Renoir did of her, he constantly pleaded with her to expose her breasts. Demurely she refused. Recalling this as an old woman, Misia's vanity took the upper hand.

"Lower, lower, I beg you," he insisted. "My God! Why won't you show your breasts? It's criminal!" Several times I saw him on the verge of tears when I refused. No one could appreciate better than he the texture of skin, or, in painting, give it such rare pearl-like transparency. After his death I often reproached myself for not letting him see all he wanted. In retrospect my prudishness seems to me stupid, since it was a question of an artist whose extraordinary eye suffered terribly when he was not allowed to see what he guessed was beautiful.

Misia had another reason besides modesty for not exposing herself to Renoir: her absurdly jealous husband. The two men got along surprisingly well, although Edwards was as uninterested in painting as Renoir was in high finance. In fact, whenever Misia managed to drag Edwards to an exhibition, he would slip off after a cursory glance to have a drink with his chauffeur. Renoir and Edwards, however, saw eye to eye on two of their favorite subjects, women and food. Yet despite his affection for Renoir, Edwards would not allow Misia to sit for the painter unless he was hovering about. He and Gabrielle (Madame Renoir's cousin and one of the painter's favorite models) would play cards in the adjoining room, but the minute the aging, arthritic painter laid down his brushes, Edwards would rush in to make certain that all was well. Nonetheless, Edwards was full of sympathy for Renoir's crippling arthritis and gallantly carried him up the grand stair-case of the Opéra one night so that the frail painter, dressed as always in his working jacket and cap, could watch the performance from their box. Edwards in full evening dress and Misia, resplendent in diamonds, were touchingly aware that they were entertaining royalty. Edwards brought doctor after doctor to see if anything could be done to relieve Renoir's suffering. When they admitted that there was no cure for arthritis, Edwards would swear at them as only he could, while Renoir nodded in sad agree-ment.

After a time it was decided that Renoir would come to the Edwardses to continue his series of portraits. For as soon as he finished one painting of Misia, he was ready to begin another. Three times a week he would be helped into the lift at 8:30 in the morning and wheeled into the apartment. Gabrielle would attach a brush to his hand, and the sittings would begin. His skin as transparent as that of a Chinese sage, Renoir would sit erect in his wheelchair and paint to the accompaniment of Gabrielle's incessant suggestions and criticisms. Renoir paid not the slightest attention. He spoke to Misia about the poverty of his youth, of the days when he earned his living by painting on porcelain, of his early ambition to be an opera singer. They talked about the younger painters, Vuillard and Bonnard, whom he admired, and about Degas, with whom he had quarrelled bitterly. Among the letters Renoir wrote to Misia, one is dated July 3, 1906: "Come, and I promise you that in the seventh portrait I shall try to make you even more beautiful. I am well and I'll feel even better if you can come to see me in Essoyes-Aube this summer. While waiting I shall work with a delicious model Vallotton sent me. . . . I shall do everything I can to show you amusing things, and we'll eat as well as possible." There were love letters as well, which sadly enough have disappeared.* After Renoir's portrait of Misia in a pink dress was finished, Misia sent him a blank check with a note reminding him of Edwards' enormous wealth. The painter filled it out for a modest ten thousand francs. When Misia insisted that it was ridiculous to charge so little, the commonsensical Renoir said, "It's a very high price; no picture by a living painter is worth more than that." With equal common sense Renoir flew into a rage when he learned that the Metropolitan Museum of New York had paid fifty thousand francs for his large painting of the Charpentier family. All he had received, he told Misia, was three hundred francs and lunch.

Misia had been unable to accept Renoir's enticing invitation to Essoyes-Aube, but the following summer she visited him on the Côte d'Azur and sat for a final portrait. Bonnard, perhaps a bit insecure at the thought of Renoir painting his Misia, wrote her:

> Our friends tell me that you are near Nice, as you had planned, and that you have been seeing the good, the great Renoir who has become your happy portraitist. They say the results are marvels. I can well believe it. It must also interest you to hear him chatter away. At least he's a man who knows what he likes.
>
> I am not yet able to say the same of myself. This year I'm leading a much more personal existence. I am installed in my own house, with lunch cooked in my own casseroles, and from time to time I choose a friendly corner where I spend the evening. The work is not going badly, and that's the main thing; every day I think I'm discovering what painting is about. It's an illusion as good as any other and helps me, after all, to pass the time not too unpleasantly.

It was the next year, 1908, that Bonnard painted the marvellous portrait of Misia that evokes the eighteenth century. There is perhaps a sense of rivalry in his Renoir-like handling of the flesh tints. But Bonnard had no reason to feel insecure. In his own series of portraits he left a unique record of Misia as a tragic muse. Especially revealing is his stark *Thadée Natanson et Sa Femme*, painted at the time of their first separation. In it one sees

---

* Jenny Bradley, the extraordinary grande dame who was Misia's friend and literary agent, told us that Misia had shown her these letters and asked whether to include them in her memoirs. Unfortunately Madame Bradley advised against it. As love letters from an old man to a young woman, she said, they were "too foolish."

Thadée and Misia descending a circular staircase; Thadée, despite his natty checked suit, all worried concern; Misia unhappy and downcast.

On December 14, 1906, the Théâtre Réjane opened with tremendous éclat. Réjane had taken the Théâtre de Paris from Edwards on a ninety-nine-year lease, and in return he had transformed it into the most splendid playhouse in Paris. The audience was dazzled by the sumptuous bar and smoking room, the magnificent flowers, the cloakroom lined with eighteenth-century armoires, and most impressive of all, the chandelier, its hundred and twenty electric bulbs casting their light on the extravagantly comfortable white and yellow brocade armchairs. The next day *Le Figaro* reported, "one would have to go back to the year 1869 to find such a sensational opening: that of the Suez Canal. And even then there was surely not so brilliant a gathering of Parisians." Literary, artistic, and social Paris, Russian grand dukes and duchesses, Briand and Clemenceau all blinked simultaneously, blinded by the magnesium flares as they were photographed from the stage at Réjane's request. The play Réjane had chosen to inaugurate her theatre was *La Savelli*, a historical melodrama which, according to one critic, managed to be "both indigestible and flimsy." But it did give the bittersweet actress the chance to tear her public's heart out. At the end of the performance Réjane stepped forward and announced with ineffable charm, "Mesdames, Messieurs, the play we have had the honor and joy of interpreting for you is signed Max Maurey [applause], the direction is signed Victorien Sardou [applause], and the desire to please is signed—Réjane [standing ovation, bravos, prolonged applause]." The verdigris satin curtain embroidered with callipygous cupids gathering grapes went down, the hundred and twenty electric lights blazed up, the string orchestra swept into "Fascination," that year's most popular song, and the audience left filled with smiling admiration for one another, for Réjane, and for Edwards' superb new theatre.

Naturally the Edwardses had been prominently on display. For once Misia was sincerely proud of Alfred, and she was moved for Réjane, fully aware of her friend's unique artistry. As Misia sat playing with her jewelled fan, she was overcome by memories. It was in this same auditorium that she and Thadée had seen the avant-garde productions of Lugné-Poë's Théâtre de l'Oeuvre. It was here that they had discovered the Scandinavian playwrights; that they had admired the incandescent Duse as Nora. Here too she had applauded Sophocles' *Oedipus*, John Ford's *'Tis Pity She's a Whore*, Byron's *Manfred*, Gorky's *Lower Depths*, Hauptmann's *Sunken Bell*, Maeterlinck's *Monna Vanna*, and d'Annunzio's *Daughter of Jorio*. Her friends' plays had been performed here as well: Henri Bataille's *Your Blood*, Tristan Bernard's *Burden of Liberty*, André Gide's *King Candaule*, and Alfred Jarry's ribald *Ubu Roi*. In those years she had been only dimly aware of Alfred Edwards. Was it possible that the stout, asthmatic man sitting next to her, the man with whom she shared such curious intimacies, had been a stranger only six years before? She thought of the day Octave Mirbeau had introduced her to Edwards in the same box. It seemed a lifetime ago.

There were two women in *La Savelli*, apart from Réjane, who caught Misia's eye. The appearance of Suzanne Avril in a supporting role carried her back to the *pension* where she had lived after her return from London. It was Suzanne who had invited her to the party where she met Thadée again, the meeting that led to their marriage. Also in the cast was a startlingly beautiful little actress named Geneviève Lantelme. Born Mathilde Fossey, Lantelme was a demimondaine. At fourteen she had been one of the attractions of her mother's brothel, but she was too gifted to limit herself to the life of a whore. Admitted to the Conservatoire, she showed such talent that after a few years she was asked to join the Comédie Française, but chose the theatre of the boulevards instead. Fierce, charming, and ambitious, she moved with an insinuating, languid slouch soon imitated by the women of Paris. Along with her engaging theatrical gift, she had something that the public relished even more: a reputation for making love to men and women with equal pleasure. Her spectacular beauty and her lurid reputation breathed sexual promise.

Edwards had been taken with her when, in the previous spring, she had first appeared with Réjane's company in Pierre Wolff's *Age of Consent*. At that time, he had sent her a magnificent bouquet of roses. The morning after the opening of the Théâtre Réjane, Lantelme received another bouquet from Edwards. This time the roses were held together by a costly gold bracelet. Another of his epic courtships had begun. Flowers and jewels arrived daily at the actress' door. At first she paid little attention, casually adding them to the tributes from other admirers. Nothing could have been better calculated to excite Edwards than Lantelme's indifference. And nothing stimulated him more than plotting a seduction. He would write a play for her, he decided, that he could easily persuade Réjane to use as a curtain raiser. It was perfect bait for the young actress. Soon they became lovers. Edwards barely had time to pull up his trousers before Misia's phone was ringing with the news. Aroused by the prospect of her first leading role, Lantelme made passionate love to her aging Romeo. After all, gratifying his sexual tastes, even his penchant for his mistress's excrement, was part of her métier. She gushed about the fifty-year-old Edwards' prowess as a lover and his genius as a playwright. Misia, on the other hand, was discouragingly sour about both Edwards' literary pretensions and his infatuation for Lantelme. In her outspoken way she made it clear that it was all *merde*. By now she had learned to get along with her husband; she was used to him; she had even become attached to him; and she did not at all mind being "the most spoilt little girl in the world." But Misia no longer had the upper hand. There was a shift in their relations that she found distinctly unsettling. It was not Edwards' waning physical interest in her that she resented, but rather his growing need for Lantelme.

Lavish gifts from Edwards continued to arrive at the young actress' door —but at quite a different door. For Edwards had installed his mistress in an expensive town house in the rue Fortuny, next door to that other lavishly kept courtesan, La Belle Otéro. There was a complication, however: Edwards had the uneasy feeling that Lantelme was still seeing her lover Paul Ardot, a handsome operetta comedian. Predictably, he was obsessed by jealousy. And now for the first time in her life, Misia too began to show symptoms of that contagious disease. Bored by her friends' innuendoes, stung by their sympathy, and curious as only she could be, Misia decided to see for herself. One day she set out to follow Edwards. It would be reassuring, in a sense, to make certain of what she already knew. As Edwards' large red car wove through the streets, with Misia in pursuit, they passed her father's house and stopped at number 29 rue Fortuny. Like a bungling detective, Misia leaned out of her taxi window to make sure of the address. Edwards, the wary tomcat, caught sight of her.

Humiliated as only a pompous middle-aged man can be when caught out, Edwards, cursing all the way, drove Misia home. Was she mad? Wasn't she ashamed, behaving like someone in a cheap novel? What would the servants think? How dare she make a spectacle of a man his age, a man in his position? Misia almost forgot that it was she who should be making the scene. "In the weeks that followed," she wrote, "it was impossible not to be aware of how upset and agitated he was." Lunch at home with Forain one day was interrupted by the telephone. Edwards rushed to take the call: it was a detective who had caught Lantelme in bed with her lover. Feverishly excusing himself, Edwards hurried out to meet the detective. "Well, that's that," Forain observed. "Until today he thought he was in love with her. From now on he won't be able to live without her." Forain was right; Edwards became hopelessly addicted. Gradually he began to treat Misia as he had treated his ex-wife. Telling her the intimate details of the affair became an aphrodisiac, a perverse doubling of his pleasure.

> Coming home to lunch each day [Misia recalled], he would sink into a chair, his head between his hands, and shout: "Good God! What's wrong with me? She's a little nobody!—and she's ghastly! She's not worth your little finger! . . . Without makeup she doesn't exist! And she's horrible, do you hear, horrible!"
>
> "Leave me in peace," I said to him. "She's ravishing, I know that, and you love her more than me."
>
> "I forbid you to speak that way," he moaned. "You're the only one I love . . . And she's trash, a horror!"

Weeping, Misia would slam the door and rush to her room. She had never paid much attention to his escapades, but now, despite his protests, she felt he was slipping away on the current of a new love. One day she secretly bought a photograph of Lantelme in a daring *décolleté*, her unruly hair tumbling about her shoulders. Misia studied it intently. The actress was devastatingly pretty, she had to admit, and—yes—disturbingly attractive. Then she would examine herself long and carefully in her boudoir mirror. The mirror reflected no signs of age, yet Misia, fifteen years older than her rival, felt old and unwanted. She longed to look like the young actress, to *be* her. Perhaps unknowingly she herself was attracted to the beautiful young woman. Slowly she unpinned her hair and let it fall *à la Lantelme*.* Then, ordering the car, she went out to shop for the provocative theatrical clothes that Lantelme wore, and the jewelled diadems that flowered into colossal aigrettes. But if Edwards noticed that his wife was imitating his mistress, he never mentioned it. Misia, who had always felt that she was doing him a favor by allowing him to idolize her, was bewildered to see her power dis-

---

* Was it at this time that Bonnard drew the profile of Misia, her hair disheveled, now in the Louvre?

appearing. She began to find him sexually attractive now that he was making love to the exciting young actress. But it was too late; she who had attracted him so easily found that her efforts to hold him were futile. She was tortured by jealousy, and jealousy, love's bad relation, began to seem like love itself. Overwrought and depressed, Misia decided to leave Paris for a while. No one knew better than she how perverse Edwards was. Without her at hand to listen to the sordid details of his affair, he would soon lose interest and realize how much he needed her. She sent a wire explaining her departure to Réjane, who answered:

> I do not want to go to sleep, *mon amie chérie*, without thanking you for your telegram. Alfred seems to me undone, nervous, embarrassed, sad. He will lose no time in going after you, finding you, and bringing you back to us, who all love you deeply—you know that.
>
> No one will feel any sympathy for him if he does not show us soon what he really is fundamentally: a good man who loves you and only you. You see, money spoils and dirties everything—it's his money that attracts the woman— You are so sensitive that you close your eyes and cannot understand what is going on.

Réjane's letter was not much comfort, as Misia's scheme to get Edwards back failed dismally. On her return to Paris she found he was more obsessed with Lantelme than ever even though he assured her that he was fed up with "that bitch." Asking her to bear with him, he swore it would all be over soon.

Perhaps thinking of his repellent coprophilia, Misia wryly observed to herself that Alfred wanted to have his cake and eat it too. Suddenly, like Thadée before him, he asked her to arrange everything, to explain his feelings to Lantelme, to tell her to let him be. Then, he promised, he and Misia would go off on a trip together. Perhaps he was right, Misia thought. In any case, it was her only hope. Since becoming Edwards' mistress, Lantelme had been given important roles in Réjane's company. The critics spoke of her brilliant and rapid success, of her beauty and charm as Suzette in Réjane's production of *Paris–New York*. She had become a celebrity, and Misia found celebrity irresistible. Consumed by curiosity, she longed to see the house Alfred had given Lantelme, for everyone said that it was a museum of priceless eighteenth-century furniture. More important, if she herself went to see Lantelme, surely she could win Alfred back. Misia had not wasted her time at the melodramas of Henri Bataille. Driving to the rue Fortuny in a splendid costume, she rehearsed her role. "I love this man, Mademoiselle," she would say with dignity, "and he loves me. You are killing him. You have a woman's heart. Give him back!" Then, in a gesture of supplication she would fling her arms out to Lantelme, who would burst into tears and throw herself into Misia's compassionate embrace.

The actual scene was quite different. When she entered the house, Misia's sable muff was taken by a footman who looked at it suspiciously, then led her into a small salon where a lady's maid examined her for concealed weapons. Misia hardly had time to glance at the Lalique vases filled with bouquets from admirers, the signed photographs, the stylish Boldini portrait of her rival, when Lantelme made her entrance. In an instant the professional actress had Misia, the amateur, floundering and forgetting her lines. Witty and offhand, Lantelme took the initiative. She covered Misia with extravagant compliments, spoke intelligently about the theatre season, and asked if there was anything she could do for her. When Misia lamely confessed that she had come to speak about her husband, Lantelme indulgently assured her that no one could interest her less. There was nothing to worry about; she was simply not attracted to him. Of course, he was a darling and terribly generous—but . . . Suddenly Lantelme took another tack. Looking at Misia with sharply appraising eyes, she said, "My dear, if you really want him you can have him—on three conditions: I want the pearl necklace you're wearing, one million francs—and you." The last condition was elaborated on with such vulgar precision that Misia was more shocked than flattered. Instantly she unclasped her necklace and put it on the table, saying, "You will understand, Mademoiselle, that I do not go about with a million francs, but you shall have the money in a few days." Ignoring the third condition, she nodded coldly and left. On her way to her rooms in the Hôtel du Rhin, she felt confused, upset, and vaguely aroused. Misia had always had a weakness for pretty women, but no one, man or woman, had ever flirted with her in such a crude way. She felt bruised and dirty, as though she had been in an accident; she must go home and wash. How she could make Alfred suffer, she thought with a certain satisfaction, if she told him that Lantelme wanted her—not him! She had barely arrived at the hotel when a letter and a box containing her pearls were delivered. The letter, on cyclamen-colored paper, was signed Lantelme. "After thinking about our meeting," she wrote, " I have decided to forget the money and return the necklace. I am holding you only to the third condition." Misia ignored the letter.

Madame Thadée Natanson au Théâtre, Henri de Toulouse-Lautrec, 1895

Misia au Piano, Edouard Vuillard, c. 1894

Misia Natanson, Edouard Vuillard, 1896
Opposite: top, *Madame Misia Natanson au Piano*, Henri de Toulouse-Lautrec, 1897
Left, *A Table Chez M. et Mme. Natanson*, Henri de Toulouse-Lautrec, 1895

La Musique, Edouard Vuillard, 1896

Misia et Thadée Natanson, Edouard Vuillard, c. 1897

La Revue Blanche, Henri de Toulouse-Lautrec, 1895

Dans le Jardin, Edouard Vuillard, 1898

Misia et Vallotton, Edouard Vuillard, 1899

Misia et Thadée Natanson, Pierre Bonnard, 1902

Top, *Misia*,
Auguste Renoir,
1904.
*Portrait de
Misia*, Auguste
Renoir, 1904

Opposite: top,
*Misia
aux Roses*,
Pierre Bonnard,
c. 1908.
*Misia
à son Bureau*,
Felix Vallotton

Misia sur un Canapé, Pierre Bonnard, c. 1914

Les Tasses Noires, Edouard Vuillard, c. 1928

Although Alfred still lunched at home every day, he had taken to spending the nights in the rue Fortuny while Misia wept in her room. But Edwards soon discovered that the latest jewel in his collection had some very rough edges indeed. Even he, who thrived on violent scenes, found Lantelme's tantrums difficult to cope with. In the book *When Paris Was Paradise*, the Belgian writer Maurice de Waleffe repeats a conversation between Lantelme and an admirer at the Grand Guignol Theatre in April 1907. Waleffe was seated in the box next to Lantelme and Edwards at the opening of Edwards' play *Perroquets Perdus* (*Lost Parrots*). When Lantelme sent her asthmatic lover to buy some chocolates, the handsome young man behind her leaned forward, saying, "What about the old man?" Voluptuously shrugging her jewelled shoulders, Lantelme whispered, "Always gasping for breath! In bed that death-rattle drives me mad. The other night I woke up; he'd stopped breathing! Without turning on the light I put out my hand to touch him. I'd hoped his body was already cold. No such luck!" Obviously Edwards had reason to be jealous of Lantelme. One day he followed her to the couturier Patou, where she was being fitted for a chinchilla coat. Knowing better than anyone that lovers used fitting rooms for rendezvous, Edwards burst in unannounced on the actress, who for once was innocent. At the sight of her eternal watchdog Lantelme flew into such a rage that even Edwards was shaken. Screaming abuse, brandishing the lethal scissors she had snatched from the startled fitter's hand, she cut the coat into shreds. But Edwards' jealousy was stronger than his fear. He collected himself, paid for the coat, and stubbornly waited to make certain that no lover was waiting in the wings.

After stimulating scenes of this kind Edwards would beg Misia to take him back. But the novelty of her husband's confessions, his assurances that she was an angel and Lantelme a devil, had worn thin. Patiently, if reluctantly, she refused. Diversion was what she needed, Misia decided. Why not go up to Normandy? So many good friends were there: Vuillard, staying with Tristan Bernard, Sem, and Lucien Guitry with his son Sacha, whom she adored. And there was always a warm welcome in Hennequeville at Réjane's. When she arrived at the Grand Hôtel in Cabourg, Misia found that Marcel Proust was staying there as well. Naturally Misia, like Réjane and Vuillard, was unaware that she would be woven into the texture of Proust's future novel. Certainly she never dreamt that Proust would use her attempt to intrigue Edwards by imitating Lantelme, but he did—in the passage where Gilberte copies the coiffure and dress of the actress Rachel to regain Saint-Loup's love. Seated in the hotel dining room, Misia breathed a sigh of relief at being away from it all. Not as far away as she thought, for as the composer Reynaldo Hahn once said, the fashionable Normandy coast was "so close to Paris and so far from the sea." As she looked around, she noticed Edwards' ex-brother-in-law Charcot, who had once urged her to become Edwards' mistress. Nodding decorously, she turned away only to see Edwards himself deep in conversation with Lantelme. And she was overcome by uncontrollable laughter when—the last straw—she saw her ex-husband, Thadée, cheerfully waving to her from a distant corner of the long, narrow dining room. That night Proust could hardly wait to write Reynaldo Hahn, *his* ex-lover. Having referred cryptically in a previous letter to "an Englishman or rational lunatic who speaks French with very suspect facility," he clarified the reference, addressing Hahn in the medieval baby talk they affected in their correspondence.

Grand Hôtel Cabourg
August 1907

My dear little Bunchtinbuls,

. . . The crude Englishman was Edwards. . . . The hotel looks like a stage-set . . . and in it are assembled as if for the 3rd act:
Edwards.
Lantelme, his mistress.
Mme. Edwards (Natanson), his last wife, separated from him.
Natanson, 1st husband of Mme. Edwards.
Doctor Charcot, 1st husband of the next-to-last Mme. Edwards (the 4th of the species, as he had already married 2 Americans, 1 Frenchwoman, and a Greek). Last night the rumor spread that Mme. Edwards had killed Edwards (the Englishman, who is really a Turk), but there was nothing in it, nothing at all.

Bonjour, Bonjour.
Munchtinbuls

Proust was being playfully inaccurate when he falsified the number and nationalities of Edwards' ex-wives and changed Charcot into the ex-husband of Edwards' ex-wife. To amuse Hahn he decribed the tragedy of Misia's marriage as though it were a Feydeau farce, using the big-city theatrical exaggeration so like Misia's own.

Late one night, when they were all safely back in Paris, Edwards called Misia's maid to ask if Madame's diamonds were locked away. Mistakenly assuming that Edwards planned to give them to his mistress, Misia angrily emptied a drawerful of jewels into a hatbox and ordered the chauffeur to take them to Lantelme. The next morning Edwards was beside himself. How could Misia send his family jewels to that whore? It was monstrous, sacrilege. This time Lantelme did not feel compelled to return the jewels; nor were there lesbian overtures on cyclamen notepaper. On the contrary, when Edwards invited her on board the *Aimée* one day, Lantelme calmly made off with a massive gold set from Misia's dressing table. In a short time the clever actress had amassed a collection of jewels worth more than she could have earned in a lifetime in the theatre. Misia never set foot on the *Aimée* again. A few weeks after the theft she found a note from Edwards in her room; he adored her, he wrote, but he was one of the damned; he was leaving her to live with Lantelme. Her humiliation was compounded by the fact that Lantelme was appearing at the Théâtre des Capucines in *Par Ricochet* (*On the Rebound*), the play Edwards had written for her. For his mistress' first leading role Edwards had callously turned the painful story of how he had taken Misia from Thadée into a drawing-room comedy. But his cynicism reached new heights, as everyone in the theatre was well aware, when he chose his seductive mistress to play the part of his cast-off wife. Misia had not felt so much at a loss since her separation from Thadée. When she received an invitation to go to Italy, she accepted eagerly. On the long trip there was time for self-pity and regret. She should never have married Alfred in the first place, she thought; it was he who had insisted. Now he had left her for a scheming little actress who didn't give a damn about him. Perhaps if they had had children . . .

She was thirty-six, heartbroken, and alone.

As she lay in her immense, lonely bed at the Grand Hotel in Rome, Misia felt a need for reassurance, for sexual adventure: a restless urge to give herself to a passing stranger, to be a little like Lantelme. She put on her dressing gown, opened the door, and peered down the empty, dimly lit corridor. A night porter passed, looked at her curiously, and disappeared. It was two o'clock in the morning, she recalled later, and she swore that the first man she saw would be asked to share her bed. "It was the only time in my life that such an idea occurred to me, and God knows what would have happened if, during the quarter of an hour I waited, shivering with fear, cold, misery, and indignation, I had seen someone other than a passing servant." Despite the apparent candor of this confession, Misia chose to omit from her memoirs the fact that it was Romain Coolus, her old flirt from the Valvins days, who had invited her to come to Italy. While she did not give herself to a passing stranger, she did console herself by sharing her bed with him. Heartbroken herself, she did not hesitate to break his heart as well. In the language of the rejected lover, Coolus complained to Misia that she had left him without news for two months. How could she put such a desert between them, he wrote, after all he had given her in Rome and Naples? He was neither hurt nor angry, he added, but hoped she would never again cause him such suffering.

In her memoirs, *Mes Cahiers Bleus*, Liane de Pougy, whose beauty Misia had admired on her first visit to Edwards' apartment, tells of another abortive adventure of Misia's, this time in the arms of a playwright famous for his love scenes offstage as well as on.

. . . an amusing story about Henry Bernstein and Misia Edwards, abandoned by Edwards for the beautiful Lantelme. She thought it would work to her advantage if she created a little scandal to excite her husband and bring him back. Drawn by the stories of Henry's passionate love-life, she chose him. . . . I had just escaped him for the sixth time and was hiding, rather bored, at the back of a small hotel in Passy. . . . The idea of Misia seemed to him a pleasant distraction and he went to meet her in Baden-Baden. The first evening Misia, with rather cautious abandon, appeared about eleven in his apartment, with her pillow and everything else she needed for the night under her arm. Henry looked askance at that and said to himself, "*Zut*—a whole night—this is going to be tough—" He liked his comfort and felt trapped. It happened again two nights running.

Bernstein, panic-stricken, sent me emissaries, letters, telegrams: "Come, my Lianon, my only love, you, the only intelligent woman in the world, come join your Henry who loves you, who is dying without you. . . ."

Misia and Henry parted very dissatisfied with one another. When they met again, each was offended, distant. Misia wanted revenge and embroiled her first husband, the Jew Natanson, in the affair. At the

Society of Authors he picked a quarrel with Bernstein, who got carried away and fell into the trap.

Thadée defended his ex-wife's virtue in a duel that ended when he drew a drop of blood from the tip of Bernstein's finger. The loquacious playwright, feeling heroic and weak from loss of blood, telephoned Liane de Pougy to tell her that he had been wounded. "Not on the tongue, I hope," said the famous courtesan, whose wit was as sharp as her wayward lover's. Clearly, neither Bernstein nor Coolus was the solution. Misia, "exhausted, prostrate with nerves and grief," felt that she "must put an end to an impossible situation." And so the definitive break came. Edwards and Misia were divorced on February 24, 1909, exactly four years after their marriage. Five months later Edwards and Lantelme were quietly married in Rouen. Presumably life in their new house in the rue de Constantine was lively. At least, with Lantelme's young lovers, her cocaine habit, and her violence, which matched his own, Edwards' interest never flagged.

Two years later, on July 25, 1911, Misia was shocked to read that Lantelme had been drowned in the Rhine. Only ten days earlier she had seen a photograph in the newspapers of the actress and Edwards with a group of friends in Verdun about to embark on the *Aimée*. Now the newspapers licked their tabloid jaws over every detail. Books were rushed into print to cash in on the twenty-four-year old actress' death. One of them, *Le Yacht Mystérieux*, tells the story in the journalistic style of the period. It begins with the assumption that Lantelme was in love with André Brulé, "the number one seducer of the French theatre." (Ironically enough, Brulé had played the role of Misia's young lover in Thadée's play *Le Foyer*.)

It was 12:30 a.m. when everyone retired. Entering her bathroom, Lantelme locked and bolted the door. . . . The heat was stifling, and she climbed up on her dressing table to open the window in spite of the torrential downpour. Then she climbed down, undressed, put on her nightgown, and combed her hair.

Tormented by the desires of a love she kept secret . . . she took a sheet of paper on which she traced these words: "My Beloved André." Pensively she searched for the next words. As no inspiration came, she opened a small bottle of white powder and poured some onto the lid in order to take a sniff, but instead of feeling relieved she felt she was suffocating. There was no air! She went back to the window and took a deep breath, leaning on the sill, her body half out of the window. What happened at that moment? Had the beautiful actress heard the Lorelei, the Siren of the Rhine, trying to lure her into the waves? Had she calculated the insurmountable obstacles that separated her from her beloved André and understood the futility of her love? Had she yielded to dizziness or felt her heart stop? Did a sudden oscillation of the boat make her lose her balance? Was she tired of pleasure, of party life? . . . Did she want to end it all?

How terrified she must have been as she felt herself fall into the water. Only her cry, the cry of a wounded bird, betrayed her anguish. . . . She struggled desperately but, sucked into a whirlpool like the whirlpool of her life, she succumbed.

Her cry of anguish was not lost in the storm. Captain Mayet and the passengers rushed out into the corridor. Where is she? She must be with Alfred. They found Edwards quietly reading in bed. Where is your wife? She's undressing. We must make sure. They pounded on her door. No answer. Edwards hurled himself against the door and broke the lock. The room was empty. "She's playing a trick on us! The window is wide open! She's fallen into the water!"

The captain turned the boat around. With flaming torches they searched the dark river, the rain pouring down. Edwards, mad with grief, went to his cabin and tried to kill himself; then, prostrate with grief, fell into bed. They heard him moan: *"Ma Ginette. Ma petite Ginette. Where are you? Why did you leave me? You knew of my boundless love! What fate has separated us forever! Come back! Tell me it's not true . . . that this is a horrible nightmare!!!"*

Why had the Grim Reaper cut down in the blossom of youth this beautiful young woman whom life had heaped with gifts and magnificent promise?

Fathomless mystery. Death lurking in the shadows watches us at every step, waiting to strike us at the moment we least expect.

The body of Lantelme, her magnificent hair streaming behind her, her priceless pearls still around her neck, was dragged up from the river. At the inquest the verdict was accidental death by drowning. The pleasure party with the shattered Edwards returned to Paris, where the yellow press exploited the affair much as Edwards himself might have done. The *Dépêche Parlementaire* wrote that Madame Edwards' death was neither accident nor suicide, that she had been murdered by a man rich and powerful enough to buy his freedom. Edwards sued for libel and the trial went on for months. In the end the newspaper was fined and Edwards was awarded damages of one franc. The case was closed, but not the mouths of scandal-loving Parisians. Misia (whose name, after all, was still Madame Edwards) was in the newspapers once again. It was painful to have her part of Edwards' notorious life served up each day with the morning coffee. For her it was an added horror that the disaster had taken place on the boat which had been built to make her happy. Rumor ran wild. Many said that Misia had pushed Lantelme overboard, although Misia, of course, had not been near the *Aimée* for years. Lantelme was buried in the Edwards family vault at the Père Lachaise cemetery. Unfortunately the papers reported that the actress' jewels had been buried with her. A few months later thieves broke into the tomb, and the newspapers had another field day. There were ghoulish descriptions of how the thieves violated the tomb and then, frightened by the noise of approaching police, ran off leaving the jewels behind. One of the policemen, overcome by fumes from the opened coffin, tried to clear the air by setting fire to some paper. Lantelme's shroud burst into flame and the fire department flooded the tomb, drowning poor Lantelme once again.

No one will ever know what actually happened when Lantelme died, but speculation continued. As late as 1930, "The Unpublished Murder of Lantelme," an article by Léon Daudet, appeared in the reactionary journal *L'Action Française*. Referring obliquely to Edwards' bizzare sexual perversion as the cause of the murder, Daudet wrote: "Edwards, according to what I have been told, was staggering around drunk. An unspeakable idea that I cannot even describe here crossed his mind, an idea that he wanted the horrified and indignant actress to put into practice. She struggled. He seized her body in spite of her protests and screams (he was a colossus) and threw her into the water." Daudet added that as "a spy for Germany and Turkey," Edwards was able to persuade the German authorities to accept his verdict of accidental death.

At the age of fifty-five, Edwards felt his life was over. He sold his house and the *Aimée* and retreated to a modest ground-floor apartment in the rue d'Anjou. There the man who had always been so flamboyantly visible lived hidden from the world, receiving the condolences of his friends in a dressing gown Lantelme herself had made for him. But he never stopped pursuing women. The man who had once been feared became a figure of fun: when he was seen with the beautiful opera singer Lina Cavalieri, Forain remarked, "I hope this one knows how to swim." *La Vente Lantelme*, a two-day sale of the actress' belongings, took place at the Galerie Drouot. Just as in the sale of Marguerite Gautier's possessions in Dumas' novel *La Dame aux Camélias*, the auction rooms were packed with prying friends and strangers inspecting the Aubusson tapestries, the Louis XVI furniture, the paintings, books, and bed linen. Lantelme's underclothes were passed from hand to hand along the rows of buyers before they were bid on. The total receipts were three-quarters of a million francs. (During the First World War the *Aimée* was requisitioned to transport wounded soldiers back from the front. Afterwards it too was passed from hand to hand, at one time belonging to the Prince de Ligne. In 1931 the boat Misia had loved so much was still afloat, rechristened *L'Améthyst*: a shoddy jewel, its lustre sadly faded.)

On March 10, 1914, less than three years after Lantelme's death, Edwards died of influenza. Notified at the last moment, Misia rushed to the rue d'Anjou, to the dark, narrow apartment that she had never seen; but she was too late. Edwards' mistress, the young actress Colonna Romano,* had thrown an evening coat over her nightdress and fled. Misia found Edwards lying in bed, his deathly green face resting on the actress' pink-ribboned pillow. The only other person in the apartment was a reporter telephoning in the next room. "*Allo! Le Matin?* Edwards is dead. *Allo! L'Excelsior?* Edwards is dead." Misia knelt and prayed at his bedside. There was a simple funeral at the Church of the Madeleine on Friday the thirteenth. Accompanied by five or six people, Edwards' body was taken to the Père Lachaise, where it was buried next to Lantelme's. In his will he left all his possessions, including the Théâtre Réjane and the Casino de Paris, to Mademoiselle Romano, "my friend in the most immaterial sense of the word." There was no provision for Misia.

---

* A great beauty, Mademoiselle Romano was painted many times by Renoir.

PART FOUR
Misia, Sert, and Diaghilev

Overleaf, Misia Edwards, c. 1910

*No race has shown more collective magnanimity
on great occasions, more pettiness and hardness
in small dealings between individuals. . . .*

*The inhabitants are brave, hospitable, and
generous, but fierce, treacherous, vindictive, and
given to acts of piracy, robbery, and wreckage.*

—EDITH WHARTON,
French Ways and Their Meaning

When Edwards left Misia for Lantelme in 1908, six years before his death, he urged her to see his lawyer about a financial settlement. But the very idea of lawyers bored Misia, and in her unrealistic way she kept putting it off. Besides, the princely check that arrived from Alfred each month was reality enough. She was financially independent, but whether she was sufficiently independent emotionally to live alone was a question that gnawed at her. Her pride had received a severe blow; she felt *déclassée* in the role of the discarded wife. Like an actress at liberty after a long run, she was both relieved and lost, and wondered anxiously what her next role would be. It was soon decided for her by the reappearance of the Spanish painter José-Maria Sert.

Sert was in his early thirties, three years younger than Misia. Short and squat—Salvador Dali later said his head looked like a potato—he was intensely, vibrantly alive. Descended from an immensely rich, austerely religious Catalan family of textile manufacturers, he decided at an early age that painting, not business, was to be his career. Equipped with a fine Jesuit education, Sert set out for Paris in 1899. With his grandiose ideas about art and life, his money and charm, and his consuming passion for women, he soon found himself in the thick of Parisian life. His oddities— sombrero and cape, alcohol and morphine—gave the color that Parisian artistic society appreciated in the budding *monstre sacré* who was to be called the Tiepolo of the Ritz. With characteristic extravagance he took the studio where Horace Vernet had once painted, in the fashionable rue Barbet-de-Jouy, and set to work on his enormous canvasses, quoting freely from Velasquez, Tintoretto, and Goya. There he received the painters Giovanni

Boldini, Jacques-Emile Blanche, Maurice Denis, and Jean-Louis Forain, as well as the composer Ernest Chausson and the writer Colette.

Of them all, it was Colette who became Sert's intimate friend. Her many letters to him are filled with advice, low comedy, and the anything-goes attitude they shared with knowing pleasure. She asks him how he will heat his studio in winter and suggests—in her best Claudine manner—having several women in his bed to keep him warm. Does he want her to go with him to shop for sheets, peignoirs, and bath towels? She speaks of her first trip to Bayreuth in a sleeping car; of the joy of lying naked as the train hurtles through the night; of Willy's rage at the overheated compartment and his complaints about the foreign sheets; of the Bayreuth shopwindow with a dreadful Art Nouveau painting of gilded Rhine-maidens with big breasts and "fat behinds" swimming in iridescent water. She describes the handsome Wagnerian opera singer Jean-Francisque Delmas, who is travelling in the same train, and depicts his early-morning appearance in a pink night-shirt, sponge-bag in hand, waiting his turn at the W.C., and imagines him enthroned on the mahogany oval brandishing his toilet paper as though it were Wotan's lance! Back in Paris, Colette writes to invite Sert to one of her Sundays where he will find beautiful women, some imbeciles, and a growing number of pretty young men. She is particularly taken with one who calls himself Natalie, eighteen years old, blond, black-eyed, red-mouthed, who (she is delighted to report) wears a handsome Lalique necklace with translucent enamel pendants around his neck. Colette insists that Sert come to stay with her at her new country house, a house so sad and calm that she longs to move there immediately.

As a favorite of the Spanish royal family, Sert had been commissioned by King Alfonso XIII to decorate the Cathedral of Vich near Barcelona. Enormous sections of this work were shown at the Grand Palais in the 1907 Salon d'Automne. They were part of a monumental exhibition that Misia saw, an exhibition which also included retrospectives of Cézanne, Berthe Morisot, and Jean-Baptiste Carpeaux as well as smaller showings of the paintings of Bonnard and Laprade (Misia's companions on the 1905 *Aimée* cruise), Rouault, Redon, and Matisse. In the October 25 issue of *La Grande Revue*, Félix Vallotton wrote:

The main attraction of the Salon (properly named!) is the loan by Monsieur Sert of fragments taken from the decoration of the Vich

Cathedral, a gigantic work which must astonish these walls, so recently devoted to a show of small sketches. To exhibit frescoes for a cathedral is not an everyday thing to do. Let M. Sert be praised for this fine gesture, even though it would be difficult to judge in advance the final effect of the colossal ensemble. The finished sections are not very attractive, and the color seems to me a little heavy and vulgar, but how can one grasp the relations of such great masses when they are on top of one's nose?

Undoubtedly with a little distance and the support of their structural frame, everything would fall into place and be properly seen for what it is worth: in any case, the model drawings are vigorously outlined and placed, and the composition indicates a skill and a taste for the magnificent which reminds one of Tintoretto.

Misia had first met Sert when Forain brought him to lunch on board the *Aimée*. Then he had just been one of the many people who passed through her life. Now it was Forain who brought Sert around once again. This time she was captivated. In a matter of minutes he took her out of herself into an absurd, amusing world of fantasy and adventure. He seemed to her "a young man, impetuous and courteous, who resembled nothing and nobody." In his thick Spanish accent he told Misia cruel, bizarre stories that enchanted her: how he had seen a stork die of hunger in front of a mound of food because its beak had been sawed off to make it lose its sense of direction; how, when he was an art student on a meagre allowance, he had fed his straw hat to his starving horse on a trip through Calabria. He spoke of the eccentricities of his native Barcelona, of the nightmarish Guell Park and the grotesque beauty of the Gaudi Cathedral. And he amused her with the story of the mad Hispano-German whose ballroom ceiling, decorated with gigantic plaster flowers, one day shed a giant petal and crushed a guest to death.

They spoke of the latest Parisian novelties, of the Pathé cinema near the Invalides which advertised an orchestra of sixty and the "largest screen in the world," and of the mercurial teen-age poet Jean Cocteau. They gossiped about Willy's scandalous separation from Colette—who, they were delighted to discover, was a mutual friend. Colette had left her husband for the Marquise de Belboeuf, known as "Missy." Even those worldly Parisians who applauded the two women when they performed their lesbian pantomimes in private salons were taken aback when they mimed the exotic *Rêve d'Egypte* at the Moulin Rouge. Adding spice to the occasion was the presence of Willy, who cheered them on as they ended their act with a frankly sexual kiss. The police stopped the show after one performance. Colette had appeared in pseudo-Egyptian costume with gold breastplates and a snake bracelet winding sinuously around her arm, but those in the know were amused to learn that she affected an even more curious jewel offstage: a gold dog tag with the identification "I Belong to Missy." Sporting a tuxedo, her normal evening wear, Missy, puffing away at her cigar, liked to reminisce about her father, "the great Duc de Morny." It was the same Morny, Misia told Sert, who had been the lover of her Russian cousin Julia Féguine, and had driven her to suicide when he decided to marry another woman.

Sert's talk, Misia later wrote, "was delivered in a tone of great seriousness, with a twinkle in his eye that gave the lie to what his mouth was saying, and punctuated by hands so eloquent that I was hypnotized by his thumbs, which turned into the air like question marks—thumbs that were animated, rough, ferocious, inquisitorial, caressing and domineering: the thumbs of an artist and, at the same time, a conqueror." Clearly Misia was aroused. She and Sert were so engrossed in each other that they scarcely noticed Forain's discreet departure. Sert's compelling talk was a prelude to passionate love-making. His "caressing, domineering thumbs" were only one indication of his sexual skill and power. Misia, who had always been uneasy about the pleasures of physical love, was overwhelmed for the first time in her life. Her feelings were intensified by the fact that Sert was leaving for Rome the next morning. To her surprise he invited her to join him there, and to her greater surprise she heard herself accepting.

The next morning, however, both had second thoughts. Embarrassed that she had so impetuously accepted his invitation, Misia was toying with the idea of changing her mind when a special delivery letter from Sert took the initiative from her. More used to casual sexual encounters than she, Sert was disturbed by the strong emotions he had aroused in her and worried about the responsibilities involved. After all, the distinguished, the exalted Misia was not just one of his *petites amies*. He tried to disengage himself by writing that he had no right to ruin her life, that he was ashamed of his behavior, that this madness must be forgotten. As Misia herself admitted, his letter was precisely what was needed to make her decide to follow him on the first available train. From a station on the way—too late for him to stop her—she wired him to reserve rooms for herself and her maid at the Grand Hotel.

The sight of Sert exuberantly waving his sombrero on the station platform filled her with excitement. It had not been so long ago that Misia, unspeakably lonely, had peered down the empty corridor of the Grand Hotel. Now the same hotel became a temple of love. Sert opened her mind and body to ecstatic thoughts and feelings she had only suspected were in her. He revealed her to herself. She had always felt that she was capable of a great love, and now at last the deep sensuality that lay within her was fulfilled. Their weeks together unfolded in a procession of pleasures. They lingered over *apéritifs* in vine-covered cafés, then dined extravagantly at Fagiano's in the Piazza Colonna. Enraptured, they walked by moonlight in the Campidoglio after making love, Misia's long white dress gracefully sweeping the marble-incrusted pavement. They gave each other pet names; she was Tosche, he Jojo. Misia's pout of boredom disappeared.

Sert played the guide, and Misia felt she had never looked at art before. He taught her to notice what she had never noticed and to appreciate what she had not expected to appreciate. An impassioned teacher, he made her feel that she understood everything, that Caravaggio, Tintoretto, and Luini were intimate friends. He pointed out the sensuous architectural tricks of the Palazzo Spada and Borromeo's Sant' Ivo. He showed her the sexually ambiguous martyrdom of Bernini's Saint Teresa in the Church of Santa Maria della Vittoria around the corner from their hotel. And when Misia hired a car and they went travelling, she marvelled at her Spanish grandee who brushed all mundane details aside with such authority—and such enormous tips. For Sert, hotels and restaurants that had been fully booked for weeks magically produced the grandest suites and the choicest tables.

Like a naïve young girl, Misia was impressed by the assurance with which he dismissed what he considered second-rate as he swept her along the galleries to what he "knew" were masterpieces. Gallantly he anticipated her museum fatigue and led her off to grimy antique shops where, their energy renewed, they vied with one another to unearth surprising treasures. Misia was reborn, brimming over with love for Sert. When the Italian trip was over, there was no doubt in her mind that she would never leave him. Besides, Misia was realistic even in her rapture, and she knew there was no one to go back to.

One of the first things Misia and Sert did on their return was to see Serge Diaghilev's production of Mussorgsky's *Boris Godunov*. The opera's first performance outside Russia promised to be the event of the 1908 spring season. Diaghilev, a Parisian before the fact, had gathered an imposing list of patrons: His Imperial Highness the Grand Duke Paul, the Grand Duke and Duchess Vladimir, the Duchess d'Uzès, the Princesses Polignac and Murat, the Countesses de Chevigné and Greffulhe, and the composers Debussy, Fauré, Saint-Saëns, D'Indy, Dukas, Messager, Glazunov, and Rimsky-Korsakov. As Misia looked about at the opulently dressed audience, she felt that it was good to be back in the most worldly, the most exciting of cities. Half an hour after the curtain rose she was so dazzled by the sight of the stage, streaming with gold, so overcome by the visceral excitement of the music, and so shaken by the fierce grandeur of the great singer Chaliapin, that she felt the need to be alone. Quietly she slipped out of her loge and escaped to the topmost gallery, where she listened to the rest of the performance perched on the stairs. As she left the theatre, the bells of the Coronation Scene still ringing in her ears, she knew she must hear the opera over and over again. She had experienced what Turgenev called "that chill and sweet terror of ecstasy, which instantaneously enwraps the soul when beauty bursts with sudden flight upon it."

At each performance (*Boris* was given seven times in five weeks) Misia immersed herself in the music. Irritated by the sight of empty places in the theatre, she bought the remaining seats and sent them to her friends so that they too could experience what the critic of *Le Temps* called "*une radieuse révélation.*"

At supper with Sert after one of the performances, Misia caught sight of a rather effete gentleman entering the restaurant. Handsome and aloof, with a white streak like a swan's feather in his black hair, he was adjusting the black pearl in his tie with heavily ringed fingers. It was Serge Diaghilev. Sert had met him the year before when the impresario had presented the first exhibition of Russian paintings in Paris. Now Sert invited him to join them, and Misia, hardly waiting for an introduction, impetuously poured out her feelings about *Boris*. Rarely had Diaghilev been praised with such perceptive fervor. She spoke of the music, the performance, and the decor with an enthusiasm and understanding that went straight to his heart. When they left the restaurant at five in the morning, Diaghilev's aloof expression had turned into a boyish grin. Impulsively Misia and Diaghilev decided they must lunch together the next day. That, they gaily realized, would be in only a few hours. Misia's Parisian frivolity and caustic wit delighted the Russian newcomer. By the time lunch was over, they felt they had known each other all their lives.

In fact the similarities in their personalities and in their lives are striking. Both were born in Russia in March 1872, lost their mothers at birth, and had fathers who soon remarried. Both their stepmothers encouraged their musical talents, and both were constantly exposed to great music from earliest childhood. Indeed, both had dreamt of musical careers and loved music with that special intensity often found in musicians *manqués*. Diaghilev had wanted to be a composer and had studied at the St. Petersburg Conservatory until he was twenty-six. He too had composed a scene from *Boris Godunov* but, like a symphony he took to Rimsky-Korsakov, it showed little talent. Rimsky had suggested cuts in the symphony. On further reflection, he said with the cruel frankness of the Russian music teacher that perhaps it would be best to cut it from beginning to end. (Diaghilev later had his little revenge when he obliged Rimsky to make cuts in the score of *Schéhérazade*.) When Diaghilev was twenty-three he wrote a letter to his stepmother that combined playful exaggeration with Russian soul baring: "I am, first, a charlatan, though rather a brilliant one; secondly, a great charmer; thirdly, frightened of nobody; fourthly, a man with plenty of logic and very few scruples; fifthly, I seem to have no real talent. Nonetheless, I believe I have found my true vocation—to be a Maecenas.* I have everything necessary except the money—but that will come."

Diaghilev's description of himself was equally true of Misia, except that money was already hers and she had already been more than generous to her artist friends. She was no more a charlatan than he, although both relied a

---

* Did Diaghilev know that the Roman Gaius Maecenas was not only a princely patron who helped shape the work of Horace and Virgil but also, according to a contemporary, Velleius Paterculus, a man "of sleepless vigilance in critical emergencies, far-seeing and knowing how to act, but in his relaxation from business more luxurious and effeminate than a woman"?

bit on fakery and neither was overburdened with scruples. Both of them took luxury for granted. With his Charvet shirts and fur-lined coat, Diaghilev was as much the dandy as Misia, dressed by Worth and Patou. Both were unconventional in highly visible ways. In Russia Diaghilev had lived so openly as a homosexual that he had been sent the anonymous gift of a powder puff. When the history of homosexuality is written, Diaghilev will be seen as one of its liberators. After all, only a few years earlier Oscar Wilde had been imprisoned for the "crime" that Diaghilev displayed with so little concern. And in her way, Misia was one of the most visibly liberated of women. Her separations from her husbands had been public scandals: she had been Edwards' mistress while still married to Natanson and was now Sert's mistress while still married to Edwards. All this at a time when Léon Blum's book *On Marriage* had bourgeois Paris in an uproar because it urged women to sleep with their fiancés.

Neither Misia nor Diaghilev was particularly gifted sexually, and both found sublimation in controlling their friends and lovers by other means. Surprisingly infantile in handling their own love affairs, they were harsh and worldly in their judgment of other people's. Cynical and irresponsible, they revelled in annihilating wit and were callously indifferent to the feelings of others. They behaved arrogantly toward anyone who did not interest or amuse them, but they could be immensely appealing to people who did. They lavished favors, money, and gifts on friends out of affection, and on enemies in the hope of disarming them. They adored gossip and had talents for intrigue which were to blossom alarmingly in the next twenty years.

Both of them had been involved with avant-garde magazines, Misia, of course, with the *Revue Blanche* and Diaghilev as one of the founders and editors of the St. Petersburg review *Mir Iskustva* (*The World of Art*). Neither, however, could be called an intellectual; their reading days were more or less over. Diaghilev was seldom seen to open a book, and Misia prided herself on being able to grasp the essence of a new volume simply by leafing through it. Yet they were both extraordinarily rich in that singular commodity called taste; they were in fact autocrats of taste, a profession in itself. In Diaghilev, taste rose to the level of creative art. Generosity and cruelty, wild enthusiasm and deadly boredom, arrogance and humility, all the heights and depths of the slavic temperament possessed them both. It was precisely Misia's slavic qualities which made their great friendship possible, for Diaghilev was never to have a true affinity with anyone who was not a Slav. There was no doubt in Misia's mind that she valued her friendship with Diaghilev above all others. Diaghilev for his part said that the only woman he could ever have imagined marrying was Misia—that she was his closest woman friend, the sister he never had.

On February 25, 1909, the day after her divorce from Edwards, Misia's father died at the age of seventy-four. With his death a certain constraint was lifted, for their relations had always been disturbing in the way that only family relations can be. Misia had married two men whom she imagined would give her the stability and protection her father had not provided. Both had failed her. Now with her father gone, she felt a curious emptiness. Yet she hoped that a new life was beginning, for she was convinced that, at last, in Sert she had found a man on whom she could rely. Sert and her father were not unlike one another. Sert too was a dedicated egotist with a taste for luxury and women who became a successful society artist. Most important for Misia, Sert had that authority without which she felt lost. For the moment, of course, marriage would be unwise. Even though Edwards was soon to make Lantelme his wife, he could hardly be expected to continue his lavish support of Misia were she to remarry. It was pleasant to have all the money she wanted without the enervating problem of how to fill her time. The languid days aboard the *Aimée*, days spent wondering if her life would always be insipid and unhappy, were behind her. As a rich, well-connected *Parisienne*, there were a thousand ways she could help the two new men in her life, Sert and Diaghilev.

Diaghilev had decided to bring the magnificent dancers of the Imperial Russian Ballet, then at its height, to Paris, where ballet had become a trivial appendage to the opera house. But with the unexpected death of his patron the Grand Duke Vladimir, his Russian subsidies evaporated. The problem was money, a problem that was always to haunt him. That winter Diaghilev's pattern was set. The "impossibilist," as the Russian painter Alexander Benois said, "has his great army on the march." Like Napoleon in reverse, Diaghilev set out to conquer Paris. He brought with him a small committee of Russian artistic advisers and engaged the impresario Gabriel Astruc to handle the business arrangements. To realize his dream Diaghilev bargained, lied, broke promises, stormed, bullied, cajoled, charmed, and mesmerized. He guaranteed money he did not have, then scurried about to raise the money he had guaranteed. He told Astruc the money would come from Russia and told the Russians it would come from France. As Serge Grigoriev, Diaghilev's *régisseur* wrote: "It appeared he had been able to do what he wanted. His great friends Madame Edwards (afterward Madame Sert) and the Comtesse Greffulhe had given him all the help they could, and their efforts had been successful. They had formed a committee of influential and wealthy people, under whose auspices Diaghilev had been able to announce his season."

The magician had done it all with mirrors. Even before the money was in his hands, Diaghilev grandly ordered the Théâtre du Châtelet to be redecorated from the proscenium arch to the topmost gallery. But if his season was to be successful, he and his committee knew that *le Tout-Paris* must be mobilized. Madame de Chevigné, the Rothschilds, the Ephrussis, and others were asked to give money and to do what came even more easily to them: to talk, to spread the word. When the dancers arrived from Russia, Diaghilev invited Misia, Cocteau, the poet Anna de Noailles, and the critics Robert Brussel and M.D. Calvocoressi to a rehearsal. The French penchant for talk had been helpful in raising money and stirring up interest, but it produced chaos at the rigorous rehearsal. Misia, normally talkative, was all eyes and ears. But Anna de Noailles, Cocteau, and Brussel, with their uninhibited "*C'est un dieu; Qu'elle est jolie! Divine! C'est génial! Eblouissant! Inouï!*" were told to be quiet in no uncertain terms. Not an easy feat for Cocteau and the Comtesse de Noailles, two of Paris' most relentlessly brilliant chatterers. The enforced silence did not prevent Brussel from flirting with Karsavina, nor Cocteau with Nijinsky. The flirtations did little to endear Cocteau to Diaghilev or Brussel to the choreographer Fokine, who, a little in love with Karsavina himself, ordered Brussel out of the theatre.

Even with the advance rumors, the feverish anticipation, and the general excitement, no one was prepared for the overwhelming success of the first performance of the Ballets Russes on May 19, 1909. Diaghilev's financial machinations were trivial compared with the pure gold he produced that night. It was a revelation to see the swift beauty of the young ballerinas and the challenging strength of the male dancers as they stamped out the rhythms of the Polovtsian Dances from Borodin's *Prince Igor*. Wave after wave of bravos seemed to match the pulsating, ever-mounting phrases of the exotic score. At last Parisians were seeing framed in a proscenium arch the fabled savagery of the Russia of their dreams. As the curtain came down, hundreds in the audience rushed backstage to get a glimpse of their new idols, Tamara Karsavina and Vaslav Nijinsky.

> I realized that something unusual was happening to me and around me [Karsavina recalled], something to which I could give no name, so unexpected, so enormous, as to frighten almost. . . . The familiar barriers between stage and audience were broken. . . . The stage was so crowded with spectators that there was hardly room to move . . . hundreds of eyes followed us about. . . . "He is a prodigy," and awed whispers, *"C'est elle."*

This and the next program, which included the Bakst-Fokine ballet *Cléopâtre*, were evenings never to be forgotten. Diaghilev and his company became celebrated overnight. A new unofficial society began to take shape: the friends of the Ballets Russes. Misia, at its center, was quickly surrounded, for it soon became evident that she was the golden link to Diaghilev. Her sumptuous drawing room in the rue de Rivoli became the informal headquarters for the Russians, much as sixteen years earlier her simpler salon around the corner in the rue St. Florentin had been the annex of the *Revue Blanche*. Diaghilev was there constantly, trailed by his band of Russian conspirators that included the painters Léon Bakst and Alexander Benois and, to the great excitement of Misia's guests, Karsavina and Nijinsky, Diaghilev's new lover. How lost Nijinsky seemed, with his shy, absent air and his total lack of French. To most of his dancers Diaghilev was a distant god, but to Nijinsky and to the lovely Karsavina, he was more than attentive and always took them to supper after the ballet. Karsavina remembered being driven home from Misia's by Proust, "shy, polite, green as a ghost." It was at Misia's too that the intoxicatingly clever Cocteau, like a brilliant gem that must be examined for its authenticity, was made available for Diaghilev's further inspection. Uniquely sensitive to Diaghilev's revolutionary way of combining the arts, Cocteau quickly found his way backstage and soon seemed a charter member of the troupe.

After the performances there were festive champagne suppers in the Bois de Boulogne or at Larue's, where Proust, sitting at a corner table writing letters and sipping a spartan hot chocolate, observed Diaghilev, Nijinsky, Cocteau, Misia, Sert, and company. "God knows Jean was irresistible at twenty," Misia said, recalling Cocteau dancing on the backs of the banquettes at Larue's. But it would take more than that, she added, for him to become Diaghilev's collaborator. Proust, of course, knew when he was onto a good thing. One might say that the main characters in his novel stepped out of its as-yet-unwritten pages to honor the Russians. The poet Comte Robert de Montesquiou—Proust's Baron de Charlus—brandished his gold-knobbed cane at the Châtelet as he screamed the ballet's praises. He had been set back on his elegant heels by the mysteriously androgynous beauty of Ida Rubinstein. Hardly surprising when one reads Cocteau's inspired description of her entrance as Cleopatra:

> The bearers set the casket down in the middle of the temple, opened its double lid, and from within lifted a kind of mummy, a bundle of veils, which they placed upright on its ivory pattens. Then four slaves began an astonishing maneuver. They unwound the first veil, which was red, with silver lotuses and crocodiles; then the second veil, which was green, with the history of the dynasties in gold filigree; then the third, which was orange with prismatic stripes; and so on. . . . The twelfth veil, dark blue, Mme. Rubinstein released herself, letting it fall with a sweeping circular gesture.
>
> She stood leaning forward, her shoulders slightly hunched like the wings of the ibis; overcome by her long wait, having submitted in her dark coffin, as had we, to the intolerable and sublime music of her cortège. . . . She was wearing a small blue wig, from which a short golden braid hung down on either side of her face. There she stood, unswathed, eyes vacant, cheeks pale, lips parted . . . and as she confronted the stunned audience, she was too beautiful, like a too potent Oriental fragrance.

Montesquiou carried Madame Rubinstein off to his *pavillon rose* in Neuilly, where he regaled her with perhaps more of his verse than she cared to hear.

One of the Ballets Russes' admirers, an enormously rich, cultivated Polish Jew, Maurice Ephrussi, invited his friends to a *soirée artistique* in the gardens of his house in the avenue du Bois. It was a magical experience to see *Les Sylphides*, led by Karsavina, against a background of massed trees alive with electric lights. Madame Ephrussi added a Proustian touch by sending Karsavina suspiciously large amounts of roses. The caustic Comtesse de Chevigné, who liked to boast that she was descended from the Marquis de Sade, and the beautiful Comtesse Greffulhe (whose sister Ghislaine had been Misia's childhood playmate in Halle) became two of Diaghilev's most generous supporters. Both, of course, were later transformed by Proust into the witty, heartless Duchesse de Guermantes. Misia, like Proust, admired both women inordinately.

Diaghilev's first season ended in clouds of glory—and debts. But as art, not money, was his preoccupation, the debts were dismissed with an aristocratic shrug. His chief concern was the next season, and the next. He had been belittling himself, it turned out, when he said he had no talents of his own. For while he was neither a poet nor a painter, composer, choreographer, or dancer, he had such extraordinary flair for combining the talents of those who were that it amounted to genius—a kind of genius that seems never to have existed before or since. Encouraged by his success, he began to make more ambitious plans. His dream was to present opera, his first love, as well as ballet, so he felt that the Paris Opéra rather than the Théâtre du Châtelet would be the ideal setting. Working behind Astruc's back despite the invaluable help his business manager had provided, Diaghilev began negotiations for a season of Russian opera and ballet. The fact that his project was in direct conflict with Astruc's plan to bring the Metropolitan Opera of New York to Paris did not seem to concern him. Astruc was so outraged by this double-dealing that he wrote an eleven-page letter to Tsar Nicholas II denouncing Diaghilev. Without Astruc, Diaghilev could do nothing; he had reached an impasse. Misia and Sert offered to help, but it was not easy. For Diaghilev, who inspired love in his friends and wary respect in his collaborators, aroused suspicion, even revulsion, in official circles. Coming to his defense, Misia spoke to Gheusi, the assistant director of the Opéra, then left for Venice with Sert. Gheusi's response was not encouraging:

27 June 1909

We received your card, dear friend, a few hours after having learned of your departure. I see that your friendly concern is following you to Venice, you and Sert. But I must tell you this: I dined by chance with Serge the Muscovite and Astruc . . . the other evening. . . . I then took the precaution of getting the opinion of Astruc himself about his slavic associate. . . .

Oh . . . My dear friend! . . . what I learned then, with no room for doubt, makes it *absolutely* impossible for me to join forces with this ostentatious, conscienceless man. And I hasten to write you so that our dear Sert, so loyal and so proud, will be warned. Benois is a perfect gentleman as well as a great artist. But the other ! ! ! Messager and Carré (who know a good deal) have also enlightened me. In short, *I must not, I cannot* be associated in any way with Monsieur S[erge] de D[iaghilev]. I'll give you more details when you return.

There will be no *official* Russian season in Paris next year. That is the *formal* wish of the Russian court and the Grand Dukes. Therefore I shall evade, with the greatest courtesy, or rather delay as long as possible, the offers in question. Then when you return we shall speak of all this again. I myself am *with* Sert, with all my heart—with you. But my strict duty is to advise you, both of you, not to get mixed up with certain others. Is that clear? . . .

Ah! How good it would be to be in Venice, with you, delicious friend, with Sert as our guide to the lively picturesque sights! . . . But that is a dream.

Misia and Sert ignored Gheusi's warning. Instead they did everything they could to help Diaghilev while he was in Russia struggling to make the necessary arrangements. Six months later when all Diaghilev's efforts had come to nothing, Misia and Sert, with the help of the Comtesses de Béarn and de Chevigné and the Marquise de Ganay, arranged a meeting between him and Astruc. Just before Diaghilev's arrival an encouraging letter reached Sert from Benois:

St. Petersburg
December 2, 1909

Bien cher ami,

It gave me great joy to read your lines, which quickened for me the picture of you I carry in my heart and all that wonderful time of the *"Saison Russe."* Diaghilev is leaving for Paris soon and will bring you good news concerning the realization of the *Dream*. All this is more or less phantasmagoric and will not cease to be so till the moment the curtain goes up at the first *répétition générale*. But that has always, always been the way he conducts his affairs, and I begin to believe he is right, seeing that, in spite of his numerous *gaffes*, his negligence, and the tricks he has the habit of playing, he also has the habit of success.

I am so accustomed to this somewhat bizarre "system" that I no longer protest but just wait patiently and with confidence. Besides, I am quite convinced that the great bullfighter will quickly dispel all your fears; at least, that's the way he operates with his close apostles.

My wife and I beg you, dear friend, to speak to Madame Edwards of our cordial devotion and to tell her that we have kept reverent memories of her rare and delightful kindness.

When Astruc and Diaghilev finally met after months of bitter wrangling, Sert and Brussel were there to help matters along. Misia's first mission as Diaghilev's emissary was accomplished. A compromise was reached and the *saison russe* was on its way.

In 1910 and 1911 a succession of ballets was unfurled before the Paris public like glittering banners from an unknown country. This uncharted land became a spiritual home for those in search of new artistic sensations. Diaghilev's ballets were far removed from the pretty little dances and neatly turned dramas of adultery that were the usual fare of Parisian theatregoers. The technical perfection and the daring abandon of beautiful bodies responding to new music were a revelation. As the seasons went on, artists and writers, high society and homosexual society (often overlapping), royalty, aristocrats, and visiting dignitaries joined to applaud with almost patriotic fervor. Ravel and Debussy; Proust, Gide, Claudel, Henry James, and Joseph Conrad; ambassadors from America, Russia, and Spain; Vanderbilts, Rothschilds, and Gulbenkians; Réjane, Lantelme, Isadora Duncan, and Sarah Bernhardt—all came to shout their approval.

There was Fokine's *Les Sylphides,* a garland of moonlit dances, so artfully choreographed that the romantic reverie seemed to come alive of itself. The tenderness of *Carnaval,* sparkling with glints of cruelty and satire, provided another proof of Fokine's genius, of his free new way of looking at dancing. But *Sylphides* and *Carnaval,* exquisite though they were, seemed effete poetry to the general public compared to the cymbal-crashing eroticism of the oriental ballets.

The French, whose love of the exotic had been nurtured on Gautier, Flaubert, Loti, and Pierre Louÿs, were overwhelmed by the orgy in Bakst's opulent harem in *Schéhérazade.* What they were seeing was an animation of their own history of painting, from Delacroix to Moreau, from Gérôme to Rochegrosse. Their erotic fantasies were brought to life in the floating, gliding, whirling, twisting, crouching, leaping, soaring bodies of the young Russians. The new Russian theatrical art was an explosion of emotion, presented with a virtuosity and an expressivity never before seen in France. The refined cruelties and sensualities of Balzac and Baudelaire were given a new erotic dimension in the living sexual thrust of the dancers. Proust, who admired Bakst "prodigiously," said of *Schéhérazade,* "I never saw anything so beautiful." And Harold Acton, a young Englishman, breathlessly describes in his *Memoirs of an Aesthete* "the thunder and lightning of negroes in rose and amber; . . . the fierce orgy of clamorous caresses; death in long-drawn spasms to piercing violins. Rimsky-Korsakov painted the tragedy; Bakst hung it with emerald curtains and silver lamps and carpeted it with rugs from Bokhara and silken cushions. Nijinsky and Karsavina made it live." Fokine's ballet to Rimsky-Korsakov's brilliantly orchestrated music was to be applauded the world over for years to come—an emblem of the Ballets Russes.* In Paris *Schéhérazade* had its effect on fashionable women, Misia among them. Dressed by Poiret in violent colors and oriental patterns, they looked as though they had just escaped from Bakst's harem as they stepped down from the running boards of their Panhards and de Dion-Boutons.

Rimsky-Korsakov's pupil Igor Stravinsky was, of course, Diaghilev's greatest musical discovery. Short, brilliant, and irascible, he produced between 1910 and 1913 the three ballet scores on which his popular fame

---

* When *Schéhérazade* was first performed in the then more puritan New York, the manager of the theatre was taken to court. The judge threatened to cancel the performances unless the suggestive silk cushions on the floor of the harem were replaced by some good, sensible rocking chairs.

still rests: *The Firebird, Petrushka,* and *The Rite of Spring* (*Le Sacre du Printemps*). *The Firebird,* performed in 1910, introduced to the world its most important ballet composer since Tchaikovsky, and for many of us the greatest composer of the twentieth century. Diaghilev felt that 1911, his third season, was the critical one. His "great army" had successfully captured the French capital, and now he repeated Napoleon's remark, "It is not enough to take the Tuileries; the problem is to stay there." *Petrushka* provided the heavy artillery. For if *Firebird* was reminiscent of Rimsky-Korsakov's oriental pungencies, *Petrushka* was startlingly original. Few in the brilliant audience that crowded into the Châtelet for the first performance of *Petrushka* could have imagined the trouble and confusion backstage. Benois, offended that his portrait of the Charlatan in the Moor's room had been repainted by Bakst, had quarreled with Diaghilev. Stravinsky was still arguing about tempi with the conductor, Pierre Monteux. The company complained that the stage was so cluttered with props that there was no room to dance. And the orchestra found the music too difficult to play. The ballet's heart-rending final scene was still being improvised by Fokine, Benois, and Stravinsky minutes before the curtain was scheduled to rise. And Diaghilev was struggling with the costumier, who threatened to remove the costumes unless he was paid at once. Twenty minutes after the house lights were lowered, the curtain was still down. There were murmurs, coughs, and a crescendo of complaints in the restive audience. Misia was wondering about the delay when Diaghilev bu·st into her loge. Those who watched as he bent over Misia's jewelled *décolletage* and whispered into her ear could not have guessed that his graceful gesture concealed a moment of financial panic. Pale and agitated, he asked if she could give him four thousand francs to pay for the costumes. "In those happy days," Misia said, "one's chauffeur was always waiting." In ten minutes she was back with the money. When the curtain finally rose, the audience was transported to Admiralty Square in St. Petersburg, where, thanks to Misia, the festive carnival crowd milling about in front of the puppet theatre was alive with the brilliant colors of Benois' costumes.

Only a week earlier, Nijinsky, graceful and almost cloyingly feminine as *Le Spectre de la Rose*, had Paris gasping at his prodigious leap. Now he touched the hearts of the audience with his poignant portrayal of Petrushka, the helpless yet indomitable puppet crushed by the indifference and cruelty of others. Perhaps three claustrophobic years as Diaghilev's jealously guarded possession had given Nijinsky an added understanding of the puppet manipulated by the Charlatan.

By the time *Petrushka* was produced, Misia had been exposed to all the Byzantine intricacies of Diaghilev and his entourage. She had learned that her friend was the absolute ruler of a court replete with slaves and favorites, intrigues and banishments, all at the whim of an implacable tyrant. And Misia, with her aigrette and diamonds, had become the benevolent consort to the monarch in his shining top hat. She played other roles as well: grand vizier and privy councillor, official hostess, confidante, and, most important, liaison officer between Diaghilev and his artists. She knew how to mollify those artists who felt cheated of money or recognition with such understanding that they came to depend on her for advice, knowing that her purse would often be open to them. Besides they felt at home with her. Misia's instinctive grasp of difficult avant-garde works made her seem like a fellow artist. Her profound frivolity, her comradely ease, and her sharp, amusing tongue were a spicy bouquet for the Russians new to the worldly capital. Like Mallarmé's description of the *Revue Blanche*, Misia was friendly and open to everyone, provided the talent interested her. Serving as a customs officer as well, Misia inspected the artistic baggage of outsiders who wanted to enter the many-faceted world of the Ballets Russes. Robert de Montesquiou had known Diaghilev ever since 1898, when he had lent Whistler's elegant portrait of himself (now in the Frick Museum in New York) to the Russian impresario for an exhibition in St. Petersburg. Even so, it was to Misia that he applied when he wanted to watch rehearsals. "I have spoken to Helleu just now, who would like to come and applaud them too," he wrote. "I should like to see the ones I do not know—*Carnaval, Schéhérazade* (or that other oriental one of Bakst), *Giselle,* or *The Firebird.*"

From the beginning Misia had been trying to interest Diaghilev in the French artists she admired: Ravel, Debussy, and Cocteau. In 1912 the seeds she planted bore fruit. The Ballets Russes presented three French ballets: Reynaldo Hahn-Cocteau's *Le Dieu Bleu* and Ravel's *Daphnis and Chloë*, both choreographed by Fokine, as well as Debussy's *Afternoon of a Faun,* which introduced Nijinsky as a revolutionary choreographer. To the general public, who expected to see Nijinsky's spectacular leaps, the static sensuality of *Faun* seemed as puzzling as the statement in the program: "*Afternoon of a Faun* should be danced in the midst of a landscape with trees of zinc." In his first choreography Nijinsky created hieratic poses that evoked a Grecian atmosphere reminiscent of the quiet, windless paintings of Puvis de Chavannes, whose works Diaghilev particularly loved. His controlled body taut, his head thrown back in an ecstasy of longing, Nijinsky moved in an onanistic dream. His fetishistic handling of the nymph's veil, leading to gestures suggestive of masturbation and of orgasm, upset those in the audience who were not prepared for such an alarmingly pagan display. The program notes gave Mallarmé's lines that explain why Debussy's composition is called *Prelude to the Afternoon of a Faun.*

> *Un faune sommeille,*
> *Des nymphes le dupent,*
> *Une écharpe oubliée satisfait son rêve.*
> *Le rideau baisse pour que le poème commence dans toutes les mémoires.*

> *A faun dozes,*
> *Nymphs tease him,*
> *A forgotten scarf satisfies his dream.*
> *The curtain descends so that the poem can begin in everyone's memory.*

The fall of the curtain did not, as Mallarmé suggested, lead the audience to his poem. Instead of a reverie there was a riot. Defying the roars of disapproval, Diaghilev ordered the ballet to be repeated immediately.

Seated in Misia's box at the dress rehearsal, Debussy was shocked. He felt that Nijinsky had been much too explicit, had interpreted the word "satisfies" too literally. Perhaps he was upset that attention was centered on Nijinsky rather than on the music. In any event, when Misia, trying to calm him, explained, "The faun has married the veil he tore from the nymph," Debussy lost his temper. "Go away," he said to her, "you are horrible," and left the theatre. Though he had accepted a place in Misia's box (it was, after all, where Diaghilev seated his guests), Debussy had been distinctly cool to her for several years. On his marriage to Madame Bardac, a rich widow, his friends had taken up a collection to help his first wife, whom he had abandoned without a penny. Knowing how touchy he was, both Misia and Pierre Louÿs had tried to conceal their generosity—Misia by giving money through Ravel. Debussy discovered the ruse and never forgave them for their considerate duplicity.

After the first performance of *Afternoon of a Faun*, the newspapers too were in an uproar. Calmette, who had kept his editorship of *Le Figaro* owing to Misia's intervention with Edwards years before, was so incensed that he wrote a front-page article denouncing the ballet as "filthy, bestial, indecent eroticism." With great nobility Rodin replied in *Le Matin*:

> Form and meaning are indissolubly wedded in [Nijinsky's] body. . . .
> He is the ideal model, whom one longs to draw and sculpt. Nothing could be more striking than the impulse with which, at the climax, he lies face down on the scented veil, kissing and embracing it with passionate abandon. I wish that such a noble endeavor could be understood as a whole; and that . . . all our artists might come for inspiration and to communicate in beauty.

According to Misia, the sculptor's praise gave Diaghilev such satisfaction that he carried the article with him wherever he went.

Some years earlier, Misia had given what she considered a smart dinner party in honor of Prince and Princess Georges Bibesco. The men, who included Proust, Sem, and the painter Helleu, wore dinner jackets except for the writer Claude Anet, who was more formally dressed in tails. When Misia teased him about being overdressed, Anet loftily replied that he was going on to the Princesse Murat's.

"Is it nice at the Murats'?" asked Misia, half naïve, half mocking.

"Nice? What do you mean by 'nice,' Misia? They're society people," he answered.

"But aren't we all society people?" Misia asked rather archly.

Anet burst out laughing. "You're fantastic! You don't understand anything! The Murats would never receive you."

Proust, one imagines, did not miss a word of this exchange. Nor did he now miss the Verdurin-like twists and turns of Misia's life. As Diaghilev's closest woman friend, she began to entertain *le gratin,* that upper crust of French society, which was discovering that it could step out of the Faubourg and remain untainted. Through Diaghilev, Misia became closely connected with Comtesse Greffulhe and Comtesse de Chevigné, with Princesse de Polignac and Princesse Murat. As a result, the members of that "society" which Anet had said would never receive her now pursued her so eagerly that she sometimes found them difficult to shake off. While she was more than pleased to be at the center of things, Misia had her own kind of snobbery largely based on what amused her and what did not.

When Misia appears in Proust's novel as the ravishing Russian Princess Yourbeletieff, Madame Verdurin is always at her side, either watching the Russian dancers from a box or giving parties for them. The Princess Yourbeletieff is based entirely on Misia, but Proust uses a device by which many of Misia's traits and the facts of her history are divided between Princess Yourbeletieff and Madame Verdurin. In the section of his book called *The Captive*, Proust gives his view of Madame Verdurin as if she, the Princess Yourbeletieff, and Misia are one.

Mme Verdurin's strength lay in her genuine love of art, the trouble that she used to take for her faithful, the marvellous dinners that she gave for them alone, without inviting anyone from the world of fashion . . . . When a boon companion . . . had turned into an illustrious man whom everybody was longing to meet, his presence at Mme Verdurin's had none of the artificial, composite effect of a dish at an official or farewell banquet, cooked by Potel or Chabot, but was merely a delicious "ordinary" which you would have found there in the same perfection on a day when there was no party at all. At Mme Verdurin's the cast was trained to perfection, the repertory most select, all that was lacking was an audience. And now that the public taste had begun to turn from the rational and French art of a Bergotte, and to go in, above all things, for exotic forms of music, Mme Verdurin, a sort of official representative in Paris of all foreign artists, was not long in making her appearance, by the side of the exquisite Princess Yourbeletieff, an aged Fairy Godmother, grim but all powerful, to the Russian dancers. This charming invasion, against whose seductions only the stupidest of critics protested, infected Paris, as we know, with a fever of curiosity less burning, more purely aesthetic, but quite as intense as that aroused by the Dreyfus case. There again, Mme Verdurin, but with a very different result socially, was to take her place in the front row. Just as she had been seen by the side of Mme Zola, immediately under the bench, during the trial in the Assize Court, so when the new generation of humanity, in their enthusiasm for the

Russian ballet, thronged to the Opéra, crowned with the latest novelty in aigrettes, they invariably saw in a stage box Mme Verdurin by the side of Princess Yourbeletieff. And just as, after the emotions of the law courts, people used to go in the evening to Mme Verdurin's, . . . to hear the latest news of the Case, . . . so now, little inclined for sleep after the enthusiasm aroused by the *Schéhérazade* or *Prince Igor*, they repaired to Mme Verdurin's, where under the auspices of Princesse Yourbeletieff and their hostess an exquisite supper brought together every night the dancers themselves, who had abstained from dinner so as to be more resilient, the great composers Igor Stravinsky and Richard Strauss, a permanent nucleus around which . . . the greatest ladies in Paris and foreign royalties were not too proud to gather. Even those people in society who professed to be endowed with taste and drew unnecessary distinctions between various Russian ballets, regarding the setting of the *Sylphides* as somehow "purer" than that of *Schéhérazade*, which they were almost prepared to attribute to Negro inspiration, were enchanted to meet face to face the great revivers of theatrical taste, who in an art that is perhaps a little more artificial than that of the easel had created a revolution as profound as Impressionism itself.

While *Rememberance of Things Past* deals with large and philosophic themes, it is also a study of snobbery, an *Almanach de Gotha*, a ledger of aristocratic society, whose cruelties, perversions, charms, and stupidities, whose grand titles and great houses obsessed Proust. He was a great writer and a snob: not an unheard-of combination. Once Misia in her outspoken way asked him if he was a snob. Apparently the question rankled, for years later he was still defending himself in a letter to her that is both illogical and flattering:

I have so many regrets. . . . the similarity of the circumstances— Ballets Russes, supper at your house—brings back to life my cherished memories and almost makes me believe in a kind of relapse into happiness. As for your question "Are you a snob?" it seemed to me very stupid the first time, but I feel I shall end by liking it because it was you I heard say it; in itself it makes no sense. If, among the very few friends who by force of habit come to ask how I am, there is now and then a duke or a prince, they are more than offset by other friends, of whom one is a footman and the other a chauffeur, and whom I treat with more consideration. The footmen are better educated than the dukes and their French is prettier, but they are more punctilious about etiquette and less simple; more easily offended. Yes, all things considered, one is as good as the other. If anything, the chauffeur has more distinction. In the end the phrase "Are you a snob?" pleased me, like one of your last year's frocks, because I found that it suited you. But I assure you that the only person whom my frequenting could make people say I am a snob would be you. And even that would not be true. And you would be the only one to think that I visit you out of vanity rather than admiration. Do not be so modest.

Characteristically, Proust's answer to Misia's blunt question was as complicated and as decorative as the stylized flowers on a Gallé vase. In priding himself on his democratic feeling about the equality of dukes and footmen, his double-edged snobbism is all too apparent. What he fails to mention is that he is sexually attracted to working-class men. After all, he had once been in love with his chauffeur. Skillfully hidden is his hostility to Misia when he suggests in his roundabout way that stupidity is becoming to her. And the letter's flattering tone is small change compared with the extravagance of his fawning letters to the titled great. If Proust used Misia as one of the models for Madame Verdurin, was he conscious that something of himself went into the making of that memorable character? Had he not maneuvered his way from the middle-class boy, lurking in a stairwell with his heart palpitating at the prospect of glimpsing a countess, to the man who basked in the splendor of the drawing rooms of the Faubourg?

It was due to Edwards' generosity that Misia was, like Madame Verdurin, in a position of power. Even after his marriage to Lantelme, Misia had continued to live in the luxurious rue de Rivoli apartment. But when the lease expired, Edwards did not renew it. In 1911 André de Fouquière's magazine *Le Tout-Paris* reported that M. Alfred Edwards was living at 29 rue de Constantine with Mme. Lantelme-Edwards, and that Mme. Godebska-Edwards was installed at 29 quai Voltaire. "It was an old apartment facing the quai," Comte Boni de Castellane remembered. "Scattered haphazardly among the Hispano-Italo-Napoleonic furnishings were antique torsos, Japanese feathered fans, and blue butterflies pinned to a silver background, looking like a flight of winged and colored pansies." Misia thought Boni a ridiculous snob, "riddled with class prejudice." Still, she admired him as the only man she knew who was "able to move from an income of ten million francs a year to the platform of a bus with perfect equanimity," when his wife, the American heiress Anna Gould, left him to marry his cousin, the Duc de Talleyrand. Edwards, aware of Sert's wealth, had cut Misia's allowance considerably. With Boni as an example, she began to sell furniture and precious objects to rich Americans when she felt short of funds. It was for the salon of her quai Voltaire apartment that Bonnard painted the panels which Misia irreverently cut up. Among her outraged friends, only Cocteau came to her defense. "Angels fly because they take themselves lightly," he said, quoting G. K. Chesterton. "Why shout, 'It's a scandal'? . . . We have Muses, more of them than we need. But how much rarer and more indispensable to the arts, which are always in danger of becoming paunchy, are those women so womanly that they bring a spirit of destruction into the temple, a spirit of frocks and scissors." Entering into the spirit of frocks and scissors himself, Cocteau playfully presented Misia with a Japanese paper fan. It was a companion to the treasured gold fan on which Mallarmé had invoked Misia's stormy piano playing. Cocteau's inscription, dated 1912, read:

> Au vide aérien de ton vol je me fie
> Fleur japonaise, aux doigts, qui renait et se fane,
> Pour prolonger ce frère où l'immortel Stéphane
> Présageait sur de l'or "les bonheurs de Sophie."

> I entrust myself to the airy void of your flight,
> Oh Japanese paper flower, which fades at the finger's touch
>   and blooms again,
> Recalling your twin on which the immortal Stéphane
> Predicted on gold "the joys of Sophie."

Since one of Misia's names was Sophie, it amused Cocteau to invert the title of the Comtesse de Ségur's book for children, Les Malheurs de Sophie, into an evocation of mischievous Misia's real-life happiness.

For Misia was happy. She had a lover, she had Edward's money without his madness, and she had her charming new apartment. As always, she was surrounded by people. Her Russians came, and her old friends as well. Her dressing table was cluttered with invitations: to Bergson's lectures, to concerts, to first nights, to costume balls. There was hardly time to play the piano or leaf through *Commedia*, *Le Bon Ton*, and the books of poems her friends sent her. An letter from the young actor Sacha Guitry, who was appearing with his wife Charlotte Lysès at the Bouffes-Parisiens, sparkles with irrepressible gaiety. He urges Misia to visit them soon. Even she, surfeited with beauty, will be dazzled by the ravishing new Pleyel piano they have just bought. Come to lunch, to dinner, come live with us he writes in his theatrical way. While he cannot promise great food, at least—he promises—there will be very little of it. He ends his letter by assuring her that the household argument is whether it is he or his wife who loves Misia more.

Réjane invited Misia to act in her company; Maurice Donnay and Henri Bataille invited her to appear in plays they planned to write especially for her. But after a few rehearsals Misia laughingly refused to continue, despite the assurances of her friends that she was born for the stage. There were proposals to celebrate Misia's beauty as well. That admirer of ample feminine charms, the sculptor Aristide Maillol, invited her to pose for him in a letter that has some of the weightiness of his monumental women: "I plan to use you as the inspiration for my Cézanne monument. Do not be angry with me for suggesting an idea that might seem to you outrageously presumptuous. The image of immortality is complete in you; there is nothing to do but copy it. Nature is the artist's inspiration. Beauty should be copied wherever it is found. It is only natural, therefore, that I should come to you. There may be innumerable difficulties, but two strong wills can straighten them out—especially yours." More demanding than Renoir, who had simply asked her to lower her dress, Maillol assumed that she would dispense with it altogether. Misia gracefully declined.

Another invitation, however, was accepted with deep pleasure. To Misia's great satisfaction Diaghilev at last asked Sert to do the sets for a new ballet. Given their close friendship, it is not surprising that Sert was chosen as the first non-Russian to design a decor for the company. It was something that he and Misia had hoped for from the beginning. In Diaghilev's first seasons, all his collaborators had been Russian. Then he began to work with composers and painters from other countries, among them some of the greatest artists of the century. Misia basked in Diaghilev's reflected glory. "Almost all those who gathered round him," she recalled, "were or became his friends; so much so that my life turned out to be closely linked with his artistic evolution."

In May 1913, in the course of two weeks, Diaghilev presented two new works that changed the course of music and ballet: Debussy's *Jeux* and Stravinsky's *Le Sacre du Printemps*, both with choreography by Nijinsky. *Jeux*, the first ballet in modern dress, was an intimate *pas de trois* with ambivalent sexual overtones. It was coolly received. The music's abstract power, like the tip of an iceberg, was barely visible to the general public. It took years for the Cubist masterpiece to disclose its subtle, revolutionary breakdown of harmonic hierarchies, its independent blocks of sound which were as novel in structure as a Cézanne painting. If *Jeux* was a hidden iceberg, *Le Sacre* was a volcano, whose burning lava destroyed the peaceful nineteenth-century musical landscape with a thirty-five-minute eruption. Misia had already heard the score, as can be seen in a letter from Stravinsky to Benois, dated November 24, 1911, from Clarens: "I had barely arrived here from Paris when Diaghilev summoned me back by telegram. . . . I went for one day and was at Mme. Edwards', where I played what I had composed of *Le Sacre du Printemps*. Everyone liked it very much." Overcome by the pounding originalty of the jagged rhythms and the dissonant, unearthly sonorities, Misia had recognized a masterpiece. Diaghilev was not as convinced. When Stravinsky first played the relentless, repetitive chords of the "Danse des Adolescentes" section for him in Venice, Diaghilev, who had a penchant for cutting scores, anxiously asked, "How long is *that* going to go on?" Stravinsky replied testily, "As long as it has to."

The premiere of *Le Sacre* created a scandal that seemed at the time as awesome as the music itself. The historic performance, with its shouted obscenities, its fistfights, its unbelievable clamor, with Nijinsky in the wings shouting the counts to the dancers and Diaghilev blinking the lights on and off to quiet the audience, with a loud joke from the balcony when the dancers, in stylized gestures, pressed their hands to their cheeks: *"Un docteur!"* then a correction *"Un dentiste!"* then another *"Deux dentistes!"* followed by laughter and catcalls; all this and more has been recorded endlessly. Ravel, who was applauding wildly—Stravinsky said he was "the only musician who immediately understood *Le Sacre"*—was rewarded by being called a dirty Jew, though he was neither one nor the other. Debussy, sitting with Misia, was saddened by the monstrous event. He had deciphered the score's complexities with incredible ease, when he played it with Stravinsky in the composer's piano-duet version. In November 1912 he had written Stravinsky: "Our reading at the piano is always present in my mind. It haunts me like a beautiful nightmare and I try, in vain, to invoke again the terrific impression. That is why I wait for the stage performance like a greedy child impatient for promised sweets." Now, listening through the hubbub to Stravinsky's literally stunning orchestration, Debussy turned to her, Misia remembered, "with a sad, anxious face" and whispered, "It's terrifying—I don't understand it." A curious statement from the man whose music, she felt, had in some ways served Stravinsky as a model. In her mind there was no confusion.

After the performance, Debussy enlarged on his disappointment in a letter to the conductor André Caplet: *"Le Sacre du Printemps* is an extraordinary, ferocious thing. You might say it's primitive music with every modern convenience." In the same vein Debussy said about Stravinsky, "He's a young savage who wears tumultuous ties and kisses ladies' hands while treading on their feet. When he's old, he'll be unbearable." Still, Debussy and Stravinsky were admirers of one another's music. In 1915 Debussy dedicated the last section of his two-piano suite *En Blanc et Noir "à mon ami Stravinsky."* And sadly enough, only five years later, Stravinsky was dedicating his *Symphonies of Wind Instruments* to the memory of Debussy. Their friendship had begun when Debussy went backstage to compliment Stravinsky at the premiere of *The Firebird*. Years later, when Debussy invited Stravinsky to a performance of *Pelléas* and Stravinsky asked him what he really thought of *Firebird*, Debussy said, "Well you had to begin somewhere." "Honest, but not extremely flattering," Stravinsky recalled. For his part, Stravinsky felt that *Pelléas* was "a great bore on the whole . . . in spite of many wonderful pages." Of such stuff are musical friendships made.

Shortly after the premiere of *Le Sacre,* Stravinsky came down with an attack of typhus. To his disappointment he was unable to go to London for Diaghilev's season—a season that was to include performances of all his ballets: *The Firebird, Petrushka,* and the controversial new *Sacre.* Diaghilev himself was half pleased, half alarmed by the *Sacre* scandal. While it had given them worldwide publicity, it created grave money troubles for the Ballets Russes. One hundred and twenty rehearsals, with Nijinsky groping his way through the incredibly complex rhythms, for only four performances was unheard-of extravagance, even for Diaghilev. A born theatre man, he knew his company could not survive on *succès d'estime* alone. London would not riot, as Paris had, but a cool British reception could endanger the future of the Ballets Russes.

Vienna had already taught him a bitter lesson. On New Year's Day of 1913, the Vienna Opera Orchestra had refused to play *Petrushka,* an infinitely more accessible work, calling it *schmutzige Musik*—dirty music. What was to prevent the English musicians from reacting like the Viennese when confronted with the insuperable difficulties of *Le Sacre*? In his high-handed way, Diaghilev decided to make cuts in the ballet without notifying Stravinsky. It is, of course, possible that he had not taken to the music as wholeheartedly as Misia had. Perhaps he felt that the score defied ballet. If he did, its history has shown him to be correct. Although many claim that Nijinsky's choreography, which has now disappeared, was a masterpiece, later versions have been disappointing. If Diaghilev had reservations about the visionary score—after all, he had contracted to produce it, not to love it—did not Stravinsky himself have reservations about Beethoven?

It was the old conflict between producer and creator. Telegrams flew from Paris to London. Stravinsky wired the conductor, Pierre Monteux, not to accept any cuts and not to be cowed by Diaghilev. Sert rather bunglingly cabled Diaghilev that Stravinsky had lost confidence in him. A network of minor composers, chief among them Maurice Delage, hovered around Stravinsky and added fuel to his angry flame. According to the conductor Robert Craft, Stravinsky's Eckermann and Boswell combined, "Sometime in 1911 Stravinsky realized the extent of Misia's power over Diaghilev and by the time of the premiere of *Le Sacre* he saw that her comprehension of it was more profound than his."

On the day after the Paris premiere Stravinsky, moved by Misia's musicianly understanding of what was incomprehensible to almost everyone at the time, presented her with a score of *Le Sacre* containing his markings for the choreography. When the difficulties over the cuts arose, Misia was able to bring the two men together and prevent what threatened to be a serious break. Her letter to Stravinsky, written the day before the first London performance, shows the turn that events had taken:

Hotel Cecil, Strand, London

My dear friend,

I wanted to wait until the first performance of *Le Sacre* to write you at length, but I prefer to do it today. For according to the news I get from Sert and Cipa, I see that you are tormenting yourself— quite unjustly, I assure you.

I believe that Delage, if it was he, would have done better not to worry you with Serge's supposed intentions, which he could not know, not understanding what was at the bottom of all this. And I do not understand why you, who know Serge, paid any attention whatsoever.

The truth, which I beg you to keep to yourself, is this: Diag[hilev] is going through a dreadful period; money problems with Beecham* which will end, I fear, in a civil-war lawsuit between them. A more or less final break with Bakst, precisely àpropos of *Le Sacre*. (He thinks it very dangerous to give it.)

The ballet is going very badly, especially the new things. A very childish public, which makes one appreciate that of Paris—though London is better behaved, with no public demonstrations. Only the opera is a triumph. Chaliapin above all. The orchestra is admirable but cannot get beyond *Petrushka*. Yesterday, a big scandal at the rehearsal of *Le Sacre* by the musicians. Monteux was forced to make a scene despite the general success of the two ballets, that is, *Firebird* and above all *Petrushka*.

In spite of all these difficulties, Serge has always protected your interests, which are his own. Keep in mind our conversation; it was right. At this moment *Le Sacre* is the vindication of his life. You must understand that he would prefer to do anything rather than sacrifice it. Because he's risking a great deal in giving it here, he is all the more determined.

I have not told him that you mistrust him, and I regret very much that Sert wired him about this matter. It made Serge very unhappy

---

* Diaghilev's English sponsor, Sir Joseph Beecham, father of Sir Thomas Beecham, the conductor of many of the Ballets Russes London performances.

and hurt him. You, of all people, should be able to understand his present state of mind.

As for me, I believe that only you can *save* him, and I also think that I prefer the worst Russian thing to any French work, no matter how inspired.

After several years, that's the conclusion I've come to. Be Russian! Remain Russian! Diaghilev can only be the soul of Russianness. There, my dear Igor, are my true thoughts on all that is happening here. I regret *very much* that you are unable to come; you would have been a great help to your friend and would quickly have sifted out the truth from all the petty cliques' gossip and meaningless drivel.

I shall return next Tuesday and hope to see you before you leave. I shall cable you the minute *Le Sacre* is given.

My dear friend, I tenderly embrace you and your wife with all my deepest affection.

Your
Misia

Petrushka was played ravishingly.

As she had promised, Misia wired Stravinsky—with more malice than tact, perhaps—in Berlin, where he was stopping briefly on his way to his family's country house in the Ukraine: "Complete success *Sacre* spoiled by your letter Monteux unjustly wounding Serge." Conceivably Stravinsky felt contrite after Misia's messages. In any case he wired Diaghilev that same day (July 12, 1913): "Sorry to have caused trouble but did not understand your diplomatic position. Cable me in Ustilug."

Back in Paris, Misia wrote Stravinsky again to explain the situation more fully:

Hôtel Meurice
rue de Rivoli
Paris

My dear friend,

Excuse me for being so late in answering your card but I wanted to write at length, and when I returned from London I was busy with a thousand things: mainly, renting a new apartment on the quai Voltaire . . . where I hope to see you very often. . . .

I left Serge rather battered, tired, not feeling very well, and worn down by his troubles: the rebellious chorus, Nijinsky insufferable and very rude, Bakst hardly speaking to him any more. Only Nouvel remained faithful, though even he had left for three days. I saw him when he came through the day before yesterday. He told me about a dreadful scandal: as the chorus refused to sing, the Coronation Scene in *Boris* was performed on an empty stage, with no chorus. (Almost no one noticed; that's the funniest part of the story.)

Tonight a grand gala, a command performance of *Boris* for the king. I think that Serge does not want to leave for Argentina, as he needs time to pull himself together and make plans for the future— for up to now he's had no serious offers. But it will be difficult, and I think that Nijinsky will never agree to go alone.

Keep these details to yourself. It is pointless for people in Paris to know all this, as even, or rather *above all*, the friends will relish it. . . .

D[iaghilev] acted very rashly in commissioning and staging French works. In the first place, your [Russian] temperaments get on badly with all others, that is, all others but your own; but we've already spoken of this and agreed. Besides, he's turned everybody against him, all those second-raters who cannot admit that Serge has any other purpose in life than to hire them and perform their works. Casella is doing his little job of disparagement, I know that.

Delage came to torment you and almost succeeded in causing irreparable damage. For I must tell you what happened after Monteux's disclosure. He actually said to Serge—in public, that is, in the middle of the rehearsal, in front of Nijinsky and the entire corps de ballet— the day of the premiere of *Le Sacre*: "I am the representative of M. Stravinsky, who has written me: 'M[onsieur] D[iaghilev] has the audacity to want to make cuts in my work. I make you responsible, etc., etc." and he added, "You can ask for my resignation and send me back." Serge replied that indeed he could envisage a lawsuit based on the grounds that he, Monteux, in the name of the French musicians, was acting against him. But most serious of all, this incident completely undermined his authority. The dancers refused to rehearse and Nijinsky spoke to him as if he were a dog.

The unhappy man left the theatre alone and spent the whole day in the park. I was astonished that he hadn't come for me as he always does; I didn't see him until quite late. I won't go on, dear friend, about the pain you've caused him, but you can be sure that I spoke to him the way you yourself would have done.

My affection and my admiration for you helped me clear up the misunderstanding and restore a little peace in the heart of your friend.

But I loathe that shabby, jealous little group that has surrounded you with pettiness.

Dear friend, the important thing now that you are at home is to get well, to write beautiful things. Serge too is hoping for beautiful things from you, I'm sure of that, in another style perhaps, but that will come of itself.

I beg you to send me your news *at length*. Don't show this letter to anyone but your wife, to whom I send a very affectionate kiss and, for you, a thousand very tender thoughts from

> Your
> Misia G. Edwards

My best regards to your mother, please, if she is still with you.

Diaghilev, as vulnerable as he was authoritative, must have suffered Tchaikovskian feelings of self-pity as he sat alone on that park bench in London. To be humiliated in front of the company so much in awe of him was extremely painful. He had gambled everything on one of the most controversial works ever written. It had taken infinite patience to watch Nijinsky trying to decipher the music and make it viable as dance. And it had taken courage to present the work to a public intoxicated by oriental bacchanales and cruel femmes fatales. Now Nijinsky, exhausted by his creative effort and restive in his submissive role, was becoming increasingly difficult. To weep in private about Nijinsky was one thing; to be insulted by him in public was quite another. And as always, the spectre of bankruptcy haunted Diaghilev.

From her vantage point Misia realized that Diaghilev was naïve enough to think he could control his two geniuses, his "creations," Nijinsky and Stravinsky. She knew that he had given everything to *Le Sacre* only to be rewarded by insults and insubordination. "How dare Stravinsky issue orders to Monteux behind my back?" he thought bitterly. On the other hand, Misia knew that Stravinsky had created a musical miracle, a prophetic utterance which might change the course of music. She could see how he found it incredible that Serge, who claimed to love it, would tamper with his creation. "How dare he cut my music?" was all he could think. Strengthened by her loyalty to Diaghilev and her love of Stravinsky's music, Misia had acted with impressive diplomacy. If she used malice in dealing with Stravinsky, it was a weapon taken for granted in the higher echelons of the Ballets Russes, a weapon that both Stravinsky and Diaghilev wielded with consummate skill. In any event, she made each of them see the other's side, no mean feat. It was profoundly gratifying to her, for she realized that the union of the irascible Stravinsky and the petulant, dictatorial Diaghilev was the summit of Ballets Russes accomplishment. In the conflict over *Le Sacre du Printemps*, Misia moved from the position of Diaghilev's understanding friend to that of his musical conscience. The story had a happy ending, at least for the moment, with a sunny note to Sert from the convalescent Stravinsky in the Ukraine.

> Ustilug, Volhynia, Russia
> July 30, 1913

My very dear friend,

Where are you, what are you doing, what are you going to do, where are you going? There: four questions which interest me and to which I should like to have a quick answer.

And our Serge, what is he doing, where is he? I have no news and that torments me, you have no idea.

Write to me, dear old boy, write!

I work, I eat, I sleep, and I never think of anything but *Rossignol*, Serge, our theatre, Misia, and you, who give me such enormous support and confidence! That's the absolute truth. That's how it is.

> Yours,
> Igor

In Nijinsky's journal, written in 1918–1919 when he was on the borderline of sanity and perhaps more self-revealing for that reason, he wrote about

Diaghilev: "I began to hate him openly. One day in a street in Paris I gave him a shove just to show that I was not afraid of him. But as I was about to walk off in the other direction, he struck me with his cane. Then at the thought that I was leaving him for good, he ran after me . . . and then I began to weep, while he swore at me, which made me feel as beaten-down as if an army of cats had begun to flay my soul; I was no longer myself. We walked slowly, side by side, and I no longer remember where we went." The journal shows that the boy who had been taken under Diaghilev's smotheringly protective wing at the age of twenty was now desperately unhappy. As he developed into the world's leading male dancer and the choreographer of *Faun, Jeux,* and *Le Sacre,* the submissive young man became increasingly independent. And not only did Nijinsky's rudeness on stage at the *Sacre* rehearsal reduce Diaghilev to tears; the impresario wept because his protégé was rude offstage as well. Lady Juliet Duff, the daughter of Lady Gwladys Ripon, recalls an unhappy episode during Diaghilev's London season: "He could make others cry, but he could cry himself, and I remember a day at my mother's house on Kingston Hill when he had a disagreement with Nijinsky, who had refused to come, and he sat in the garden with tears dripping down his face and would not be comforted."

Lady Ripon had been responsible for bringing Diaghilev's company to London for the first time in 1911 to participate in the gala season that marked the coronation of King George V. As Diaghilev's patroness, she became Misia's closest English friend. "Whenever she came to Paris [Misia wrote], she notified me in advance so that I could arrange a dinner for her with 'new people.' Everyone interested her, provided he was first-class. A brilliant politician, a sensational beauty, an inspired artist, and an astonishing fortune-teller interested her equally. She was so far removed from any prejudice that she did not even know the meaning of the word 'snobbism.' And if she was delighted to meet Philippe Berthelot or Marcel Proust at my house, she was equally enchanted to become acquainted with the music-hall singer Damia." As unconventional as Misia herself, Lady Ripon arranged for Misia and Sert to be accepted by English society, and even by royalty, at a time when unmarried couples were not usually welcome in such exalted circles. At a dinner for Queen Alexandra, Lady Ripon, grandly disregarding protocol, seated Nijinsky at her right. It was even more shocking than the presence of the unmarried lovers, but "no one," Misia said, "batted an eye."

When the 1913 season closed, Nijinsky joined the company for the three-week trip to Buenos Aires, where they were to begin their South American season. Diaghilev, who had a superstitious fear of crossing the ocean (a fortune-teller had predicted that he would die on the water), decided not to sail with the troupe. Instead he joined Misia and Sert for their annual stay in Venice, which had become their summer city. There they met daily with Lady Ripon, Bakst, and the poet Hugo von Hofmannsthal to discuss *La Légende de Joseph* the ballet Diaghilev hoped would become the chief attraction of their German season. Richard Strauss was commissioned to write the music. The librettists were to be Hofmannsthal and the art-loving diplomat Count Harry Kessler. Bakst would design the costumes which, together with Sert's decor, would evoke the splendors of Veronese. Nijinsky was to dance the title role and choreograph the ballet.

The biblical legend of Joseph and Potiphar's wife touches on themes that recur in many of the ballets Diaghilev chose for Nijinsky. They are themes strangely parallel to the two men's life together—and strangely prophetic. In *Cléopâtre* death is the price the young slave pays for a night of love with the Queen. In *Schéhérazade* the slave who has sexual relations with the Sultan's favorite is killed on the Sultan's orders. In *Petrushka* the puppet's love for the heartless doll is confined to frustrated longing, but even at that, he dies and his lifeless body is dragged off by the charlatan-puppeteer. And in *Joseph* the shepherd is destroyed even though he rejects the advances of the king's wife. In each of these ballets there is a lowly young man and a vindictive, powerful older man. Clearly the arch-misogynist Diaghilev found Nijinsky ideally cast as the victim of predatory females. In choosing these roles for his young lover, Diaghilev seemed to be warning him against what he regarded as the lethal dangers of sex with women. It is hardly surprising that Nijinsky wrote in his journal, "When he told me that to love women was an abject thing, I believed him."

It was, in fact, because of a woman that Diaghilev's plans for Nijinsky foundered. One September morning in Venice, the impresario telephoned Misia and asked her to play for him, as she often did, a score he had just received. "I can see myself," Misia wrote in her memoirs, "coming into his hotel room in my white batiste dress, swinging my parasol. He was still in his nightshirt, Turkish slippers on his feet." Diaghilev was in a happy mood. As Misia played, he opened her parasol and did an elephantine dance across the room. Misia, as superstitious as he, was terrified and begged him to shut the umbrella. At that moment a telegram arrived. Deathly pale, Diaghilev handed it to Misia. It was a message from Nijinsky announcing his marriage in Buenos Aires to Romola de Pulszky. Romola had studied dancing in Budapest, and acting in Paris with Réjane. Although Miss de Pulszky was not gifted enough to be in the company, Diaghilev had given her permission to take classes with his dancers and sail with them to South America. What he had not realized was that, like a femme fatale in one of his ballets, she had been stubbornly, secretly trying to make a conquest of his passive lover. And now the slave had escaped. Diaghilev, the Pygmalion whose pudgy fingers had molded Nijinsky into what Rodin called perfection, felt his creation slipping out of his hands. Sobbing shamelessly in Russian despair, he bellowed accusations and recriminations; he cursed Nijinsky's ingratitude, Romola's treachery, and his own stupidity for allowing Nijinsky to travel without him.

His friends, Bakst and Sert among them, were called in for a council of war. Everyone excitedly tried to recall Nijinsky's state of mind when he left Venice. Like a character in Gogol, Bakst felt that the chief question was: Had Nijinsky bought new underpants before he left? That would show he had meant to elope. The underpants problem was examined from every angle until, Misia recalled, "Diaghilev burst out again: to hell with their talk of underpants when he was in the depths of despair!" The marriage must be stopped. Telegrams must be sent. Vaslav must be rescued from the Hungarian's clutches. But it was too late. Nijinsky had committed the unpardonable sin: he had yielded to a woman. Shortly afterward, Misia and Sert took Diaghilev to Florence and Naples where "overcome by sadness and fury, he gave himself to a wild orgy of dissipation. But he was beyond consolation."

Diaghilev's friends took malicious pleasure in the scandal. A heartless letter from Cocteau to Misia began: "Is Vaslav's marriage a farce? What a pity if he should cease to be Moloch's grumpy Ganymede. . . . A friend wrote me from Florence, 'I saw a big ogre who fattened up little boys in the street before eating them. It was Diaghilev.'" But Diaghilev was heartless too. In his jealous resentment and wounded pride, he decided the way to punish Nijinsky was to dismiss him. Nijinsky had been art and love indissolubly entwined, and there is no doubt that Diaghilev was shattered by his defection. Yet "Strangely enough," Grigoriev wrote, he

was "like someone who had shed a load and can at last breathe freely."
With frozen composure Diaghilev ordered Grigoriev to wire Nijinsky that
his services were no longer required. It is possible Diaghilev had begun to
tire of the tensions of living with the troubled dancer. Or perhaps he had
had enough of the scandals provoked by Nijinsky's ballets and longed
for an unequivocal Fokine success. In any case, after a four-hour telephone
conversation he persuaded Fokine to stage *La Légende de Joseph*. No one,
Diaghilev announced, was irreplaceable. In December he left for Russia to
look for a new Joseph.

At the Moscow opera, an extra carrying a ham on a platter caught
Diaghilev's eye. He was a boy of compelling presence and beauty, the
eighteen-year-old Leonide Massine. A few nights later there he was again,
this time dancing the Tarantella in *Swan Lake*. Massine had decided to be
an actor, but in no time he found himself transported to St. Petersburg to
audition for Fokine, who accepted the half formed dancer reluctantly. After
the audition, Diaghilev took the boy straight to the Hermitage Museum and
from there presumably to bed. Massine's education had begun. *La Légende
de Joseph* was given in Paris, with Strauss himself conducting, in the spring
of 1914. By then it was obvious that Diaghilev's instinct had been sound,
though Massine's acting was more remarkable than his dancing. Still, the
unsmiling, grave beauty of the boy, scantily clad in a shepherd's tunic, made
a deeper impression than Strauss, Bakst, or Sert. Parisians renamed the
ballet *Les Jambes de Joseph*, turning Joseph's legend into Joseph's legs.
Nijinsky was in the audience, in the awkward situation of watching a ballet
that had been intended for him. During the intermission he went to Misia's
box to greet his old friends. But Romola, always one to collect injustices,
recalled that Misia's guests, "including Cocteau, gave him a cool reception."

In June 1914 Misia and Sert went to England with Diaghilev for the London premiere of Sert's ballet. According to Massine, the English public
"seemed to respond to Strauss's music . . . and to Sert's decor with more
enthusiasm than the Parisians." London had been well prepared by the

unusual amount of publicity Diaghilev arranged for Sert, Fokine, and Massine. Showman that he was, he used all his tricks to turn the lukewarm reception in Paris into the legend he hoped the ballet would become. At the first London performance Diaghilev received a telegram from Count Kessler warning him that war was imminent and the fall season in Germany might be cancelled. Telling the company of Kessler's message, Diaghilev said, "The dear count must be sick." But it was the world that was sick. A few weeks later war broke out. When the London season ended on July 25, the company disbanded with plans to meet in Berlin in the fall. On July 28 Diaghilev turned up at Misia's apartment to hear Erik Satie and the Spanish pianist Ricardo Viñes play Satie's *Trois Morceaux en Forme de Poire*. Misia was pleased as they sat listening to the charming score. She had been urging Diaghilev to consider Satie's music for a ballet, and now she could see that he was going to say yes. Suddenly Satie and Viñes were interrupted by a friend who burst in to tell them that Austria had declared war on Serbia. Misia recalled that her first thought had been: "What luck! Oh God, let there be a war." She was not alone. For many Frenchmen, war meant adventure and a welcome chance to teach the Germans a lesson. Her wish, "childish as well as unconsciously cruel," was soon fulfilled. On August 3 Germany declared war on France. The day before, when the newly mobilized troops were leaving for the border, Misia was caught up in the frenzied excitement that swept over Paris.

On the *grands boulevards,* in the midst of a rapturously enthusiastic crowd, I suddenly found myself perched on a white horse behind a cavalry officer. I wound some flowers around the neck of his gala uniform, and the general exaltation was so great that not for a moment did I think it strange. Nor were the officer, the horse, or the crowd around us in any way astonished, for the same sight could be seen all over Paris. Flowers were being sold at every street corner: wreaths, sheaves, bouquets, and loose bunches, which a minute later reappeared on soldiers' caps, on the tips of their bayonets, or behind their ears. People fell into one another's arms; it did not matter who embraced you; you wept, you laughed, you were crushed, you were moved to tears, you were almost suffocated, you sang, you trampled other people's feet, and you felt that you had never been more generous, more noble, more prepared for sacrifice and, in short, more wonderfully happy!

That evening Boni de Castellane, Réjane, and her son Jacques dined at
Misia's. Jacques, the boy who had declared his love for Misia on board
the *Aimée* nine years earlier, was now a tall, handsome young man of
twenty-one. Upset that her son was about to enlist, Réjane swore to put
an end to all the nonsense. She would simply go to the Kaiser and, like
a heroine out of Racine, plead with him to stop the war! Many others
were as naïvely optimistic. They imagined their soldiers in glorious operetta uniforms going off to battle, a rousing song on their lips. The
fighting would take place offstage, and in no time the gallant, smiling
victors would come marching home with a sling on one arm and a beautiful
girl on the other.

To the surprise of Parisians, the offstage battle came terrifyingly near.
When the wind was blowing in the right direction, the curious made
expeditions to the Bois de Boulogne in the hope of hearing the rumble
of cannons. In September the first German plane flew over Paris, dropping
three bombs. Beside the body of an old woman, the only casualty, a note
was found: "The German Army is at your door. There is no choice but
surrender. Lieutenant Von Heidssen." Soon more bombers appeared. Every
time the sirens sounded, Misia would go to her window to watch the antique
dealer from the shop below. Dressed in a loud, checked shooting jacket, he
paced up and down the quay and waited for planes. Whenever he sighted one
of the low-flying craft, he shouldered his rifle, took careful aim, and fired.
His gesture did not seem futile considering the flimsy look of the wooden
crates that hurtled through the air.

By the end of August hundreds of Belgian refugees were arriving, haggard, frightened, clothed in rags, carrying nothing but a briefcase or a
wicker basket. The Grand Palais and six schools were transformed into
hospitals. Cinemas and restaurants were closed, and the streets were sad
and empty. Newspapers printed instructions for knitting (the ladies of the
Franco-British Society were making woolen underpants for the kilted Scot-
tish Highlanders). The public was carefully shielded from the horrors of
the war, the severe defeats and reversals the French Army was suffering.
Misia, however, knew only too well what was going on. At the center of
things as always, she became a political hostess overnight. Aristide Briand,
Georges Clemenceau, his first secretary Georges Mandel, the minister of the
interior Jules Pams, the diplomat Philippe Berthelot, his young assistants
Paul Morand and Alexis Léger (the poet later known as Saint-John Perse),
and the air-force ace Roland Garros all met at Misia's. As the Red Cross

was not yet functioning and ambulances were desperately needed, Misia decided to do her bit. André Gide described her in action in his Journal of August 3, the day war was declared. Trying to volunteer his services at Red Cross headquarters, Gide was "nabbed by Sert and Madame Edwards, who here as everywhere, immediately took a conspicuous role. Given private authorization and provided with Red Cross badges, she had gone in her automobile from hotel to hotel, requisitioning a great quantity of sheets and towels which she brought to the organization. She produced something even better: an entire hotel, the Hôtel du Rhin, which, yielding more out of fear of being sacked because of its German name than from any burst of generosity, put at the disposal of the Red Cross, all its rooms, its beds, linens, etc." Misia, of course, was not unknown at the Hôtel du Rhin, her old pied-à-terre.

As a friend of General Gallieni, the military governor of Paris, she was given permission to go to the front to give first aid to the wounded. Know-, ing that the couturiers had been forced to close down, she persuaded them to donate their delivery vans, which she quickly converted into ambulances. It was a bizarre group that Misia commandeered to transport the wounded back from L'Haÿ-les-Roses. Leading the way in her Mercedes were the designer Paul Iribe at the wheel, dressed like a deep-sea diver, and Cocteau in a smart male nurse's uniform run up for him by Poiret. In the back seat were Misia in a business-like tweed suit and Sert in pale grey knickerbockers, his enormous Kodak at the ready, bickering with Cocteau, whom he loved to tease. Trailing behind were Misia's twelve improvised ambulances. It is hardly surprising that they were constantly stopped by sentries who took them for spies.

Jacques-Emile Blanche never painted Misia but he did paint Sert. Still, there is a telling portrait of her in his memoirs, *Cahiers d'un Artiste* (*An Artist's Notebooks*). She is thinly disguised in a chapter called *Chez Sonia*, but let us drop the mask and call her by her real name. Dated November 26, 1914, the entry describes a meeting of a group of volunteers at Misia's apartment.

I haven't heard laughter since the war began. Ghéon's laugh sets the porcelain vases, the pendants of the boat-shaped crystal chandelier, and the Coromandel screens to vibrating as much as the métro, which makes the house shake. In his patriotic optimism he makes predictions, agitates, condemns the lukewarm, shouts in a heroic, dionysiac frenzy. . . .

He arrived with Gide. Gide too is very excited, but serious, and congratulates himself that he is living in these prodigious times. Five men—stretcher-bearers, doctors—bend over maps under the large lampshade. Thin faces, haggard, weather-beaten: these poets and artists are making plans for a convoy soon to leave for the front. They are the same men who gathered around the now-closed piano last May when Stravinsky played *Le Sacre du Printemps* at Misia's party.

An atmosphere of army barracks and hospitals has tarnished this apartment, where the lacquer, the mother-of-pearl, the gold, the Venetian chinoiserie, the Bonnards, and the Renoirs are buried as if under a film of gunpowder. The fish have died in the empty aquariums; the salon of ribbons and tassels, silk and blown glass, is now a soldier's coatroom, a workroom where the spools of yarn, the stockings, and the forage caps are of pretty, colored wool because the "boss" simply could not knit with ugly colors.

Misia was in Rheims during the first bombardments; she strolled about in the machine-gun fire and the flames. If her house were to catch fire, she would stay there, the better to watch it burn. How could she bear to have anything happen anywhere, and not be present?

Misia's tour of duty as a nurse began in a burned-out railway station [at L'Haÿ-les-Roses] where the dying lay helpless. Is that a Negro stretched out on the straw? No, it's a German whose skin is covered with flies, "a very distinguished young man" (Misia says)—dazed—unable to believe that it is not a dream: the stinking waiting room, the feeble lights hanging from the beams of a roof pierced by shells. Misia frees two dying men from the dung heap where they lie. One, a German, has no arms; when she hoists him into an automobile, he seems to be trying to support himself on his missing hands. For one kilometer the enemy fires on the automobile, relentlessly trying to kill the wounded for the second time.

Even the most nervous and the most timid are pulled to the edge of the crater by curiosity; it galvanizes them and makes them able to bear the explosions of the powder magazines in the tidal wave, the downpour of shellfire.

"Look here, this is not for women, this filthy mess! It's unbearable, unbearable!" says Misia.

But she began again the next day, just as she had the day before and would again the day after.

"Just imagine, the Bishop of Meaux at dawn, in his violet silk robes, giving us his amethyst ring to kiss before deigning to give communion to the dying—each man takes communion, lined up along the walls of Rheims Cathedral as if they were in a hospital ward. One takes communion not only *for oneself* but *for the others*. It's the millennium, the end of the world," she says.

Then I open the doors to the balcony to look at Paris plunged in darkness. The Seine is invisible except when passing steamers, which run until nine o'clock, shine their searchlights on the waves. Paris is constantly on the alert for zeppelins. From this terrace Misia and her friends have followed the bombers battling over the Cour du Carrousel. What a sight when the air commander's fleet ventures forth! Whales, sharks in the clouds, the monster Fafner over the Louvre, waddling along with his giant body of aluminum and gutta-percha, darting electric rays from his beacon eyes over the sleeping Ile de la Cité. This war, staged by Wilhelm, looks to Misia like a Berlin Secessionist poster. These props of terror belong in the theatre, as do the artillery's polyphony. . . .

The Germans grind their heels in our faces, trample our bodies, and declare themselves the victors. . . .

"We'll get them all the same!" someone roars. Someone else says there is no such thing as a specifically German genius, even among the greatest composers. We talk nonsense.

Misia, the mistress of the house, loses her patience.

"All the same, we mustn't let patriotism turn us into idiots! You and Saint-Saëns [who led the movement to prohibit German music in France during the war], I'm fed up with you all. I can't bear the idea of seeing any of you after the war."

A letter from Diaghilev urged the exhausted Misia to come to neutral Rome for a rest. "I have received a mad telegram from Misia," Diaghilev had written Stravinsky on November 1, "saying she will not leave Paris because it is now the most beautiful city in the world." For Misia, to be in the eye of the storm was to be alive. To be useful, to relieve the misery of dying soldiers, was a marvellous sensation. It could not be called a pleasure; it was too horrible for that; but it was a more profound satisfaction than she had ever known. A few days later she left for the front again. The hundreds of wounded filled her with pity. With such limited space in the convoy, how was she to choose among the poor wretches who looked at her imploringly? Every trip was made in the dark, with no headlights, on gutted, poorly marked roads. Worse still, General Fevrier of the *Corps Sanitaire* had ordered the wounded smuggled into Paris by night like contraband goods. Parisians were not to be demoralized by the truth.

Through the horrors of these expeditions among the dead and the dying, it was Cocteau who was the life of Misia's party, as it were. Without his youthful vitality and the bubbling, surprising imagery of his wit, she could never have survived "the fatigues, the irritations, and the sleepless nights." Playful, tender, and gay, he won Misia's heart all over again. And she his, for they had had their differences. The year before the war Cocteau, filled with admiration for *Le Sacre*, had asked Stravinsky to collaborate on a ballet for Diaghilev to be called *David*. Stravinsky was half-interested but gave Cocteau only vague signs of encouragement. It was difficult for the young poet bursting with ideas to deal with Stravinsky's indifference. When he heard that Stravinsky had not produced a note of music for *David*, Cocteau wrote Misia for help: "If you knew what I am preparing—what I am building! I am as dreadfully sad as Nietzsche when he thought of Wagner after the Bayreuth nightmare. It is unthinkable, it seems impossible that our encounter should remain fruitless. Igor will come to his senses. If you could bring him forth from the void where *David* exists, you would be delivering him from an evil spell. I embrace you with tenderness and confidence. Oh God, my nerves!!!"

Presumably with Misia's help, things took a turn for the better, since Cocteau wrote her later: "*David* will be a great surprise to you. Prodigious. . . . Need I tell you, dearest Misia, that it belongs to you? . . . Igor and I dedicate the work to you. . . . Our enthusiasm knows no bounds." It would be an understatement to say that Cocteau was exaggerating Stravinsky's enthusiasm since the composer had never shown much interest in *David*. And Diaghilev, who did not like Cocteau much, liked the idea of Cocteau's ready-made package even less. He preferred to choose his own artists. When nothing came of it, Cocteau was bitterly disappointed and blamed Misia as well as Diaghilev. He wrote Stravinsky, "I find Serge intolerable. Misia is completely under his thumb, and she too is becoming offensive." Cocteau was apt to feel that Misia was a troublemaker when her schemes to help him failed, and an enchanting friend when they succeeded. But now on the new battlefront, the real one, Misia impressed Cocteau so deeply that he felt she had the dimensions of a heroine. When he wrote *Thomas l'Imposteur* in 1923, he planned to use Stendhal's *La Chartreuse de Parme* as a model. "I tried in vain," he said later, "to keep my mind on La San Severina, but Misia automatically became the Princesse de Bormes." Describing her in the novel, Cocteau wrote:

> She touched what was not to be touched; she opened what was not to be opened. She walked and talked on a tightrope in the midst of a glacial silence, with everyone hoping she would break her neck. Having first amused people, she then disturbed them. Her colorful high-relief personality offended some but seduced others. These others were the elite. Thus from imprudence to imprudence she unknowingly wove a magic spell. Mediocre people avoided her and only people of quality remained with her. Seven or eight men, two or three warmhearted women became her intimates. They were exactly the group that a socially ambitious and intriguing woman would have wanted as friends but would never have had. . . .
>
> This woman could not care less about having the seat of honor at a fête; she preferred the best seat. It is generally not the same. At the theatre she wanted to see rather than to be seen. Therefore artists loved her.

Artists loved her, but not all of them. Nor did they all love Cocteau, for that matter. Gide for one was put off by both Misia and Cocteau's mocking, irreverent manner. In his journal of August 20, 1914, he describes meeting Cocteau for tea: "I did not enjoy seeing him again even though he made himself extremely agreeable; he simply cannot be serious and to me all his aphorisms, his witticisms, his reactions, and the extraordinary *brio* of his customary way of talking were as shocking as a luxury article on display in a period of famine and mourning." Misia, a casual friend of Gide's since the *Revue Blanche* days, found his Protestant rigidity, his suspiciousness, his tortured self-questioning, prissy and distasteful. Nor did his covert homosexuality appeal to her as much as Cocteau's open love of handsome young men. On the other hand, Misia, Sert, and their friends did not measure up to Gide's exacting standards. On August 26 Gide noted that although Madame Edwards said she had seen Belgian children whose hands had been cut off by German soldiers, the report had never been authenticated. Misia and Cocteau's veracity on this point became an obsession with Gide when neither was able to produce the photographs they swore they had seen.

Gide listened more sympathetically when Misia "spoke with the liveliest passion of the Polish cause." Descended as she was from generations of patriots fighting for Polish independence, she complained bitterly of Russia's promise to free Poland. What guarantees did they offer? The Tsar had not even signed the agreement. Ever since Poland had been divided by the Germans, Austrians, and Russians, it was always the Russian sector, Misia insisted, that was the most miserable. Gide quotes her as saying, "And it's the country which took from our people all freedom of thought and religion; which even wanted to suppress our language; which now has promised us freedom with no guarantees!" When Joseph Retinger, Misia's cousin, escaped from Poland and made his way to Paris, Misia took him to see Philippe Berthelot in the hope that the diplomat would support the Polish cause.* "But what could he say?" Gide wrote. "Mme. Edwards was indignant that he would not commit himself. One would have wished that France would ratify the Russian gesture, but France feared future diplomatic complications and refused to make a statement."

In her role as political hostess, Misia began to see a great deal of Hélène and Philippe Berthelot, for whose home Sert designed murals in his best Tiepolo manner. A witty, cultivated man, Berthelot was given to reciting from memory phenomenally long passages of Mallarmé, Musset, and Claudel while glancing through official dispatches. Though he was second in command, it was said that he actually ran the ministry of foreign affairs. He struck Gide as being "completely insensitive" and very conscious of "his superiority and that of his family, his friends, his taste, etc." Gide's journal of November 12, 1915, about an evening with the Berthelots at Misia's is the most graphic of all descriptions of her. It tells us a good deal about Gide as well.

---

* Berthelot's assistant Paul Morand recalled that when Misia was at the Hôtel Meurice in 1916, Boni de Castellane would meet Retinger there to discuss the possibility that he, Castellane, might be proclaimed king of Poland.

Mme. Philippe Berthelot arrived in a fur-trimmed dress, straight at the waist, a kind of solid-color apple-green silk chemise; apologized, as she did every other time I have seen her, for being in a "tea gown" and, like the other times, Mme. Edwards cried out, "But I, too, my dear! I'm in a *robe de chambre.*" She wore an extremely low-cut blouse, filled in with transparent gold lace, a cream-colored silk skirt, very short, edged with fur, and over it all, a kind of coat with wide sleeves, also edged with fur, noticeably shorter than the skirt. The two women sit pressed one against the other with the gestures of odalisques. Mme. Edwards laughs and clucks and coos, puffing out her neck, and letting her neck loll on her bare shoulders. Sert is there; plumper, more sententious than ever. I make an effort, in vain, to concentrate on what he is saying. He harangues me relentlessly on the superiority of "baroque" art, and exudes boredom as much as I do. It seems to me that after living in France as long as he has, he could have managed to lose a bit of his accent. . . .

They asked me to go to the piano so insistently that it was very difficult for me to refuse. To encourage me, Mme. Edwards sat down with a volume of Chopin and played several mazurkas, flowingly and with charm, but in an "artistic" manner, with that *tempo rubato* which I dislike so much, or, to put it more exactly: no longer taking any account of the beat, and with sudden accents, pauses, and effects more suitable for displaying the temperament of the performer than the quality of the piece. This all took place between two *salons,* in a minuscule room lined with gold cloth, on a piano completely out of tune. The Philippe Berthelots having left, I wanted to slip out after them, but since it was raining torrents, Mme. Edwards insisted on sending for a car and, while waiting, dragged me to the piano in the other room, the big *salon* with the Bonnard decorations. I began the Prelude in E Flat Major; but, just as it sometimes happens to me that when speaking with an Englishman I take on an English accent, I adopted, out of politeness, the same *tempo rubato* that Mme. Edwards had just used, and stopped after twelve measures of sheer agony.*

The car that took me toward Auteuil ran out of gasoline and broke

---

* In view of Gide's superior attitude about Misia's style of playing Chopin, it is amusing to remember that Stravinsky said, "That Gide understood nothing whatever about music in general is apparent to anyone who has read his *Notes on Chopin.*"

down two kilometers from the Villa [Montmorency] so that I had to walk the last two kilometers in the middle of the night in a pouring rain. I was unable to close my eyes all night and I'll be dragging myself about all day with a headache and a grudge against myself and my hosts of yesterday.

Two months before Misia infected Gide with her contagious *rubato*, she and Sert had gone to Rome to meet Diaghilev and Massine and drive with them to Switzerland. Travelling through Italy, the two couples stopped to visit museums in Bologna, Ravenna, Padua, and Verona. While Diaghilev referred to his guidebook, saying, "Let's see what Mr. Baedeker has to tell us," Misia deferred to Sert, her personal Baedeker, who offered fascinating footnotes of his own. The trip ended in Lausanne, where Diaghilev and a nucleus of his company had found a refuge from the war. Misia and Sert stopped at the Hôtel Beau Rivage Palace in Ouchy near the Villa Belle Rive, where Diaghilev and Massine were installed. Lydia Sokolova, an English ballerina in Diaghilev's company, described it in her memoirs, *Dancing with Diaghilev*, as "a spacious villa on the lake's edge with marble floors and masses of greenery and flowers." It was the first time since he had left Russia that Diaghilev lived in a house rather than a hotel. "Of all the years we travelled with Diaghilev," Sokolova recalled, "those six months were the happiest, and I believe if he had been asked later he would have said the same."

Living nearby were Stravinsky, Bakst, Diaghilev's new Russian painters Mikhail Larionov and Natalia Gontcharova, the Swiss conductor Ernest Ansermet, and the Italian ballet master Enrico Cecchetti, who gave Massine daily lessons. Since it was almost impossible to arrange performances because of the war, Diaghilev and his company devoted their time to creation and rehearsal. With no income to support his dancers, he often went to Paris to try to raise money. Everyone knew when the trips were successful, because Massine would appear wearing a new sapphire ring. It amused the company that the rings Diaghilev gave him were set in platinum, whereas Nijinsky's had been set in mere gold.

Not surprisingly, Misia and Sert had blamed the lukewarm reception of *La Légende de Joseph* on the substitution of the inexperienced Massine for the great Nijinsky. Although Massine's vivid personality had carried the day, they still had misgivings about Diaghilev's judgment, which was warped, they felt, by his infatuation. But Diaghilev, who liked to say, "Give me six months and I can make a choreographer out of anyone," had gambled and won. Massine's unique talents as dancer and choreographer had begun to emerge and Diaghilev was eager to show Misia and Sert the work they were doing.

MISIA TO COCTEAU

Beau Rivage Palace
Ouchy-Lausanne

Mon cher petit Jean,

We arrived here the day before yesterday with no trouble, and for the first time in my life I understand the charm of Switzerland, partly, perhaps, because I am leaving again tomorrow for Italy.

Excellent hotel on the lake, mountains, good air. One finds again everything that's not the war. And then there's the spectacle of Serge, which nothing can equal. Imagine a large house on the edge of the lake set in a park, with Serge as master of the house and, as mistress, a young Russian, the wife of an embassy councilor in Rome, who fell madly in love with them all in Rome this winter and who for the past two months has been here keeping house for him. Some painters, the Stravinskys, Massine, make up an extraordinary group that never stops working. But it was Stravinsky who provided me with an overwhelming experience. Imagine the most beautiful work of our greatest musician, with the quality of *Petrushka* as seen through *Le Sacre*. Yesterday he played *Les Noces Villageoises* for me in a small house, charmingly arranged, with Catherine, the children, and domestic objects so simple that they added to my joy. It was there that this marvel was born. He has opened yet another door, and there everything is permitted, everything is sonorous, joyous, and each note takes you by surprise, just as you would wish—and overwhelms you.

He is preoccupied at this moment with another work to which he attaches great importance, and just as I feared, he will not commit himself to *David* just now. That's the only reason I did not insist on his doing it immediately. I shall tell you his reasons, to which absolutely no objection can be made. I delivered your letters, which were not read in my presence. Stravinsky seemed to be very much affected by them and told me he would write you.

Last night, a dress rehearsal for us of what has been done these past months. Something completely new, very beautiful, in which Massine proves that he really is someone. And how prejudiced we were against him, Sert and I!!

Serge fatter and fatter, his clothes tighter and his hat smaller, rather "circus director," as Igor says, has again found a way to surprise us. . . .

I am overcome by anguish again this morning, and Switzerland irritates me once more.

The neutrality of the Swiss newspapers drives me mad, and the lake, once again, is implacably boring. . . .

Affectionate kisses,
Misia

For Misia, *Les Noces* was Stravinsky's response to her earlier injunction, "Be Russian! Remain Russian!" Diaghilev, whom she considered the "soul of Russianness" reacted to the music as emotionally as she. "When I first played *Les Noces* to Diaghilev—in 1915, at his home in Bellerive, near Lausanne—" Stravinsky later said to Robert Craft, "he wept and said it was the most beautiful and the most purely Russian creation of our ballet. I think he did love *Les Noces* more than any other work of mine. That is why I dedicated it to him." One can see from Misia's letter to Cocteau the qualities that made both Diaghilev and Stravinsky value her opinion: her understanding of, her at-homeness with, and her enthusiasm for challenging and difficult new works. Equally important, Diaghilev valued Misia's frankness. She was as passionate and as impulsive as he in her likes and dislikes, and it never occurred to her not to tell him exactly what she thought. But when Misia—as Cocteau said—touched what was not to be touched, the results were often disastrous.

MISIA TO STRAVINSKY

(probably written July 19, 1916)

My dear friend,

. . . How I should love to see you, both of you; to chat with you at length; to get some respite, near you, from the noise and confusion here in Paris, the frightful center of futility: of the disabled soldiers, the wretched and the poor who are struggling in the hope—quite simply —of getting something to eat. Yesterday I spent an atrocious evening, in which you were involved, my dear Igor, and that is why I am writing to you. I beg you to understand through my words, which can only give a factual account, that my great unhappiness is caused by my great love for what you have given me; my respect for your name alone makes me exigent.

Well then, yesterday afternoon I heard there was a concert at Poiret's art gallery, where they were to play Satie, then your quartets. You can imagine that I dropped everything and threw on my clothes to get there in time to hear some of it. You see the sad truth in the enclosed program.* When they got to you, my poor ears had been subjected to every possible nightmare—and my eyes, too. Why did you get mixed up in all this, dear Igor? What sense is there in this poorman's sauerkraut? At last, *your* first measures—but the charm came to an end immediately, as the piece was too short to have any line. I detest the second piece, you understand, I *detest* it with a passion, yes, yes! Why do you write such things? At least don't let them be played in the midst of these brutes, who are as stupid when they laugh at something as when they admire it. I found it hard to understand the third piece, in which you seem to be flagellating yourself but which, had I heard it elsewhere, would have moved me a great deal—I think.

Dear friend, no one, not even Catherine, can love or be more sympathetic to what you do, so do not mistake this for anything but love,

---

* The program Misia sent Stravinsky is dated July 18. She probably arrived in time to hear Satie's *Gymnopédie* and *Sarabande* and works by Henri Cliquet, Roger de Fontenay, Darius Milhaud, and Georges Auric. The program ended with Stravinsky's *Trois Morceaux pour Quatuor à Cordes*, performed by Yvonne Astruc, Darius Milhaud, Arthur Honegger, and Félix Delgrange.

for as I re-read it, I see that I am talking nonsense. Whatever stand you take, whatever banner you represent will carry all before it if you are composing for yourself and *for yourself alone.*

Serge completely carried away by *Les Noces Villageoises,* completely!

I shall see him soon, as he should be coming back for a few days. Let me know how you are feeling; I kiss you both with all my heart.

Your
Misia

Pleased as Stravinsky had been by Misia's enthusiasm for *Les Noces,* her impatient dismissal of his *Pieces for String Quartet* aroused in the composer a thumpingly dissonant reaction.

STRAVINSKY TO MISIA

Morges, July 24, 1916

My dear Misia,

Your letter has brought on an abscess which I shall burst open with these lines. You tell me at the end of your letter that you are writing nonsense. That is not true, it is not nonsense, it is much more disagreeable than that, and makes me detest your letter. I no longer recognize you. And why do you write that Diaghilev is enthusiastic about *Les Noces Villageoises?* I hope not about *Le Coq et le Renard,* which I am writing for Madame de Polignac, and not for him.

Unless you are mistaken about the title. But even that would astonish me very much as in Madrid that work left him completely indifferent (naturally, as does everything I write that is not for him). And if it's a question of the *Noces Villageoises* as you say, his enthusiasm seems to me quite suspect and inappropriate. For one speaks with enthusiasm of a work that has impressed one recently, whereas the *Noces Villageoises* was played for him seven months ago at your apartment on the quai Voltaire before his departure for America: since then I have not played it for him.

Here's an end to these lines but the pain that your letter gives me will remain forever. I am going to burn it* and never want to think of it again.

Your faithful
Igor Stravinsky

Two more words: it's becoming increasingly difficult for me to come to an understanding with D[iaghilev].

I feel that we are rapidly growing apart. Art in itself no longer interests him. He is tired of it.

And besides it's very tiresome always to hear the same talk about "the young" and "the old"—one must be young, Diaghilev says—that's stupid and untrue and tragic at the same time. He no longer gets any pleasure from his work. His life is burned out and I think of all this very often, with profound bitterness.

There, my dear, my latest impression of your Serge.

And another thing: I do not understand your rage against my pieces for quartet. Really, my dear, you should have been able to understand before pouncing on this poor quartet (which was composed for you—it's piquant, isn't it—to be played in your Chinese salon; do you remember?) that my works are always very difficult and before being played they require my personal supervision, which was not available this time. I can imagine how badly they played for you?!!! Your brother spoke to me about it because they had already been played for him last winter, and he did not recognize them when I played them for him on the piano.

The letter with its four codas, so unlike Stravinsky's concise musical procedures, was deserved. Like many an amateur of art, Misia was naïvely unaware that often the artist, as Gertrude Stein said, wants nothing but praise.

---

* Stravinsky obviously did not burn Misia's letter. Instead he took it with him in his various moves from Switzerland to France to Hollywood to New York, just as he did with thousands of the letters, photographs, and documents he possessed. Historians can only be grateful.

Telegram from Misia to Stravinsky

Your note has made me ill by its incomprehension of mine, which was simply an excess of admiration for you, dear friend.

Misia's *gaffe* was soon overlooked—along with Stravinsky's *Pieces for String Quartet*, one of the great composer's less memorable works. The real problem lay between Stravinsky and Diaghilev, who, like some brothers, had mixed feelings of love, rivalry, and antagonism. (They were, in fact, distantly related.) Diaghilev had not created Stravinsky's genius. But he had introduced it to the world, and like everything he loved, he wanted to own it exclusively, to guard it jealously. After the first concert performance of *Le Sacre*, which received an ovation in contrast to the stormy reaction to the ballet, Diaghilev saw Stravinsky being carried on the shoulders of his admirers and caustically remarked, "Our little Igor now has to have the police to escort him out of his concerts, like a prize fighter." Just as he never forgave Nijinsky for straying from the fold, he could not help being childishly resentful when Stravinsky accepted commissions from others, though he was in no position to commission anything himself. If he wanted a poorly paid court genius, Stravinsky was not his man. Certainly Diaghilev was unfeeling about the musician's financial problems. For his part, Stravinsky had never quite approved of Diaghilev, whose under-handed way with money put him into a financial panic. He found Diaghilev's open homosexuality an invitation to derision, a Stravinskian speciality. One of the composer's earliest memories of Diaghilev was of the narcissistic array of mirrors in his Petersburg flat. Later he mockingly recalled Diaghilev's entering a restaurant on the Nevsky Prospekt, "bowing to right and to left like the Baron de Charlus" and his feeling that Diaghilev "wanted to sin": a touchingly prudish attitude from the composer of *Le Sacre*.

But during the difficult war years money was the real bone of contention between the two men. And it was to Misia that Stravinsky turned when he was in need of help.

Morges
Place St. Louis 2
January 8, 1918

My dear Misia,

It is very painful for me to speak to you about all the misfortunes that have struck us in this dreadful year, and now this horrible humiliation we are going through. Added to that, the absolute lack of money and the absolute impossibility of getting any. Since July, not a penny from Diaghilev, who owes me thirty thousand francs and who is in a critical situation himself. Madame Errazuriz [a rich, stylish Chilean—a friendly rival of Misia's], who still owes me a thousand francs, has not sent me anything for four months. . . . I really don't know what to do, where to turn for money. Therefore I had the idea of asking if it would be possible for you to find some for me somewhere in the form of a loan, to push back the frightening spectre of destitution that threatens us.

My dear, pardon me if I embarrass you with this request, but there is truly nothing else I can do. I should be infinitely happy to have a short note about this, or a telegram if possible. Please send me your news. It is a very, very long time since I have known what is happening to you. I feel very abandoned by all of you. *Je vous embrasse.*

Your
Stravinsky

Misia did not abandon him. Instead, with enchanting tact, she sent him a check, pretending it was from an anonymous admirer. She also tried to arrange a concert of his music in the hope that performances would bring him additional money.

STRAVINSKY TO MISIA

Morges, January 29, 1918

My dear Misia,

I have already wired you all my gratitude for your great kindness and I shall repeat it to you once again here. But I shall not hide from you the fact that I feel very embarrassed. I can guess the name of this admirer who has sent me two thousand francs, of which I acknowledge the receipt, as well as the thousand francs from Madame Errazuriz. In fact when I asked you to arrange a loan for me, it never occurred to me to ask you for it personally. I know that your means are not unlimited, especially in these times. I cannot tell when I shall be in a position to return this sum to you—and that embarrasses me horribly. . . .

I embrace you with all my heart. Believe me, your old and faithful friend.

Igor Stravinsky

I embrace Sert.

After the Revolution, neither Diaghilev nor Stravinsky received further income from Russia. It was an extremely difficult situation, for Stravinsky had his wife and children to support, and Diaghilev his family of artists. As Russia was not a member of the international copyright agreement, no one was legally bound to pay Stravinsky performance rights for *Firebird*, *Petrushka*, or *Le Sacre*, all of which had first been published in Russia. Diaghilev took advantage of this financial loophole, and often presented Stravinsky's ballets without paying him. Again and again, Stravinsky turned to Misia for help.

Morges
July 25, 1919

My dear Misia,

It is thanks to you and to your great friendship and kindness to me that this disagreeable business is beginning to be settled, and I hope that very soon it will be settled completely. I would never know how to express to you all my gratitude, not only for having intervened with Diaghilev to ease the pressure of my financial problems, but also for having relieved me of this painful task. . . .

Your
Stravinsky

October 30, 1919

. . . I think it would be more dignified on Diaghilev's part to admit frankly that *his tricks have failed*, instead of lying to everyone. Ansermet has written him a letter, a letter Diaghilev will not dare to read to anyone.

Excuse me for always bothering you with these interminable stories but I am not at fault. In all justice the blame must fall on Diaghilev.

Your old Stravinsky

In still another letter a few months later (January 18, 1920) Stravinsky writes Misia that if Diaghilev does not send him the monthly payments they had finally agreed on, he will not go to Paris, as Diaghilev had requested, "in spite of all my longing to come to Paris and the great joy which awaits me—to see one another . . . I embrace you, my dearest, with all my heart and I hope all the same that we shall see one another soon. Your Stravinsky. Are there rooms at the Meurice, as that is where I should like to stay?"

With all their financial problems it seems never to have occurred to either Stravinsky or Diaghilev to travel any way but first class. It was not only Stravinsky who had been complaining to Misia.

BAKST TO MISIA

December 20, 1914
Hôtel du Parc
Geneva

My dear Misia,

You are an angel to have answered my letter. I am here waiting to go to Rome with Stravinsky for his concerts (I have some portraits to do down there) and I am delighted not to go alone because I am trying as hard as I can to avoid that filthy exploiter whose name is Serge.

Among other things, do you think he has paid me? Not on your life: he has only given back what *I lent him*. But both he and his money disgust me. Especially after having sold a good many pictures

in America during the summer (think of it!!!) I am in a position
to throw his money in his face!

Misia's reaction to these complaints was not only to help the artists but
to spring to Diaghilev's defense. "After all," she wrote in her memoirs, "at
the end of a season in which he had collected four million gold francs to
keep the troupe alive, he considered himself the most fortunate of men if
he had 10,000 francs left to spend the summer in Venice." She felt that
Diaghilev was far from being the "filthy exploiter" that Bakst called him.
For her, he was an idealist, a perfectionist who had sacrificed his personal
fortune to make everything as beautiful as possible for his artists, only to
have most of them, like Bakst, vilify him. Clearly, Misia's first loyalty was
to Diaghilev. Theirs was a friendship that began on a note of profound
exaltation and continued with the same passionate intensity to the end. In a
sense, their rapport was based on the chemistry of irony and laughter. No
one escaped their lighthearted, if dangerous, malice. Many of their friends
found it irritating to see them constantly whispering and gossiping, laughing
at secret jokes. From the heights of Mount Olympus it amused Diaghilev
and Misia to manipulate the lesser gods who surrounded them. Hurling an
occasional thunderbolt delighted them even more. Like Jupiter and Juno,
they enjoyed a violent quarrel from time to time, but for the most part
they saw eye to eye. As the center of his particular universe, Diaghilev expected everything and everyone to revolve around him. He was childishly
irritated when Misia went off to Spain with Sert just when he wanted her
to be in Italy with him. Telegrams of recrimination pursued her. If all else
failed, Diaghilev, who was normally too impatient to write letters, was
reduced even to that:

> . . . I know nothing more absurd than the kind of fate that makes
> you arrive in a city at the exact moment in which I must leave it, or
> that obliges you to leave another exactly when I arrive and when I
> need you most, if only for a few hours. Honestly, in these past weeks
> you have shown such indifference to everything important to me,
> everything dear to me, that it would be best to have a heart-to-heart
> talk.
> I know perfectly well that a friendship cannot last for centuries, but
> there is one thing I beg of you: never tell me again that you have

been "urgently called away," because *that I know in advance*. I can, automatically, predict those "urgent calls" with absolute certainty— besides I do not consider them "calls," except in the sense that they call forth laughter from the friends to whom I have prophesied them.

In Sert's case I can understand perfectly that he can be called away by his work, but that you, *you* treat me this way, that is to my mind as unfriendly as it is undeserved. So you see, there are times when the truth seems to me more important than anything.

These quarrels only intensified their friendship. Diaghilev always needed someone to help clarify his instinctive judgments, his hunches, his enthusiasms. For this Misia was ideally suited: unlike his artists, she had nothing to gain. And so their discussions—of a possible musical score, a sketch submitted by an artist, a new dancer presented for her inspection— were often on a purely aesthetic level. When Misia had a protégé of her own to push, however, her cunning knew no bounds. Their artistic colloquy took place at the busy corner where art and gossip meet. Decisions would be made at rehearsals, during ballet intermissions, at supper parties, or on the telephone. If Misia knew how to criticize, she knew even better how to assure Diaghilev of her admiration for the "chain of miracles" he produced. Perhaps what stimulated him even more than her extravagant praise, sincere though it was, was her enticingly malicious way of flirting with him. One day she said that it was his work, not he himself, that was important to her, and that she could not mean much to him either, since he never bothered to write her but just bombarded her with telegrams. This teasing provoked a touchingly adolescent response:

You claim that it is not I whom you love, but only my work. Well! I must say the opposite about you, because I love you with all your numerous faults and I love you the way I would love a sister, if I had one. Unfortunately, I do not have one, so that all this love is crystal- lized in you. Please remember that not very long ago we *very seriously* agreed that you were the only woman on earth whom I could possibly love. That is why I find it so unworthy of a "sister" to make such a fuss simply because I do not write to you.

When I do write—and you know how rare that is—it's exclusively *to say something* and not to talk about my box-office success in London (of which news has certainly already reached you), but rather to confide in you my hopes, my plans, and my projects.

In at least one of Diaghilev's projects, the ballet *Parade*, Misia's role was somewhat more complex than that of a simple confidante. On May 18, 1917, in the third year of the war, the curtain of the Théâtre du Châtelet rose on that concise, mysteriously telling ballet. At last Cocteau had succeeded in astonishing Diaghilev with a brilliantly original scenario. In so doing, he helped to provoke a scandal which he liked to think was almost as satisfyingly tumultuous as that of *Le Sacre* itself. "Our wish," Cocteau wrote, "is that the public consider *Parade* as a work that conceals poetry beneath the coarse outer skin of slapstick. . . . *Parade* brings together Erik Satie's first orchestral score, Pablo Picasso's first stage decor, Massine's first Cubist choreography, and a poet's first attempt to express himself without words." There were those in the audience who recognized *Parade* as a milestone in the history of the arts. But others felt that such frivolity at the height of a tragic war was so unpatriotic that its perpetrators should be deported. *Parade* was announced as "a *ballet réaliste* by Jean Cocteau," but for the program notes Apollinaire invented a new word, *sur-réalisme* (super-realism), to describe its magical fusion of decor, scenario, music, and dance, which he felt had a poetic reality more intensely valid than reality itself.

For this ballet Picasso painted a lyric front curtain: an Italianate landscape as a background to an alfresco meal served by blackamoors to a Venetian boatman, a bullfighter with a guitar, and a group of circus performers in harlequin costume. The scene is dominated by a pale Pegasus licking its foal. A winged ballerina stands poised on the horse's back. The curtain rose on a Cubist evocation of New York skyscrapers set at crazed angles. Even more astonishing, two end men, "managers" encased in towering Cubist constructions, presided over the sideshow booth of a cheap travelling fair. One by one the acts were presented to lure passers-by inside. The performers, appearing in eccentric mimetic dances, included a pair of acrobats, a dizzy American flapper, a fire-eating Chinese magician (danced by Massine), and that old circus trick: two men as a horse. In his infectiously brash and jazzy score, Satie had written the *Ubu Roi* of music. Brushing the past aside, he composed a work as seemingly simple and repetitious as a baby's rattle. On closer study the score reveals a mathematical asymmetry and a spare orchestral transparency that are the emblems of a new aesthetic. The ballet is light and comic, but it has resonances that are still with us today. It influenced a new generation of French composers and anticipated *musique concrète*. And it opened the path to ballets that deal with everyday life.*

The events leading to the creation of *Parade* were even less dignified than the ballet itself. In fact, the making of *Parade* was an almost farcicial example of the backstage intrigue that seems as fundamental to a ballet company as the five positions. In-fighting and behind-the-scenes treachery made for a power struggle that Cocteau was to refer to as the "greatest battle of the war." He might with greater accuracy have called it a comedy of bad manners. Appropriately, it began on June 28, 1914, the day that Archduke Ferdinand was assassinated. On that day, as we have seen, Misia had Erik Satie play his music for Diaghilev, and planted the seed for a Satie ballet in Diaghilev's mind; but the scheme had to be put aside with the outbreak of war. At that time the eccentric composer's original talent was recognized only by those in the know: among them Debussy, Ravel, and Stravinsky, all of whom were influenced by the hypnotic purity, the anti-Wagnerian aspect of Satie's music. A refined and subtle spirit, Satie was always desperately in need of money and recognition. His wit, his charm, his pince-nez, his stiff collars, and his dozens of umbrellas are as legendary as his daily bottle of brandy and his terrifying readiness to take offense. Paul Morand, who met Satie at Cocteau's apartment, wrote that he looked "like Socrates: his face is made of half-moons; he scratches his billy-goat's beard between every two words. . . . Above all, he wants to give the impression of being crafty . . . the semi-failure, the man whom Debussy has always crushed and who suffers from that."

In 1916 Diaghilev, responding to Misia's continued enthusiasm, again

---

* In 1973, fifty-six years after its creation, when *Parade* was revived by Massine for the Joffrey Ballet in New York, it was still startlingly fresh and innovative. At that time Massine said that he had re-invented many of the steps. He added, "I was just a young greenhorn when I first choreographed it."

took up the idea of a Satie ballet. The alert was sounded and Cocteau pricked up his prehensile ears. Still smarting from the failure of his ballet *Le Dieu Bleu* and the frustrations of the abandoned *David*, Cocteau at twenty-seven was determined to fulfill Diaghilev's historic injunction: "*Etonne-moi*, Jean!" Here at last was his chance to "astonish" Diaghilev, to climb back on the Ballets Russes's bandwagon. According to the young artist Valentine Gross, Satie and Cocteau had met at her home as early as October 1915 to discuss working together. Now they agreed that Cocteau would devise a scenario for the ballet Satie was to write. But how to break the news to Diaghilev, who had never asked for Cocteau's collaboration? Through Misia, of course— and so the intrigue began. At Cocteau's suggestion they decided to conceal this first meeting from Misia, for they all feared that she would try to destroy any ballet not hatched under her wing. (As Diaghilev was in America, it is likely that Misia was behaving in a more proprietary way than usual.) In any case, Cocteau was convinced that Misia had intrigued against him in his abortive collaboration with Stravinsky. It was soothing to the young poet's vanity to blame her rather than face the fact that neither Diaghilev nor Stravinsky had ever shown any enthusiasm for *David*. Through Cocteau, Picasso was later chosen to design the sets and costumes—his first work for the theatre. It was a coup that Cocteau, not unnaturally, boasted about for the rest of his life.

As in many theatrical collaborations, everyone connected with the ballet wanted top billing and credit for originating the ideas. In an atmosphere of shifting loyalties no one drew the line at lies and subterfuge. Back-biting and bitchery were the order of the day. Misia, usually helpful, became meddlesome. Satie, the benign Socrates, became malignant. Picasso, whose only loyalty was to himself, behaved treacherously to Cocteau. And Cocteau, who said, "The art of life is to know just how far to go *too* far," went even farther. As Diaghilev wisely observed, "In the theatre there are no friends."

The letters that flew back and forth during the planning of the ballet read like an eighteenth-century epistolary novel. There is a conspiratorial, *Liaisons Dangereuses* tone in the correspondence between Satie and Cocteau and between each of them and Misia and Valentine. The ladies were the *commères*, the two end women of the offstage minstrel show that preceded *Parade*.

The conspiracies begin on a courtly note.

SATIE TO MISIA

May 1916

Chère dame,

What you said to me, at your house, about the "Ballets Russes" has already produced a result: I am working on a thing that I plan to show you very soon and that is dedicated to you as I think of it and as I write it.

All this, dear Madame, gives me the greatest pleasure. Are you not a magician?

SATIE TO MISIA

[n.d.]

Chère dame,

I am coming on Tuesday, isn't that right? If so, not a word to the others about what I've prepared for you. My little idea for the "thing" has ripened so well that I could play it for you right to the end. (There's a bit missing in the middle but I count on you not to tell anyone.) And I want it to please you. . . . Diaghilev is not a man to go back on his agreement, I imagine?

Bonjour chère dame,
E. S.

SATIE TO COCTEAU

April 25, 1916

Cher ami,

Forgive me—sick—grippe.
Impossible send word except by telepathy. All right for tomorrow.
Valentine Gross tells me marvellous things. You are the *idea* man.
Bravo!

SATIE TO COCTEAU

June 8 [1916]

Cher ami,

For heaven's sake stop worrying, don't be nervous. I am at work. Let me do it my own way. I warn you, you won't see the thing until October. Not a note before that. I tell you so under oath. Will it be all right if I mention that you are the author of the scenario? I need to. Madame Edwards is all for the project. . . . You *must* trust me.

COCTEAU TO MISIA

[n.d.]

Chère Misia,

A letter from Erik Satie absolves me from my vow of silence. One evening in your house, by thrilling coincidence, Satie asked me to collaborate with him at the very moment I was about to ask him the same. That little miracle happened in the presence of Valentine Gross, who thus learned of the matter. I kept the secret until I was sure that the work was well on the way, having suffered from being overhasty with Igor. This was also Satie's explicit wish. Moreover, though nothing is left of *David, David*'s failure surely served to make possible the birth of the new work—there are mysteries that are beyond human understanding. You will be the first to hear it, so I am telling you about it at once—dropping my incognito (*for you alone*) the moment Satie asks me. We won't take less than your "love"—mere "approval" would kill us poor Arcueil-Anjou minstrels.* It is a very short work which resembles the composer—everything goes on behind the eyeglasses.†

---

* Satie lived in the working-class suburb of Arcueil, Cocteau in the fashionable rue d'Anjou.

† According to Francis Steegmuller's remarkable biography of Cocteau, "It is not certain that this letter was ever sent. It is not among those which Misia prints in her memoirs. Two slightly different versions exist, both formerly among the papers of the late Valentine Gross Hugo, to whom Cocteau apparently submitted the drafts for approval. . . . Valentine once told the present author that she herself had sent a lying letter, composed by Cocteau, assuring her that it was at Misia's house rather

After receiving Valentine's "lying letter," Misia wrote to Cocteau, who was shuttling back and forth between Paris and his military duties at the front. As she received no answer—perhaps for once he was at a loss for words—she wrote again.

MISIA TO COCTEAU

Paris
Sunday
June 1916

Mon cher petit Jean,

... I answered your letter after receiving a long letter from Val[entine] about Erik Satie and you. I will just tell you again that I already knew about this collaboration. Although I have not said anything to E. S., I know that if he wants to do something for Serge, your presence would be useless. I shall pass over this however. . . .

I expect Serge this week and hope to work all this out once and for all. Satie comes to see me fairly often and I still have great hopes of him. He is both candid and crafty and I hope he will disentangle himself from the wretches who surround him. . . .

Igor passed through Paris on his way to Spain to see Serge (who came back from America on an Italian boat loaded with munitions but preferred DEATH to the dreadful boredom of America and just couldn't wait). So he went to Spain where he has been with Stravinsky ever since.

Therefore I asked Stravinsky to support Satie and he was so enthusiastic that he even thought of combining this project with the new work that was commissioned from him by Polignac [*Renard*] to make a short and perfect evening. . . .

I embrace you with all my heart
Your
Misia

Tell me as much as possible about yourself.

---

than in her own that *Parade* had really been conceived. Perhaps that took the place of anything signed by Cocteau himself."

In Valentine Gross's copy of Misia's memoirs, opposite a quotation from a Cocteau letter—in which he wrote, "My meeting with Satie was all lightness and happiness"—Valentine pencilled an indignant "What lies!"

Understandably, Cocteau was upset to hear that Diaghilev did not want him, but it was always Misia's way to be brutally frank. The tone of her letter shows, however, that her frankness had nothing to do with her affection for Cocteau. Her first concern was to convince Diaghilev to put on a ballet by Satie; her second and more delicate task was to soften Diaghilev's attitude toward Cocteau. Evidently she succeeded, for when Diaghilev finally gave him his chance, Cocteau wrote from the front to thank her.

COCTEAU TO MISIA

[n.d.]

. . . Your letter arrives as if by carrier pigeon and reassures my heart. Far from everyone, in the land of cannibals, one is tortured and begins to doubt even the most faithful. . . . Satie is an angel (well disguised). . . . My part of the work doesn't make things easy for him—quite the contrary. If only our collaboration could move you the way it moved me the day I told him what he must write. . . .

I can guess from his postcards that things are going the way I most want them to.

Cocteau was in for a disappointment that he could not blame on Misia. He may have received encouraging postcards from Satie, but at the same time Satie, far more crafty than he was candid, was telling Valentine Gross that things were not going at all the way Cocteau thought they were. Valentine, moreover, was passing the information along to Cocteau.

COCTEAU TO VALENTINE

July 30, 1916

. . . I feel terribly alone and anguished—I beg you to let me hear from you, exorcize the devil, see Satie, learn what is going on. If this thing fell through it would be the end of me.

SATIE TO VALENTINE

August 8, 1916
Tuesday, 3:12 p.m.

It's happened! I've broken with Aunt Trufaldin [Misia]. What a bitch!

Of them all only Satie had cause to be angry with Misia, for she had committed the cardinal sin of interfering with his creative activity—and with the possibility of his being paid for a new composition. One can only suppose that Satie had played parts of *Parade* for Misia. She loved his *Trois Morceaux en Forme de Poire* with its alternating sections of expressive lyricism, hypnotic stillness, and high-stepping music-hall gaiety, but his new style may have alarmed her. *Parade*'s daring ingenuousness, its single measures repeated endlessly like a wallpaper design, made what seemed to her an aesthetic rather than a musical statement. And she might well have been afraid that Diaghilev would find it more gaga than Dada. She made no secret of the fact that she and Diaghilev might prefer to use some of Satie's old pieces instead of the new work. "Satie is old—let him stay old—it's so good that way," she was heard to say. It was enough to infuriate any artist. Satie was deeply hurt and began to call her names that fell below the standard of his usual exquisite wit. Misia was demoted from "*chère dame*" and "magician" to "Aunt Trufaldin" after the deceitful servant in the *commedia dell'arte*. Like naughty children, Valentine and Cocteau joined in the game. From now on in their correspondence with Satie, Misia was not only "Aunt Trufaldin" but "Abortionist," "Sister-in-Law," and "Aunt Brutus," while Sert, of course, became "Uncle Brutus." And Satie's *mot*, "Misia is a lovely cat—so hide your fish!" was soon being repeated all over Paris.

As for Cocteau, it must be remembered that Diaghilev had never asked him to work on the Satie ballet, any more than he had asked him to collaborate with Stravinsky. In both cases the young poet had pushed himself forward uninvited, behind Diaghilev's back, and then felt betrayed when he was not made welcome. Besides, Cocteau had stepped on Sert's toes (and Diaghilev's!) when *Le Mot*, the magazine he and Paul Iribe published, attacked *La Légende de Joseph* in a jingoistic display of anti-German feeling. That Misia continued to promote Cocteau's cause with Diaghilev after that was a gesture of real friendship on her part. Despite these complications, some progress was being made.

COCTEAU TO VALENTINE

August 9, 1916

Very good day's work with Satie. Erik-Trufaldin catastrophe not serious and very serious.

COCTEAU TO STRAVINSKY

August 11, 1916

Satie and I are collaborating on something for Serge, since Serge, despite the abyss that I feel divides us, is still the only impresario with genius.

COCTEAU TO VALENTINE

August 13, 1916

My dear Valentine,

Nothing very new except that Picasso keeps taking me to the [Café] Rotonde. . . . Misia is now inseparable from Apollinaris [Apollinaire]. What is she up to with him at Maxim's? She has quite abandoned Saint-Léger for him. Our good Satie . . . is composing marvels for me and refuses to see Aunt Brutus. A long letter to Igor S. in which I let him know that I am far from being a party to inept intrigues. To tell you the truth, Diaghilev—that Italian tenor—finds it clever to attribute to me all the blunders of the quai Voltaire [Misia], all due to my influence, he says—and naïve Igor accuses me of treachery.

Still, it's a great thing to be in the thick of the dog fights of great art.

JOINT POSTCARD FROM COCTEAU AND SATIE TO VALENTINE

August 24, 1916

Picasso is doing *Parade* with us.

COCTEAU TO VALENTINE

August 31, 1916

Picasso and Satie get on like Misia and Serge. Picasso is moulting, undergoing a transformation—Saturday night we begin real work.

Little did Cocteau realize the ominous undertones of Picasso and Satie's burgeoning friendship. When he brought off his great coup and arranged for Picasso to do the decor for *Parade*, Cocteau could not have anticipated the game of musical chairs that followed. Picasso had his own ideas for the scenario and Satie preferred them to Cocteau's. Picasso and Satie felt that in "their" ballet, Cocteau's "presence would be useless," just as Misia and Serge had thought in the first place. It was civil war in the none-too-solid ranks.

COCTEAU TO VALENTINE

September 14, 1916

. . . Make Satie understand, if you can cut through the aperitif fog, that I really do count for something in *Parade*, and that he and Picasso are not the only ones involved. . . . It hurts me when he dances around Picasso screaming, "It's you I'm following! *You* are my master!" . . . Does he hear anything I say? . . . calm him in his inordinate hatred for the Aunt. Sh! Burn this, for the work is going ahead, and that's the main thing. Picasso is inventing marvels.

SATIE TO VALENTINE

Thursday—September 14, 1916

Chère et douce amie—

If you knew how sad I am! *Parade* is changing for the better, behind Cocteau's back! Picasso has ideas that I like better than our Jean's! How awful! And I am all for Picasso! And Cocteau doesn't know it! What am I to do? Picasso tells me to go ahead, following Jean's text, and he, Picasso, will work on another text, his own—which is dazzling! Prodigious! . . . Now that I know Picasso's wonderful ideas, I am heartbroken to have to set to music the less wonderful ideas of our good Jean —oh! yes! less wonderful. What am I to do? What am I to do? Write and advise me. I am beside myself.

SATIE TO VALENTINE

Wednesday, September 20, 1916

Chère amie,

It's settled. Cocteau knows everything. He and Picasso have come to terms. How lucky! Did I tell you that I got along well with Diaghilev? Still no money from him. Our "Aunt" is in Rum—I mean Rome.

COCTEAU TO VALENTINE

[September 22, 1916]

. . . You were probably worried about Satie—let me quickly set your mind at rest. Caught between Picasso and me, our good Socrates from Arcueil has lost his bearings—our different vocabularies make him imagine that one of us is talking white and the other black. Have decided with Picasso to lie to Satie so that he'll be able to go ahead without getting confused.

COCTEAU TO MISIA

[n.d.]

Dear Misia,

Come back soon—I'm impatient to hug you and to laugh and kiss away a thousand misunderstandings that have been exaggerated by distance and fatigue. Very good meeting with Serge and Massine—the latter's fresh intelligence and general air I like very much. I have the impression that Serge likes our work and that he understood perfectly the seemingly very simple motivation I provided for the union of musician and painter. I stand between them, giving a hand to each. . . . For the first time I feel myself in rapport with Serge—a very nice feeling.

SATIE TO COCTEAU

[n.d.]

My "sister-in-law" is no longer dangerous, I think. What luck!

Finally, in February 1917, Diaghilev invited Cocteau, Satie, and Picasso to come to Rome to work with Massine on *Parade*. "Will I really go?" Cocteau wrote Valentine. "I wonder: Aunt T. is in charge! ! !" Go he did; but Satie, despite the fact that he had been shopping for luggage, remained behind. When asked if he knew Rome, Satie replied, "By name—only by name." From Rome, Cocteau wrote Misia, "Picasso amazes me every day. To live near him is a lesson in nobility and hard work." But there was one more problem to be worked out. The possibility that Cocteau might be called back to France to resume military duty disturbed Diaghilev, who felt that *Parade* could not be completed without the poet's help. At last Cocteau had made himself indispensable.

CicerO TO MISIA

CenterCenter

CenterCenter

CenterCenter

CenterCenter

CenterCenter

CenterCenter

COCTEAU TO MISIA

[n.d.]

Dear Misia,

Reassure Serge that if my stay here upsets the War Ministry too much, since the work is going very well (Massine soaking up my ideas) no matter what Diag thinks, my absence could no longer hurt *Parade*....

It's boring to be far away from you.

Apparently Misia spoke to Berthelot at the War Ministry and succeeded in extending Cocteau's leave.

COCTEAU TO MISIA

[n.d.]

Dear Misia,

... Thanks for Berthelot. Serge was really worried that I might leave the work incomplete. I think you will be happy with it.

The Chinese magician is done. Massine was supposed to play the acrobat but he demonstrated the role of the Chinese with such talent that I begged him to dance that role....

Write a little postcard, you are my *other* family, you know that, and just the sight of your handwriting moves me. Bakst has a cold—he buys special handkerchiefs that "don't excite the nose" and is living in a brothel. He explained to us . . . that when young he posed as Antinous at drawing school since at that time he looked as much like Sarah Bernhardt as two peas in a pod.* Serge nearly died laughing and the meal was interrupted as the waiters were doubled up with laughter themselves. . . .

---

* According to Paul Morand, Bakst was "a rumpled, tubby man with spectacles, sparse red hair, a ridiculously dapper military mustache, and a comical lisp."

I shall return soon in spite of Serge. . . . Uneasy far from home. In the Pincio I dream of the quai Voltaire.

Embrassez Mons. Sert
Jean

At last *Parade* was completed. When, at the first performance, Misia and Sert "received" in the foyer of the theatre—Misia in full regalia, with a silver tiara—Cocteau could not resist saying that she looked like the mother of the bride. As the ballet unfolded, Misia might well have been reminded of Cocteau's behavior during the past year, for the characters he had devised hawk their wares in much the way that Cocteau himself had done in selling his act to Satie and Picasso, to Misia and Diaghilev. Like his characters, Cocteau had used coquetry, sleight of hand, acrobatics, and slapstick, with that overlay of mockery that was his own cynical, slightly sinister veneer.

All the same, by this time Misia and Cocteau had made up their differences. She was to remain his close friend for life, while Valentine Gross broke with Cocteau six years later. And Misia and Picasso became so attached to one another that he asked her to be a witness at his wedding to Olga Kokhlova, one of Diaghilev's Russian dancers, and godmother to their son Paolo. Valentine married the artist Jean Hugo, a great-grandson of Victor Hugo, with Cocteau and Satie as best men. The couple had met in Cipa's apartment, where Jean first saw Valentine seated on a leather sofa under a portrait of Misia's father. Jean Hugo became one of Misia's closest friends, but Valentine never liked her. When Misia's memoirs were published after her death, Valentine was still complaining. Spitefully she marked the margins of her copy with short, corrective splutters of rage.

After the reviews of *Parade* appeared, Satie, who never forgave a slight, sent an insulting postcard to a critic who had treated his score harshly. "*Monsieur et cher ami*," Satie wrote, "You are nothing but an ass-hole and an unmusical one at that." The critic sued for libel and Satie was sentenced to a week in jail. His friends were horrified, and Cocteau was not above turning to "Aunt and Uncle Brutus" for help. Cocteau's was the last word, a postscript to the intricate parade of letters.

COCTEAU TO MISIA

Poor Satie. Were you told that we *all* stopped by to see you after the verdict? Satie did not want to bother anyone beforehand (alas!) as he

thought the matter was not very serious. . . . What's to be done? If only
he could be kept out of prison. . . . Just now Sert telephoned. I've told
him to arrange something. . . .

Fortunately something was arranged, either by Misia and Sert or by the
combined efforts of the group. Satie was given a suspended sentence and
spared the humiliation of going to jail.

During the making of *Parade* Misia met Gabrielle Chanel, who was to
become her closest woman friend. Chanel was slender, with a small aristocratic head poised on a long, graceful neck. In profile she looked as
distinguished as a Gainsborough duchess; but full face, with her mocking
dark eyes, wide mouth, and knowing expression, she was the embodiment
of the seductive street gamine. Born a peasant, she had been a singer, an
entertainer, a cocotte, and a milliner by the time Misia met her. Now, in
1916, Chanel was transforming herself from the classic little milliner-cocotte
into a leader of fashion. For ten years she had been living with Etienne
Balsan, an upper-middle-class *bon vivant*, in his château at Royallieu near
Paris where horses, gambling, and making love were the chief diversions.
Among the visitors at Royallieu was Arthur Capel, an Englishman known to
his friends as "Boy." After a time, both men apparently shared Chanel in
a lighthearted *ménage à trois*. Balsan had installed her in the ground floor
of his Paris apartment, where it amused his society friends to buy her pretty
hats. But Boy fell in love with her and set her up in a shop of her own
behind the Hôtel Ritz. Soon her cleverness, her beauty, and her revolutionary sense of style became the talk of fashionable Paris. It is curious that
these two grand men, who felt that they were conferring honor on the little
milliner, are remembered as footnotes in the history of their *petite amie*.

In the late forties when Misia was dictating her memoirs to her friend
Boulos, she included a chapter on Chanel with whom she had been in-
extricably bound for over thirty years. Out of the usual unkindness of her
heart, Chanel insisted that the chapter be omitted. She would tell her own
story, she announced; she too was writing her memoirs. Misia was deeply

offended. "But they're already written," she said. "All you have to do is publish your account books." Misia not only removed the chapter from her book
but never referred to Chanel by name, even in the episodes where she appears.
Here is the missing chapter.*

It was toward the middle of the 1914–1918 war that I accepted an
invitation to dine one evening at the home of Cécile Sorel, then at the
summit of her glory. Our national Célimène† lived on the quai Voltaire
in an apartment where the windows were lavishly draped with somewhat
moth-eaten leopard skins. At table my attention was immediately drawn
to a very dark-haired young woman. Despite the fact that she did not
say a word, she radiated a charm I found irresistible. She made me
think of Madame du Barry. Therefore I arranged to sit next to her after
dinner. During the exchange of banalities appropriate to a first meeting
in a salon, I learned that she was called Mademoiselle Chanel and had a
milliner's shop in the rue Cambon.

She seemed to me gifted with infinite grace and when, as we were
saying goodnight, I admired her ravishing fur-trimmed, red velvet coat,
she took it off at once and put it on my shoulders, saying with charming
spontaneity that she would be only too happy to give it to me.
Obviously I could not accept it. But her gesture had been so pretty that
I found her completely bewitching and thought of nothing but her.

The next day I could hardly wait to go to see her in the rue Cambon.
In her little boutique one found sweaters, hats, and accessories of all
kinds. When I arrived, two women were there talking about her, calling
her "Coco." I don't know why the use of this name upset me so, but my
heart sank: I had the impression that my idol was being smashed. Why
trick out someone so exceptional with so vulgar a name? I was indignant! I was still in a rage when at last I saw again the woman I had been
thinking about since the night before.

Magically the hours sped by, even though it was I who did most of
the talking, for she hardly spoke. The thought of parting from her
seemed unbearable, and that same evening Sert and I went to dine at

---

* It was generously given to us by both Monsieur Paul Uldace, the painter who is
Misia's literary heir, and Madame Jenny Bradley.

† The actress was noted for her interpretation of Célimène in Molière's *Le Mis-
anthrope.*

her apartment on the quai de Tokyo. There, in the midst of countless Coromandel screens, we found Boy Capel, who represented important British interests in Paris.

Sert was really scandalized by the astonishing infatuation I felt for my new friend. I was not in the habit of being carried away like this, and I myself was rather surprised that a woman I had met the night before could already fill such a place in my thoughts!

Not long afterward [three years later, in December 1919], Boy Capel was killed in a dreadful automobile accident. Coco felt this loss so deeply that she sank into a neurasthenic state, and I tried desperately to think of ways to distract her.

As it was the season of parties and balls, I had the Machiavellian idea of going to Rebattet, at that time the most fashionable caterer in Paris, and asking for the list of parties scheduled at the homes of the wartime *nouveaux riches*, whom naturally we did not know. Armed with this information, I decided one evening that we would go to a costume ball at the Blumenthals', a frightfully rich and snobbish couple to whose home, of course, we had not been invited.*

It took a good deal of pleading to persuade Sert to dress up as a Negress dragging along a hurdy-gurdy. It was in this getup that he accompanied Coco and me to the house of the victims in question, who took such a dim view of the situation that, after a dreadful fuss, we were thrown out by the servants.

Not at all discouraged, I dragged my group to various other "routs" —without much more success—landing finally, when the night was almost over, at the house of some simple middle-class people whose name I did not even know. They received us with open arms, and we were given a delicious supper!

The Count and Countess de Beaumont had asked Sert to take charge of the decorations for a great ball they were to give that spring. One day when I brought Coco Chanel along to their house, we discussed the party at length and they asked her too for suggestions. But two days before the ball, I discovered that she had not been invited, and I decided in that case I would not go either. Instead, with Picasso and Sert as our

---

* An amusing note on Misia's small Parisian world: when the Blumenthals' son Cecil married Mimi Pecci, a great-niece of Pope Leo XIII, and was granted the papal title Count Pecci-Blunt, his wife became Misia's closest friend in Rome.

escorts, we mingled with the chauffeurs crowded in front of the house to watch the costumed guests make their entrances. Rarely have I been so amused.

I know perfectly well that in those days "society people" would never dream of inviting "tradespeople." Then again, the latter would never permit themselves to recognize or greet you, except in their own establishments. Consequently Count de Beaumont was probably behaving naturally in not sending Mademoiselle Chanel an invitation; but she was *my* friend, so I felt hurt that an exception had not been made for her.

It was in this frame of mind that Sert and I took her to Venice the following summer. I immediately gave a huge dinner party to introduce my new friend to the *"gratin"* gathered there. I invited Princess de Poix, Count and Countess Volpi, the Prince of Greece, in short, the smartest people I could find! Thanks to her unaffected charm she had a great success, and after that Italian season it was out of the question, once she was back in Paris, that anyone would dream of not inviting her!

Today, when couturiers are not only invited everywhere, but are almost the only people to give lavish parties to which everyone rushes, it is difficult to imagine the vast privilege conferred on Mademoiselle Chanel toward the end of the war, when the doors of the salons opened for her! It was certainly without precedent and the forerunner of a good many upheavals.

At the same time that she penetrated the famous, carefully guarded "game preserve," Coco came to know Diaghilev at my house, as well as the whole group of artists that gravitated around the Ballets Russes. And they found in her a faithful, a very generous friend. Stravinsky in particular fell desperately in love with her! Afterward she was to give him a house in Garches and, frequently, financial help too.

It was just after the war that Mademoiselle Chanel, whose establishment in the rue Cambon was rapidly expanding to dizzying heights, transformed women at one stroke by eliminating their corsets, their whalebone stays, their chokers—and even their hair. Gone were the flashy frills and furbelows—vanished miraculously along with the cinched petticoats and the bodices laced to the point of suffocation. Women's bodies took on a new shape; bosoms and bottoms disappeared

—while legs suddenly appeared where formerly one had only glimpsed a chaste ankle. . . .

On matters of style, Chanel unquestionably laid down the law in that period.

Coco always had a genius for discovering the essence of something gigantic in the most minuscule idea suggested to her. If the grain of sand you offered her had some interesting quality, she could turn it into gold. I should like to give an example that is almost miraculous.

One day a friend,* secretary to the empress, came to see me reeking of *Violettes Impériales*. He had been diligently going through the papers of the beautiful Eugénie, to whom he was devoted, body and soul. He seemed literally embalmed in the perfume of the woman whose grace illuminated the Second Empire. "Just imagine, Misia," he said, "I discovered an astonishing beauty formula among the letters of our dear great empress. The faith she had in it is my best guarantee of its effectiveness. But you'd better read this document and tell me as a friend, since we're alone, if it wouldn't be possible to sell this lost formula to some cosmetics house—without revealing the name of the illustrious person who used it to keep her beauty alive." With these words he handed me a sheet of paper:

THE SECRET OF THE MEDICIS

Shortly before the war, excavations performed in the underground passages of a famous royal château on the banks of the Loire brought to light several manuscripts by René the Florentine, Perfume-Maker to Queen Catherine de Medici.

Among those manuscripts there appeared the *Secret of the Medicis*, the famous toilet water which made it possible for Queen Catherine, for Diane de Poitiers, and later for Queen Marie de Medici to brave the years, yet to keep, even in old age, a ravishing skin and the complexion of a young girl.

The *Secret of the Medicis* is not an ordinary beauty product nor a perfume. It is an essence unlike any other cosmetic, learnedly compounded in a completely special way which proves that René

---

* Lucien Daudet, secretary to the Empress Eugénie, wife of Napoleon III. The empress had recently died.

the Florentine had raised his art to the level of a science.

Using the *Secret of the Medicis* twice daily guarantees permanent, indestructible youth. This toilet water without rival tightens and nourishes sagging skin, cleans the pores, and clears the complexion in an incomparable way. It is the only product men should use for protection against razor irritation. It is not a makeup and leaves no trace. If at first the secret formula produces a burning sensation, it is only a sign of the bad condition of the skin. Then the treatment should be prolonged and the dosage increased.

My first reaction was to try to control the irresistible laughter that shook me. The second was an inspiration. "You want six thousand francs for this formula," I said to him; "You shall have it." I had just thought of Coco. Since everything she touched succeeded, why not launch a Chanel toilet water based on this formula?

I was no longer thinking of the friend who was visiting me, still less of the Medicis and dear René the Florentine! I rang, asked for my coat, and ordered the car. Ten minutes later I was sitting opposite Coco and busily explaining, with all the glib poise of a first-class travelling salesman, the marvellous success she could have by creating a Chanel toilet water based on the unbelievable *Secret of the Medicis*. Her name was then on everyone's lips and in itself a guarantee of success.

I did my job so well that René the Florentine amused her as much as he amused me! Painstakingly we experimented with a very severe bottle, ultra-simple, almost pharmaceutical, but in the Chanel style and with the elegant touch she gave to everything.

A few weeks later, *L'Eau de Chanel* made its appearance. It succeeded far beyond our wildest hopes. It was unbelievable, almost as if we had won first prize in a lottery! "Why don't you really go in for perfumes?" I said to Coco. "It seems to me, after the success of *L'Eau de Chanel*, that René the Florentine is the goose that laid the golden egg."

At that moment Mademoiselle Chanel, who at first considered the toilet water a plaything, had the genius to see the future possibilities of this new idea. And from the start her perfumes were so successful that Chanel Number 5, Number 22, and *Bois des Iles* were soon in demand on all five continents.

And that is how the sorceress, with a flick of her wrist, started with the minuscule idea the *Secret of the Medicis* had given me and created an industry of such importance that, one by one, all the fashion houses followed in her path. Thanks to her, they managed to balance their budgets during the years when they were threatened with bankruptcy!

I am only telling the story of the most resounding of Coco's miraculous achievements. But think of costume jewelry—where did that begin? It would take a whole book for me to explain what women, elegance itself, and even the city of Paris owe to Coco! But I very much hope that it is she who will write that book one day.

In my book I just would like to show the important role that such a woman played in our time. I felt it so strongly that, from our first meeting, I could hardly wait to make others aware of it. One could say that it is easy to help a beautiful diamond to shine. Still, it was my privilege to help it emerge from its rough state, and—in my heart—to be the first person dazzled by its brilliance.

Misia could hardly have chosen a better image than the diamond. Like a diamond, Chanel was hard, brilliant, expensive, and, in the eyes of many, uniquely beautiful. It is true that Misia gave the rough stone two of its most brilliant facets: an entry into high society and, more glittering still, an introduction to Diaghilev and his circle of artists. Together she and Sert gave Chanel an infinitely more precious gift: they opened her eyes to art, both past and present. Chanel was an incredibly quick and responsive pupil. Unfortunately, Misia was as proprietary about her new protégée as she had been about *Parade*. It irritated Chanel when Misia demanded gratitude for what she gave, despite the pleasure she took in the giving. And there was always that unremitting urge in Misia to be credited, to be recognized for discovering and guiding unknown talent. It was the Diaghilev in her. Omitted from Misia's telescopic memoir of Chanel were the subterranean depths of their friendship, a mixture of love and hate, with overtones of sexual intensity. For over thirty years the two women were locked in an embrace that seemed at times the embrace of lovers, at other times a struggle to the death. Despite her independence, Misia throughout her life was in search of tyrants. To be tyrannized was, for her, a requisite of love. In the silent young Chanel she had recognized, with uncanny intuition, the woman who was to join her father, Edwards, Diaghilev, and Sert to complete the quintet of *monstres*

sacrés that formed the deepest attachments of her life. In her relations with
each of them, there was a power struggle. To captivate, to disarm, to tyran-
nize the tyrant were among her most urgent needs.

In Paul Morand's book, *L'Allure de Chanel*, he recalls Coco telling him
about her first trip to Venice with her usual combination of vivacity and
malice. Travelling in Sert's automobile with its diplomatic license—a guarantee of privilege he always managed to have—was festive. The car bulged
with the pictures, statues, Capo di Monte porcelain, rare books, and crates of
oranges that the affluent bohemians collected as they motored about. *"Ce
dîner est à môa, Madmachelle,"* Sert would say in the Spanish accent Coco
imitated so killingly. *Grand seigneur* that he was, he paid for everything and
left huge tips everywhere. He insisted on ordering magnificent wines and
lavish meals even though they all ate and drank sparingly. They would drive
miles out of their way looking for an inn Sert remembered, and when they
could not find it, he would turn a fiasco into a feast by buying a suckling pig
and roasting it at the side of the road. "You must admit that Jojo makes
everyone else seem dull," Misia said. Coco agreed. Untiringly, Sert showed
them the art he loved so much, and he seemed to know everything: the lives
of the saints, the engravings Dürer made at fourteen, the travels of Antonello
da Messina, the technical tricks of Caracci and Tintoretto. In the middle of
an inspiring morning in a museum, Misia, suddenly bored, would say, "Let's
get away from all this junk, these Botticellis and Leonardos, and do some
serious shopping." Then Chanel would complain that Sert "sneakily put
deposits on all the objects he was mad about" in antique shops to prevent
her from buying them. But even this underhanded maneuver was training for
her sharp, acquisitive eye.

Sert was "an enormous gnome," Chanel told Morand, "who carried in his
hump, as if it were a magician's trunk, both gold and garbage, extremely bad
taste and exquisite discernment, diamonds and shit, kindness and sadism . . .
good qualities and faults on a dizzying scale." All the same, Chanel thought
Sert a great gentleman. He was never petty; gossip bored him; he was extravagant and immoral, like a man of the Renaissance. Even his colossal frescoes,
she felt, did not express the full scale of his personality. Always a realist,
Chanel did not bother to conceal her contempt for Sert's painting. "I know
you loathe it," Misia whispered, "but don't let him know." Nor did Chanel
make a secret of her physical repulsion for Sert. "A hairy monkey," she
called him, "round-shouldered, with a dyed beard . . . who never bathed,"

and who smelled more like a Renaissance man than the fastidious creator of perfumes would have liked. One night they arrived in Rome exhausted and ready to sink into the comforts of the Grand Hotel. No, no, they must see Rome by moonlight, Sert insisted. It was ineffably beautiful and much more important than a bath or a rest. Standing in the Colosseum, he enchanted the two women with descriptions of imaginary fêtes he would give among the ruins that he called the skeleton of the city, "just as bones are the skeleton of a face." Then, with macabre Spanish relish, he turned to Chanel. "You," he said, examining her closely, "you, with your good bones will make a beautiful corpse."

When they first met, Misia was in her mid-forties, Chanel ten years younger. By then Misia's pout of dissatisfaction had turned to clear-eyed pessimism, her impertinent irreverence to occasional cruelty. The girl who "did not know what money was" had learned, through Diaghilev and Sert, to manipulate it. She had developed her taste for dramatic incident and preferred an all-out explosion, any time, to the tedium of tranquillity. Her fear of boredom had become so strong that she felt it lying in wait even when she was most amused. Restless when she had guests, she would suddenly appear dressed for another party, and say, "Don't leave. I'll be right back." As befitted a queen of Paris, she had become a law unto herself. Unlike Diaghilev, Chanel, and Sert, she had no career, no all-consuming interest. But between slavic bouts of indolence—she spent her mornings in bed, receiving friends—she was all activity. And she still inspired love. Among her new young admirers were the poets Max Jacob, Pierre Reverdy, and Alexis Léger, and the writer-diplomat Paul Morand. Morand—whose father, the director of the *Ecole des Arts Décoratifs*, had been a friend of Misia's father—was a dapper, handsome young man-about-town. His wartime diary, *Journal d'un Attaché d'Ambassade*, contains many worldly vignettes of Misia:

November 4, 1916

Lunched, quai Voltaire at Misia's; Misia in a light-colored dress, among her rock crystal and her lacquers, in her somewhat precious *rococo* setting. She's just returned from Italy and Spain. She describes Venice. Everyone has fled; only the working people remain. Daily bombings, announced by an ear-splitting siren. *Lucia di Lammermoor* being played at Florian's behind blackout curtains. The orchestra stops and people take shelter in sand-bag trenches prepared in advance. She visited Mme. Fortuny in the old Fortuny palace. A bomb fell near them and demolished Salviati, but not the hideous mosaic façade, which remained intact. "Publicity for Salviati," Misia says, "everybody will have a house built of Salviati mosaics." She has seen d'Annunzio, who has not been wounded at all, but suffered a detached retina during an airplane flight.

Misia's niece, the young Godebska . . . is leaving for London to visit the Arnold Bennetts.

On November 22, after lunching with the Aga Khan, Morand went to see Misia, who was not feeling well. "As it bores her to be ill at home, she has moved to the Meurice. The Meurice is a bizarre caravansary where the Rostands, [the Maharaja of] Kapurthala, and the Italian ambassador are all staying, side by side."

November 25, 1916

Went to see Misia in her room at the Meurice; very 1895, very Renoir, with her ample bosom, her hair covering her forehead and piled up on top, and picking her teeth with a scissors. Her brother, Godebski, was there with his daughter. . . .

Misia recalled this story from Wilde: a sailor went each day to the sea and, on returning, said that he had seen the Sirens. One day he returned and said nothing; for this time he had seen them.

"J.-E. Blanche and Gide," Misia says, "are both very stingy. They each make fun of the other's avarice and tell the same story (an omelet that each succeeded in getting the other to pay for), and each attributes it to the other.

Misia says: "I think Léger was in love with me. Hélène Berthelot assures me that it's so.* He kissed my arms, and the night before a trip to Spain, did not want to leave."

---

* Perhaps Madame Berthelot was not exaggerating. When Léger left for China to work in the French legation, he wrote Misia: "Dear friend whom I love and whom I

November 27, 1916

"To live in a hotel," says Misia, "what a dream!" And pointing at a tiny green plant, "Would I ever have thought of having that at home? Would I ever have thought of owning a palm tree?" A knock at the door. An old manservant enters.

"I'm here to clean the palm tree, Madame."

Misia, the nomad, is exultant: "See! Would I have a special man at home to clean palm trees?"

December 13, 1916

To amuse her, took to Misia's yesterday the lion cub that Hélène* bought at a charity sale. I find Misia in bed at the Meurice. I put the lion on the white velvet quilt and he roars. Misia, screaming, emerges from the sheets in her nightgown. In the next room her dogs, mad with fear, jump to the ceiling. The terrorized lion cub forgets himself on the bed; an appalling smell fills the overheated sickroom. Lucien Daudet, very calm, says, "All the corpses his ancestors have eaten are coming out!" . . . "He's ruined my twelve-hundred-franc quilt," says Misia. "Paul brought this lion just to have it make *caca* on me!" And we give it to the lift boy, who very proudly takes it down to the Meurice cloakroom.

I leave with my lion and take him back to the Ritz. Hélène is not pleased. "My lion doesn't smell as bad as hers," she says drily, meaning Sert.†

---

shall not see again for such a long time, why was I not able to drive with you along the roads of France!" He spoke of all the infinite sweetness of his feeling for her, adding: "Tell me, Misia, that you will come to Peking one day and we shall go to the cinema with Jacques-Emile Blanche, with Cocteau, with Guillaume Apollinaire, with Boy, with anyone you wish, provided that you are there, Misia, who come from no place on earth."

* The Rumanian Princess Soutzo, a friend of Proust. She later became Morand's wife.

† In 1975, when we were leaving the Morand house in the avenue Charles-Floquet, Monsieur Morand, after describing at length the extraordinary quality of Misia's charm, pointed to a shadowy corner of the vast, dimly lit room where a barely distinguishable figure lay on a chaise longue. "Too bad my wife is blind and deaf," he said. "As she loathed Misia, she would have had some very interesting things to tell you."

On Christmas day Morand "lunched with Misia; at her bedside Loche Radziwill,* Jean Cocteau, and little Mimi Godebska." Two days later Morand and Misia spent a few moments at the Alhambra music hall. "We watched a contest between the champion woman orange packer from California and the champion builder of orange crates, presented by a burly impresario with a megaphone. 'The invasion of the American style is beginning,' said Misia, adding sardonically, 'Very promising.'"

At this time Misia was shuttling back and forth between the Meurice and her apartment in the quai Voltaire. For one thing she loved living in hotels, and for another coal was rationed and it was difficult to heat her apartment. Despite the fuel shortage, she gave a New Year's Day party at her apartment to usher in the year 1917. Morand came, although he had a fever and headache.

January 2, 1917

I dragged myself about all night, *chez* Misia, who was dressed up like a Christmas tree. Charming party: the older people in the red dining room, the young in the room with the nativity figures. Retinger . . . Jean Cocteau, Mimi Godebska, Valentine Gross at our table. Jean Cocteau is tipsy and pounds on the table shouting, "We'll get them!" Someone says, "Now let the year of victory end and the year of peace begin!" In a word, very low morale. . . . Then Cocteau and Saglio-Drésa have a violent fight about the Cubists and turn their backs on one another.

From Misia's at seven in the morning I go straight to work at the Quai, where I bury myself in New Year's telegrams from all our embassies.

---

* The Polish Prince Léon Radziwill, married to his cousin Dolly Radziwill, one of the five women Misia said she most admired. The others were the English Marchioness of Ripon, the Belgian Comtesse Greffulhe, the French Comtesse de Chevigné, and the Venetian Contessa Morosini.

April 10, 1917

Went to see Misia. She is in bed, buried in pink pillows and lace, sick with a stalactitic cold; even her colds are *rococo*. What I admire in Misia is that *joie de vivre* always concealed behind a mask of ill-humor; that perfect poise, even in moments of despair. And then Misia is Misia, someone with no equal and, as Proust says, a monument. Misia will take her place in the history of taste, of Parisian art, more important than all the Deffands and all those silly women of the eighteenth century.

Misia has the full bosom of the statues with which her father, the sculptor, decorated the roof of the Monte Carlo casino.

She speaks enthusiastically about the Russian Revolution, which she sees as an enormous ballet. Bakst, she says, turns out to be the brother-in-law of the minister of war, Diaghilev is related to Rodzianko, who has wired him in Rome to offer him the [ministry of] fine arts. The whole Gorky set—Argutinsky, Benois, Bakst—steps to the forefront! Stravinsky, who is in Rome, has been commissioned to write a new national anthem based on the "Volga Boatmen." . . .

Misia states that her family's vast properties in Poland have been confiscated and that she is having Maître Clunet, the great international lawyer, prepare a claim to regain the land in case of an eventual division of the crown properties.

She says the Tsar has been robbed . . . deprived of everything . . . that the Revolution is the triumph of Rasputin, who always said, "If I disappear, you will disappear. . . ." In the middle of her speech Sert arrives. . . . He has bought all the balloons from a vendor in the Tuileries. Overjoyed, Misia forgets her cold and stands in her bed, plays with the multicolored bunch of balloons, ties her griffon to the string to see if he'll float in the air. But the dog is too heavy. Upon which Boy, Madame de Villa Urrutia's woolly gray puppy, jumps at the balloons, tries to bite them, breaks one, and runs away, howling.

April 29, 1917

Lunched at Cocteau's with J.-E. Blanche, who has just arrived from Barcelona. He speaks of "Sert's enormous fortune" with that childish admiration he has for the rich.

On June 15, an exceptionally hot evening, Misia gave an early dinner party on the terrace of her quai Voltaire apartment. The guests were going on to Morand's to hear Cocteau read his latest work, *Le Cap de Bonne-Espérance*. Dinner was served by Misia's Polish butler, who was dressed in white, a novel idea. It was a town picnic: blue-and-white checked table-cloths and even a bird, Misia's blue macaw, screaming at the sight of his dinner of buttered bread. The guests were given lobsters on silver platters. Misia maintained her rosy Renoir look, fresh and summery in a pink linen dress. Eugenia Errazuriz, whose chic was resolutely more advanced, looked more like a Van Dongen in her blue straw hat, her dress of black-and-white checked mattress ticking, and a slash of carmine on her lips. Sert arrived disgruntled. One of his paintings had gone for four thousand francs at a charity auction, while a Boldini was sold for three times as much. "Let us go to table, Madame," he said grumpily to Misia. When the ladies discussed the new fashion for bobbed hair, Misia said it was not for her: "What suits me, you know, is to look like a housemaid."

The news of the evening was Misia's announcement that she had sold the remaining fifteen years of the lease on her apartment to an American for forty thousand francs, an impressive sum in those days. "He's mad!" she said. "Besides, I was a fool to take a twenty-five-year lease. I should have known I'd be fed up with it long before that. But every time I do something foolish, it works out marvellously." (Misia soon took another apartment on the quai Voltaire, "with a better view," she wrote Stravinsky.) Before Misia and her friends went on to hear Cocteau, they gave him a thorough Parisian going-over. "He feels the need to please everyone," Misia complained, "Picasso, Madame de Chevigné, the Marine sharp-shooters—he's wasting the best years of his life trying to please instead of trying to displease." (Misia had a point. It was the trap that Picasso and Stravinsky, the two geniuses Cocteau most admired, never fell into.) Morand recorded the arrival of the guests at his apartment in the Palais Royal: "Valentine Gross, with her wide-open eyes, her face painted like a doll's, her hair smoothly parted in the center; Edith de Beaumont . . . ravishing, looking like Titian's *Man with a Glove*; Etienne de Beaumont, his hands crossed over his stomach, and then Porel, then Gautier-Vignal. Sultry. Not a breath of air, not a sound."

And so the reading began. *Le Cap de Bonne-Espérance* was a long series of poems, a memorial tribute to the handsome pilot Roland Garros, for whom Cocteau had felt a romantic attachment. Misia too had been attracted to the war ace who was entrusted with the air defense of Paris. Between Garros' dangerous missions, Cocteau had often brought the young hero to see Misia. With a calm, sad smile, the daredevil flier would lie under the piano while he listened to Misia play. Once she asked him to take her up in his plane. "Dressed in the most peculiar getup," Misia wrote, "I took a seat next to him in one of those fragile machines that could accurately be called deathtraps. He wanted to impress me with his aerial skills by showing me all kinds of loop-the-loops, and I have never been so frightened in my life. The adventure left me green with terror; it took me several days to get over it." Shortly afterward Garros was captured and spent over two years as a prisoner in Germany. In a sense this was fortunate, as the life expectancy of ace pilots, once they began active duty, was estimated at three weeks. After a fantastic escape, Garros returned to Paris physically shattered. Aviation had made enormous strides during his imprisonment, and he was out of his depth. His friends begged him not to return to the fighting. "Stop Garros at all costs," Cocteau wrote Misia. "Tell him we shall need heroes in peacetime, too." "But it was useless," Misia wrote. "For a long time I had seen the mark of death on his face. He was killed on his third flight."

When Misia moved out of her apartment that summer, she gave her aquarium to the Berthelots. Morand found Monsieur Berthelot installing it in his salon: "The water was spilling all over the Chinese rug and down into the garden. Misia is to bring the fish tomorrow. Berthelot on his hands and knees mopping up the rug. 'The role of the diplomat is to mop things up,' he says."

Worlds removed from Paul Morand's mundane preoccupations and his smart snobbishness was the poet Pierre Reverdy. Alternately attracted and repelled by the glittering world of the rich and the great, he once wrote, "Life in society is one huge adventure in piracy and cannot be successful without a great deal of conniving." Misia knew this only too well. And like Reverdy, she also knew the rewards of friendship with someone who strove for spiritual and artistic grace. Among her young writer friends it was perhaps Reverdy—sad, mystic, voluble, and impassioned—to whom Misia felt closest and whose work she most admired. In 1917 Reverdy founded a little magazine called *Nord-Sud* after the métro line that ran like an artery between Montmartre and Montparnasse, the two artistic centers of Paris. *Nord-Sud* printed the works of the new art movements, Dada and Surrealism. Its pages were illustrated by André Derain and Fernand Léger, by Juan Gris and Georges Braque. It published Max Jacob and Guillaume Apollinaire and introduced Louis Aragon, André Breton, and Tristan Tzara.

Misia was moved by Reverdy's modesty; he was, as he said, "the one who only came to see, not to be seen"; and she was taken by his dark gypsy eyes and his gleaming white teeth. But it was what she called "the radiant beauty that never dies," his Mallarméan use of silence, his haunted fantasy that made her feel she must help finance his short-lived though inspired review. It was like the early days of the *Revue Blanche*. But it was not like Misia just to give money; she went further, talked it up, and asked her friends to subscribe. She also sent him a monthly check that enabled him to make long retreats at the Abbey of Solesmes. In gratitude Reverdy copied out and bound a small volume of his poetry for her. And just as she had done with Renoir, she paid the poet the largest sum she could persuade him to accept. It was an endearing kind of generosity rare among artists' friends, who tend to expect a reduction in price, a *prix d'ami*, as one of the reassuring privileges of friendship. Like Diaghilev, Reverdy respected Misia's artistic judgment.

> I was anxious to know your feelings about my book [he wrote]. I am happy that it moved you and that the life from which it springs and the sincerity which—in the absence of talent—has given it birth should have found an echo in the life and in the sincerity which are yours.
>
> From your letter I see that your life, however blessed with pockets of light, is not without its dark colors and layers of bitterness.

Reverdy's first sensitive, lyric letters to Misia are filled with his admiration and gratitude. Later, surely more than a little in love with her, the poet wrote from his retreat in Solesmes:

> I love you so much, I think of you with so much tenderness. You cannot imagine how much or in what way. Sometimes one of your

phrases, a word you have spoken to me, strikes my heart, and then this sweetness is mixed with the bitterness of not being able to embrace you, to put my hand on yours, of not being able to see you.

How often have I cursed the obstacles that separate me from you: my extreme sensibility, the social differences, my stupidity amidst the people among whom I should have to bear to see you live. You have sometimes reproached me for not coming to see you more often. But you did not realize that I would have wanted to have you all to myself and that you would have had to sacrifice everything, all at once.

Dear friend, so tenderly loved, know that into my life, which never ceases to be a silent torture, you have brought something meaningful—happiness, and also suffering—for it is true that one does not really love without suffering and you are among those whom I love to the point of suffering.

I often miss you. My arms, my lips, and my heart miss you. You are a part of my life. The blue part.

Misia, who was fond of saying, "I've had only husbands, never lovers," introduced Reverdy to Chanel. Chanel, who had only lovers, never husbands, found no difficulty in adding him to her list. Theirs was a real love affair, unlike the poet's fantasy love for Misia.

PART FIVE
Madame Sert

Overleaf, Misia Sert, c. 1925

The twenties were born prematurely with the end of the First World War. France, which had been reduced to a bloody battlefield, now became a place of celebration. Like a ship in peril it tossed overboard whatever baggage seemed unnecessary. In life as in art, old respected values were the first to go. New conventions were born. A certain savage frenzy, offspring of the war's brutality, replaced decorum. Manners became freer. The clever insult replaced the gallant compliment. Dope became fashionable. American and Soviet influences began to shape French behavior and thinking. The flag of sexual freedom was hoisted. Isadora Duncan had long before kicked off her shoes to celebrate one aspect of this liberation, while Diaghilev and Gertrude Stein had lent their not inconsiderable weight to another. And Cocteau, the prince of homosexuals, was now the loquacious symbol of what had once been the love that dared not speak its name. Always a little behind the avant-garde but ahead of society, Cocteau in the twenties was the epitome of the advanced artist as homosexual hero. His chic bag of magician's tricks seduced everyone, from Oxford undergraduates to aging Parisian duchesses. Picasso, always ready with his picador's *banderillo*, could not resist saying, "Cocteau was born with a pleat in his trousers. He is becoming terribly famous: you will find his works at every hairdresser's."

Bernard Shaw, when asked to name the two most important living women, unhesitatingly answered, Curie and Chanel. And he was not far wrong, for Chanel in an incredibly short time had become the fashion wonder of the world. By divesting women of their full-blown sails and turning them into sleek little yachts, she had shown them another channel to freedom. Shorn of their mysterious trappings, they looked breastless, hipless, and, with their short hair and pullovers, as free as adolescent boys. In art, the image had already been taken apart and put back together in new and sometimes mystifying ways. Debussy, Stravinsky, and Schoenberg had done much the same for music. And now Diaghilev, the genius synthesizer, daringly combined the new elements of art, music, and dance to make delectable, and often moving, spectacles for the general public. It was he who helped popularize the talents of Picasso, Braque, Matisse, Chirico, Derain, and Miro, to say nothing of a formidable list of composers and choreographers. Once again Paris was the liveliest city in the world. Everyone wanted to live there: Gertrude Stein and James Joyce; Pablo Picasso and Juan Gris; Max Ernst, Marc Chagall, and Sergei Prokofiev; the

Rumanian Constantin Brancusi, the Dutchman Kees Van Dongen, and the Cuban Francis Picabia. Struggling artists, rich Americans, South American millionaires, Russian aristocrats in exile—all made Paris their new home.

A home away from home for many of them was a night club called Le Boeuf sur le Toit. One of Cocteau's most diverting inspirations, it was named after a tango-ballet he and the composer Darius Milhaud had created for the Théâtre des Arts. Noisy, small, and amusing, it was the perfect *club sans club*. "Ain't She Sweet," "Hallelujah," "Constantinople"— tinny, perky, and sad—were mixed with Bach, Mozart, and Johann Strauss by the inimitably light pianists Wiener and Doucet, who played like angels and looked like Mutt and Jeff. A Dada song called "Eat Chocolate, Drink Cow" and another simply called "Dada, Dada" made for a deliciously smart din.

Strangers spoke to strangers. The club was there for everyone, and everyone came: ravishing women, poets, musicians, art dealers, painters, journalists, pederasts, transvestites, theatre people, the grand, the rich. Through the cigarette smoke one could glimpse the new Paris. There were Arthur Rubinstein's frizzy head and Marie Laurencin's smart new bob; Picasso in a red sweater, Satie in his stiff collar and blue serge suit; the Prince of Wales with his girl friends, Maurice Sachs (the Genet of the twenties) with his boy friends, and the painter Pascin with his black friends. Gide, the observer, came in his black cape; Cocteau wittily played the drums with the black jazz band, while the dancer Serge Lifar played footsie under the table. There were Etienne de Beaumont with his sleek hair and exaggerated gestures, his wife Edith looking like Joan of Arc, the Princesse de Polignac looking like Dante, and little Lucien Daudet looking like Beatrice; the teen-aged poet Raymond Radiguet with his monocle being looked over by Diaghilev with *his* monocle. There were the young composers: good-natured Francis Poulenc roaring with laughter; cherubic Georges Auric with his sharp tongue; Germaine Tailleferre, fresh and pretty; Stravinsky, short and dapper. Picabia described his hundred automobiles. Pierre Reverdy with his brooding eyes out-talked a chic and grinning Chanel. Yvonne Printemps' tinkling laugh could be heard, as could the cavernous voice of Sert telling his extravagant stories. This was the new Paris family, and Misia, as she had always done, chose her favorites. To the old intimates—Diaghilev, Cocteau, and Chanel—she added Poulenc, Auric, Marie Laurencin, Serge Lifar, and the unsavory but gifted writer Maurice Sachs.

The year 1920 was a signal year in Misia's life, for on August 2 she and Sert were finally married. It was an animated, very Spanish wedding celebrated in the dreary, if fashionable, Church of Saint Roch in the rue du Faubourg St. Honoré. The twice-divorced bride was forty-eight, the bachelor groom forty-five. They had lived together for twelve years. Skeptical but optimistic, Misia listened to Sert's solemn vow of eternal fidelity, although fidelity, she well knew, was not his forte. In the words of his biographer, Alberto del Castillo, Sert was "accustomed to render fervent, intense, and multiple homage to the cult of feminine beauty, always and without interruption throughout the entire course of his life." Sert, too, was optimistic. "She is the only woman capable of understanding me and putting up with me," the incorrigible Don Juan said with childish pride. And indeed, for twelve years Misia had watched his *petites amies* come and go. She had taught herself—with some bitterness, as Reverdy had observed—to disregard his little infidelities, even to view them with grudging admiration. They proved he was "*un vrai* he-man," as she liked to call him. Besides, she was convinced that she knew how to handle him. Proust, about whom Misia said, "He liked me only because I was rich," sent Misia an exalted if ironical letter of congratulations.

Chère Madame,

I was very touched that you took the trouble to write and tell me of this marriage which has the majestic beauty of something wonderfully unnecessary. What wife could Sert have found, and you what husband, so predestined, so uniquely deserving of one another? I knew Sert when I believe he did not yet know you, and I thought: this, and this, and this, might please him. But, all this is combined and elevated to the ideal only in Madame Edwards. She is, for me, fated to be his wife. And he, her husband. That is why I never saw either of you without speaking of the other. You tell me that you have brought St. Roch into all this. La Scuola di San Rocco brought you together. It is only just that St. Roch has blessed you, as well as countless others, among whom no one has a warmer admiration, for you and for Sert, than your respectfully devoted

Marcel Proust

I was very happy that your beloved Poland has been saved.

In her earlier marriages Misia's youthful beauty had made her indispensable to her husbands' happiness. Now in middle age Misia had learned to make herself indispensable in other ways. Through clever manipulation and a certain faith in Sert's work—who but he, after all, was painting frescoes and decorating cathedrals?—she had helped to make him a great international success. In so doing, she had caught him in a golden web of favors rendered. They were a perfect team: he the artist as *grand seigneur*, she the companion of his art, the entrepreneur selling his work. As early as 1913 Jacques-Emile Blanche had watched the team in operation and recorded his impressions. Blanche was in London to paint portraits of Thomas Hardy and Henry James and to help Sir Saxton Noble decorate his houses. To his chagrin, Blanche found that the Serts were in town, working the same rich vein.

Blanche had unsettled the Noble household—a tactical error in his wife's opinion—by introducing Karsavina to Sir Saxton, who took to haunting the ballerina's dressing room. Madame Blanche was even more upset when her husband told her he was lunching with Sert. According to Blanche's memoirs, she said, "Sert? Another of your blunders! Sert and Misia, too, no doubt? They're at Claridge's . . . plotting and planning again, looking for places to decorate, for commissions in England. Fortunately the Nobles have nothing to decorate." But Madame Blanche underestimated the Serts. It was not long, Blanche wrote, before he heard from them again. "At 2:30 José-Maria and Misia telephone. They're at Kent House with Saxton and Blomfield [his architect], measuring, plotting." Moreover, the Serts adroitly disarmed the Blanches by persuading Sir Saxton to arrange a gallery for Blanche's paintings above the music room at Kent House.

The Serts' "plotting and planning" bore fruit—and not only with the murals he executed for the Saxton Nobles. Commissions began to pour in. As Misia said with immodest accuracy, "From the time we met, his career rose prodigiously." The walls of the rich began to luxuriate with hundreds of Sert's elephants, camels, and mules, dwarfs and Herculean giants, acrobats and blackamoors, nude gods and goddesses under palm trees and parasols, popes, bishops, and cardinals, mythological and biblical scenes, lanterns and billowing curtains: all the trappings of Tiepolo, Veronese, Goya, and Velasquez—but alas, without their quality. The theatricality of the work prompted Degas, when he visited Sert's sumptuous studio, to say after long examination, "How very Spanish—and in such a quiet street!" But no one could outdo Forain, whose talent for disparagement almost surpassed his gifts as a painter. Asked how the overblown murals could be transported, he said, "Don't worry. They're collapsible." Not surprisingly, the Montmartre and Montparnasse painters looked down their noses at Sert's work and his worldly success. "Sert paints with gold and *merde*" was an often repeated quip that many were happy to take credit for.

But there were others who thought that with Sert, the golden age of painting had returned. Gide, Proust, and above all, Claudel admired him. Gide hoped to have Sert as the designer of a projected staging of his *Perséphone*. Proust admired his costume designs and visited his atelier when he needed details for a description of a great painter's studio. And Claudel collaborated with him in the theatre and published ecstatic appreciations of his paintings. Sert's works remain impressive in their vastness, their sequential insistence, and, in the best of them, their grand fantasy. If the color is poor, the draughtsmanship is masterly, and the problem of handling large spaces is wonderfully solved. Perhaps most admirable was Sert's determination to pursue his own vision of art. Never did he consider joining the avant-garde bandwagon or deserting his own ideal of beauty. His works suited the rich by lending an imposing air to their vast salons in Barcelona and Buenos Aires, in Paris and London, in Palm Beach and Long Island. Shades of Cyprien Godebski!

Through the years Sert carried out commissions for Lady Ripon and Sir Philip Sassoon in England, the Errazurizes in Argentina, the Beckers in Belgium, the Rothschilds, Wendels, and Polignacs in Paris, the Cosdens and Mackays in America. All these and many others ordered frescoes for their ballrooms, pavilions, music rooms, and imposing staircases. Sert's patrons valued his works so highly that they tended to transport them—though his murals were hardly as collapsible as Forain claimed—from continent to continent. Charles Deering, who had commissioned decorations for his castle in Sitges near Barcelona, shipped them to his house in Chicago in 1924. The loss of this "national treasure" was violently debated in the Spanish chamber of deputies. When King Alfonso abdicated, the Harry Phippses bought the twenty-eight large panels he had commissioned. The Phippses moved them from Spain to Long Island, while Mrs. Harrison Williams moved her Serts from Long Island to Capri.

As his reputation grew, Sert decorated public buildings: the town hall in Barcelona, the Palace of the League of Nations in Geneva, and in New York, Rockefeller Center and the grand ballroom of the Waldorf-Astoria Hotel, which was named the Sert Room.* "It's not everyone who has a room named after him during his lifetime," Sert said, adding with appealing irony, "of course, people only look at the pictures between sips of champagne." At the time of his negotiations with the Waldorf, Sert was entertaining some clients at the Hotel Ritz in Barcelona. After dinner Sert the raconteur was interrupted by an agitated waiter who announced a long-distance call from New York. Calmly stirring his coffee, Sert went on with his stories. Several cups of coffee later, and after much prodding from the *maître d'hôtel*, Sert excused himself and strolled to the telephone booth, where he coolly agreed to paint the Waldorf murals for a hundred and fifty thousand dollars—the equivalent of over half a million dollars today. It was possibly the highest fee any artist had ever received for wall decorations. But Sert's frescoes for the Cathedral of Vich formed the cornerstone of his life. It was a project that occupied him for almost forty years. Begun before he met Misia, this work was disrupted by political upheavals in Spain twenty years later, then largely destroyed by bombing during the Spanish Civil War. Heroically, indomitably, with almost religious fervor, Sert began all over again. He was still at work in Vich when he died.

Shortly after their wedding, the Serts went off to Venice, taking Chanel along as Misia's *dame de compagnie*. Each day they joined Diaghilev to meet with the international set that flocked to the Piazza San Marco as faithfully as the local pigeons. But being more adventuresome than most, the Serts did not restrict their travels to Venice's fashionable outdoor salon. They went to England and Switzerland. They drove through Rumania and visited Constantinople. They cruised the Mediterranean and admired the sights in Tunis. "How sorry we are that we can't go to Egypt with you!"

---

* Long a landmark, the Sert murals were removed in the 1970s and given to a Spanish dealer who was willing to pay the cost of dismantling them. He shipped them to Barcelona where they were sold for a huge sum.

reads a note signed "Picasso, his wife, and his son," with a postscript inviting the Serts to join them in Dinard. Sert made several trips to South America, and in 1924 he and Misia made their first crossing to New York, where the Wildenstein Gallery had a tremendously successful show of his work. Sert went to Spain three or four times a year, often taking Misia with him.

MISIA TO COCTEAU

> Hotel Casino
> Alhambra Palace
> Granada
> September 1st.

Dear Jean,

At last a word from you, from your star to mine, for Andalusia in the month of August lies somewhere between Africa and the moon. Nothing can give you any idea of our automobile trip—a kind of sublime catastrophe. No one has ever been able to describe this country, which is the strangest and the most special I have ever seen. Don't know if you would like it—you're too French, but all the same! . . . The exaltation and the union of this sky and this land—blessed and cursed at the same time.

The Alhambra is particularly moving for other reasons, and awesome for the general beauty one sees there. I'm in all the photographs as Schéhérazade to Serge, who is passing through. The bells and the scents make one swoon with voluptuousness, and nowhere else is there such a sense of the lust for life and its terrifying joys.

I am unable to calm my nerves or to accustom them to this paroxysm, and my eyes constantly fill with tears. . . . No dancing in Granada. The gypsies are rather fake, and music is heard only in the distance.

After their marriage the Serts took their first apartment together: a suite of rooms in the Hôtel Meurice overlooking the treetops of the Tuileries, though Sert kept his studio in the rue Barbet-de-Jouy. Just as his paintings were inspired by Veronese and Velasquez, his extravagant way of life was modeled after Rubens. Like Rubens, Sert filled his home with precious objects and his studio with hardworking assistants who realized his sketches and shipped the results all over the world. Those Parisians for whom interior decoration is the eighth and liveliest art marvelled at Sert's decor. At the Meurice and in his later apartments, his willful sense of disproportion worked startlingly well. A Greek marble weighing half a ton would be placed on a fragile chimneypiece, and huge oriental vases seemed to crush the gilt-encrusted black lacquer armoires they rested on. Massive pieces of rock crystal were placed in front of fireplaces to refract the light in magical ways. Rock-crystal chandeliers illuminated tables of tortoiseshell or malachite and elaborately carved Louis XV consoles bearing ancient Chinese terra-cotta animals that Sert had somehow managed to smuggle out of the Forbidden City.

It was all rich, original, and staggeringly grand: an Ali Baba's cave, as Misia admiringly said. But all that glittered at the Serts' was not necessarily gold. An El Greco of doubtful lineage prompted the remark, "If it's not real, it's more beautiful than if it were," from Cocteau, whose special province was the blurring and blending of the real and the unreal. Possessed by his possessions, Sert took to storing the overflow in warehouses all over Europe: furniture, candelabra, paintings, *objets d'art* of gold, marble, ivory, and velvet; even a rare collection of Neapolitan nativity figures. Misia, on the other hand, tended to give superfluous objects to friends or, with her antique dealer's instinct, sell them to rich Americans, carelessly stuffing the profits in drawers or behind Sert's priceless books.

In the 1920s Misia was at the zenith of her powers. Loved, feared, and respected, she had become an elder statesman in the Diaghilev circle; and like elder statesmen, she had an aura of other times. Certainly she was not a typical twenties girl despite her long cigarette holders and her strings of pearls knotted below the waist. Not for her the flat-chested flapper's slouch; her erect and noble carriage, the still-radiant complexion, the graceful gestures of a woman accustomed to admiration—all were reminiscent of an earlier day, of corseted ladies in flowered hats. Misia was a liaison between the Belle Epoque and the twenties. As private opinion in those days was more powerful than public criticism, she was cultivated, especially in avant-garde circles, in much the way that critics are now. For Misia was an arbiter of taste. In 1917 she had gone to an evening of short plays organized by the actor Pierre Bertin and his pianist wife, Marcelle Meyer. The program included Max Jacob's *La Femme Fatale*, Satie's *Le Piège de Méduse*, for which the composer wrote both text and music, *Les Pelicans* by Cocteau's protégé, the fifteen-year-old poet Raymond Radiguet, and *Le Gendarme Incompris*, a joint work of Radiguet and Cocteau. In the role of Baron Méduse, Bertin made himself up to look like Satie and did such a telling impersonation that everyone in the select audience roared with laughter except the touchy master of Arcueil himself.*

Misia, equally touchy, was offended by the irreverent spoof of Mallarmé's *Ecclésiastique* in *Le Gendarme Incompris*. Jean Hugo remembers that a certain unfortunate Mademoiselle Le Chevrel was about to applaud when she caught Misia's pitiless look of disapproval. "She understood immediately and her hands, instead of applauding, fluttered about her temples to indicate that the play was mad."† Though Misia disapproved of the play, her sharp ears did not miss the exuberant charm of the incidental music by the eighteen-year-old Francis Poulenc. She passed the word along, and eventually Diaghilev commissioned Poulenc to write the ballet which became *Les Biches*. Poulenc was a member of the group of young composers christened *Les Six* in 1920. How they got this name is recorded by the composer Darius Milhaud in his memoirs *Notes Without Music*.

> After a concert at the Salle Huyghens, at which Bertin sang . . . and the Capelle Quartet played my Fourth Quartet, the critic Henri Collet published a chronicle in *Comoedia* entitled "Five Russians and Six Frenchmen." Quite arbitrarily he had chosen six names: Auric, Durey, Honegger, Poulenc, Tailleferre, and my own, merely because

---

* Almost sixty years later Bertin, who adored Satie, told us that it had taken months to repair the damage. He also sang for us some Satie songs he had introduced, performing them with a dazzling sense of style.

† The composer Henri Sauguet told us that when he had his first performance in Paris, Misia, sitting in the front row, made a rude, *c'est la barbe*, gesture of disapproval which cowed the entire audience. Two days later when she was seated next to him at a lunch party, she apologized. "I was naughty with you," she said, and turning on the full battery of her charm, won his affection for life.

we knew one another, were good friends, and had figured on the same programs; quite irrespective of our different temperaments and wholly dissimilar characters. . . . Collet's article excited such worldwide interest that the "Group of Six" was launched, and willy-nilly I formed part of it.

Les Six were protected by Satie, publicized by Cocteau, and pushed by Misia. She interested Diaghilev in three of them, with the result that his company performed ballets with scores by Milhaud and Auric, as well as Poulenc, in 1924—all with choreography by Nijinsky's sister Bronislava.

Georges Auric was the child prodigy of the group. At twelve he had written the first article ever published on Satie's music. Impressed by the unknown critic's perceptive analysis, Satie wrote for an appointment. Georges answered the door of his parents' apartment dressed in his first pair of long trousers. Satie, who loved children, beamed, patted him on the cheek, and asked for Monsieur Auric the critic. *"C'est moi, le critique,"* said the pudgy little fellow—and a devoted friendship began. From then on Satie lunched with the Auric family once a week and regularly downed an entire bottle of brandy, to the child-composer's startled admiration. By the time Auric was sixteen, Misia and Cocteau had arranged for him to play for Diaghilev. During the First World War, when performances of Wagner were forbidden in France on patriotic grounds, the boy wrote to Misia (as one anti-Wagnerian to another) on music students' stationery with a brooding picture of Wagner at the top.

22 December 1915

Madame,

First of all, please excuse this probably very useless letter and my permitting myself to trouble you in this way.

But since you were kind enough to enable me to play my *Noces de Gamache* for Monsieur Diaghilev a month ago, I venture to ask you (on the off chance) if it would be absolutely impossible to see him again for a moment.

I can well imagine that he is very busy with the coming performance and do not wish to bother you.

But since Cocteau, I believe, is not here at this moment, I don't hesitate to send you these *few* words, for which you will forgive me, *n'est-ce-pas*, while you admire the *Hun* who is *thinking* in his corner up above.

Once again, all my thanks for your warm welcome recently.

I send you my respectful greetings,
Georges Auric

The very quality that irritated Stravinsky—Diaghilev's insistence on the newest by the youngest—was a godsend to *Les Six*. A new French era began for the Ballets Russes, an era ushered in by *Parade*. Debussy left the first performance of that pivotal ballet muttering that its success with the young was beyond him. And an outraged woman screamed indignantly at the cheering Apollinaire, "So that's French Art?" "That's it," he said, grinning. The cheeky little masterpiece had somehow cleared away both the Wagnerian underbrush and the Debussyan haze. A new kind of French music was born: fresh, jazzy, unpretentious, ideally suited to the "modern-dress" ballets that stemmed from *Parade* and *Jeux*. A brittle, bittersweet gaiety succeeded the pre-war exoticism. If Satie was the mentor of *Les Six*, Stravinsky was their idol. His stringent musical procedures, his acid dissonances, and his complicated cross-rhythms became the air they breathed. Auric spoke of Stravinsky in another letter to Misia: "As a child, during the war, and today, I considered him, I consider him now, and I think I shall always consider him one of the greatest geniuses who can console us for the mediocrity of art and artists—which I forget as soon as I hear ten measures of *Sacre* or *Rossignol*, in which I find the most comforting distraction from so much death and horror."

A few weeks before Misia's marriage, Milhaud, a friend of her brother Cipa, came to the Meurice to play a ballet he had written to a scenario by Paul Claudel.* Milhaud recalls:

Diaghilev, who was strongly influenced by [Cocteau], was distinctly attracted by the amusingly direct art personified by Poulenc and Auric; on the other hand, he was not very fond of my music. Nevertheless, to please José-Maria Sert, who was a great admirer of

---

* When Claudel had been sent to Brazil as ambassador in 1917, Milhaud had gone along as his secretary.

Claudel's, he asked me to play *L'Homme et Son Désir*. The performance took place in Misia Edwards' drawing room. . . . She was a great
friend of Diaghilev and lent him devoted assistance in putting on his
shows. He placed great confidence in her judgment, which was trenchant. Like Diaghilev himself, she was always on the alert for the
novelty of the day, or rather of the latest minute, and if she liked a
work, she would take it up. . . .

It was therefore amid an atmosphere heavy with skepticism and
unspoken reservation that I played my score. The icy silence that
followed it was broken by a conversation in Russian between Diaghilev
and Massine. I soon realized that my symbolic and dramatic ballet no
longer corresponded with the needs of the day.

Possibly Diaghilev failed to realize that when *L'Homme et Son Désir* was
played on the piano without singers and percussion, the music lost its
quiveringly sensual quality. Besides, Milhaud's elegance and patrician
simplicity eluded Diaghilev, though at Misia's insistence he later commissioned Milhaud to write the ballet *Le Train Bleu*, which had a libretto by
Cocteau, costumes by Chanel, and a front curtain by Picasso.

For his 1920 season Diaghilev asked Ravel to complete *La Valse*, a score
which the composer had been thinking about for some years. But the fate
of *La Valse* was even sadder than that of *Daphnis and Chloë*, which had
been overshadowed eight years before by Debussy's *Faun. La Valse* was an
inviting score, and pedigreed as well, dedicated as it was to Misia. But
after his unhappy experience with *Daphnis*, Ravel had forebodings rather
like the sinister rumblings in the music itself.

Ravel to Misia

A thousand thanks for your reassuring letter. But what can I do? I
have reason to be anxious: poor *Daphnis* had a good deal to complain
about from Diaghilev . . . even though it was not always his fault.

Now let us talk about *Wien* . . . pardon me, it is now called *La
Valse*.

First I must ask you to excuse me, but I don't know if Serge is in
Paris, and as you know, he never answers my letters.

My choreographic poem will undoubtedly be finished and even

orchestrated by the end of this month, and I could let Diaghilev hear
it any time after that.

As always, it was on Misia's piano in Misia's salon that Diaghilev listened
to the new score. With him were two or three handsome male secretaries,
the pianist Marcelle Meyer, Poulenc, and Stravinsky—an intimate group,
but there were tensions. Close friends since 1913, Stravinsky and Ravel
had become estranged and had not seen one another for some time. The
situation was especially painful for Ravel because Diaghilev's successful
revival of Stravinsky's *Le Sacre* a few weeks earlier had been substituted
for the revival of *Daphnis* that Diaghilev had originally promised Ravel.
The young Poulenc, of whom Ravel said, "the good thing about him is
that he creates his own folklore," was already a musical and social figure
around town. He was tall, jaunty, shy, and infinitely amused by social
nuance. Ravel's audition made a deep impression on Poulenc, as he later
recalled in a radio interview:

> Diaghilev planned to stage *La Valse* at the Ballets Russes with decor
> by José-Maria Sert, who was Misia's husband. Ravel arrived very
> simply, with his music under his arm, and Diaghilev said to him,
> "Well, well, well (with that nasal voice), well, my dear Ravel, what a
> joy to hear *La Valse. . . .*"
>
> And I, who knew Diaghilev very well at that time, noticed him
> fidgeting with his false teeth and his monocle. I saw that he was em-
> barrassed, that he didn't like it, that he was going to say—"No." When
> Ravel had finished, Diaghilev said something to him which I consider
> very accurate; he said, "Ravel, it's a masterpiece, but it's not a ballet,
> it's a portrait of a ballet; it's a painting of a ballet." . . .
>
> But what was extraordinary is that Stravinsky did not say *one
> word!* Nothing!
>
> It was in 1921, I was twenty-two years old, I was flabbergasted. . . .
> And that was a lesson I've never forgotten, a lesson in modesty; be-
> cause Ravel very calmly took back his music—without worrying about
> what they thought of it—and left very quietly.

Misia later told Poulenc that she had fought Diaghilev "tooth and nail"
over *La Valse*, but there was no moving him. As Diaghilev never staged the

ballet,* it meant a quarrel with Ravel that was never resolved. Misia ironically observed that it was one of the rare disagreements between Diaghilev
and a collaborator in which money was not the problem. Poulenc himself
came frequently to the Serts' to play snatches of the ballet he was writing
for Diaghilev. A brilliant improviser, he would play an approximation of
what he intended to write, and then, when asked to repeat a passage, would
improvise something quite different. Misia and Diaghilev did not hesitate
to point out to the young composer that they detected a bit of *Mavra* here
or a dash of *Petrushka* there. (Stravinsky's reaction was an amused "better
to imitate something good than to write something original and bad.") And
so Poulenc, wise as he was witty, decided not to show them the score until
it was complete. Possibly forewarned by Cocteau and Satie, he wrote a
letter to Sert explaining his position: "Tell [Misia], please, that if I
have not played her my ballet—which is dedicated to her—it's because
Les Biches is not quite finished, and since I consider your wife to be one
of the rare people who really know and love music, nothing would have
intimidated me more than to show her an unfinished work. As soon as the
last bar line is drawn, it will be my joy to play it for her."

On the Serts' honeymoon trip to Venice, Chanel had sat tongue-tied and self-
effacing as she listened to Diaghilev's interminable discussions with Misia
about the money needed to re-stage *Le Sacre du Printemps*. One morning
after their return to Paris, Chanel called at Diaghilev's hotel. He did not
recognize the name, and when he came down to the lobby he was surprised
to see Misia's silent friend. She had thought a good deal about *Le Sacre* she
told him, and would like to help—on condition that he never mention it to
anyone. By "anyone" she meant Misia. But as soon as she left, Diaghilev
undoubtedly rushed to the phone to tell Misia what he had in his pocket, for
Chanel had presented him with an extremely handsome check. It was Chanel's

---

* Had Diaghilev lived to see George Balanchine's masterly *La Valse* in 1951, with
the unforgettably exquisite Tanaquil Le Clercq, even he might have admitted that
there were choreographic possibilities in the music which he had failed to recognize.
Poulenc, who did see it, found it one of his "greatest ballet experiences."

first gesture of competition with Misia: a gesture that combined generosity, bribery, and social maneuvering. In one stroke she had cut through the formalities of making friends with Diaghilev as deftly as she had cut through the frills and furbelows of women's clothes. It was a giant step in transforming herself from Misia's little dressmaker-companion into Diaghilev's indispensable patron and friend.

So began a political power struggle. With her check Chanel tipped the balance of power although she never succeeded in toppling Misia from her throne. Chanel conquered but Misia continued to reign. Chanel knew that Misia would resent her secret dealings with Diaghilev, that Misia would feel it was her right to deliver the check herself as something she had persuaded her friend to contribute. But Chanel suspected Misia of even deeper perfidy. Just as Satie and Cocteau had been convinced that if Misia could not take the credit for *Parade* she would throw her weight against it, Chanel felt that if Misia could not take the credit for the gift she would have preferred it not to be given. Possibly Chanel was correct. For once the two women—never noted for their ability to keep a secret—did not discuss the matter. But there was another factor in their relation to Diaghilev. In his mind, Chanel stood for fashion and industry—treacherous shallows which did not interest him particularly, whereas in Misia's hierarchy of values, art came first and fashion was just an amusing diversion. Chanel thought Diaghilev's frayed overcoat was shameful; Misia found it endearing and loved him all the more for it.

Chanel was like a brilliant pupil who was outstripping her teacher in both fame and fortune. She found it maddening that everyone she met had known Misia for years—and very well; that whenever she opened a new door she found Misia already inside. But in spite of their competitive feelings, neither could live without the other. Throughout their lives they remained the best of foul-weather friends, coming to one another's rescue at the first sign of a crisis. Early in 1920 Chanel bought a house in Garches near Paris and asked Misia to decorate it for her. In a generous gesture Chanel installed Stravinsky and his family there, since the composer's lack of money was even more dramatic than Diaghilev's. As late as 1933 Stravinsky—then in his fifties and universally recognized as one of the century's greatest composers—was still in need of financial help.

STRAVINSKY TO MISIA

February 6, 1933

Dear Misia,

I'm dreadfully sorry always to be asking you for something or bothering you with my petty affairs, but you know that Chanel has not sent us anything since the 1st and so we are without a radish to live on this month; therefore I ask you to be kind enough to mention it to her. . . .

I thank you in advance for all your kindness, which is so great that one easily gets into the habit of counting on it, and I embrace you thousands and thousands of times, very warmly.

Igor

Chanel's succession of lovers—Pierre Reverdy, the Grand Duke Dmitri, the Duke of Westminister, and later Paul Iribe—fascinated Misia, who was an insatiable confidante. No one enjoyed scandal more than she, unless it was Chanel. Together their gossip was dazzling, almost creative in its intensity. Conjecture passed for truth, meanness for wit. Around them rose an odor of sulphur along with the perfumed pungencies that Chanel so successfully purveyed. Chanel's incredible success as a leader of fashion fascinated Misia even more than her elaborate love life. Rapt with admiration, Misia watched as Chanel imposed an expensive simplicity, an almost poor look, on rich women—and made millions in the process. Her genius, her generosity, her self-madeness combined with her lethal wit, her sarcasm, and her maniacal destructiveness intrigued and appalled everyone—Misia most of all. Chanel gave presents without grace ("I'm sending you six Venetian blackamoors," she would say. "I can't stand them any more.") and then capriciously took them back as if the gifts had been loans. She would impulsively present a platinum cigarette case to a friend and then, two months later, accuse her of stealing it. Misia's once shy creature had turned into a non-stop talker, a relentlessly clattering ticker tape announcing that everyone's stock had fallen except her own.

Sert was almost as involved with Chanel as Misia was. In fact the Serts became Chanel's family, and as in many families, there was mistrust, rancor, and rivalry as well as love and admiration. For Chanel and Sert, style was all-important. Belonging as she did to a younger generation, Chanel struck a more modern note, but when she bought a splendid apartment in the rue du Faubourg St. Honoré with her new millions, she relied on the Serts to help her make it one of the most beautiful in Paris. As soon as they had installed the piano Misia had chosen and set up the last Coromandel screen, Chanel's house became a constant meeting place for the friends. Picasso had a room there for a time, and so did Misia. The apartment became for Chanel what La Grangette at Valvins had been for Misia, with the difference that Chanel created a scented, fashion-world version of the unpretentious bohemia that Misia had known as a young woman.

Although both Chanel and Misia seldom made a move without consulting the other, Chanel, like Cocteau, tended to blame Misia when things went wrong. Stravinsky had been in love with Chanel, and the perfidious Misia— or so Chanel chose to think—had intrigued against her. Yet meddlesome as Misia was, it would be difficult to imagine that she was powerful enough to deflect the passions of such a strong-willed man. During the Stravinsky-Chanel affair, the composer left for Spain and Coco promised to join him. But at the last moment she decided it would be more amusing to drive to Monte Carlo in her new Rolls-Royce with the Grand Duke Dmitri. Misia wired Stravinsky, "Coco is a little seamstress who prefers Grand Dukes to artists." Stravinsky was so enraged that Diaghilev wired Chanel, "Don't come; Stravinsky will kill you." Or so Chanel claimed. Whether Misia sent the telegram to alert an unsuspecting lover or to comfort a rejected one, no one knows. Misia herself denied ever having sent a wire. In any case Coco and Misia had one of their most violent arguments and did not speak for weeks. As always, the silence was finally broken by a telephone call and the friendship was renewed once again. Coco and Misia were seen together so constantly and their relations were so highly charged that it was said they were lovers. Who knows? Perhaps they were. Certainly they were gossiped about. To this day many of their friends insist that they were sexually involved, while others, with equal conviction, swear that they were not.

In 1920 Diaghilev presented his first ballet season after the war. With *La Boutique Fantasque, Le Chant du Rossignol, The Three-Cornered Hat,* and *Pulcinella,* Massine proved himself to be even greater than Diaghilev had predicted six years earlier. His ebullient choreography based on characterization and gesture, his sombre beauty, and his fiery dancing made him the man of the hour. Perhaps his most rousing success was *The Three-Cornered Hat.* Massine was as hardworking as he was inspired, and while in Spain he had mastered the techniques of Spanish dancing in a phenomenally short time. Just as the public had once been transported by the exoticism of Diaghilev's oriental ballets, now they were carried away by the heel-clicking excitement of the dancing, the rhythmic fire of Manuel de Falla's music, and Picasso's brilliant costumes and subtly colored decor: a pink and ochre archway against a pale blue sky.

The triumph of the ballet carried over into the supper party Misia gave after the first performance. Arthur Rubinstein played Falla's music *con amore.* Picasso borrowed Misia's eyebrow pencil and drew a crown of laurel leaves on the composer's bald head. Everybody kissed everybody else, then kissed again. It was all gloriously Spanish. Under his black dinner jacket Picasso wore a café waiter's red sash, which—with his dark, burning eyes—made him look like a bullfighter at the moment of truth. According to Paul Morand, all the women there were a little in love with Picasso, and Picasso was more than a little in love with Misia. The relation between these two lawless creatures was complicated, but they had a kind of tacit understanding. Sert, whom Picasso ironically called Don José, stubbornly insisted that Picasso did not know how to draw. And Misia, who tried to convince herself that Sert was *the* great Spanish painter, was reluctant to face the uncomfortable truth. But she was too sharp not to have overheard Cocteau humming a malicious little ditty he had invented about Sert: *"Il était un Catalan / Qui n'avait aucun talent"* (He was a Catalan who had no talent). Despite Sert's high fees and fashionable success, Misia knew that to compare his academic skill to Picasso's astounding originality was rather like comparing her father to Rodin. She herself said about a small Picasso she owned, "Those few inches of painting seemed to me the most precious object in the world."

Nothing could have made Misia more aware of the discrepancy in their work than two Massine ballets that were based on eighteenth-century Italian music: *Le Astuzie Femminili,* an opera-ballet by Cimarosa, and *Pulcinella,* Stravinsky's trenchant, witty reworking of Pergolesi. Although the performances were only twelve days apart, the decor and costumes—Picasso's for *Pulcinella* and Sert's for *Le Astuzie*—were light-years apart in quality. Lydia Sokolova, despite her success in *Le Astuzie*, complained that "Sert designed for us the most hideous costumes we had ever been called upon to wear," while Picasso's designs, which he said he liked better than any of his other work for the theatre, made ballet history. Seated in Misia's box at the first performance of *Pulcinella*, Picasso turned to the gifted young artist Jean Hugo and said, "Are you still painting by hand?" This malicious opening salvo did not prevent Jean Hugo from enjoying the ballet or the party afterward given by the Persian Prince Firouz. (Firouz was one of those wealthy foreigners upon whom Paris society conferred the honor of allowing him to entertain them.) A caravan of cars went out to the village of Robinson, where there was a rather dubious establishment run by an ex-convict named René de Amouretti. The Beaumonts, the Picassos, the Serts, Diaghilev, Stravinsky and Massine, the Princesse Murat, Misia's friend the American heiress Hoytie Wiborg, Lucien Daudet, Jean Cocteau, his young lover Raymond Radiguet, Auric, and Poulenc were among the guests.

"Prince Firouz was a magnificent host," Jean Hugo said in his memoirs, *Avant d'Oublier*. "A great deal of champagne was consumed. Stravinsky got drunk, went up to the bedrooms, took the pillows, bolsters, and mattresses, and threw them over the balcony into the room below. There was a pillow fight and the party ended at three in the morning." Although the seventeen-year-old Radiguet was the quietest person there, he had the most to say about the evening. In fact, the party would long have been forgotten had he not immortalized it in his novel, *Le Bal du Comte d'Orgel*. In its pages Etienne and Edith de Beaumont are disguised as the Comte and Comtesse d'Orgel, and Hoytie Wiborg becomes the mannish American Hester Wayne. Hoytie Wiborg was a handsome lesbian who had bounded rather clumsily into Misia's life and was determined to stay there. Her passion was so strong that Misia, laughing and swearing, would sometimes have to fight her off with her fists. For Misia's friends, Hoytie was the epitome of the hopelessly awkward, hard-drinking American. Although she irritated Misia, who called her *l'emmerdeuse*, she was to become a lovable nuisance, a permanent fixture in Misia's life. Once they shared a sleeping compartment on a train to Venice. As Misia settled in for the night, Hoytie descended from the upper birth, pounced on her, and, panting and heaving, declared her love. "Oh, all right, if that's what you want," Misia said. A short time later she added annihilatingly, "Is that all you know how to do?" Mercilessly Misia told the story around town. It was the only time she admitted having been to bed with a woman.* Some of her friends, hearing the tale, wondered if Misia had had greater expectations.

With the help of Chanel's money, Diaghilev set Massine to work on a new version of Nijinsky's *Le Sacre du Printemps*. Unfortunately, Massine was also preparing a new version of the drama that had shattered the Diaghilev-Nijinsky union. Massine, a prudish, tightly buttoned-up young man whose incandescent warmth was reserved for the stage, had submitted to a relationship with Diaghilev even though the impresario attracted him as little as Potiphar's wife did Joseph. Massine's years with Diaghilev had made him the most famous choreographer and male dancer in the world. But he had been deprived of women, since Diaghilev was as possesively obsessed with him as he had been with Nijinsky. Lydia Sokolova, who danced the Chosen Virgin in the revival of *Le Sacre*, remembers Diaghilev's icy rage when he surprised her in a kiss with Massine. But it was Vera Savina, another English dancer in the company, who had caught Massine's eye. "She was the only person in the company who had no idea of Massine's situation," Sokolova wrote. "But Massine had fallen in love with her. Without realizing any of the implications, she must have been flattered."

After the first orchestra rehearsal at the Champs-Elysées theatre, Sokolova happened to go down to the stage after most of the dancers had left.

It was about six in the evening [Sokolova wrote] and the place was dark. Vera Savina was standing in the far corner of the stage when Mme. Sert suddenly came through a door nearby. Misia Sert was a clever, attractive woman of the world, besides being Diaghilev's devoted friend, and there were no secrets between them. Crossing the stage, I overheard Vera say, "Mme. Sert, have you seen Mr. Massine?" "No,

---

* By a curious coincidence, Hoytie's fortune came from the Wiborg Company for whom, in the nineties, Lautrec had made a poster with Misia as his model—years before Hoytie and Misia ever met.

Verotchka. Did you want him for anything in particular?" "I have an appointment with him." At this, of course, Mme. Sert pricked up her ears—and so did I. "Oh? Where is your appointment?" "At the Arch *de* Triumph, but it's such a big place I don't know exactly where to meet him." "Then," said Mme. Sert, "I should stand right in the middle of the arch, if I were you." I was staggered by this but said nothing. I imagined Misia hurrying off to tell Diaghilev about the appointment, and Vera standing in the center of the Etoile, waiting in vain.

Misia's ruse may have kept the lovers apart, but only momentarily. At supper in the Hôtel Continental after the opening performance, Diaghilev, Stravinsky, Chanel, and the Serts sat stunned when Massine, somewhat drunk, jumped onto the piano and announced that he was going to marry Sokolova. But Diaghilev soon realized that Massine was trying to put him off the scent and that it was Savina, not Sokolova, who was his rival.

A series of sordid episodes followed. Detectives were put on the trail. Massine was beaten up by hired thugs. Diaghilev humiliated himself in front of the company by kneeling down to tie Massine's shoelaces when Massine ordered him to. In a drunken moment, Diaghilev pushed Massine onto a bed with Savina and said, "If that's what you want, take her now." Massine's love for Savina was more than Diaghilev could cope with. With the gracelessness of the proverbial wife who marries beneath her, he said, "He was nothing when I met him." "Haven't I done everything for Massine?" he complained to Grigoriev. "Didn't I make him?" As for Massine's contribution, it was "nothing but a good-looking face and poor legs." Grigoriev was ordered to dismiss him. After Massine left, Savina joined him, and they were married. Diaghilev's valet told Sokolova that his master nearly died of grief.

The next month Diaghilev announced once again that no one is irreplaceable and began to look for other choreographers and other lovers. His requirements were specific. One day a young man whom he was considering as a private secretary was ushered into his hotel room. Diaghilev was at his desk writing and did not look up. The applicant cleared his throat to attract attention. Still without looking up, Diaghilev muttered, "Take off your clothes." After a few awkward moments the young hopeful cleared his throat once more. Diaghilev screwed in his monocle, saw that the young man's body was too hairy for his taste, and said, "Put your clothes on," as he went back to his letter. The young man understood that he had not been hired.

Instead Diaghilev engaged Boris Kochno, a handsome seventeen-year-old Russian poet. Misia approved of the bright, sensitive, eager young man, and they became friends. But since she had watched Diaghilev's other protégés come and go, it did not occur to her that this one would be there to the end. For the first week Kochno was given no duties; he sat idly by while Diaghilev wrote his own letters. Finally he asked timidly, "Monsieur Diaghilev, what do you expect your secretary to do?" "That's for you to find out," Diaghilev replied ambiguously. For Kochno it was a valuable answer; he set about creating a role for himself that brought an infusion of new life to the Ballets Russes. He wrote the libretto for Stravinsky's opera *Mavra* and was to provide the "poetic argument" for many Diaghilev ballets, including the Rieti-Chirico *Le Bal*, the Nabokov-Tchelitchev *Ode*, and the Prokofiev-Rouault *Prodigal Son*—all with choreography by George Balanchine, the last and greatest of Diaghilev's choreographers.

A few years earlier, Misia had become friends with Raymond Radiguet, an even younger poet than Kochno. When Radiguet was only fourteen he had been brought to see her by Max Jacob, and she was charmed by the shy, stubbornly silent boy in his too-large coat with his father's hat hanging down over his ears. In the six years remaining to him, Radiguet lived a long life and produced two extraordinary novels. He was so precocious at sixteen that Apollinaire said in his sweetly ironical way, "Don't despair; Monsieur Rimbaud waited until he was seventeen before writing his masterpiece." In January 1922 Cocteau, Radiguet's protector, lover, and one might almost say inventor, gave a reading of the boy's first novel, *Le Diable au Corps*, at Jean Hugo's studio in the Palais Royal. The Picassos, the Serts, and the Beaumonts were there. "Radiguet kept a sharp eye on the listeners through his monocle," Hugo recalls. Despite everyone's astonishment at Radiguet's talent and the psychological insights that he set out with classical clarity, Madame de Beaumont fell asleep in the middle of the reading. This did not escape Radiguet. He had not been studying the Beaumonts through his monocle out of idle curiosity and in his second novel he was to transform them into luminous literary characters. As a result they are better known to the world as the

Orgels than by the historic name they were so proud of. Radiguet become a mascot, a kind of adopted son, for Cocteau's friends: Misia, Chanel, Max Jacob, Paul Morand, and Poulenc and Auric, both of whom wrote songs set to Radiguet's poems. It was while working on his second novel that he wrote to Misia, "touched by the affectionate messages" she had given Jean for him: "It's not very gay to be laid low, as I am, by the disease of silence and not to dare to see those whose company one enjoys most for fear of boring them. However, as soon as I come back, I shall selfishly come to see you. Jean is returning with some very beautiful poems and two magnificent novels [*Le Grand Ecart* and *Thomas l'Imposteur*]. But I have written only one, about which I shall not be happy unless it does not displease you."

In this novel, *Le Bal du Comte d'Orgel*, Radiguet, painfully aware of his youthful awkwardness, wrote: "Of all the seasons, the spring, though the most becoming, is the most difficult to wear." Spring, alas, was the only season Radiguet was to know. To the horror of his friends who felt such special tenderness for him, he died unexpectedly of typhoid fever in December 1923 at the age of twenty. No one could believe the news. He died alone in a hospital in the middle of the night while Cocteau, unable to watch his friend's suffering, stayed in the rooms they had been sharing in the Hôtel Foyot. During his short illness Misia and Chanel were often at his bedside. Misia remembered his face so distorted with pain that the nun in attendance had to leave the room. When she came to see him after he died, Misia said, "I am not superstitious, but his expression is not the same. He is at peace."

Chanel took charge of the funeral. The church of St. Philippe du Roule was filled with white flowers except for some red roses that lay on the white coffin. Grief-stricken, Radiguet's family and friends (among them Picasso, Brancusi, and the black jazz band from the Boeuf sur le Toit) watched the white hearse pulled by white horses make its way through the streets in the December rain. Radiguet's father wrote to Misia a few days later:

Madame,

We had wished, on the very day of the magnificent funeral of our beloved son, to express to you all the gratitude that we shall always feel to you as well as to Mlle. Chanel for all that you have done.

The same day that our poor child had to be taken to the hospital, Cocteau told him not to worry, that two angels were watching over him, taking care of him, curing him. Those two angels did everything possible. Alas! nothing could save him. But he did not suffer, he did not know he was dying. "Everyone is so kind to me!" he said the night before he died. And there were tears in his eyes when he heard your names.

I cannot express in long phrases, Madame, the feelings I have—that we all have, my wife, my children, and I—when we think of you.

Our beloved Raymond lived for only twenty years, but he knew all the joys; all his dreams were realized, no sorrows, and up to the last minute, thanks to you, he was cared for with unparalleled devotion. . . . This letter is very incoherent. Please forgive me. How can we ever tell you how much we owe you!

My despair is great. How much greater it would have been if our adored Raymond had not had the care he was given, the funeral—a true apotheosis—that you wanted him to have.

Please accept, Madame, the assurance of our eternal gratitude.

M. Radiguet

It was Misia's friend Etienne de Beaumont who, like the Comte d'Orgel in Radiguet's novel, "opened the ball after the war." Beaumont, the Diaghilev of costume balls, staged his parties elaborately, even calling on Cocteau, Sert, and Marie Laurencin to design them. His rivalry with Diaghilev blossomed in 1924 when Beaumont, who was immensely taken with Massine, organized the *Soirées de Paris*, evenings of ballet with Massine as their central figure. Here too he borrowed from Diaghilev, using such Ballets Russes artists as Satie, Milhaud, Cocteau, and Picasso. Jean Hugo recalled the second of the *Soirées de Paris*: "At the first appearance of Massine, Beaumont cried: 'Bravo!' and applauded noisily. There was no echo. Misia had entered. She was the Ballets Russes incarnate, which Massine had betrayed. She did not go unnoticed, and when the curtain fell, many hesitated to applaud." At the Beaumont balls the guests were the well-born, the talented, and the amusing: a typical Parisian cocktail. Exclusive in the Proustian sense, the parties depended for their excitement almost as much on who was *not* invited

as who was. Incredible amounts of time and money were spent in the preparation of the costumes. Just as in the theatre, there was a full dress rehearsal.
The night of the ball, groups of guests made their grand entrances in carefully co-ordinated costumes. Announced by footmen in livery and powdered
wigs, they paused for applause or laughter, then descended the staircase into
the ballroom.

At one of the costume balls—which the French aptly call *travestis*—
Max Jacob appeared as a monk, Jean Hugo as an Imperial Guard, and Lucien
Daudet (who had sold Misia *The Secret of the Medicis*) as the *Spectre de la
Rose*. At the end of the evening the effete Daudet was stark naked. The
guests had plucked the rose petals his devoted mother had sewn onto his
tights, and eventually the tights disappeared along with the roses. Misia's
nephew Jean came to the Beaumont's *Bal des Jeux* as a house of cards,
Radiguet as a shooting gallery, Auric, Poulenc, and Milhaud as football
players, and the Princess Soutzo as a Christmas tree. Jean Hugo attended the
Bal de Mer dressed as one of four waiters from Prunier's who bore a large
tray. On it was perched the Maharanee of Kapurthala, disguised as caviar.
Hugo was somewhat tipsy and let his corner of the tray drop. When the
maharanee almost fell to the floor, the maharajah was heard to mutter, "In
India he would have been put to death at once." The Duchesse de Gramont
was determined not to miss the Beaumont's Louis XIV Ball even though she
was in mourning. She solved this challenging problem by organizing an
entrance that represented the beheading of John the Baptist. Dressed in the
black costume of an executioner, hood and all, she appeared carrying a
platter with a wooden head of John the Baptist that looked suspiciously like
Beaumont himself. Tall, manly Jean Hugo, with his grandmother's fan
fluttering in his hand, obliged the duchess by appearing as Herodias in a
rented wig and a dress with floating panels borrowed from the Comédie
Française. As Salomé, the Prince de Chimay covered his face with veils but
liberally exposed the shapely legs he was so proud of. Hidden all evening in
a bedroom like children at a costume party, they missed Marie Laurencin as
Molière's *Malade Imaginaire* attended by Radiguet, as "measles," with red
spots painted on his face.

In 1921 the tireless Beaumonts had given a New Year's Eve party. According to Jean Hugo:

Proust was expected: Etienne de Beaumont announced, "Céleste
[Proust's housekeeper] just telephoned for the tenth time; she wants to

know if it's draughty and if the herb tea for which she gave the recipe is ready."

Finally at midnight there was a kind of stir in the crowd and we knew that Proust was there. He had entered with the New Year, the year of his death. . . .

His pale face had become puffy; he had developed a paunch. He spoke only to dukes.

"Look at him," Picasso said to me, "he's pursuing his theme."

Indeed, Proust, the spectral image, was tying up the loose ends of his novel. His last volume, *The Past Recaptured*, may seem full of unbelievable coincidence and startling revelation, but a glance at Misia's world makes it appear more than plausible. Was Proust imitating life or was life imitating Proust? Who could have foretold that Misia, who had once been assured that society would never receive her, would now reign as one of the queens of Paris? Or that Chanel, whom Misia had not been permitted to bring to the Beaumonts' a few years earlier, would soon employ Beaumont to design jewelry for her? Or that this peasant girl from the provinces would refuse to marry the Duke of Westminster? Or that Léon Blum, the *fin de siècle* dandy of Misia's *Revue Blanche* days, would become the Socialist leader of France? Or that Picasso, so courageous in his art, would not have the courage to help his dear friend Max Jacob when Jacob was on his way to certain death in a Nazi concentration camp? Or that the Catholic rightist Sert would save Colette's Jewish husband Maurice Goudeket from the same fate? Or that the dying Jewish composer Darius Milhaud, nostalgic for his youth, would tell his wife he would like to see his old friend Paul Morand, an archcollaborationist, even though they had not spoken for years? Or that Proust himself, the amateur who dabbled in literature, would write the greatest French novel of the twentieth century? (And could anything be more Proustian than the quick transference of Edwards' obsessive jealousy from Misia to Lantelme?)

Proust of necessity was becoming more and more a recluse. To conserve his strength during the noble race against death that enabled him to complete *Remembrance of Things Past*, he left his sickbed only to gather a final touch for one of his characters. As he had already written what he wanted to say about Misia, he could spare her no further time, although in a card to Sir Philip Sassoon he wrote, "How stupidly my life is arranged that I never see

Misia whom I love." Proust's last letter to Misia* was in answer to her invitation to a Christmas party the week before his appearance at the Beaumonts':

> It is a good many years since I have gone to a party and I do not think that I could begin again on December 24th. But for the first time I am tempted. Nothing would please me more than to come to you, than to see you. It is one of the very few things that would give me pleasure. . . . There are days when I recall your cruel and beautiful face with astonishing clarity. Other times, less. Are you still a friend of M. Sert? I admire him prodigiously, but he is rather disagreeable with me and has said that *no one* is more antipathetic than I. What exaggeration.

How amazing, Misia thought, that ill as he was "he still had the courage to be flirtatious about Sert." But then, Misia was always aware of the fact that Proust—like Gide and Cocteau—was more flirtatious with her "he-man" Sert than they were with her. Misia felt that Sert's

> cultivation and Jesuit training made it possible for him to slip in and out of the labyrinth of Proustian complications as easily as a fish in water. My health, my laughter, my gaiety shocked Proust a little. . . . Perhaps he admired me a bit, but I was too all-of-a-piece, too violent in my tastes and preferences for his subtle, devious mind not to rebel. . . .
>
> The same God who arranged for Molière to draw his last breath on the stage should have allowed Marcel Proust to die at a ball.

In contrast to the studied grandeur at the Beaumonts', Misia entertained with impromptu gaiety. In the early twenties she gave a ball to launch Joseph Czapski, an appealing young Polish painter. He and a group of fellow artists had arrived in Paris penniless, but luck smiled on him and he met Misia. After her inevitable question, "What do you live on?" was answered with

---

* Madame Jenny Bradley, a friend to almost every important French and American literary figure in the last half-century, told us that Misia once startled her guests by saying, "I have many letters from Proust that I've never bothered to open." Misia countered the cries of disbelief by asking her niece Mimi to get them. When several packets neatly tied in ribbons were brought in, Misia asked, "Anybody want them?" Madame Bradley wanted them desperately but was too shy to say so. Others, less diffident, made off with them.

discreet despair, Misia gave him a monthly allowance and went into action. She introduced him to Picasso and Sert and invited him to bring his group to lunch with some of her rich lady friends. By the time lunch was over, Misia had sold a painting by each of the impoverished young Poles. Not content with that, she hired a barge that was moored at the Pont Alexandre III, asked the jazz-loving Polish artists to be the orchestra, hung their paintings all around the dance floor, and invited *le Tout-Paris*. Just as the guests began to inspect the paintings, there was a power failure and the boat was plunged into darkness. Not in the least disturbed, Misia stuck candles in empty wine bottles, told the orchestra to strike up, and a memorable evening began. Lifar danced with Misia, Count Harry Kessler recalled in his journal *In the Twenties*, and

> Diaghilev came to our table and tried to speak in the teeth of the frightful din of the jazz, which itself faced competition from the wind and the rain lashing against the boards of the barge. . . . All that was needed to carry the dramatic character of this Polish entertainment to its logical conclusion was for the hull to spring a leak. . . . At the end when the cloakroom clothes rack collapsed, everyone was scrambling around on the floor in the darkness and looking for hats and evening cloaks among the wreckage.

By the time the sun rose, all the guests had fox-trotted, tangoed, mazurka-ed, flirted—and promised to buy more pictures. The party was such a success that festivities aboard the gallery–night club continued for a week. It was art, pleasure, and profit combined and, for Czapski and Misia, the beginning of a lifelong friendship.

Among the guests at Misia's ball were her brother Cipa and his family. Mimi, now in her early twenties, had surpassed her Aunt Misia's fondest expectations and become a real beauty. Blond and blue-eyed, she sang Ravel and Fauré with charming delicacy and wrote engaging short stories. But her modesty, her vagueness, and her naïveté worried and irritated Misia. For Mimi had inherited her father's sweet nature and, like her father, did not have an ambition in the world. "What I could have done if I'd had those looks!" Misia would say impatiently, and even Cipa would embarrass his daughter by complaining that there were too many beaux and no serious prospects. To the family's relief, in 1925 Mimi made a brilliant marriage

Top, Sem (the cartoonist), Lucienne Bréval (the opera singer),
Misia, and Alfred Edwards on the deck of the *Aimée*.
Bottom, Alfred Edwards

Misia, during World War I, carrying a wounded man on her back
Opposite, the actress Geneviève Lantelme

Above, a Sert mural from
Sir Saxton Nobel's London residence, Kent House
Opposite: top, Marie Laurencin's drawing of Misia,
with Mallarmé's quatrain at lower right.
Misia's passport photograph

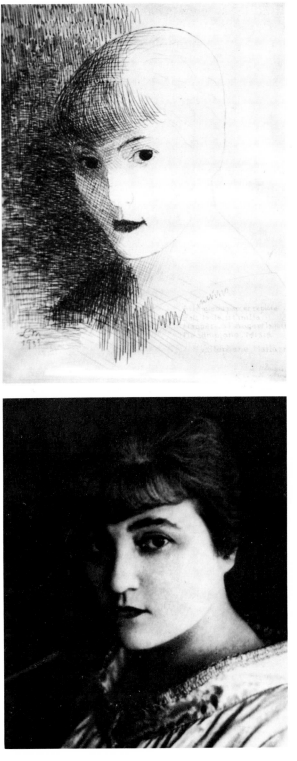

Misia Godebska de Profil, Pierre Bonnard, c. 1900

La Ronde Célèbre,
Mikhail Larionov, 1924
Right, Sert, Léonide
Massine, Misia, and
Serge Diaghilev,
in a drawing by Cocteau

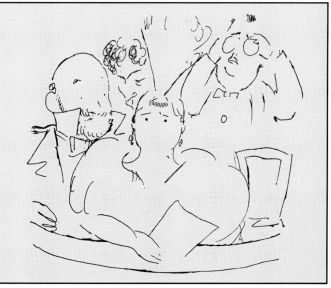

Opposite: top, Roussy Mdivani and Serge Lifar at a costume ball
Below, Leonide Massine
Above, Misia and Diaghilev on the train to Venice

Opposite, the Lido: Diaghilev,
Coco Chanel, Misia, and
Contessa Vendramina Marcello
Above, Chanel and Misia
Right, Chanel

Opposite, clockwise from top left: Jean Cocteau,
Erik Satie, Marcel Proust, Igor Stravinsky
Above, Diaghilev's funeral.
Behind Misia is Boris Kochno. To the right of Misia,
Lifar and Diaghilev's cousin Koribut-Kubitovich

Misia with her niece Mimi Godebska Blacque-Belair

to Aiméry Blacque-Belair, an army officer and the son of a general. It was all the Godebskis had hoped for. The marriage took place in the chapel of Les Invalides. It was formal, smart, and replete with generals and statesmen. General Maxime Weygand was there, and Marshal Louis Lyautey stood up for Aiméry, who had served under him in Morocco. Mimi was as beautiful as a bride should be in her wedding dress, a present from her aunt. Misia gave Ida an embroidered Chanel coat with a fox-fur collar and hat, then outdid the mother of the bride by appearing in a silk cape trimmed in chinchilla with a toque to match. No one seems to have noticed that Mimi, always submissive, was marrying to please her parents and Misia rather than herself. The couple settled on the quai de Bourbon. Following the family tradition, they had a literary salon of their own, where they received Maurois, Mauriac, and the Princesse Bibesco. Blacque-Belair was later elected to the Chamber of Deputies as the deputy from the Seine, and Misia felt that Mimi was on her way.

There were, of course, more edifying events than Mimi's society wedding, Misia's bohemian barge party, and the Beaumonts' frivolous costume balls. Evenings of music were presented at the imposing house of the Prince and Princesse Edmond de Polignac. The Polignacs were an extraordinary couple whose marriage had been engineered by Robert de Montesquiou—and a fine arrangement it turned out to be. For while the prince liked men and the princess liked women, they were devoted to each other. The prince was a gifted amateur composer in the Satie style; the princess was an American, Winaretta Singer, heiress to the sewing machine fortune. Theirs was a union the French liked to call the marriage of the sewing machine and the lyre.* A great patroness of the arts and one of Diaghilev's chief supporters, Princess Winnie, as she was affectionately called, commissioned many compositions: Stravinsky's *Renard*, Poulenc's *Two-Piano Concerto*, and Satie's masterpiece, *Socrate*, among others. Over the pilaster capitals in the Polignac's mirror-lined *grand salon à la Versailles*, Sert had painted Sapphic creatures voluptuously disporting themselves with monkeys and bacchic masks, to the delectation of the princess.

Before Diaghilev's 1923 Paris season began, he asked the princess to arrange a private hearing of Stravinsky's *Les Noces* so that the dancers could

---

* Isadora Duncan was the princess's sub-rosa sister-in-law through her liaison with Winaretta's brother Paris Singer.

familiarize themselves with the complicated score. It had taken Stravinsky eight years to arrive at the final instrumentation: voices, winds, percussion, and four pianos—a startlingly original, if cumbersome, combination. The piano parts were played by Poulenc, Auric, Marcelle Meyer, and Hélène Ralli on the latest musical invention, Pleyel double-pianos, each containing two grand pianos joined together in one enormous case, rather like Siamese twins. When in 1915 the composer had suggested, as only he could, the force and rhythmic vitality of his score on the upright piano in his tiny studio in Morges (a room he had wall-papered with his own hands), Misia and Diaghilev had been moved to tears. Now, at the Polignacs', as Stravinsky conducted with his peculiarly propulsive rhythmic intensity, they found themselves thrilled anew, unprepared for the granite-like sonorities he had devised. Originally intended for Nijinsky, *Les Noces* inspired his sister Bronislava to her greatest choreographic achievement.

At the end of the season Diaghilev was asked to stage a gala evening in the Hall of Mirrors at Versailles: a benefit for the restoration of the palace. It was the apotheosis of his worldly success. For three days he prepared a fête in much the way that Lully had done for Louis XIV. Président Poincaré, members of the cabinet, the diplomatic corps, and the inevitable *Tout-Paris*, magnificently dressed, were greeted by Diaghilev, with Misia easy and graceful at his side: king and queen for a day. But after all, had not Misia, in a moment of boredom *à la* Turgenev, asked Diaghilev to marry her, and had not he, teasing and tender, replied, "How can I marry my sister?" The evening was a triumph. A glittering international audience paid huge sums for the spectacle and supper that followed. At one end of the room a broad staircase had been built leading down to a stage. The performance began with the appearance at the top of the grand staircase of a singer, bewigged and feathered, dressed in royal blue and gold. As he descended at a stately pace, singing a seventeenth-century air, his blue cape emblazoned with *fleurs de lys* spread out behind him. By the time he reached the front of the stage, the train of his cape, held up by little black pages, had become wider and wider and finally covered the entire stage and staircase with blue velvet and gleaming gold. Clearly, Diaghilev knew where art and the Folies Bergères meet. By the time his dancers made their spirited entrance to an infectious Tchaikovsky polonaise, their swirling images reflected in the great mirror-lined room, the audience was ecstatic. As they left through the magnificent courtyard lit by blazing torches, they knew that Diaghilev had shown them what grandeur was.

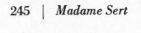

After years of wandering, Diaghilev longed to find a home for his company. Once again he turned to the Princesse de Polignac. Through her husband's nephew, Prince Pierre de Monaco (the father of Prince Rainier), she arranged for the Ballets Russes to spend six months each year in Monte Carlo. There the company could unpack and feel that at last they had a permanent home. The year of Diaghilev's first Monte Carlo season, 1924, included not only revivals of two Sert ballets (*Las Meninas* and *Le Astuzie Femminili* in a revised version called *Cimarosiana*), but the first ballets of Misia's young protégés, Poulenc, Auric, and Milhaud.

Of the new French ballets, Poulenc's *Les Biches* was choreographically and musically the most successful. The composer's biographer Henri Hell describes it as a twenties "*fête galante* where, as in certain paintings of Watteau, one could either see nothing or imagine the worst." If *Les Noces* was a powerful cornerstone of those years, *Les Biches* was a sparkling ornament. Chic, insinuating, and as potent as a blues, the music was perfectly married to the evanescent pastels of Marie Laurencin's decor. In an astonishing about-face after her powerful *Noces*, Nijinska's light and witty choreography with its tantalizing suggestion of perversity in high places, of vamps and gigolos, was a mirror of a good part of the audience. It tickled them to see themselves depicted with such spicy playfulness. And of course it never occurred to them that it had taken seventy-two rehearsals to achieve such frothy, effortless perfection. "*Les Biches* moves *les riches*," Marie Laurencin wrote Poulenc.

Marie Laurencin was one of Misia's great enthusiasms. They had known each other since the days of Apollinaire, who had been Marie's lover. Asked why she had never married him, she gave as her fanciful reason, "I detest that third person called 'the couple.'" A gamine as perversely ambiguous as Colette's Claudine, Marie made a charming drawing of Misia and sent her dozens of playfully flirtatious letters, letters that have the blurred enchantment of the designs she made for *Les Biches*. In one, where she pursues her thoughts on "the couple," she speaks of being alone with her Japanese nightingales, birds that sing only when separated, and of her relief that since they have been reunited, the noise of their song has ceased. Another letter begins by saying that because of her high cheekbones she will not be able to see Misia and ends with Dada assurances of her love, despite the fact that she is not the inventor of face powder.

During the preparation of *Les Biches*, Misia and Marie went each day to the atelier of Vera Sudeikina, who executed the costumes for the ballet.* Marie Laurencin had brought a bouquet of the prettiest costume sketches imaginable, but they were so amorphous that they were impossible to realize with any accuracy. Each visit produced new ideas from the overflowing fantasist, enthusiastically abetted by Misia. Finally Madame Sudeikina wrote Diaghilev that she could not be responsible for all the changes. One particular change made by Laurencin and Misia created a sensation. They simply eliminated—with a snip of what Cocteau called Misia's irreverent scissors— the long train from the evening dress that the superb Vera Nemtchinova wore, turning the costume into the first mini-skirt. Shocked dowagers stamped out of the theatre, shaking their heads in disapproval, but Cocteau was inspired to write: "When that little lady emerges on her pointes from the wings, with her long legs, her too-short jerkin, and her right hand, white-gloved, held up near her cheek like a military salute, my heart beats more quickly."

Misia and Diaghilev, now in their fifties, had arrived at the watershed of their lives, with its first glimpses of the downward slope. In each of them essential and similar changes were taking place. They became more intractable, crueller, more imperious. His rages, foul-mouthed and uncontrollable, became more frequent; her restlessness knew no bounds. Although Misia still recognized talent in the young, her bursts of enthusiasm, her almost physical love affairs with the new in art, became rarer. Diaghilev began to suffer a similar atrophy. It was the normal flagging of energy, the disillusion of

---

* A statuesque blonde, Vera was the wife of the painter Serge Sudeikine, designer of the Art Nouveau decor for Diaghilev's 1913 ballet *Salomé*. Because of her extraordinary beauty, Diaghilev had engaged her to mime the role of the Queen in his 1921 revival of Tchaikovsky's *The Sleeping Beauty*. The ballet was partially re-orchestrated by Stravinsky, whom she later married.

Madame Stravinsky told us that at a time when neither her first marriage nor Stravinsky's was going well, Diaghilev introduced her to Stravinsky, explained that he was "very moody," and asked her to be "nice to him." "And so," she continued, coquettishly batting her great blue eyes, "I *was* nice to him." Her devotion to the great composer, and his to her, continued to the day of his death, although they did not marry until they came to America in 1940.

middle age. A certain passion that went with their fresher, more potent years was gone. A nagging suspicion remained that life had been more beautiful, that art had been greater. For Misia, the great experiences of her youth—Mallarmé, Ibsen, and Verlaine, *Pelléas, Boris,* and *Le Sacre*—were never to be equalled. For Diaghilev, the idols of his early years, Wagner, Tchaikovsky, and Mussorgsky, became more and more important. Nor was their point of view unjustified. After all, Proust towered over Radiguet; Renoir and Lautrec were greater than Marie Laurencin; and *Les Six*, fresh and innovative though they were, could not be compared to Stravinsky. The cooling of their ardor gave Misia and Diaghilev an objectivity that stood them in good stead. The twenties were to be grateful for their impeccable judgment, even if it seemed patronizing at times. To compensate for their sense of nothing's-what-it-used-to-be, they tended to inflate their latest protégés in public. In private, however, they were apt to call the works of their new favorites charming little turds, *des petites crottes adorables.*

Misia, though she had grown thicker, looked extraordinarily youthful, but Diaghilev was showing his age badly. Vainer than ever, he refused to have his portrait painted and like Dorian Gray, never looked in a mirror. His aloofness, except when warmed by Misia's presence, became more pronounced. Surrounded by new young men, he was embarrassed by his middle-aged stoutness and his ill-fitting false teeth. Munching endless chocolates and sniffing cocaine, he suffered from diabetes and boredom. Deeply superstitious, he was never without a cane so that he was always touching wood. Lovers appeared and disappeared. Perhaps because they were truly homosexual and available, they did not stir him to the heights of neurasthenia that the reluctant Nijinsky and the unwilling Massine had aroused. A baleful haze of decadence hovered in the atmosphere. There was something pitiful about the fat, aging man who exacted sexual dues from ambitious and beautiful young boys. Collecting rare books, which he looked at more than he read, became his absorbing new interest. And though he leaned more and more heavily on Kochno for artistic advice and intellectual comfort, he never lost either his flair or his absolute control over the Ballets Russes. His new dancers—Lopokova, the perfect Spessivtzeva, Danilova, Doubrovska, the child prodigy Markova, Dolin, and Vladimirov—his painters, new to theatrical design—Derain, Matisse, Juan Gris, Max Ernst, Miro, Chirico, and Tchelitchev—all were brilliant choices of the twenties.

There were two young men who made the last years of the Ballets Russes

memorable: Serge Lifar and George Balanchine. It was Balanchine who was
to take Diaghilev's lead, carry the ballet into uncharted waters, and make the
twentieth century an unparalleled era of dance. With Alexandra Danilova,
Tamara Geva, and Nicholas Efimov, Balanchine had escaped from Russia
and made his way to Berlin, the German provinces, and finally the Empire
Theatre in London. The word was out. Kochno was sent to look them over.
He wired Diaghilev, who sent for them, and an audition was arranged in
Misia's apartment. Balanchine recalls the momentous occasion in his no-
nonsense way. His shirt open to the waist, he led his dancers through the
exotic, daringly original steps he had devised to Rachmaninoff's *Elegy*
and Arensky's *Egyptian Nights*. From England he had sent a romantic
photograph of himself, long-haired, with coat collar turned up. He remembers a splendid apartment, a rich and smiling hostess, and Diaghilev's
disappointed, "Oh, but I thought you were darker." "I was not his
type," Balanchine told us drily when he described this first meeting.
Quick to sense Diaghilev's disappointment, he realized that the success
of the audition would depend on talent alone. Equally quick, Diaghilev
knew talent when he saw it. To his questions, "Can you choreograph
quickly? Can you stage operas?" Balanchine, twenty years old, unhesitatingly answered yes. Diaghilev's nod of approval shaped his life. Misia
too sensed genius in the young dancer. Stravinsky, aware of Balanchine's
unique musicality, wrote Misia to ask if she would arrange an appointment
with the young choreographer. And so began one of the most glorious collaborations in ballet history.

As for the other newcomer, Lifar, it was not Diaghilev alone who took to
him. From the moment Misia and Chanel saw him, they too were captivated.
At a rehearsal of *Le Train Bleu* in which the dancers wore Chanel's stylish
bathing costumes and sports clothes, Lifar remembers hearing Misia say to
Diaghilev, "But he's charming, this little Russian; just look at him," and
Chanel adding, "Yes. There's your dancer." Lifar was the only one of the
new dancers who became part of Diaghilev's charmed circle. His easy social
manner, his instinct for flattery, his Byzantine beauty, and the fact that he
was the apple of Diaghilev's eye made him a delectable household pet for
the friends. It amused them to see the outward signs of Lifar's rise to court
favorite: straightened teeth, smart plus fours, and paintings given him by Diaghilev, the master appraiser. His superb acting, his indefinably fascinating
presence, and his beautiful body soon made him a favorite with the public

as well. Diaghilev had again molded a unique dancer. At Chanel's, of an evening, he and Misia would perform a parlor trick that everyone found ravishing. While Lifar reclined on the piano, Misia would play the opening measures of Debussy's *Prelude to the Afternoon of a Faun.* Languorously, Lifar would remove his jacket, then descend from the piano with magnificent animal grace to dance a one-man version of Nijinsky's sensually potent steps.

It was about this time that the Serts acquired a Russian household pet of their own, a handsome nineteen-year-old girl named Roussadana Mdivani. Like a stray cat, one day she wandered into Sert's new studio in Montparnasse, was picked up, examined, fondled, and adopted. To Sert's satisfaction she turned out to have a pedigree: she was a Georgian princess. Her value soared despite the fact that the Mdivani pedigree was somewhat suspect. Roussadana's father, Zacharias Mdivani, was a general and had been an aide-de-camp to the Tsar. His wife, half Georgian, half Polish, had borne him five children: Nina, David, Serge, Roussadana—called Roussy—and Alexis. The story goes that when someone telephoned and asked for Prince Mdivani, the general answered, "You must mean one of my sons." In a similar vein he said that he was the only person in the world who had inherited a title from his children. Despite the general's modesty, his children chose to call themselves princes, astutely aware that the title to which they had a vague claim was a social asset to struggling exiles.

Before the Revolution the Tsar had appointed General Mdivani governor of the province of Batum, and the family moved to a remote, ruined castle belonging to their Moslem grandfather. Young toughs of the castle, the two older boys, David and Serge, were attractive, swaggering marauders. They rode like Cossacks, fought like hellcats, and seduced every peasant girl in sight. To the relief of the district, while still in their teens they were sent off to school in Massachusetts by an American millionaire. In a few years, their seductive powers undiminished, they became known as the marrying Mdivanis, taking heiresses and film stars as their wives and exchanging the wild steppes of Georgia for the manicured polo fields of Long Island and Beverly Hills.

After the Revolution the general's wife and the other children escaped to Constantinople on the last Italian ship to leave Russia. A very stout lady, Mama Mdivani spent her days playing patience, reading risqué novels, nibbling on Turkish delight, and drinking a little more vodka than was good for her. The children had the time of their undisciplined lives, organized only when Mama, who was mad about the cinema, insisted that they go along to keep her company. There was little money even for that, as Madame Mdivani in her odalisque way had distractedly smuggled out of Russia a trunk full of party favors instead of the family jewels and silver. The enterprising youngsters solved the problem by putting up posters in exchange for free tickets. Undaunted by their unaccustomed poverty, Roussy and Alec took to the streets of Constantinople. There they were adopted by the polyglot sailors of the bustling port, who shared their rations with the adventurous children. Roussy and Alec worked up a thriving little business: Roussy, in a pleated skirt with ribbons in her hair, would smile enticingly at passersby, then spit on their shoes when they were not looking. Up popped Alec, rag in hand, and offered them a shine. The children loved their rough-and-tumble life and adored each other. It was a wild spree without governesses or tutors: a prelude to the permanent vacation they were to seek all their lives.

The Roussy who rang the bell of Sert's new studio in the Villa Ségur in 1925 had grown into an intriguingly handsome young lady. Tall and slender, she had ash-blond hair streaked with gold, large eyes grey as slate, and the seraphic, turned-up smile of an archaic statue. She was a sculptor and ostensibly had come to ask for technical advice and inquire about studios, since her own was too small. Perhaps, Mdivani-like, she was simply curious to meet the rich, famous painter. "How can one man possibly need so much space?" she asked with an enchanting smile as she looked covetously around the impressive two-story studio. Struck by her beauty and charm, Sert cleared a corner of his studio with a grand gesture, and soon they were spending the afternoons together. Ingenuous and playful as a kitten, Roussy tumbled into Sert's bed. The lessons in art turned into lessons in love.

Before long this latest in the list of Sert's escapades became something more serious, a fact he carefully concealed from Misia. Secret loves breed violent passions, and in no time Sert was in love as only a man of fifty can be with a girl of twenty. He could tell his cruel, amusing stories once again, dazzle her with his erudition, and astonish her with the extravagance of his presents. In contrast to Misia's knowledgeable view of his work, the unquestioning admiration of his sensitive protégée gratified his vanity. Aware that many women visited Sert's studio, Misia made a point of never turning up unannounced. It was out of respect for his work, she told herself. In any case she felt that his casual adventures were no threat to her. But there was something alarming in his boyish excitement when he spoke of the gifted princess, and for the first time Misia felt threatened. She decided that it might be a good idea to meet the girl. An encircling tactic would be best: she would gather the enemy to her bosom, make her a friend, and praise her to Sert. One afternoon Misia drove up to Sert's atelier and caught sight of a tall, blond girl shielding her face with a handbag as she ran across the street. Misia knew it must be Princess Mdivani. The next day Misia telephoned to ask if she could call on her. Armed with a gift, she arrived at Roussy's tiny studio. The young sculptress was at work on a bust of the Japanese actor Sessue Hayakawa, who was attended, as always, by his silent samurai lover. Roussy, her pet monkey perched on her shoulder, seemed perfectly at ease. It was Misia who felt uncomfortable, just as she had years before when she confronted Lantelme.

But something unexpected interfered with Misia's worldly plan: she fell under the spell of Roussy's luminous beauty. Suddenly she felt that it would be impossible to intrigue against the attractive young girl, a girl who could not possibly mean her any harm. It was another of Misia's instant infatuations. She longed to take the girl to her bosom, but not as an enemy; to make her a friend because she was the most enchanting creature she had met in years. Yes, she would praise Roussy to Sert, but sincerely, out of the fullness of her heart. They would both love her. Misia always felt that whenever she followed her impulses, everything worked out perfectly. Recklessly she invited Roussy to dinner with Sert that night, to lunch the next day, to a ball she was giving the following week. Roussy, whose mother had recently died, explained that she was in mourning and refused the invitations. But there was no resisting Misia when she set out to be charming. Besides, it was in the Mdivani blood to respond to generosity. Finally Roussy agreed to come to lunch if she could bring her sister. Nina, a manipulative mother to her younger sister, dominated the conversation while Roussy remained silent. On the way out, Nina, who knew a good connection when she saw one, invited the Serts to dine at the Ritz to meet their father. They found him a charming, distinguished gentleman of the old school.

Misia was moved when she saw how deeply Roussy missed her mother.

Overcome by tenderness, she felt that here was the daughter she had never had. She invited the girl everywhere. Soon the Serts and Roussy were an inseparable trio, an arrangement that did not go unnoticed by their gossip-loving friends. Half princess, half street urchin, Roussy brought sunshine to the Sert's heavily curtained rooms. Stories of her exotic childhood and her escape from Russia, whispered confidences and infectious laughter, improvised poems in invented languages, warm kisses, impulsive hugs—a battery of youthful Tartar charm captivated the Serts. They liked to think that they had seen everything, but they were in for a few surprises. One day they caught sight of Roussy and her brother Alexis careening wildly around the Place de la Concorde in two open cars, inches apart, holding hands like lovers: a modern Siegfried and Sieglinde. "Promise never to do it again," begged the terrified Serts, who had bought Roussy the car. Lightly she agreed, kissed them both, and ran off to Rumpelmayer's. When she returned, choking with laughter, she told them that her monkey had made a mess all over the pastry counter, then knocked the chocolates he hadn't eaten onto the floor. Despite a certain edge of hysteria, her high spirits were so contagious that Misia and José-Maria couldn't help being amused.

The relations of the trio became so entangled that they were at a loss to understand their own motives and emotions. Sert knew Misia's weakness for taking up new friends with the intensity normally reserved for lovers; he had seen it when he introduced her to Diaghilev. Uncontrolled enthusiasm was part of her charm. Once before, and only once, when Misia had first met Chanel, Sert had been shocked by her passionate feeling for another woman. Yet he had never imagined that she might take to one of his mistresses in the same way. Misia's almost sexual attraction to Roussy only served to heighten Sert's desire for the girl. Accustomed to respect from the young, the Serts found that Roussy's naturalness, her informality, even her disrespect made them feel young again. When she was not with them, they spoke of her constantly—Misia taking the lead in pointing out the poetry of Roussy's charm. But she was with them more and more. Though Misia was infatuated, she did not forget that it was Sert whose bed Roussy shared—with Misia's tacit agreement. Generous by nature, Misia felt she was behaving nobly by giving so much to the man she loved. And the more entrenched Roussy became in their lives, the more profoundly Misia felt that she loved Sert, and the more Sert felt torn between his two loves. He was in the pleasant if awkward position of having two women—women who adored each other—both in love with him.

Misia was relieved when summer came. Roussy was going away with her family, and the Serts would be leaving for their annual trip to Italy. Much as they enjoyed the season in Paris, they had always looked forward to the summer. It was such luxury to get into the car that had been specially built for them, and be driven wherever their fancy led. They would stop for lunch in restaurants they had discovered years before. Then, when it was too hot to go sight-seeing, they would draw the curtains of their hotel room and make love, just as they had on their first trip together. And when they reached Venice, Coco, Diaghilev, and all their friends would be waiting for them. By the time they returned to Paris, everything would be as before.

All that spring Coco had kept Misia on the phone for hours, telling her she was mad, an idiot to play such a dangerous game. Perhaps Coco was right, Misia thought; things were getting out of hand. A summer without Roussy might cure Sert of his infatuation. As the chauffeur loaded the dogs and luggage into the car, they were unaware that Roussy had slipped into a corner of the Meurice lobby. Like a wistful child whose parents are going off without her, she watched the festive departure.

During the trip they spoke of Roussy constantly. It was difficult to say which of them missed her more. When they returned to Paris nothing had changed. Naïvely, Misia underestimated the selfish power of sexual love. Sert's physicial need for Roussy was not to be diverted. Misia was torn between love for the girl and a longing to have her vanish from their lives forever. When in 1925 friends invited the Serts to Biarritz for Christmas, José-Maria was reluctant to leave Paris. But he could give no reason for staying behind, and so they went. Once again Misia hoped the change would do him good. He must realize that he was making a fool of himself and of her. Surely he would come to his senses; surely the infatuation would end. Then she would show him how generous she could be. Nothing would make her happier than to adopt the poor little princess. She would take her to Chanel, who would know exactly how to dress her. Misia assumed that if she deposited favors her credit would grow, not realizing that all the clothes, the jewels, and the presents she gave Roussy only made the girl more beautiful in Sert's eyes. She would introduce Roussy to charming boys of her own age and arrange a brilliant marriage for her. Sert would be proud of their protégée.

In Biarritz something happened that put an end to her fantasies. While putting away one of Sert's suits, Misia found a letter to Roussy that he had not yet mailed. She made the fatal mistake of the unhappy wife: she read it. The letter left no doubt in her mind that Sert planned to leave her and marry Roussy. Hatred, jealousy, resentment, and self-pity engulfed her. Yet at no time in her life had she felt so intensely in love with Sert. How could words in a letter hurt so much? After all she'd done for him, after all she'd given him! It must be a mistake. "A few miserable words, written in a moment of madness—could they wipe out twenty years of love?" she wondered. Impulsively she scrawled across the pages of his letter, "It's impossible. I know you still love me. We belong together. Whatever happens, I am yours." Stuffing it back into his suit pocket, she turned and caught her reflection in a mirror. She was getting old. Sert never spoke of the letter or her message.

When they returned from Biarritz, Roussy came to see Misia every day. She was as affectionate as ever, but the strain was beginning to show. High-strung and irritable, she smoked without stopping. At odd hours she would say she was starving, bolt down astonishing amounts of food, and run off, leaving Misia more charmed than ever. There were times when Misia did not know whom she loved more, Roussy or Sert. They were her family. But Roussy had an adoring family of her own who disapproved of what seemed to them a futile *ménage à trois*. When the girl threatened suicide, they knew that steps must be taken. Urged on by Nina, Roussy decided to join her brothers. Their brilliant marriages were proof that the streets of America were paved with gold. Roussy would be commissioned to make busts of the Mellons and the Carnegies. Attractive young millionaires would throw themselves at her feet. All she had to do was lift her little finger, and she too could be one of the marrying Mdivanis. Hurt and puzzled by her uncertain position and by Sert's indecisiveness, Roussy finally announced that she was leaving for New York. The Serts went to the boat train to see her off. Roussy stood on the platform, shivering with cold. Just as the train was about to leave, Misia impulsively took off her sable coat and wrapped it protectively around Roussy's shoulders. Silently the Serts returned to their Ali Baba's cave at the Meurice.

For the first time since they had met, Misia and Sert had nothing to say to one another. With Roussy gone they both felt a deep sense of loss. All that winter, telegrams arrived from America. Sert hid them clumsily, secretly hoping, perhaps, that Misia would find them. But Misia did not have to read them to know that her husband was suffering terribly. Both felt guilty and unhappy: Misia because she was depriving him of what he wanted, Sert because he was making the two women he loved unhappy. In Venice the following summer, Sert was not himself. Although he was incapable of speaking of what troubled him, one evening Misia found him quietly weeping alone at the window. You are weeping for me, she thought, since in your heart you have already abandoned me. And still neither of them could speak. When they returned to Paris, they found Roussy waiting. She had been away for almost a year, yet she and Sert took up where they had left off. As before, she came to see Misia constantly. Nothing had changed.

Just before leaving New York, Roussy had caught a bad cold. She could not shake it off. Weeks went by, and her throat was still inflamed. Her doctor suggested that she see a specialist in Switzerland. Misia immediately took charge, and the two went off to Berne—Misia tenderly attentive, Roussy endearingly grateful. It all seemed perfectly natural. Over tea one afternoon, Roussy suddenly confronted Misia with the truth they had been avoiding for so long. "He loves me and I love him," she said, her grey eyes meeting Misia's with candor. "I want to marry him. He wants it too." She had returned from America, she said, where she had refused a brilliant marriage, because Sert had written that he would die if she married anyone but him. Misia replied that she understood Roussy's adoration of Sert only too well. She loved her all the more for it. But was Roussy sure of Sert's intentions? He was old enough to be her father. For that matter, wasn't Misia herself too old to be abandoned? Besides, Sert was a devout Catholic; divorce was out of the question. Despite all this, Misia assured Roussy that she would never try to keep Sert against his will.

Yet she did. Once more Sert reassured her, and once more Misia hoped that the love she lavished on Roussy would force the girl to give Sert up. Shortly after Misia and Roussy returned from Switzerland, Roussy fell ill once again. Misia took her to a doctor who performed a minor operation in his office. On the way back to the Mdivanis, Roussy felt faint. Frightened, Misia took her to the Meurice instead, and put her to bed. Roussy's illness became worse; the Mdivanis were called in. The doctor said that if Madame Sert had told him that the princess had a permanent fever, he would never have operated. Suspecting Misia of the worst, the Mdivanis turned on her. Misia was furious. What did she know about operations and permanent fevers? How dare they accuse her of trying to harm Roussy, when the truth was that they had neglected the poor girl and she was the only one who had tried to help? Still, Misia was terrified; she swore to herself that if God allowed Roussy to recover, she would give Sert his freedom. The girl did recover, though slowly. In the spring the Serts took her to the seashore for weekends and by the time summer came, Roussy was practically living with them at the Meurice.

Roussy and Misia clung to each other, both of them waiting to see which would loosen her grip first. Naturally there were dark rumors. Some claimed that they were having an affair, that Sert was a voyeur who enjoyed watching them make love. Others said that Roussy was simply a fortune hunter determined to break up the Serts' marriage. Still others swore that it was a sinister *ménage à trois*, that the jaded older couple drugged the young princess, kept her locked up in their apartment, and used her for their perverted pleasures. Certainly it was true that the three of them were taking drugs. Sert had always used cocaine; Misia was beginning to find release in morphine; and the volatile Roussy, whose high spirits gave way more and more frequently to bouts of depression, was willing to try anything. Misia, who had been gossiped about all her life, was not prepared for the viciousness of the attacks. But when the Serts left for Venice, Roussy went along. It was her first trip to Italy. In Florence an incident occurred that haunted Misia for the rest of her life. She spoke of it years later in a letter to Sert.

My God! how vividly I remember that bedroom, with the shutters closed against the early afternoon heat, where for the last time I was yours. . . . Suddenly a faint creaking revealed her presence: she had crawled in on all fours to make less noise! You were not even angry. And when evening came, I felt that your concern was only for her. She had disappeared from the hotel and we waited for her in a dreadful silence. . . .

From that day on, mute and implacable, tragedy shadowed our lives. It stalked us, encircled us, showed us no mercy. The word I was hoping for, which you could still say to avert it, to save me, you did not utter. All at once life no longer had any meaning. It was nothing but an agonizing wait. You had to choose, and it almost drove you mad.

As a devout Spanish Catholic, Sert's situation was complicated. He had applied for an annulment, but he knew it might take years to come through. With accommodating flexibility and a push from Roussy's conniving sister Nina, he found a Jesuitical loophole: civil divorce and remarriage in a Protestant country. Nina's husband, Charles Huberich, an American lawyer who lived in Holland, was able to make the arrangements. Till the last moment Sert begged Misia to stand by him and promised never to leave her; but Misia, defeated by Roussy's calm assurance, knew he would. Nightmare trips to The Hague followed: applications for divorce and legal attempts at reconciliation. Finally on December 28, 1927, Sert divorced Misia and it was all over. That evening the triumphant Mdivanis gave a dinner party. It was a strange group that assembled in the dining room of the hotel where they were all staying: Sert, the woman he had just divorced, the woman he soon would marry, his prospective sister-in-law and brother-in-law, who was also his divorce lawyer. Misia had come partly out of gallantry and partly because she could never bear to be left out. Halfway through the meal she broke down and left the table. Curiously, it was Roussy who rushed to comfort her and who shared her room that night. "I can't bear it; I love him so! I love him so!" Misia sobbed as she lay cradled in Roussy's arms. "Don't cry," Roussy whispered. "Now there will be two of us to love you. We'll never leave you. We owe our happiness to you."

The day Sert left the apartment in the Meurice, a small suitcase in his hand, was a fatal one in Misia's life. She lost her balance and was swept along on a current of irrational hopes and futile dreams. Here was a peculiar dilemma: she loved both her husband and the woman who had taken him from her. Slowly and painfully she returned to some semblance of her former self. She mended, she functioned, she was Misia, but she was never quite the same. She clung to her unhappiness as though it were a treasure. Not surprisingly, she fell ill. Chanel insisted that Misia come to stay with her. Dutiful visits from Sert while Misia was at Chanel's were no comfort, for he seemed distracted and in a hurry to leave. Roussy came too, but Chanel refused to let her see Misia. Not wanting to upset Misia further, Chanel did not tell her of these visits. When Misia found out, she was beside herself.

How could anyone dare to keep us apart, to let her believe that I had closed my door to her! My only thought was to get up as soon as possible, to find her again, to leave the house where she was not welcome.

Chanel was contrite and offered to invite Roussy to lunch. Misia agreed, on condition that Coco would not criticize Roussy in any way.

I could not have borne anyone to pass judgment. Having adorned her with every gift, I couldn't allow anyone to touch my idol. Her mere presence calmed my anguish, gave meaning to my life. She was like a mirror, giving me back my youth. With her I found my gaiety again. And how could I not be convinced that she loved me? Had she not accepted all I had given her? She must have adored me to accept such a sacrifice on my part. For she was fully aware of my despair.

Misia was fascinated by the thought of marriage and romance—even her rival's. As if she were marrying off a daughter to a man she approved of, she kept herself occupied with preparations for Roussy's wedding. She took her to Chanel for her trousseau, went to all the fittings, and even persuaded Coco to reduce her prices. It had not been difficult, for Chanel too was a little in love with Roussy. She found her ideal model in the tall, elegant girl who wore clothes with such nonchalant distinction. Together Misia and Sert chose the superb ruby necklace that was to be his wedding present to the bride. Misia even helped him buy the ring. The wedding took place in The Hague on August 18, 1928.

Chanel knew how lost Misia must feel now that Sert and Roussy were married, and suggested that Misia spend the summer with her. Her lover the Duke of Westminster (the richest man in England) was expecting them in London and at his fishing lodge in Scotland. Misia was grateful to be included, but Eaton Hall, Westminster's vast country house with its gloomy gothic shadows, did not please her. It was for the Macbeths, she complained testily to Coco, for blood-stained hands and guilt-ridden insomniacs. Nor was she amused in Scotland by the shabby tweeds, the hearty breakfasts, the salmon fishing, the endless rain, and the English jokes whose meaning escaped her. Misia stubbornly refused to be distracted. To be with Sert and Roussy was her only thought. Persistently she turned over the possibilities in her mind. She and Roussy had exchanged roles, that was all. Once the three of them were together again, everything would be fine. Hadn't they promised they would never abandon her?

Roussy and Sert had, in fact, promised more than they meant. Foolishly, if halfheartedly, they had invited her to join them on a cruise to Greece and Turkey. Even more foolishly, Misia had accepted. Her days in Scotland were spent waiting for a telegram from Sert. When a wire finally came asking her to meet them in Genoa, Misia in her pathetic eagerness arrived three days before the newly married couple. Almost farcically—or had they deliberately neglected to book a cabin for her?—there was no room in first class for Misia. So it was she and Roussy who shared the bridal suite, while Sert squirmed in gentlemanly discomfort in a small cabin below decks. Misia tried not to think they were sorry she had come; but gradually, horribly, it occurred to her that she had assumed the role of the unwelcome mother-in-law. All the same, she could not let go. She preferred the sickness of imposing herself on them to the deathly emptiness of living without them. Aware that she was an intruder, she tried to convince herself that she could be happy in the shadow of their lives.

Paul Morand was bemused by the spectacle of Sert and his "two women." In his poetic memoir *Venises*, he describes a visit they made to their friends the Baroness Catherine d'Erlanger and her lover Albert Landsberg at the Villa Malcontenta. With its overgrown lawns sloping down to the Brenta, Palladio's magnificent villa was in a state of picturesque disrepair. Bertie and Cathy were living like gypsies. Surrounded by packing cases, camp beds, Brazilian hammocks, and rustic chairs, they had decided to restore the villa to its former glory. "Keep your knives," the hosts announced after lunch on a Ping-Pong table. "We're going to scrape the walls for Veroneses." The baroness and her children scratched away while Sert, the pasha, sank "into a sagging armchair, with his two wives, Misia and Roussy, stretched out at his feet. Diaghilev, his white lock standing out against his dyed hair, his ribboned monocle in his eye, studied the ceiling while Lifar and Kochno scraped the plaster from the walls." Diaghilev must have understood Sert's ambivalent situation: for he also had a pair of jealous competitors for his affections, the two young men searching for hidden murals. No Veroneses came to light, but the Zelottis and the Francos, the frescoes of Aurora, of Philemon and Baucis, that were eventually uncovered were delightful!

In the summer of 1929 the Duke of Westminster invited Chanel and Misia to join him on a cruise along the Dalmatian coast. Westminster's yacht *The Flying Cloud* was a far cry from Misia's old *Aimée*. Even Misia and Coco were impressed by its ornate luxury. The crew of forty, the massive furniture, and the canopied beds were perfect targets for their irreverent ironies. One day in the midst of their conspiratorial laughter, the ship's wireless operator handed Misia a radiogram from Venice: "Am sick; come quickly. Serge." Misia was alarmed. When she had last seen Diaghilev a month before in London, he had looked "drawn and at the end of his tether." Despite his deteriorating health, he had been planning ballets with Hindemith and Strauss. More exhausting still, he was pursuing young men. His latest protégé was a Russian composer, Igor Markevitch—gifted, handsome, and seventeen years old. After the London season Diaghilev's doctor prescribed a rest cure, but instead he took Markevitch on a strenuous cultural pilgrimage. For the aging Pygmalion, illness was to be ignored; it was far more important that the young composer hear Wagner in Munich and Mozart in Salzburg. Molding, shaping, loving the boy would be cure enough.

As soon as the *Flying Cloud* reached Venice, Misia and Coco rushed to the Grand Hôtel des Bains on the Lido, where Kochno and Lifar were staying with Diaghilev. When the two women entered the small bedroom, they found him in horrible pain, frighteningly haggard, and drenched in perspiration. Although the heat was overpowering, he was wearing his dinner jacket in bed to keep from shivering. It was touching to see his eyes light up the way they always had for Misia, though his mouth was twisted in pain. "Oh, how happy I am to see you," he whispered. "I love you in white. Promise me you will always wear white." But later in the day the light went out of the sick man's eyes and he relapsed into a delirious fever. Misia's heart sank when she realized he was speaking of himself in the past tense: "I loved *Tristan*—and the *Pathétique*—that's what I've loved most, all my life. What? You don't know it! Quick, go hear it and think of me, Misia." Suddenly turning to face her, he said in Russian, "I feel drunk." Afraid of breaking down, Misia slipped out to buy him a sweater. The sight of her elegant friend looking like a derelict in his rumpled dinner jacket had unnerved her.

Lifar told her about the terrible ordeal of the past weeks. He had nursed Diaghilev day and night, reassured him, listened to his wandering memories: of his student days, his trip down the Volga, his first trip abroad, his triumphs in Paris. Then, as though to keep death at bay, Diaghilev had sung Tchaikovsky's *Pathétique* in a loud, raucous voice. Terrified as he was of dying, he had begged to be moved to the other bed in the room despite Lifar's superstitious fear that to change beds meant the end was near. Lifar refused; then, to his horror, he found the dying man trying to crawl from one bed to the other. Misia sent for German doctors and engaged an English nurse to relieve Lifar and Kochno. After a while Diaghilev's condition seemed to improve. Chanel, reassured, left on the *Flying Cloud* while Misia stayed behind. But Diaghilev took a turn for the worse. With his two young friends on either side and Misia at the foot of his bed, the night passed.

Misia spent the next day, August 18, at his bedside. About ten in the evening she went back to her room at the Hotel Danieli to get some rest. But toward midnight Kochno telephoned to say that Diaghilev had fallen into a coma. Quickly she returned to the Lido. At three in the morning, as Diaghilev seemed to be sinking, Misia sent for a priest. When the sleepy, irritable priest was told that Diaghilev belonged to the Russian Orthodox Church, he refused to do anything. Her nerves at the breaking point, Misia screamed at him until he agreed to perform the last rites. It was a night Misia was never to forget.

At dawn his heart peacefully stopped beating. The sun's first rays lit his forehead at the moment his breathing stopped. Suddenly, flooded by sunlight, the sea was gloriously ablaze. The nurse bent over Diaghilev to close his eyes, now blind to the triumph of light. It was then, in that small hotel room where the greatest magician in the world of art had come to die, that a phenomenon took place, an essentially Russian phenomenon such as one finds in Dostoevsky's novels.

Serge's death must have been the spark that caused the explosion of pent-up hatred in the two boys who had been so close to him. In the tense silence of this only too authentic drama a kind of roar broke out. Kochno threw himself on Lifar, who was kneeling at the other side of the bed. Shaken by rage, they rolled on the floor, tearing at each other's clothes, biting one another like wild animals: two mad dogs fighting over the body of their master. After the first moment of shock, the nurse and I had all we could do to separate them, and get them to leave so that she could lay out the body.

My spirit emptied of emotion, I left, to wander about aimlessly. A bench in the sun—I don't know how long I sat there. Then I remember a tram, a gondola, the cemetery—to find a plot of ground for him, that was the last and frightful service I could perform for the friend who had been so close to my heart for over twenty years.

As always with Diaghilev, there was little money. Misia gave the six thousand francs he had to Kochno and Lifar. She gave the money she had brought from Paris to the Baroness d'Erlanger and asked her to pay the funeral expenses. Then left with nothing, she decided to raise a loan on her diamond necklace. On her way to the jeweller's she ran into Chanel who, following a presentiment, had persuaded Westminster to turn the *Flying Cloud* around and bring her back. Chanel of course offered to help. Nine years ago she had paid her entrance fee into Diaghilev's charmed circle, and now in a sense she was repaying him for the deep pleasures with which he had enriched her life.

That afternoon a few close friends met in Diaghilev's hotel room for a private service. The next morning a coffin was brought to the hotel before dawn, for death in this festive corner of Venice was not permitted to dampen the guests' holiday spirits. The body was placed in a large funeral gondola and taken to the Greek Orthodox Church. After the solemn mass the coffin was carried back to the black gondola with its gilded winged angels. Escorted by priests, Diaghilev's body floated across the lagoon to the small Russian cemetery on the *Isola di San Michele*, an island as mysteriously remote as Roerich's *Isle of the Dead*, that Symbolist entrance to the other world. In the first of the three gondolas that formed the cortege were Misia, Chanel, Kochno and Lifar. As their gondola made its way, lunging and gliding, the voices of the chanting priests could be heard over the water. It could not have been more unreal, more sadly beautiful, more justly theatrical. Even the Ballets Russes theatrics at the burial—Kochno and Lifar crawling on their knees to the gaping hole in the earth, Lifar trying to throw himself into the grave—were a fitting end for the strange great man who had meant so many things to the little group at the graveside.

Diaghilev's death signalled the end of a princely era. As a young man he had written of his desire to be a Maecenas. He became one: a mythic aristocrat, coolly and gracefully straddling the world of art. With a few props he created an international illusion. A top hat, a monocle, white tie and tails, a fur-lined coat—and he was the elegant, the luxurious king of culture. Like royalty, he expected others to foot the bills; it was not for him to carry money in his pocket. As the years went on and his clothes became a bit threadbare, his teeth false, and his paunch prodigious, he still—with his Russian aloofness and his almost frightening formality—gave the illusion of fastidious, distant royalty.

Unlike many a Maecenas, he left an incontestable legacy. For Diaghilev had seen a vision of a new drama without words: drama that would explore the expressivity of the body in fresh and miraculously telling ways. By combining great painting, music, and choreography, he developed an art form that told the world of things hitherto unexpressed. He used the associative power of bodies in motion much as his contemporary Freud used the dream and the associative power of words: to explore the subconscious. Psychological motives and human relations are the province of spoken drama, but Diaghilev's chosen choreographers—Fokine, the Nijinskys, Massine, and Balanchine—found physical ways of making us understand what cannot be stated in mere words. Just as Catherine the Great collected works of art, Diaghilev collected artists. In addition to the composers and painters, the dancers and choreographers whom be nurtured, he left a heritage of uncompromising ideas and ideals for dance and theatre that nourishes us to this day. The Ballets Russes, his beautiful creation, was the golden cornerstone of our unique century of dance. With the death of Diaghilev a certain glamour went out of the world. Misia spoke of this in an introduction she wrote for the catalogue of the Diaghilev exposition at the Musée des Arts Décoratifs in 1939.

It is now ten years that you are gone, dear Serge. And we are left without a magician. The last time I saw you, do you remember, it was the eve of your death, in Venice. . . .

We have been reliving old memories: you spoke to me then—you who discovered, one by one, all the composers who were to turn the music of our time upside down—of your secret preference for Tchaikovsky's *Pathétique* and for *Tristan and Isolde*. Works of love.

Your whole life was inspired by love. It was in you like a fever that you communicated to artists, artists chosen by your love, which demanded that they give the best of their souls.

For twenty years my eyes watched the prodigies of creation that you provoked in the midst of indescribable storms.

You were right. Works of love never perish. Those that were born of your love have outlived you, prolonging in our hearts the miracle of your existence.

After Diaghilev's funeral, Misia and Chanel left Venice on the *Flying Cloud*. Misia was in despair. She felt the need to share her grief with Sert, but he and Roussy were happily driving through Spain in their splendid new car. At each port, at each hotel, Misia inquired for an answer to her wires. But the consolation she hoped to get from Sert was not to be hers. Instead, another blow awaited her in Paris. At the time of their divorce in Holland, Sert had told her that he was applying for an annulment from the Church as well. Because it was never mentioned again, Misia had dismissed it from her mind. She clung to the idea that since Sert was a citizen of Catholic Spain where divorce was not recognized, she was still the real Madame Sert; his civil marriage was just a game they had all played, and one day the game would end, Roussy would somehow disappear, and she and Sert would be together again. When she returned after Diaghilev's death, she was summoned by the Archbishop of Paris to a hearing of Sert's application for annulment. Alone with four priests in red robes, Misia listened to a detailed description of her internal organs and the reasons she could not bear children. It was this inadequacy that gave Sert grounds for annulment. "I could hardly believe my ears," she wrote, "when the interminable report came to an end, and I was asked if I acknowledged the truth of what I had heard. I quickly said yes, signed everything I was asked to sign, and ran out, suppressing a wild desire to laugh. It was not until the next day that I was overcome by hopeless sorrow."

When Fira Benenson, a young Russian friend, offered her an impressive sum to help launch a fashion house in New York, Misia accepted. Encouraged by her friends, she thought that with a change of scene she might forget herself in work. "The *Aquitania* is about to depart," she wrote Vuillard. "I leave Europe with a violent desire to return as soon as possible and send a last greeting to you as my dearest friend." She sailed for America half-hoping that Sert would stop her. But he took the news of her departure calmly. The following spring he wrote her in New York that he and Roussy had been married again in the Spanish church in Paris. The casual tone of his letter upset her; the two people who had sworn that they would never abandon her seemed now to be treating her as though she were just another name on their mailing list. Unhappy as she was, however, Misia still led the worldly life. New American friends, visitors from Paris, fashionable dinners, concerts, and theatres, even negotiations to arrange new commissions for Sert, made her feel she was still alive. Of all her diversions, the evenings spent at the Casino in the Park with her old friends Jean and Baba Faucigny-Lucinge amused her most. They were captivated by the engaging jazz pianist Eddy Duchin, and Misia invited the handsome young man to lunch at her hotel, then asked him to teach her to play jazz. After a few lessons Duchin was as impressed with her Gershwin as Liszt had been with her Beethoven fifty years before.

Misia did her work in New York, but she was bored and longed for Paris, Sert, and Roussy. When at last she went to see them in their magnificent new apartment, it was clear that their life was complete without her. Somehow it was their enormous, ornate bed that made her realize she was unwanted. "God alone knows," she wrote, "why this piece of furniture astonished me so: it was the bed that suddenly made me feel abandoned, alone, and almost old."

PART SIX
Misia

Overleaf, Misia in Venice, c. 1947

In the late twenties Vuillard painted his last portrait of Misia. The interior we see is her relatively modest apartment in the rue de Constantine near the Invalides, the apartment she had taken after her divorce from Sert. As in the early portraits, Vuillard reveals as much about himself as about his model. Youthful charm and spontaneity now discarded, the picture is all sobriety and directness. A lacklustre atmosphere hovers over the canvas like stubborn truth. The girlish Misia he had painted so lovingly has become a watchful woman, authoritative, playing her cards close to her ample chest. Seated at her dining table like a chairman of the board, she is seen with her niece Mimi, now a grown woman, looking submissively down at her. The feeling of emptiness in the painting suggests the loneliness of both painter and model. Is it lost youth, lost love, or lost time that the painter is describing?

Misia's situation inspired two plays as well: in 1933, Alfred Savoir's *Maria*—originally called *La Donneuse (She Who Gives)*—and in 1940, Cocteau's *Les Monstres Sacrés*, subtitled *Portrait of a Play in Three Acts*. Unlike Vuillard, Cocteau chose to paint Misia as a woman of blazing temperament, a celebrated actress, a Parisian deity who sacrifices herself on the altar of love. And there is justness in his choice. For Misia never lost her élan, her inimitable wit, or her ability to dominate the scene. Even in her lowest moments she always put on a good performance. While Cocteau has changed the details of the Misia-Sert-Roussy drama and given the characters other names, the essential truth of their story is in the lines they speak. In one scene Roussy tells Misia she is Sert's mistress, and Misia replies:

> Be quiet. (*She paces up and down.*) When the Empress Elizabeth was assassinated she thought she had merely been struck. She walked for a long time with the knife in her heart. They removed the knife and she was dead. I am walking with your knife in my heart. When it's taken out no doubt I shall die. Till then I feel giddy . . . light-headed.

A revealing scene between Misia and Chanel follows:

> MISIA (*Esther*): . . . It's perfectly normal that extraordinary things happen to me. I'm an exceptional person. Oh! Don't think I'm

boasting. I meant to say that, unfortunately, I'm exceptional and that, unfortunately, I can't live by the rules. I must make my own. And it's not easy, I assure you.

CHANEL (*Charlotte*): It would be a fine thing if everyone talked the way you do.

MISIA: I'm not everyone . . . and I regret it. Other people's decent behavior would be obscene in me. And I want to behave decently, do you understand? . . .

CHANEL: How shocking you are! . . .

MISIA: I shock you . . . because I go about, exposing my soul, right here in the house, and that's not done. . . .

CHANEL: . . . Why did you lure her here to be thrown into his arms? That's what I can't understand.

MISIA: It was irresistible. There are forces that . . . draw us to catastrophe.

CHANEL: Ah, you admit it's a catastrophe.

MISIA: Yes, it's a catastrophe. But I will do everything in my power . . . to live with it . . . to tame it.

CHANEL: A domesticated catastrophe. . . .

MISIA: Why not? I can't force myself to hate him or to hate the little one. . . . I would be lying. I love them both. I love to love. . . . I have a rage to love, like Verlaine. And you hate love. Everyone hates love, tries to spoil it, to kill it. . . .

CHANEL: No one will understand you, believe you. . . .

MISIA: Naturally I'm struggling, naturally I'm suffering. It would be too simple otherwise. Last night . . . suffering made me cry out. I called him. He came. He fussed over me. He wanted to stay with me. It was I who forced him to leave, to go back to her room.

CHANEL: You don't have a shred of decency.

MISIA: God preserve me from that. If I had kept him, I would have thought he stayed with me against his will and she would have resented me for it.

CHANEL: You're too much!

Les Monstres Sacrés, a rather Henry Bernstein–like play, is one of Cocteau's minor works. Metamorphosis and the brilliant juggling of unexpected images and ideas were more in his line. Yet he made the distinction between truth and slander with his usual adroitness. There is love and sympathy in his portrait of Misia. Alfred Savoir did not manage the distinction as sensitively, or as tactfully, in *Maria*. In fact, Misia stormed out of the theatre halfway through the first performance. Savoir, a successful playwright, had been in and out of Misia's apartment for years. It was even said he was her lover. Like Cocteau, he found the Sert *ménage à trois* irresistibly theatrical. In his play the trio is found in bed together; Sert believes that his two women are having an affair; in short, the world's suspicions are given a thorough airing. Both playwrights, however, came to the same conclusion: Misia had a rage to love, a rage to give. "I gave my husband everything, including the woman he loves," Savoir has Misia, *la donneuse*, say.

Quite understandably, the real-life Roussy found Misia's interfering love intolerable. As did Sert. He had been illustrious always, but marrying a princess gave his name a new international lustre. Exalted by aristocratic notoriety, he began to live a more conspicuously extravagant life. He and Roussy took a grand apartment on the Place du Palais Bourbon, where Sert's interiors were photographed by *Vogue* as the epitome of elegance. Later they moved to an even grander apartment on the rue de Rivoli, where Sert was able to give free rein to his awesome sense of the luxurious.

Commissions poured in at higher and higher fees. With the money he received for decorating Rockefeller Center in New York, he bought a large property on the sea near Barcelona, a stretch of beach that was all coves and bays and limpid water. There he decorated his house, the Mas Juny, with such daring simplicity that it was considered by many the most beautiful seaside villa in Europe. Geared to the fashion world, the rich, and the vaguely talented, Sert had moved from Misia's lightness, with its solid base of art, to Roussy's frivolity, with its nihilistic base of chic. Gradually Roussy came to feel that Misia—always there, always expecting to be included—was, as Cocteau described her, "like someone waiting for a table in a crowded restaurant, whose presence prevents the diners from enjoying their food." Included less and less often, Misia floundered about gracelessly. Gifts were fruitless; there was nothing for *la donneuse* to give that others were not providing. Roussy's smart young friends supplied amusement. Chanel, who adored her more and more, gave her magnificent clothes. Sert and the Mdivanis gave her love, and covered her with jewels.

New to Sert was the tawdry café-society world of Roussy's brothers, those skilled marksmen in the predatory profession of fortune hunting. Tough Hollywood actresses and bewildered young heiresses spent vast sums to buy their rather dubious titles and favors. Theirs was a world whose only standard was gold. It was comically unexpected that Roussy's sisters-in-law were Pola Negri, the great movie vamp, and Mae Murray, famous for her bee-stung lips. Roussy felt a passionate, almost incestuous attachment to her youngest brother, Alexis. In 1931 at the age of twenty-two he bagged his first American heiress, Louise Van Alen of the Astor family. With his nineteen-year-old wife's money, he established himself in a princely house. Grand parties, liveried servants, and coats of arms emblazoned on the silver, the bed linen, and the polo ponies' blankets soon made Alexis seem a prince indeed. Eighteen months later he divorced Louise for someone richer: the Woolworth heiress Barbara Hutton. His brother Serge, reluctant to see the Van Alen millions disappear from the Mdivani clutches, married Louise himself four years later.

Even the Mdivanis must have been amused when young Alec, signing his marriage settlement of a million dollars, said, "I'll sign anything blindfolded because I love Barbara and that's all that matters." As fortune would have it, Barbara inherited an additional forty-two million dollars on her twenty-first birthday, and Alec persuaded her to settle another million and a quarter on him. Perhaps it had occurred to him that there were other things besides love that matter, after all. It was natural for Roussy to be engrossed by her brothers' financial-sexual gymnastics, and natural too that her family insist she drop Misia. Not that she removed herself completely; on the contrary, they saw one another a good deal. There is a revealing three-minute film made in 1934 of Roussy, Misia, and Colette.* The three women appear in the window of Misia's apartment. Colette sits immobile, her arms resting on the window ledge. Roussy, playing with her pet monkey, is gay, young, totally absorbed in the monkey's antics. Misia hovers attentively in the background, moving with startling lightness: an older woman of immense distinction. One can readily see the problems Sert must have faced when he exchanged a fascinating, many-faceted woman for a narcissistic, perversely alluring girl. And one wonders what thoughts lay

* Taken by Bobsy Goodspeed Chapman, who brought a movie camera to Paris in the thirties and recorded many of the most distinguished people in the arts. Her film documents are now in the collection of the Film Library of New York's Museum of Modern Art.

behind Colette's wise and weary gaze, for she loved Misia. After Sert had married Roussy, Colette had written to Misia as the person, among all those who suffer the strange, dramatic twists of fate, of whom she thought most often. Discreetly she added her wish that one day Misia would open her heart to her.

In February 1933 Misia and Marcelle Meyer gave a two-piano concert in the grand ballroom of the Hôtel Continental. The recital was to benefit Mademoiselle Meyer, a gifted pianist who was having trouble with her career because she chose to play Satie and Stravinsky instead of Liszt and Chopin. Though Mademoiselle Meyer was by far the greater pianist, it was Misia, as usual, who stole the show. And Misia was the first to admit it:

> I must put all modesty aside and say that it was truly a triumph. The ballroom, dazzlingly elegant, was filled to the bursting point. In front of the endless line of private cars at the entrance, one heard the chauffeurs of "great houses" say that they would never have believed such luxury could still exist after the 1914 war. . . . Sert, who had been more excited from the first moment on than if it had been he who had to perform, was now wreathed in triumphant smiles! And Roussy—as if she were twelve years old again—jumped for joy and covered me with kisses. . . .
>
> Perhaps [Marcelle's] playing was somewhat lacking in sensitivity, but I compensated for that so well that we made a team the impresarios fought over. . . . Offers for engagements began to pour in. But after a second performance at the Théâtre des Ambassadeurs,* given this time in a completely professional manner to a packed house, I ended my short career, thinking I had done all I could for Marcelle.

Jean Cocteau, always devoted, not only made a charming drawing of Misia rehearsing in a cloche hat and her inevitable diamonds, but wrote a pen portrait for the newspaper *Paris-Midi* as well:

> So here we are, face to face with one of those women in whom Stendhal recognized a certain genius: a genius in the way she walked,

---

* At this concert Serge Lifar danced his solo version of *Afternoon of a Faun* while Misia and Marcelle played Debussy's two-piano transcription of the score.

laughed, put one in one's place, handled her fan, entered a car, designed a tiara. . . . But I did not realize that her vague, aerial genius, that genius which expressed itself sometimes by insolence, sometimes by making Chinese trees with branches of feathers and pearls—I did not realize, I repeat, that this gift extended itself to true genius and that the pianist who played for us at home was, in fact a real pianist. . . . [She] drew forth from her Pleyel preludes and mazurkas of Chopin, displaying their ribbons and pearls as no one else could: drew forth the storms and joys of her piano, displaying the heritage of her race. She bewitched us in the true sense of the word.

In spite of Misia's desire to put Marcelle Meyer forward, everyone spoke of "Misia's evening, Misia's concert, Misia's talent." This response to beautiful music in a worldly setting was a tribute to a woman who had helped make Paris shine: an admiring acknowledgment of a *Parisienne* who knew how to fight other people's battles better than her own. Gracefully, Marcelle Meyer insisted that Misia play the encores alone. Max Jacob wrote poems for the occasion. Lifar coached Misia in her bows. Poulenc turned pages for her. Everyone who was in Paris came to the concert, and those who were away sent messages. Colette, who bought a new dress for the occasion, missed the concert because she was giving lectures in Valence, Grenoble, and Lyon. Stravinsky had written from Switzerland, "And you, dear Misia, I hope so much that you are well; you must be working magnificently at your piano, for the day of the concert approaches! And I very much hope to be in Paris for that!"

Deprived of Sert and Roussy and with Diaghilev gone. Misia lost her *raison d'être*. She had no further function; no one needed her. All that was left to her was the futile pursuit of the newly married couple, the quest for diversion, and increasing doses of morphine. In 1931 while Sert and Roussy were putting the finishing touches to their house in Spain, Chanel invited Misia to go to Hollywood with her. Ironically enough, it was Misia who was now Chanel's *dame de compagnie*. They had met Samuel Goldwyn in Monte Carlo, where—despite the Depression in America—he had offered Chanel a million dollars to dress his film stars. Goldwyn staged a triumphal tour, an extravaganza of commercial make-believe, for his two French imports. Hollywood royalty turned out to meet them: Garbo, Dietrich, and Claudette Colbert; Fredric March, George Cukor, and Erich von Stroheim. Chanel found it all a little beneath her; Misia enjoyed it enormously. But when they went to visit Roussy's brother David, Misia was depressed to see him living in a kind of "fake mosque of unimaginable hideousness," surrounded by family souvenirs and photographs brought from Russia. In a Proustian moment she was stripped of her last illusions about the Mdivanis. The vulgar, provincial bric-a-brac was all that remained of the intoxicating fantasies that Roussy had spun when they first met. Recklessly she wrote Sert to tell him of her revelation: of the shabby pretentiousness of the Mdivanis. Inevitably the letter fell into Roussy's hands. Misia had only gained another disadvantage.

In 1935 Barbara Hutton sued Roussy's brother Alexis for divorce. With his customary extravagance and his Hutton millions, he took an apartment in the Place du Palais Bourbon. There, attended by two silent Indian manservants, he settled down in garish oriental splendor. That summer he and his mistress, Maude Thyssen, visited the Serts in Spain. Driving in his Rolls-Royce one day he struck a culvert. The car turned over five times; Baroness Thyssen was thrown clear, but Alexis, whose head went through the windshield, was killed instantly. When his shattered body with its almost severed head was brought back to the Mas Juny, Roussy was inconsolable. Childishly, hysterically, she clung to the idea that somehow Sert would be able to save her brother. When she saw that he could do nothing, Roussy lost her faith—in him, in everything. Without the brother she loved with an almost unnatural fierceness, Roussy lost her will to live. She locked herself in her room, and refused to eat or to see anyone for a week. Sert had a doctor come from Paris but he could do nothing as Roussy was determined to destroy herself. When reports of her insomnia, drugs, and suicidal self-neglect reached Misia, she immediately took the train to Barcelona. But Misia was the last person the Serts wanted to see, and she was ignominiously shunted off to a hotel. Later when they were all back in Paris, Roussy still refused to see Misia, but did not hesitate to call her in the middle of the night to speak of her anguish. In a sense Misia had become her mother: a mother she felt close to, but whose presence she could not bear. As though

Alexis' death were not tragedy enough, the following year Roussy's brother Serge was killed in a fall from his horse while playing polo in Florida.

In 1938 Roussy and Sert cruised the Mediterranean in their Venetian fishing boat that Sert had transformed into a yacht. Painted black with red and gold sails, it was named the *Saint Alexis* after Roussy's brother. With them were Igor Markevitch and his wife Kyra.* In spite of her constant fever, Roussy would swim for hours. Disturbed by her cough, her irritability, and her wraith-like appearance, the Markevitches persuaded her to see a lung specialist in Switzerland. Apparently this idea had never occurred to Sert, who tended to ignore illness. X-rays revealed that Roussy was in an advanced stage of tuberculosis. When she returned to Paris, she took to her bed and stubbornly refused to have a nurse. But now when her visitors left for the day, she would telephone Misia and whisper, "Come quickly. I'm alone." While Sert slept, Misia spent the nights with Roussy. "As she smoked without stopping and dozed off, burning the sheets [Misia wrote], I was always afraid that she might really set the bed on fire. And so I remained almost all night, kneeling at her side, telling her stories. She became a child again and never tired of listening to me till dawn. Then, as she dropped off to sleep with the first light, I would steal out on tiptoe."

Gaunt and haggard, Roussy was fading fast. To those who loved her she had taken on a new, ethereal beauty, but Claudel, who did not approve of her, painted quite a different picture in his journal of July 13, 1938: "Sert's wife, once so beautiful, now terrifying. As in a Chinese legend, a vampire who reveals her true self little by little." It was essential to get Roussy to a hospital but impossible to persuade her to go. Finally Chanel took matters into her capable hands. She told Roussy that she herself was ill and begged the sick girl to come with her to a Swiss clinic. Misia wrote later: "Thank God she believed the story of our friend's illness. . . . A few days later, unable to bear it, I left for Prangins. When I arrived at the clinic, I was not permitted to see her. Nor did I ever know whose orders prevented me from visiting her. Twice I went back, always in vain. I was told that the smallest emotional upset could be fatal to her." Misia suspected that it was not the doctors but Chanel who would not let her see Roussy. Back in Paris she telephoned Chanel at the clinic and was told, "Only a miracle can save her."

---

* Markevitch, Diaghilev's last protégé, had married the daughter of Nijinsky, Diaghilev's first protégé.

Superstition and religion were closely allied in Misia. Perhaps a pilgrimage and prayers would bring about the necessary miracle. And so Misia, exhausted and sick at heart, took a train to Lourdes. There she bought a candle so heavy that "two men were needed to carry it to the grotto." Suddenly she felt a stabbing pain in her eyes; everything looked blurred and distorted; her head ached horribly. Whether it was the strain of despair or of remorse, from that moment Misia's sight was permanently damaged. It was as though she could no longer bear to see things as they really were. When she returned to the rue de Constantine, a telegram was waiting for her. Roussy had died the day before, December 16, 1938. She was thirty-two. "I put the telegram in my pocket. Unable to hear or see anything, dry-eyed, I left the room in silence. Stretched out on my bed, I sank into a stillness that I wished could be complete and eternal." Roussy's friends mourned her deeply. For them she had been a graceful, ravishing creature, as spontaneous as laughter itself. The Mdivani family came to Sert's apartment to console the widower—and lay claim to Roussy's valuables. As they fingered the rubies, diamonds, and pearls that Sert had given her and appraised the furniture with knowing eyes, they became more and more clamorous in their conviction that all Roussy's possessions belonged to them. Sert found them odious and sinister and would not give an inch. In the end, little was exchanged except recriminations.

Misia, who in her complicated way had loved Roussy as much as she loved Sert, was overcome by a sense of futility and desolation. She had given Sert to Roussy and now they were both lost to her. All the suffering she had gone through seemed pointless. Even Roussy, trying to comfort her, had once said, "You love him too much. He isn't worth it any longer." Misia was sixty-six and alone. When her brother Cipa had died the year before, Colette had written her compassionately of the several kinds of solitude Misia had come to know, and of the pain they both suffered as they watched the ranks thinning around them. But it was Sert's unfeeling remark after Roussy's death, "After all, if you had really loved me, you wouldn't have let me go," that made Misia feel there was still another kind of solitude to endure.

It was during this bleak and embittered period of her life that Misia turned to her niece for comfort, but there was little comfort there. Mimi's marriage had not been going well, and she had become the mistress of the critic Pierre Brisson. Misia, who detested him, was one of those people who are least generous with their own families. Certainly she did not stint on money and gifts—she had more or less supported the Godebskis for years—but she was pitiless about what she considered her family's shortcomings. Misia was convinced that Mimi had made a dreadful mistake. She had drifted into a love affair with a priggish *petit bourgeois* journalist who had a string of mistresses, and as Misia said, "never gave her so much as a bunch of violets." And so Mimi found herself being ridiculed and threatened. "What a pretty neck Mimi has," said a friend. "Yes, perfect for the guillotine!" Misia snapped.

If Misia was cruel to Mimi, she was poisonous to Brisson. But Brisson was as dangerous an enemy as Misia herself and, as critics often do, he had the last word. He published a *roman à clef* called *Le Lierre* (*The Ivy*), in which he describes his affair with Mimi and his hatred for Misia and Sert. He shows them living in a gloomy house filled with monstrous fake antiques. The character based on Misia (Did she belong to the third sex? the author wonders) is a cadaverous, loathsome creature of the night who lives on other people's blood. Her rages are terrifying, her ambition uncontrolled, her conniving cleverness relentless, her destructiveness absolute. Sert is portrayed as a pretentious manipulator who sells fake Tiepolos, Raphaels, and Nattiers for enormous sums. The couple are determined to marry their niece to one of his rich but shady associates. "Sometimes I feel she's trying to break my spirit," the heroine says of her aunt. "She keeps telling me how stupid my life is."

In Brisson's quiet, rather stylish novel, the lurid caricatures of Misia and Sert stand out like fire and brimstone. Heartless, invidious arch-snobs, they lavish extravagant gifts on their niece but stop at nothing to destroy her love affair—just for the sadistic pleasure of keeping her under their thumb.

After Roussy's death Sert turned to Misia, who continued to live in the rue de Constantine but gradually took on the role of hostess at Sert's apartment. Things were not as they once had been, however. Sert was desolate, and Misia, still in love with him, could not reconcile herself to their separate

lives. Now that he was alone, she saw no reason to have two apartments. He was her husband, she felt, not just a friend with whom
one dined at Maxim's. But dine at Maxim's they did. Then he would
drive her home, and she would be left to brood about the coolness of their
warmed-over relationship. Still, as the old intimacy renewed itself and
Sert began to discuss his work with her again, she felt that she was at least
useful to him. "After all, it's only with you that I have any fun," he would
say. Then as her eyes lit up only too eagerly, "But think how boring it
would be if we were an old couple in bedroom slippers, sitting around the
fire." Longing to say that nothing could bore her less, Misia for once held
her tongue. There was in reality little time for fun in Sert's life. To distract
himself from his grief, he plunged into work, carrying out commissions all
over the world with almost superhuman energy. Every time he left Paris
Misia felt abandoned, yet she admired his dedication.

Misia herself, of course, was no longer at the center of the stage. She had
become a link with the past, an object of almost historic interest to the
young. Her role as hostess to musical, artistic, literary, and elegant circles
had been taken over by three younger women. Music became the province
of Marie-Blanche de Polignac, the niece of Misia's friend the Princesse de
Polignac. Painting and literature were taken over by Marie-Laure de
Noailles, granddaughter of her friend the Comtesse de Chevigné. Style and
fashion belonged to Marie-Louise Bousquet. In a sense, it took three Maries
to make one Misia. In the mid-thirties when Roussy was avoiding her, Misia
had begun to look for other surrogate daughters. Among the attractive
young women she took up were Diane de Rothschild, the playwright Marcel
Achard's wife Juliette, the Russian beauty Lady Ia Abdy, Georges Auric's
wife Nora (a Russian beauty herself, and a talented painter), Henry
Bernstein's lovable daughter George, and Denise Mayer, the sensitive,
highly cultivated wife of René Mayer, later France's Président du Conseil.
All of them found her a sympathetic listener as full of fun and as young in
heart as they: a combination of godmother and girl friend. They were
amused by her sharp tongue, touched by her kindness, and fascinated by
her past. Above all, they found her natural and direct despite the stylized
world she lived in. Misia had adoptive sons as well: Max Jacob, Marcel
Achard, and the painter Christian Bérard, among others. Once she said
regretfully to Bérard, "If only I'd been born earlier, I could have sat for
Manet." A few days later the witty Bérard amended history with a charming

portrait *à la* Manet of Misia as she might have looked in the past, just as once Lautrec had painted her as she might look in the future.

Misia's last great friend was Sert's secretary, Boulos Ristelhueber, the son of a diplomat. Sensitive and extremely cultivated, he was a delicate, startlingly pale and thin young man. He was sympathetic, bizarre, and heavily made-up. His friends called him "the Ectoplasm" or "the most elegant of our ghosts." Nor were these names mere euphemisms, for Boulos padded out his income as the ghost-writer for Lifar's memoirs as well as Misia's. Hardly a day went by that he did not visit her. They had much in common: friends, music, and drugs. Boulos took drugs, it was said, because he was in constant pain as the result of an automobile accident. But drugs were not unheard of in their circle: Sert, Cocteau, Auric, Kochno, even the level-headed Chanel did not neglect this means of escape. For Chanel drugs were harmless sedatives; for Misia their purpose was forgetfulness. There was a great deal besides Roussy's death and her changed relations with Sert that Misia preferred not to think about. Her sight was deteriorating. Her bright eyes, which had been among the first to recognize the beauties of Vuillard and Bonnard, could now barely distinguish the outlines of the pictures she loved. From Switzerland, where she went for an eye operation, she wrote in a pathetically large, unsteady hand to the wife of the playwright Henry Bernstein, the disgruntled Casanova of her unsatisfactory escapade in Baden-Baden many years before.

Thank you, dear Antoinette, for such a kind letter.

I do not know if you'll be able to read this, written with a trembling heart and hand. I was mad to come here—the operation a complete failure and so terrible that I'll never be myself again.

They are trying to save the right eye with daily injections directly into the eye, and in three weeks I hope to be dead or out of here.

Besides, to be away at this moment is real torture. The quarter-hour of *Soldat* was sheer rapture. How pretty Paris must be—and they speak French there. Kiss George. . . .

My dear, I can hardly write another word but only want to tell you that I love you both so tenderly.

Your
Misia

Not long after her return from Switzerland, Misia suffered a heart attack. Sert wrote to his sister:

April 1939

Dearest Dolores:

I was planning to leave for Spain, but a grave misfortune has kept me in Paris. For the last four days a dreadful heart attack has kept Misia hovering between life and death, and at best she won't be out of danger for at least three weeks. She is in bed, completely immobilized, and the doctors are keeping her under constant sedation to prevent the worst.

The poor woman was so deeply affected by Roussy's death and suffered so much that first she lost an eye, and now she has had a hemorrhage in the heart like the one she had in the retina. This being the case, I've changed my plans. As her niece and nephew are not in Paris, I must take care of everything. It is God's wish.

The specialists say there is some hope in spite of the gravity of her situation. Do not worry, but trust in God.

Un fuerte abrazo de
Jo

Misia recovered, but with her damaged eyesight and her weakened heart, she was sadly diminished. This was Misia's condition when the Second World War began in the fall of 1939, and she was no better in the following spring when Paris was occupied by the Nazis, those "overgrown homosexual boy scouts," as Misia called them.

As she and Sert watched the German troops goose-stepping by from his balcony overlooking the Place de la Concorde, they felt stunned and humiliated. But Sert was not stunned for long, since his was the accommodating nature of the perfect collaborator. Though violently anti-German and a professed pacifist, he cynically came to terms with the German authorities. There was a rumor that he would be commissioned to decorate important public buildings, but nothing came of it. Perhaps he was too canny to commit himself so openly. In any case, and by whatever mysterious means, he soon became one of the most privileged people in Paris. There were moments during the Occupation when two of the few places in starving Paris that had unlimited amounts of food were the Spanish embassy and Sert's apartment. "Have you laid in a supply of fuel for the winter?" one of his less fortunate Spanish friends asked sarcastically. "For a man like me, that kind of thing is never a problem," was Sert's arrogant answer. The horrors of the war and the Occupation depressed him deeply; yet his cruel, selfish nature and his loyalty to Franco seem to have given him the indifference of the extreme rightist to common people. In marked contrast, Misia—perhaps remembering her Jewish grandmother—was a fierce champion of the Resistance. Bedridden a good deal of the time, she stayed close to home in relative comfort. The comfort, of course, was provided by Sert. Like many another collaborator, he played an ambiguous game with the occupying forces. The aging satyr did not hesitate to take as his mistress Marie-Ursel, the Baroness Stohrer, wife of the German ambassador to Spain. In fact, he hoped she would divorce her husband and marry him. In his inept way he tried to hide the affair from Misia. "Don't tell anyone you've seen us together," he said to Lifar when he and his baroness met the dancer at a party in Venice given by high-ranking fascists. But of course Misia knew.

Sert had been named neutral Spain's ambassador to the Vatican. Riding about in his chauffeur-driven limousine, dining in *grand luxe*, ordering his gold leaf from Italy, his brushes from London, and his canvasses from Switzerland—these were the seignorial rights that Sert regarded as his due. The largesse he dispensed in his lordly way was in brutal contrast to the deprivations suffered by almost everyone else in war-torn Paris; nevertheless, it was very much welcomed by his friends. Misia, with no fight left in her, tried not to think about his position. When she spent weekends, which sometimes became weeks, at Sert's apartment, she was a little awed by the unending luxury, but her chief feeling was simply gratitude. For her, more than ever he "represented a kind of miracle outside time and space."

When Sert saved Colette's husband Maurice Goudeket, he was already in a deportation camp waiting to be sent to Germany. Colette had frantically appealed to everyone she knew—and she knew everyone—but it was useless. Goudeket was almost lost when it occurred to her to ask her old friend Sert for help, and Sert managed to rescue him. "I am sure," Misia wrote, "that even I do not know how many people were released from prison through him, or how many he saved from being deported or an even worse fate. As for those who, during the months of famine, lived on provisions brought by the truckload from Spain, they will not readily forget him." But Sert could not save all their friends. In 1944 Misia received a heartbreaking letter from Max Jacob. The Jewish poet had become a Catholic, but that did not prevent the Nazis from tracking him down to the village of Saint-Benoît-sur-Loire, where he was living as a lay brother.

MAX JACOB TO MISIA

. . . In my anguish, I call for help. . . . The friendship you have so often shown me is strong enough in my memory for me to have the audacity to depress you with the spectacle of my suffering . . . my family's home ransacked, destroyed with all the souvenirs of my childhood. My older sister has died of grief. My brother-in-law dead in a concentration camp. My brother taken off to prison. . . . I've borne it all, resigned to the curse on my poor race. But now the crowning horror: my youngest sister, my favorite, the one I called *"ma petite,"* has been arrested with no pretext, taken to the Dépôt, then to Drancy. It's for her that I ask your intervention before they drag her off to Germany to die in some dark cell. . . . The poor creature has only known unhappiness; her only son is in an insane asylum.

Chère amie, permit me to kiss your hands, the hem of your dress. . . . I beg you, do something.

"As soon as I told Sert about this letter," Misia recalled, "without thinking for one second of all the trouble he would bring upon himself by intervening for a Jew under the German terror, he immediately pulled every string he knew. Alas, poor Max was dragged off to Drancy himself, and the order for his release which Sert was finally able to obtain arrived too late." Misia felt the bitter injustice, the futility, and the waste in the death of a true poet. Each year on the anniversary of Max Jacob's murder, Misia read through the poems he had written for her, then went alone to church to have a mass performed in his memory.

———— ⚜ ————

In the first years of the Occupation, Boulos Ristelhueber kept a diary in which Misia figures prominently.

EXCERPTS FROM BOULOS' JOURNAL, 1940–1941

June 14, 1940

The hallucinatory column of smoke has disappeared. The layer of soot that floated in the sky has settled on the city pavements. Our nostrils are choked by burning coal, our heads are hot, our hearts cold. And the Germans are in Paris.

Is this really Paris, this sinister desert watched over by a few concierges? Aside from them, the only people left are Marie-Laure de Noailles,* Edith de Beaumont, Serge Lifar, the Serts, Valentine Hugo, Walerik,† and me. Everyone buried in his corner.

After this frantic flight from the city, I ask myself what madness possessed all these people who are now racing along the roads of France. Is it because I am so sick? Not for an instant have I had the slightest desire to stir from here. My God, what for? And how I congratulate myself that I've kept Marie-Laure here, in spite of the dreadful scene with Bergery,‡ who begged her with tears in his eyes to leave!

I shall never forget the abortive departure we made five days ago. That road to Fontainebleau, more congested than the Flea Market; the mattresses, the hand carts, the automobiles overloaded to bursting; the faces, like those in the Stations of the Cross; the poor trudging along; the shrieking horns; the limousines, unable to move in the general confusion . . . how shameful, that mass of humanity,

---

* Boulos was living at the Vicomte Charles de Noailles' impressively beautiful house in the Place des Etats-Unis. Noailles' wife, Marie-Laure, was the daughter of an extremely rich Jewish-American banker named Bischoffsheim. Brilliant, talented, and perverse (she was, after all, a descendant of the Marquis de Sade) she emerged in the thirties as one of the most talked-about women in Paris. She looked like Louis XIV and was as autocratic as he with friends and lovers. She and her husband were friends of Misia, Sert, and Roussy. Since she was half-Jewish, it was owing to her exalted position, her vast fortune, and her cynical willingness to collaborate with the Germans that she was able to survive in Paris during the Occupation.

† Walerik Dobujinsky, the son of the painter Mstislav Dobujinsky, who designed two of Diaghilev's 1914 productions: the Fokine ballets *Papillons* and *Midas*.

‡ Gaston Bergery, later Misia's lawyer. During the Occupation he was named French Ambassador to the Soviet Union. He and his charming American wife Bettina Jones were great friends of Sert and Roussy, whom they often visited in Spain.

quaking with fear, fleeing from the unknown to the unknown! I am sure that no plague, no cataclysm, ever provoked such an exodus.

Only ten miles after the Lion de Belfort I stopped the car and suggested we turn around. Marie-Laure said to me: "You're a fake. Admit that you never had any intention of leaving Paris." I admitted it—while the maid trembled at the thought of going back to Paris and vomited up everything she had eaten.

Sert comes at noon and offers to take us in his car to see the Germans parading at the Etoile. Marie-Laure and Serge go with him. I prefer to go on foot with Walerik.

The troops appear as in a Wagner opera. Ponderous and arrogant, they pass with the sound of an earthquake. Rows of Wotans and Lohengrins in gleaming steel helmets, supernaturally beautiful. Endless lines of enormous horses with long manes pulling cannons with gaping black mouths. At the top of the Arc de Triomphe, half of which is covered with sandbags, an enormous flag with a swastika and a tiny little photographer recording the spectacle for *Wochenschau*, the illustrated German weekly.

December 16, 1940

At Misia's at seven o'clock. Antoinette Bernstein very gloomy and dull. Then a marvellous evening alone with Misia. She does me a world of good.

December 17, 1940

Paris sadder than ever. An atmosphere of catastrophe. False rumors running wild. One knows nothing, nothing.

December 19, 1940

Lunch at Misia's. Serge Lifar speaks about the concert tonight at the Chaillot. It seems that Karajan, who is going to conduct a Bach mass, is a revelation. Naturally this festive little evening will be a *Soldatenabend* and the French, those miserable second-class citizens, won't be invited.

December 20, 1940

Dined with Misia in her bedroom. Picasso sinks onto her bed and speaks of his unhappy divorce from Olga which has never been resolved. Perhaps, he says, he will end his days with her and their monster of a son.

Misia tells him that when she was in Switzerland for her sinister eye operation, the monster in question came to see her and told her—with a cynicism beyond praise—that he made a living selling drugs. (In fact, the clinic he's in now is costing Picasso a fortune in Swiss francs.) She told him that rather than risk prison for paltry profits, he could make much more money by stealing one of his father's paintings and selling it. Picasso pretends to be revolted by this suggestion.

What a curious mixture of kindness and cruelty he is. It seems that one day when he lived with Fernande, he adopted a waif, a little girl on whom he lavished affectionate care. Six months later, suddenly feeling he'd had enough, he deposited her on a park bench and calmly walked off without turning around!

The story of his divorce from poor Olga is really marvellous. She had beautiful long hair that he loved more than anything. One fine day, Olga began to talk of cutting it. Then she never stopped boring him by asking what he thought of the idea. Very coldly he took a pair of scissors and cut her hair off.

That evening he took Olga and the boy to the Opéra-Comique to hear *Pagliacci*. When they got home, he undressed Olga very affectionately and made love to her. The next morning the servant announced, "There's a gentleman waiting in the salon who wishes to speak to Madame."

"You go," she says to Picasso, "I'm not dressed." He replies, "Certainly not; it's you he wants to see."

Ten minutes later she returns from the salon, quite pale, with a paper in her hand that the gentleman has given her: it's a summons announcing a suit for divorce instigated by Picasso. He's working at his easel and singing *Pagliacci* at the top of his lungs. She packs her bags and goes with their son to live at the Hôtel Californie!

Misia tells us that at the time of the hearing she found it disgusting that no one would testify for Olga. Picasso's lawyer explained to the court that she spent her life throwing vases at his head and never missed a chance to make scenes in public. . . . Misia went to testify for her and to say that she thought her incapable of breaking any dishes. . . .

"But then, Madame, what in your opinion drives her husband to ask for a divorce?"

Just in the nick of time Misia remembered that she was testifying *for* Olga. She had been about to say, "But your honor, simply because she is the most *emmerdante*, the most boring, woman I've ever known."

"What a shame," cries Picasso, "that you didn't say that! You really are unforgivable. You gave false testimony!"

December 21, 1940

Rather sad lunch tête-à-tête with Jean Cocteau. . . . Went with him to see how the work is coming on his tiny apartment in the Palais Royal. . . . I deposited him at Colette's . . . and went to see Jean Marais . . .

At four o'clock called on Coco Chanel, so nice to me that she did me good. She has great hopes that her perfume business will soon be straightened out. Perhaps one day I'll work for her? . . .

December 26, 1940

So convinced of the pointlessness of everything that I don't get up till two in the afternoon. Go to Misia's. She is in bed . . . for the same reason. She claims that we are the first victims of an epidemic: the symptoms will be precisely the refusal to get out of bed.

December 27, 1940

Misia is more beautiful than ever, decked out in all her finery to dine with the Barnses. She is beside herself about the anti-Jewish laws that turn Paris into a prison, the exact negation of what our city is. She is so right!

December 28, 1940

The rumor is still going around that all France is about to be occupied. At last night's dinner at the Barneses', Misia openly confronted an important German official and asked him if it is true. He replied that it is not impossible. . . .

Misia speaks against the narrow concept of the "man of integrity," making a distinction between honesty, which has a precise meaning, and integrity, which has a hollow ring.

Hélène Berthelot tells us a very amusing story about Poincaré, the man of integrity *par excellence.* She went to visit him in Lorraine and dined alone with Poincaré and his wife. The house and the food were monastically simple, as suits a retired man of integrity. For dessert, as they were three, they were served three pieces of fruit: a pear, a peach, and an apple. Hélène Berthelot, being the guest, was served first. She took the peach. Upon which Poincaré burst into tears. . . .

Spent the evening at Misia's with Coco Chanel and François d'Harcourt. Coco goes into a long tirade against the Jews. The conversation is dangerous, given Antoinette's origins and the presence of the duke.* Fortunately she was sidetracked when everyone agreed that Catherine d'Erlanger's emeralds are nothing but bits of green bottles. . . .

Sert's chauffeur drove me home in such blackness that half the time we were on the sidewalk.

New Year's Day, 1941

Thick snow. Paris covered in white: grey-green uniforms everywhere. With its deserted streets—just a few horses and men pushing hand carts—Paris looks like a city in east Prussia.

January 5, 1941

At six o'clock, called on Coco, who sits at the piano and picks out some Bach with two fingers. I find Misia half-asleep. . . . Sert takes the three of us to a sumptuous dinner. A pre-war atmosphere: gypsy orchestra, red banquettes, a chauffeur who knows one—impossible to believe one's eyes. We discuss Jean [Cocteau] at length and I argue about him with Coco. I find it impossible to destroy our friends systematically, the way she does. It makes one squirm. I know she really is very fond of them, but that doesn't prevent her from talking about them as unkindly as possible. I feel I must tell her so.

* The Duc d'Harcourt's wife Antoinette was a Rothschild.

January 8, 1941

Misia has me stay on to dine with Antoinette d'Harcourt, and Coco
Chanel. Despite the lack of food, electricity, and fuel, in three minutes
she runs up an exquisite supper, with candles and a nice fire. A peaceful evening: we spoke only about the Aurics and Louise de Vilmorin.
Fairly neutral territory.

January 11, 1941

At Misia's: she is sad. Sert is going to Spain for two weeks. . . .
We go, Cocteau, Jean Marais, and I, to an all-night pharmacy to
fill a prescription. While it is being made up, we notice a box of soap,
a rare commodity that is not allowed to be sold. After long delibera-
tion, in a bit of a cold sweat, Marais and I decide to steal it. At the
door we show our loot to Jean. From his pocket he produces a tube
of face cream that he has made off with on his own!—
Going home at night on the métro. A nightmare.

January 12, 1941

Strange lunch at [the ballerina] Suzanne Lorcia's with Serge Lifar
and Paul Morand. . . . She has a very expensive apartment and offers
us enormous amounts of caviar, champagne, and truffles, with great
sweetness but in the language of a concierge. Morand [who made no
secret of his pro-Nazi feelings] seems very much at home there. He
pinches the maid's behind, and his favorite cigars are kept for him
in a special drawer. He tells us that Europe will definitely fall to the
Germans. "As of now, the English are already beaten and nothing
will prevent Hitler's supremacy." *Bravo et merci!*
I am terribly far from thinking as he does. Besides, it seems to me
that everything he says smacks of the comfortable opportunism of a
man over fifty who has decided never to lack for anything.
Serge is still in a state of euphoria. He says to me: "The boss is
expecting me in Munich soon." It's Hitler he's referring to.

January 22, 1941

I go to dine with Jean Cocteau. . . . He shows me some great photographs of the old days. I've never seen such a collection: Gide at fif-

teen with long hair *à la* Lamartine . . . Georges Auric and Raymond Radiguet, stark naked in a small clump of reeds. Carpentier at the time of his first communion, in boxing shorts. Marie-Laure coiffed with cherries under a neon light. Misia and Coco in ju-jitsu outfits. Picasso looking romantic with his tall Fernande. The Cocteau family in black stockings, short trousers trimmed with braid, and Irish lace collars . . .

January 24, 1941

I take Serge to lunch at Misia's. One of her good days. Full of ideas. And so seductive! . . .

January 26, 1941

Arriving at Coco's, I overhear astonishing vocal exercises. Two witches with dyed red hair are installed at the piano, one seated, the other leaning on it. Coco is listening like a good pupil to their instruction. She's having a singing lesson.

"It's unbelievable," Misia says to me on the way home. "At fifty-four!—And she seriously thinks that her 'voice' has a future!"

January 27, 1941

Misia is in bed. She tells me she is haunted by the thought that she might die before Sert's return. You can say what you like about her theatricality, her love of publicity, the games she plays, the knowing way she runs her life; but I cannot help admiring, with no reservations, the special kind of love Misia has for Sert. A domestic drama that has lasted for more than thirty years on the same exalted plane, and still means more than those so-called "true loves" that last six months.

February 4, 1941

A "French Gestapo" has been organized that has already made 1,400 arrests. Very promising.

February 6, 1941

What good luck! Sert will be back from Spain in a week and Misia will be herself again.

February 12, 1941

Misia feels we are heroes to remain here now that people are arrested and disappear for no reason whatever.

There were two pleasures that Misia could still enjoy despite her fading vision. One was playing the piano; the other was making miniature trees, like fanciful Japanese bonsai, out of jade and coral. The piano was a private pleasure, sometimes shared with intimates. The trees she sold to rich Americans or gave to friends like Colette, who was having eye problems of her own. Colette describes in the last page of her *Journal Intermittent* how lightly and gallantly Misia carried her near-blindness.

August 15, 1941

Now that she can hardly see, Misia displays the utmost grace in the way she moves about, picks up fragile objects, handles them, avoids the arm of a chair, puts her confident hand on a light switch.

Sometimes she leans forward to look at her feet—her pretty feet!—as if she were at the edge of a brook. In her apartment, all crystal and mother-of-pearl, she seems to see better than we, who are not bold enough to touch the king-fisher feathers, the flowers of semi-precious stone, the little coral trees brought to life by Misia's magically lucid hands.

At my house she guesses where the door knobs are, senses where the edge of the rug is, goes straight to the nicest chair, walks ahead of us down the staircase she has climbed only once. How much more moving than complaints we find her noble coquetry.

Once again, as I have often done, I beg her: "Misia, show your legs." She lifts her skirt on the most beautiful columns that ever supported a woman's torso, allows us to admire them for a moment, then goes to play the piano standing up.

There is an Italian musical term—such as one finds in a Liszt waltz—that is the only adjective to describe the play of her hands: *volteggiando*—flying about.

The day Paris was liberated, Sert invited fifty people to his apartment to see de Gaulle's troops march through the Place de la Concorde on their way to the Arc de Triomphe. Some of the guests watched with joy, others with apprehension. The collaborationists—Lifar, Chanel, and Beaumont—hoped that Sert would work a reverse miracle and protect them from the Free French as effectively as he had protected his liberal and Jewish friends during the Occupation. Dazzled by Sert's magnificent tortoiseshell dining table set with heavy gold platters of ham, sausages, and fresh fruit from Spain, his guests felt the war was truly over. But in the middle of the celebration, the windows began to shatter all about them. It was gunfire from the overly exuberant liberating army. Everyone rushed for cover, hiding under tables and in closets, as bullets, missing them by inches, lodged in the tapestry on the wall behind them. Everyone but Sert, that is, who in his *macho* way stood coolly taking in the sights as he leaned on the balcony he had draped with antique velvet. Misia was lost in admiration. When the fusillade was over, Sert apologized for the inconvenience in his courteous Spanish manner and invited everyone to join him for lunch.

Sert had not been caught by the bullets whizzing around his head, but nonetheless he was a doomed man. Seriously ill with jaundice, he was told by his doctor that only complete rest and a careful diet could cure him. He ignored the warning, went on working obsessively, travelled about Europe, enjoyed his morphine and absinthe, and ate whatever he pleased. Almost to the last day of his life he was climbing ladders to put the last strokes on his murals in Vich. On November 27, 1945, he was dead. Misia, who was on her way down to see him, arrived too late. She had not realized that he was close to death and had lingered in Paris to buy new clothes for the trip. Unable to believe that he was gone, she attended the solemn Spanish mass and saw Sert, garbed in the robes of a Capuchin monk, laid to rest within the walls of the Vich Cathedral, the cathedral he had spent a lifetime decorating. "With him," Misia wrote, "disappeared all my reasons to exist."

Paul Claudel to Misia

Brangues
December 14, 1945

Dear Misia,

Alas, I cannot come to Paris now. Everything is arranged for my trip to Switzerland, and all my plans are made. But at the beginning of February I shall go to Paris and my first visit will be to you. I can gauge by what this disappearance has meant to me what it must mean to you. Now I know what it is to lose a brother.

I did not know that Sert had occupied so large a place in my heart. I wept all night. And then the good Lord, slowly and patiently, in His own way, began to explain things to me, and I in turn should like to explain them to you.

Dear Misia, do you remember the day when I came to lunch at Sert's and he was late? And suddenly he came in with a kind of shimmering light on his face. He had a sheet of paper in his hand. It was the sublime front curtain he had sketched for *Le Soulier de Satin*. His hands were still black with charcoal. And I looked with emotion and respect at those hands from which so many masterpieces have sprung.

And I think now: when he appears before God, when the Holy Virgin presents him to Her Son, he has only to show Him those blackened hands, those worker's hands, those generous hands, those radiant hands, and to say, "This is what I have made of the hands with which You have extended my eyes, my brain, my heart."

Dear Misia, what does it matter after all? We do not have so much longer to live, you and I. Between him and us there is no longer such a distance, such a path to travel, however bitter, however desolate it may be for you; I understand it—poor friend. For the moment, the veil that separates us from him is impenetrable. But we too, thank God, have the faith that has been the strength, the greatness, the light, the *raison d'être* of this beneficent and heroic destiny.

We know that where he is now, there is a greater awareness, a greater love, and a greater need than there has ever been. There is a secret understanding between us and him such as life was unable to give; there is something that, from now on, enables us always to be as one with him. There is a certain profoundly moving radiance of intermingling waves.

May God bless you. I do not ask that He dry your tears. Tears are sweet when one loves.

A bientôt
P. Cl.

This letter from the man Misia ironically called "God the Father" moved her deeply. It had taken a rare spirit, a poet, to understand and condone the tears she shed for a man whom—in a sense—she had lost twenty years before. No one else had appreciated the slavic sweetness of her tears. If those twenty years of tears had been perverse, there was a tenacious truth in them. For this capricious woman—who could take people up with an almost terrifying passion, then drop them with a grimace of boredom—had been faithful to Sert, and to Roussy. Certainly her fidelity was tinged with neurosis, but it had its share of nobility.

In his will Sert left his studio in the Villa de Ségur to his assistants, with instructions to destroy all his paintings and sketches. (As is so often the case, these instructions were ignored.) His property in Spain was left to his sister Dolores, along with one hundred and fifty thousand dollars he had in America—a sum left him by Roussy, who had inherited it from her brother Alexis. The Mdivanis felt, just as they had at the time of Roussy's death, that everything that had once belonged to her was rightfully theirs. Only after prolonged and sordid litigation did Dolores finally receive her money. To Misia, Sert left his apartment at 252 rue de Rivoli with all it contained: the valuable furniture, the equally valuable library, the *objets d'art*, and the paintings, among them El Greco's *San Maurizio*. Spendthrift that he was, Sert had gone through his millions as quickly as he had earned them. It was just this reckless prodigality that Misia had loved in him. That she herself was left with a relatively small amount of money did not worry her. For with her professional antiquarian's eye she saw that the contents of the apartment could keep her comfortably for the rest of her life. In fact, during the next five years she was able to sell one of Sert's grand commodes or Louis XV chairs whenever she felt she needed money. Reverdy had once written her: "Time that passes, dear Misia, is not to be compared with time that lasts." And it was true for her when now, at seventy-three, she installed herself in Sert's Ali Baba's cave—just down the street from the opulent apartment where she had reigned as Madame Edwards, and just around the corner from the *Revue Blanche* "annex" where she had spent her youth with Thadée. In Sert's apartment, time paused mysteriously. Reverdy's "time that passes" and "time that lasts" had become one. The rooms were haunted. Sert's masculine authority and Roussy's infectious gaiety lurked in the shadows. Sert's possessions, once enlivened by his presence, now seemed ominously impersonal. The apartment was a warehouse of memories. There stood the splendid armoire whose price, she recalled, he had lied about so abominably: "part of his game, his pleasure in astonishing me." And there was the regal bed, shrouded in seventeenth-century velvet, that he had shared with Roussy. It was inconceivable to Misia that she should sleep in it. Feeling that she was still an intruder, she quickly chose a small back bedroom for herself and had it done up in pink and black.

Misia knew that she would be lonely in the cavernous stretches of Sert's apartment and invited her niece Mimi to live with her. Mimi had divorced Blacque-Belair and broken with Pierre Brisson, and so she was pleased, in her rather dissatisfied way, to be of practical help to her aunt. Unfortunately, she did not amuse or stimulate Misia; that was left to Boulos, whom Misia inherited along with Sert's apartment. With time running out, Misia was to enjoy one last romantic friendshp. Their *amitié passionnée*, as Boulos called it, was hardly a love affair, but just because it was not, Misia revealed more of herself to him than she had to the men with whom she had been passionately involved. There was great solace in recounting her memories to the strange, exquisite young man who made a cult of her past but was too sensitive to pry into those devious motives of her behavior that she preferred to conceal even from herself. And Boulos was grateful to Misia for her understanding of his tortured emotional state. "I regret more each day that I did not know her before my soul was so sick," Boulos wrote in his journal. "Without upsetting the perilous structure, Misia has already cleared away the litter, the problems I would never have had the courage to attack. I must try not to tire her. . . . I come to her like a patient who stubbornly refuses to say what he's suffering from, won't allow himself to be examined, and pretends to be cured. Easy for the doctor!" Yet, how often he must have smiled to himself while she was dictating her memoirs to him: at her picture of herself as a helpless pawn, trapped between Edwards and Thadée; at her all too human wish to justify herself in the eyes of the world; at the way she so coquettishly lied about her age; at her sly concealment of her worldly ambition and the cruel streak in her nature. Boulos must have known, too, how important the touchstone of memory was to Misia—how in remembering her past she felt again the thrill of the power she had once enjoyed. In the late afternoon when the hours of remembering were over, they would greet the twilight together with the drugs that gave them respite from a present that both found too painful to bear. Boulos would go to the study to transcribe what Misia had said, and would reappear in the evening to read what he had written to Chanel, Mimi, the actress Gabrielle Dorziat, or whichever friends were visiting. And Misia, always capricious, always exigent, would laugh and say, "Oh no! That's not what I meant. That's not it at all!"

Misia often said, "Every woman decides to be either eighteen, thirty, or eighty for life. Unfortunately," she would add, looking fierce, "poor Coco chose to be eighteen, the most difficult age. *I* decided to be thirty." Now that Misia was much closer to eighty than to thirty, she still looked startlingly young. Old friends dropped in at teatime just as they had before the war, and once again Misia's apartment became a place where history and gossip meet. But now conversation was apt to turn most often to politics, and to the uncertain future of the many collaborationists who crowded the apartment. Misia was careful to invite *collaborateurs* and *résistants* on different days. Inevitably, however, their visits sometimes coincided; then with her usual aplomb she simply herded them into different rooms. There were times when Etienne de Beaumont held court in one room while Lady Diana Cooper presided in another. Misia smiled knowingly at the incongruities of post-war life: at the banality of France becoming Americanized; at the adjustments (so like those between the Dreyfusards and their enemies) between patriots and Collaborationists as they made their uneasy peace.

Chanel had taken a German lover during the Occupation and was under a cloud. She had been arrested for a few hours shortly after the Liberation and was still shaken by the experience. Two young liberators dressed in sports shirts and sandals had led her in disgrace through the lobby of the Ritz Hôtel. With snobbish disdain she reported that the most ghastly thing about her arrest was hearing her armed captors say *tu* to the doorman. A few days later the American G.I.'s were buying Chanel No. 5 as avidly as the Germans had during the Occupation. Lifar, who had been made the director of the Paris Opera Ballet under the Germans, still spoke of the golden hours he had spent alone with *der Führer*. "Only two men in my life have caressed me like this," he would say as he ran his hand lasciviously down the arm of the nearest attractive young man, "Diaghilev and Hitler!" As shrewd as he was boastful, he claimed that he had accepted Hitler's invitations to tête-à-têtes in order to assassinate him, not to work for him. "But God stopped my hand when I was ready to strike," he said piously in *Ma Vie*, the book Boulos helped him to write. (As late as 1978 he was still complaining that for ten years after the war, Parisians would cross the street to avoid him when they saw him coming.) Although Misia admired de Gaulle and was eager to meet him, it amused her to hear Beaumont's arrogant views on the changing world. When she asked what he thought of de Gaulle and his Army of Liberation, Beaumont made her guests feel complacently superior to the new democratic ways when he explained: "You know, Misia, in the old days Mother used to invite the common soldiers of the local garrison to our château once a year. Now, *ma chère*, it's the garrison every day."

Misia still made the rounds of the antique shops and went to small dinner parties, though fewer were given in those lean years. Denise Mayer recalls going with her to a concert of the Orchestre du Conservatoire conducted by Charles Munch. Wrapped in her sables in the unheated Théâtre des Champs-Elysées, Misia loudly voiced her disapproval of Munch's interpretation of "her" *Sacre du Printemps*. The audience too reacted coldly, not owing to fear of Misia's opinion, as in the old days, but because of the freezing temperature in the hall. For the sad truth is that Misia was no longer an arbiter of taste. She was no longer the woman who, after the thunderous ovation at the premiere of the imposing Honegger-Claudel oratorio, *Jeanne d'Arc au Bûcher*, had all Paris laughing when she said, "This brings together the three biggest bores in the world, Claudel, Honegger, and Joan of Arc."

In a way, Misia's last visit to her old friend Picasso was her farewell to the avant-garde. Like many an older person, she was convinced that anything she didn't understand lacked quality. For her, Picasso's late works were bad jokes perpetrated on an unsuspecting public.

I wanted to see Picasso in his studio in the rue des Grands-Augustins [Misia recalled in her memoirs]. I crossed the large courtyard of the shabby yet sumptuous house that suited him so well and climbed one of the most beautiful staircases in Paris to reach the floor where he worked. He showed me the lofty rooms with ceilings held up by enormous wooden beams, the little corner where his treasures were kept—small African statues, simple objects carved from materials polished by time—and farther on (with what childish glee), a bathroom with washbasins where boiling-hot water came out as soon as he touched the tap, so that we found ourselves in a steam bath. (He was especially proud of this last detail. . . .)

With the hands that moved me so, he took down some canvasses to put them within sight of my failing eyes. There were dozens and dozens of them. How I should have liked to be able to tell him that I adored them! How happy he would have been to see me carry one off! . . . Alas, in all that he was doing, there was nothing that I could have lived with. I loved him far too much to be able to deceive him about my feelings.

When he saw me out and kissed me at the door, I saw his large, clear eyes cloud over with tears. What wouldn't I have given to be able to say to him: "I adore that painting over there!"

I found myself back in my car, weeping uncontrollably over all that might have been.

With her slavic temperament Misia was not ashamed of tears. "You *should* weep, you *must* weep," she told friends who bore the tragic personal losses of the war with what seemed to her unnatural stoicism.

More and more, Misia confined herself to Paris. Even short excursions were apt to tire her, although she was still endlessly restless. She would visit friends in the country, then leave before dinner with the excuse that country air was too pure for her and that she missed the microbes of Paris. She made one last trip to Venice, the city she "could not live without," for, like Diaghilev at the end of his life, Misia found that the sights and sounds of her youth meant more to her than ever. A photograph taken by Horst in 1947 shows her standing on a boat-landing opposite the Dogana and the Church of Santa Maria della Salute. It is one of Misia's last portraits. Slender, elegantly dressed in white, with heavy clusters of pearls about her throat and her small dog at her feet, she smiles an all-knowing smile of enigmatic tenderness: a tragic muse caught in a wistful moment. Unseen behind her on the right is the Abbazia, the former abbey that Sert decorated for Alexis Mdivani and where he and Roussy had once splendidly lived. To the left, far beyond the Arsenale, lies the Isola di San Michele, the sad little island where Diaghilev is buried—and where Stravinsky would be buried twenty-four years later.

Venice was more than the backdrop for this photograph. Venice, whose light was like the iridescent mother-of-pearl with which Misia surrounded herself; the city whose palaces floated in their own shadows, creating a world of mirrored unreality: Misia's world. Venice, a city of strange complexity: the city she had known she would adore even before she saw it. Fifty years earlier, just before leaving with Thadée for their first trip to Italy, she had written to Vallotton, "I am beside myself especially at the thought of Venice. . . . I dream of serenades, rope ladders, gondolas, and palaces. What will all these dreams lead to?" And then again:

> Our last day in Venice, my dear friend, and I want to devote some of it to those I love. What things, what things we've seen! My dear Vallo! Venice is so much more beautiful, not only than I had imagined, but than anything I believed possible. First, our arrival. I flung myself into a gondola, and just the idea that it was real, that I was really in it, was so overwhelming that it was painful. . . . We spent a week in ecstasy. At times I closed my eyes, unable to bear so much splendor. And at the slightest thing, for no reason at all, I would weep for joy.

On Misia's last day in Venice in 1947 there was no weeping and little joy. Horst recalls how Misia, half blind, led him to her favorite paintings in the Accademia Museum and spoke of them with passion. She remembered details she could no longer see and illuminated their subtle beauties with penetrating awareness. Horst photographed her as she turned away from the arched splendors of a Renaissance painting. Slender, sad, and vulnerable, her mouth drawn down in a thin line of disillusion, Misia looks as though she has seen everything and is ready to make her last farewells. When he led her back to her hotel room, she spread her Italian money on the bed. "Take it," she said. "You will come back to Venice one day. I have no use for it."

If Venice was illusion, Paris was reality. Misia's trip to Venice recalled her lost youth; her return to Paris was a return to old age. It was perhaps now, when the gap between thirty—the age Misia had decided she would always be—and seventy-five, her real age, could no longer be bridged, that her addiction to drugs took full possession of her. The indignities of old age depressed her more and more: constant fatigue, the indifference of the young, falling down in the street and being led home by strangers. And so she began the final descent through drugs to self-destruction. The doses became stronger and more frequent. It was Misia's way of escaping the natural sequence of life, of waylaying the truth with dreams. But drugs could not protect her from the harshness of reality. In 1949 her niece Mimi was killed in an automobile accident on her way back from a christening in

Brussels. Her death left Misia more alone than ever, for Mimi had become an essential part of her life. As she stood at Mimi's grave she knew she had sometimes been cruel to her niece, yet she felt she loved her tenderly.

Getting drugs was dangerous, but Misia took for granted that her privileged position would keep her out of trouble. After all, she was hurting no one but herself. Reckless and impatient, she made no attempt to hide what she was doing. Chatting at dinner parties or wandering through the flea market she would pause to jab a needle right through her skirt. Once in Monte Carlo she walked into a pharmacy and asked for morphine while a terrified Chanel pleaded with her to be more careful. But carefulness was not in Misia's nature, nor could she control her habit. When she answered the door one day, she was confronted by the police. She was under arrest because her name had been found on a drug dealer's list. That night she found herself caged in with drunken whores, derelicts, and fellow addicts. It was the final, the saddest, blow. She who took deference for granted, who wore privilege like a badge, who made her own laws, was reduced to an anonymous cypher, a criminal among criminals. Powerful friends intervened, of course, but Misia spent twenty-four hours in the filthy cell before she was released. She never recovered from the experience. More dependent on morphine than ever, she trembled whenever the doorbell rang. She began to neglect herself, forgetting to eat, dressing carelessly.

Aware of the risks they ran in Paris, Misia and Chanel had for some time been making trips to Switzerland to get the drugs they needed. How the two old friends had changed over the years! Chanel's gamine beauty had turned into simian chic, her shrewdness to vindictiveness. Misia, once full-blown and radiant, had wasted away to thin pessimism and disillusion. Her sunbursts of enthusiasm had disappeared along with her energy. Drugs were like heavy curtains that she drew to shield herself from the light. Yet a stranger who looked at the two women in their train compartment could have guessed little of this. There they sat, deep in talk and laughter, distinguished, elegant, and unimaginably worldly. Habit, that weaver of old friendships, had made them as indispensable to each other as the drugs they were about to buy. But with all the changes in Misia and Chanel, how much like themselves they remained! Chanel was still trying to wrest the crown from Misia, unaware that it was no longer there. She was still sharing her secrets with Misia—and she knew that when Misia died she would never again tell the whole truth. When she was with her fellow collaborationist, Paul Morand, she still criticized Misia's friendships with Jews and homosexuals. She still complained that Misia was a perfidious devourer of people, a parasite of the heart. And she still called her Madame Verdurinsky. But despite her hatred, whenever she needed someone to love, it was to Misia she turned. For her, she told Morand, Misia was all women and all women were in Misia. Then, taking back the love she had given Misia as if it were a platinum cigarette case, she added, "We love people only for their faults; Misia gave me ample reason to love her."

In September 1950, on her return from a trip to Switzerland with Chanel, Misia, exhausted, took to her bed. Early in the morning of Sunday, October 15, her maid telephoned Denise Mayer to tell her that Madame Sert was dying. The priest had already performed the last rites. Madame Mayer went to her immediately. She found Misia very quiet, breathing normally, her mind clear, fully aware that death was coming. *"Tu sais, ce n'est pas beau, la vie,"* Misia said to her; and for a long time afterward, Denise Mayer wondered whether that was Misia's true feeling, that life was not beautiful, or whether she had been trying to be brave, to show no regret about dying. When someone told her that Chanel was on her way, Misia, too weak to cope with Chanel's chatter, sighed and said, "Coco! That will finish me!" Suddenly she turned to Denise and said, "Take something for yourself, something from this room—quick, before she gets here." Madame Mayer's eye fell on a votive offering that hung on the wall beside Misia's bed: a heart-shaped locket with the initial M inscribed in mother-of-pearl. She put it into Misia's hands and said that it was the only thing she wished to have: Misia's heart. Misia pressed her hand and said that she was happy for Denise to have it. Some days later, when Madame Mayer opened the locket, she was startled to find that it contained a photograph of Roussy.

Chanel arrived at the end of the afternoon, along with a few of Misia's other friends. Among them was Paul Claudel.

CLAUDEL'S JOURNAL, OCTOBER 15, 1950

I go to see Misia in Sert's old apartment, rue de Rivoli. She looks astonishingly young. She has fulfilled all her religious duties. Jean Cocteau, whose hands I admire; Chanel, a skeleton; Madame Mayer. She leaves her entire fortune and Sert's as well to ————— —————, who lives with her.

The missing words were Boulos Ristelhueber. Late in the afternoon Misia stopped speaking. Shortly afterward, all the friends left. Gradually Misia's breathing grew weaker and weaker; then, very late at night, it quietly stopped. Early the next morning Coco took charge. With her peasant's respect for death, the high priestess of fashion performed her last rites. She had Misia's body moved to Sert's canopied bed, dismissed everyone from the room, and set to work to make Misia beautiful for the last time. Deftly she arranged Misia's hair, rouged her cheeks, and put on her jewels. When she threw open the doors after an hour, the assembled friends could only gasp in admiration. There was Misia, more beautiful than ever, dressed in white and lying on a bank of white flowers, with a pale-pink satin ribbon across her breast. On the ribbon lay a single pale-pink rose. It was Chanel's last offering of peace and love.

The funeral was held nearby in the Polish church in the rue Cambon. Misia's body was taken to the small country cemetery overlooking the Seine near Valvins, where Mallarmé and Mimi lay buried. It was half a century since Misia, feeling young and immortal, had wept at the grave of her beloved poet—but only a year since, frail and defeated, she had buried her lovely niece. For some years afterward, friends who visited Misia's grave in October always found a fresh pink rose lying on the simple tombstone. Then one day that too disappeared. No one ever discovered who the mysterious mourner was. Could it have been someone who had known Misia when—still Mademoiselle Godebska—she had received a bouquet of flowers from Mallarmé, with a couplet that is like an evanescent symbol of birth and of mortality?

> *Chaque autre fleur ne saurait méconnâitre*
> *Que Misia fit gentiment de naître.*

> *Each other flower cannot help but know*
> *That Misia has been born, and sweetly so.*

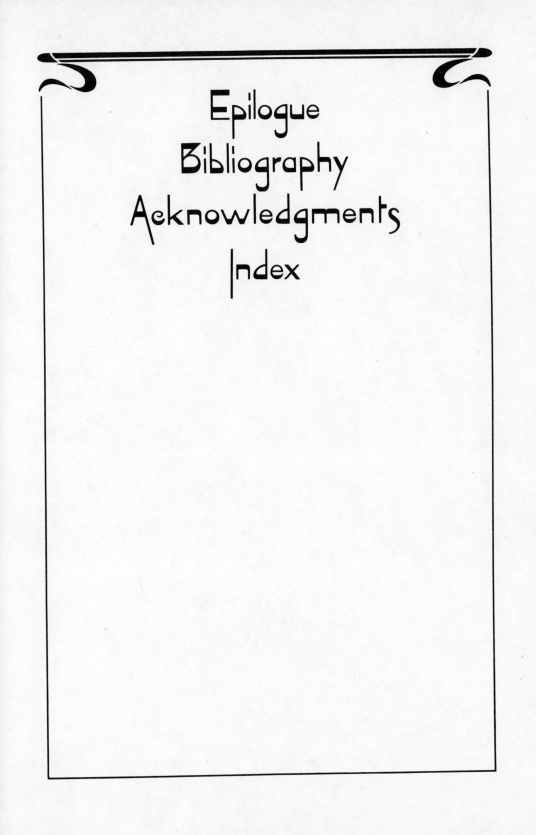

Epilogue

Bibliography

Acknowledgments

Index

Epilogue

IN SEARCH OF MISIA

WE NEVER MET MISIA, although we might easily have done so. Yet it has been our privilege to know many of her friends, some of whom became our friends as well. Most of them shared their memories of Misia with us. Because their testimony has been as valuable a source for our biography as the references to Misia in books, we should like to speak of those people first. As we look back, it seems to us that Misia's path and ours crossed in mysterious ways. It was music that led us into Misia's world: the world of Diaghilev and Stravinsky, of Debussy, Ravel, and *Les Six*, of Vuillard, Renoir, and Toulouse-Lautrec; of that Paris where Proust's tone and resonances still echoed.

In 1946 we were about to give our first two-piano concert in New York, a program that included one of the first performances of Stravinsky's *Sonata for Two Pianos*. The composer had come from California on a visit, and we were eager to play the sonata for him. We went to the apartment of Kyriena Siloti, whose father Alexander Siloti had conducted the first performances of Stravinsky in St. Petersburg. There a very Russian scene awaited us. Seated about the room were the Stravinskys with a dozen of their friends, all of whom had covered their heads with newspapers. As we entered, we too were given newspapers to hold over our heads with one hand while we greeted the guests with the other. The protective covering was welcome, as it was the moment when our hostess's pet birds took their daily hour of free-flying exercise and bathing in bowls of water strategically placed about the room. It was a somewhat spattering experience, one that the Russians enjoyed enormously. When the birds had been coaxed back into their cages, Stravinsky said he was ready to hear the sonata and his two suites of piano duets that he called *Pièces Faciles*. The intensity with which he listened to the music, and his ideas about rhythm and counterpoint struck us with the force of revelation. It was a moving experience for two young musicians to play, for the man they admired above all living composers, the *Trois Pièces Faciles* that he himself had played with Diaghilev in

1915. As Stravinsky was leaving New York before our concert, he suggested we meet again at the apartment of George Balanchine so that he could hear the rest of our program. We began with Satie's *Trois Morceaux en Forme de Poire* (Misia's favorite of Satie's compositions, we learned later, and the work she had him play for Diaghilev in the audition that led to the ballet *Parade*). Our dress rehearsal ended with Vittorio Rieti's *Second Avenue Waltzes*, the music Balanchine used in its orchestral version for his ballet *Waltz Academy*. In addition to the Stravinskys, Balanchine's guests included Rieti and Alexandra Danilova. Thus we found ourselves playing for the choreographer, composer, and prima ballerina of *Le Bal*, a Diaghilev ballet of the late twenties. Later that evening we listened to the first reading of Hindemith's *The Four Temperaments*, music Balanchine had commissioned and subsequently used as the base for a dance masterpiece. As one of Diaghilev's last projects was a Hindemith ballet, when Balanchine invited us to watch rehearsals of *The Four Temperaments* we felt we were assisting at the birth of a brilliant child after the death of its spiritual father.

In the spring of 1948 we sailed for France to spend the first of many long summers in Europe. Our boat train reached Paris at midnight. Early the next morning we telephoned Germaine Tailleferre, the only woman member of *Les Six*. We told her that friends had sent her a package from New York, and she asked us to lunch. When we arrived there was an animated party in progress. It was our first taste of the life that Misia knew: that particularly Parisian mixture of worldly elegance, artistic cultivation, caustic wit, and superb food. The package we were carrying was the score of Virgil Thomson's opera *The Mother of Us All*. After lunch Georges Auric sat at the piano, carefully turned the music upside down, and improvised a Thomsonesque accompaniment while Francis Poulenc "created" the roles. He sang a nonsense-syllable imitation of Gertrude Stein's English in a hilarious falsetto, and was especially compelling in the role of America's pioneer suffragette Susan B. Anthony. Thus on our first day in Paris we were entertained by three of *Les Six*, for whom Misia had done so much. (In the years that followed, these three, as well as Darius Milhaud, not only wrote two-piano music for us but also told us about Misia.) Before we left the party, Madame Tailleferre invited us to drive with her and her daughter to their country house near Grasse. We spent our days rehearsing on the pianos in that house with its view of lavender-covered hills and the sea beyond. It was a curious sensation to read Gide's *Journal* there and to come upon the entry of September 11, 1941, in which he speaks of his joy in playing Chopin on the same pianos. "The other day, alone at Germaine Tailleferre's, while waiting for her, I re-read the delicious sonata in B Flat. . . . How I should like to take up the piano again. . . . What prevents me? . . . My obsessive fear of disturbing the neighbors." Germaine told a different story. Whenever Gide called, she assured him that his musical visits did not inconvenience her in any way. But Gide insisted on being alone with such devious delicacy that Germaine and her family felt obliged to while away the afternoon in Grasse so that the considerate writer could feel he was not disturbing them. At Germaine's suggestion we gave an informal concert at her house for a small group that included several of Misia's friends: among them Marie-Blanche de Polignac and Colette. No sooner had Colette seated herself near the pianos than the cat of the house, with infinite feline wisdom, jumped onto her lap and installed himself there, to her evident satisfaction. Although it did not occur to us to ask Colette about Misia, we find the account of Misia's gallant behavior in *Journal Intermittent* the most touching of all descriptions of her.

Germaine had invited Picasso to her musicale, but he was unable to come and suggested instead that we all visit him the next day in his studio in Vallauris. The bronzed painter welcomed us from the top of the steep wooden ladder that led to the atelier where he was making ceramics. Our conversation was constantly interrupted by the noise of breaking dishes. "Don't be disturbed, it's only the baby," Picasso said, pointing to his infant son Claude, who sat contentedly among the ruins of Picasso plates. With a shrug, his father added, "I can always bake more of them." Germaine and Picasso had been friends in the days of the Ballets Russes, but they had not seen one another for almost twenty years. The painter was struck by the resemblance of Françoise, Germaine's teen-age daughter, to the young Germaine he had last seen. "*You* are the one I recognize," he said to Françoise, then turning to Germaine accusingly, "Not you!" Picasso's outspoken acknowledgment of the passage of time upset him as much as it upset Germaine; nonetheless, he returned to the subject again and again. When he was told that we were musicians, he asked if we knew Stravinsky. We said that we had seen the Stravinskys in New York only a few weeks earlier. "How is he? Is he still composing?" asked the designer of *Pulcinella*. We assured him that Stravinsky had never stopped, that his music was as beautiful as ever. "And Madame Stravinsky, who is she?" Picasso asked. We were taken aback. "Why, she's Madame Stravinsky," we said, "Madame Vera Stravinsky, the same Vera he's been with for years." Picasso seemed startled by such marital constancy. *"Toujours la même Vera!"* he exclaimed. *"Tiens!"*

Thirty years later, in 1978, the "same Vera" Stravinsky put at our disposal the many letters from Misia that her husband had saved. When we dovetailed them with letters from Stravinsky that Misia had saved, they gave us a clearer understanding of the entire *Sacre* contretemps. Vera Stravinsky also allowed us to tape her reminiscences of Diaghilev, Stravinsky, and Misia and gave us permission to quote from *Stravinsky in Pictures and Documents*, the book that she and Robert Craft had just completed. Craft guided us through the Stravinsky archives with meticulous skill, then produced a photograph of Misia and Sert taken by Stravinsky and another of Misia at Diaghilev's funeral. Both are reproduced in this book.

After a summer in Provence we drove back to Paris, stopping on the way at Poulenc's house in the Loire valley to play his two-piano concerto for him. Between the magnificent lunch and the superb dinner, Poulenc sang for us his *Huit Chansons Polonaises (Eight Polish Songs)*. Each of them, he explained, was dedicated to one of the extraordinary Polish women of Paris, Misia and her sister-in-law Ida among them. He told us about Misia's role in bringing young French composers to Diaghilev's attention. Then he sang for us his "Carte Postale," set to words of Apollinaire. It is a melancholy fox-trot dedicated to Madame Cole Porter. In his book *Journal de Mes Mélodies*, Poulenc wrote about this song: "Imperturbable rhythm. Thought of Misia Sert at the piano as painted by Bonnard." Poulenc and the baritone Pierre Bernac gave their first American tour of song recitals that fall and looked us up when they arrived in New York. We spent an amusing evening together—at least, they seemed to be amused when the restaurant we went to served veal kidneys with béarnaise sauce. Stimulated by this unorthodox combination, they agreed to be taken down to Chinatown, then up to the Savoy Ballroom in Harlem to watch the jitterbugging and listen to the jazz. *"La trompette est parfaite!"* Poulenc shouted in approval. The Poulenc-Bernac concerts across America were received with an enthusiasm that was matched by Poulenc's reaction to every aspect of American life. *"J'adore Hollywood!"* he announced to the assembled reporters who met his train. "I want to marry Greta Garbo and live here for the rest of my life." As soon as he returned to Paris he went to see Misia. Many years later Denise Mayer told us that she had happened to call on Misia at the same time and found her helpless with laughter at Poulenc's stories. "You must listen to this," Misia said. "He's just discovered America."

During our memorable first stay in France, the Comtesse de Polignac suggested that we rehearse on the piano in her music room whenever we were in Paris. (Her house in the rue Barbet-de-Jouy was across the street from Sert's first studio, where he had entertained Colette in the early 1900s.) Each morning promptly at ten, the butler appeared to ask if we would like a glass of champagne. He seemed bemused by our prim refusals. Before lunch the countess would look in and ask us to play for her. Then one of us would join her in a Schubert piano duet or accompany her in songs of Debussy and Fauré. It was an inspiring house to work in. The manuscript of the Poulenc two-piano concerto (dedicated to Marie-Blanche's "Aunt Winnie") was available in the study adjoining the music room. The dining room was decorated with Bérard murals, the library was filled with paintings by Renoir, and the music room itself contained magnificent Vuillard portraits of Marie-Blanche and her mother Jeanne Lanvin. During the eight Sunday evenings we spent in that room in September and October 1948 (and the many "Sundays" in later years), we performed for *le Tout-Paris musical.* "Who would you like to meet?" Marie-Blanche would ask. "Louise de Vilmorin? Jules Supervielle?" Although the Aurics, Poulenc, and Henri Sauguet were "regulars," it never seems to have occurred to anyone to invite Misia. Perhaps she was already too unwell. (Marie-Blanche's privately—and posthumously—published *Souvenirs d'Edouard Vuillard* gave us a most helpful impression of what it must have been like for a beautiful young woman to pose for that sensitive master.) When we returned to give our first public concert in Paris in June 1949, Poulenc appeared backstage. "*Je vous couvre de merde,*" he said in an exaggeratedly extravagant version of the French "Good luck." To our great delight he re-appeared at the intermission and announced that he would write a two-piano sonata for us. After the concert we were given a supper party by Edmonde Charles-Roux. Did she know then that she would write a biography of Chanel? Certainly it never occurred to us that one day we would write about Chanel's friend Misia. But in retrospect it almost seems as though the long arm of coincidence crooked its finger and beckoned us in Misia's direction.

That summer we rented a villa on the island of Ischia, a house we shared with the poet and dance critic Edwin Denby. Our talks when the day's work was done, and his analyses of ballet, gave us new insights into the heritage of Diaghilev. Although we had been told that pianos could easily be rented in Naples and shipped across the bay, there were none available. The owner of the villa said, "The postmistress has a small upright, and the German baroness who lives nearby might agree to let you have her grand. I've arranged for you to have tea with her." After an exchange of visits, the baroness said she would be happy to help us. She seemed less disturbed than we when her piano was dismantled and carried up the steep, rocky path to the villa on the back of a donkey. Not until we began to write this book many years later did it occur to us that she was the same Baroness Stohrer whom Sert had wanted to marry in the last year of his life, and that in 1949 we had been preparing concerts on the piano of the woman who had been Misia's rival for Sert's affections only four years earlier!

In October 1952 we began a tour of European concerts in Paris with music by two of Diaghilev's composers in two theatres where the Ballets Russes had performed. First we played Poulenc's two-piano concerto at the Sarah Bernhardt theatre, and the next evening in the Théâtre des Champs-Elysées we presented a concerto Vittorio Rieti had written for us. We were staying at the Hôtel du Quai Voltaire, and it was at a bookstall on the Seine, almost directly opposite Misia's old apartment, that we found the book of memoirs which has been our most important source: *Misia par Misia*. Like so many others, we fell under Misia's spell. Now we began to question our French friends in earnest. "I regret that I never took you to see her," Poulenc said. We regretted it more than he. When we left for concerts in Barcelona, both the Comtesse de Polignac and the Aurics gave us letters to their friends Alberto and Margarita Puig-Palau. "They're wonderful," Marie-Blanche assured us. "They travel with their gypsies." In fact the hospitable Spaniards arranged a private flamenco performance for us that lasted till dawn. Then they invited us to come with them to their house by the sea. It was none other than the Mas Juny, the villa that Sert had created for Roussy. It was through the Aurics too that we met Jean Cocteau, who seemed to us the quicksilver epitome of charm and elegance. Cocteau asked us to record the musical background for a film he planned to make: We would improvise jazz variations on the song "Japanese Sandman"—or rather one endless variation that with hypnotic monotony would serve as the sound track for the entire film. Reluctantly we confessed that we had no gift for jazz. "But you're Americans, aren't you?"

was his thunderstruck reply. It was rather satisfying to us that in this small way we had managed to "astonish" Jean. (In 1954, however, we did participate in a film, another thread connecting us to Misia. It was a documentary about Darius Milhaud. Following a sequence in which Milhaud and Paul Claudel discussed their artistic collaboration, we appeared to greet the poet, then quite old, and the composer as representatives of "young musical America.") Cocteau spoke to us of Misia, and suggested that we read the novel and the play he had written about her. These works, *Thomas l'Imposteur* and *Les Monstres Sacrés*, were to provide us with vivid fictional portraits of Misia. (Years later we were received at Cocteau's house in Milly-la-Forêt by his heir Edouard Dermit, who put the Cocteau archive with its many letters to and from Misia at our disposal.) Georges Auric, sensing our disappointment at not being able to work with Cocteau, offered to write a partita for two pianos, and it was through that composition that we first saw Misia's nephew. For after the premiere of the Auric *Partita* at Aix-en-Provence, Misia's friends Charles and Marie-Laure de Noailles invited us to stay with them at their château in Hyères. It was there that we met Jean Godebski, the child for whom Ravel had written *Ma Mère l'Oye*. Jean seemed to us a most romantic character, a painter who lived in the Camargue and rode wild horses.

Misia kept us company on our travels, for wherever we went there she was, looking at us from the walls of the local museum, or in private collections. Paintings of Misia can be seen in Paris, New York, London, Lyons, Los Angeles, and Leningrad; in Berne, Brussels, Dresden, Karlsruhe, Zurich, and Tel Aviv; in Fort Worth, Houston, Norfolk, Palm Beach, San Diego, and Merion, Pennsylvania. Through the years we found more and more passages about Misia in the books we read, but it was not until 1974 that we decided to write the story of her life. We spent three winters in Paris looking for the material we needed. Francis Steegmuller, whose biography of Cocteau provided us with invaluable source material, sent us to see Jenny Bradley. This extraordinary woman has known almost every important literary figure in Paris since the days when Anatole France would take her, then a little girl, to the Louvre on Sunday afternoons. We spent many hours with Madame Bradley, who knew Thadée as well as Misia. She gave us her copy of Misia's unpublished chapter on Chanel and a passport picture that Misia claimed was her favorite photograph of herself. It was Madame Bradley who told us that we must see Jacques Porel, Réjane's son, and read his memoirs.

In the winter of 1975 Porel came to lunch with us at the apartment of our friend Alice Delamar, at the corner of the rue Gît-le-Coeur and the quai des Grands Augustins. He took advantage of the unseasonably warm weather to walk from his flat in the rue Cambon. The handsome eighty-two-year-old gentleman, who wore his hat in the jaunty manner of the Belle Epoque, was visibly moved as he pointed at a bridge on the Seine and said, "The last time I walked across the Pont Neuf was seventy years ago, after a cruise on Misia's boat which was always moored there, on the quai des Orfèvres." We are grateful to Porel for allowing us to quote the description of that trip from his book *Fils de Réjane,* and for the picture he evoked of the passion that Misia inspired in the heart of a twelve-year-old boy. Alice Delamar suggested that we interview her friend Bettina Bergery, for Bettina and her husband Gaston had been close to Roussy and Sert. An extraordinary *raconteuse,* Bettina gave us a vivid idea of Vichy France as well as of the relations between Misia and Roussy. As Gaston Bergery had been Misia's lawyer, we were able to study Misia's passports and her last will.

When we were asked to present a series of concerts in the Théâtre de la Ville, we invited many of the people who had known Misia. It was there that we first saw Misia's niece Annette Vaillant, the daughter of Thadée's younger brother, Alfred Natanson. Our many talks with her, together with her enchanting memoirs *Le Pain Polka,* have been our most reliable source for information about the remarkable Natanson family. With unparalleled generosity Annette Vaillant made it possible for us to re-photograph many of the sensitive pictures her father took, developed, and printed of Misia, Thadée, and their families and friends in Villeneuve-sur-Yonne. But no one was more helpful to us than Denise Mayer, who went to endless trouble and took great pains to help us understand Misia, to introduce us to Misia's friends whom we did not know, and to find the book or article that might supply a missing bit of information. She went with us to visit Misia's houses: Le Relais at Villeneuve-sur-Yonne and La Grangette at Valvins. Together we made a pilgrimage to the cemetery of Samoreau to see the graves of Misia, Mimi, and Mallarmé. One day Denise Mayer said, "It would be interesting for you to speak to Madame Simone, the actress who created the role of Misia in Alfred Savoir's play *Maria.* But she is ninety-eight; I shall see." The next day Denise reported that she had telephoned to ask Madame Simone if she would be too tired to receive us. The actress replied, "Why should I be tired? Forty of my pupils are coming to see me at four o'clock. Let your friends come at six." We thought a long interview would be an imposition and took along only one short reel for our cassette recorder. Madame Simone was reclining on a chaise longue when we entered her room. She was slender, blonde, blue-eyed, and beautiful. She spoke with the precise diction of an actress trained in an earlier time—and she spoke without pause for almost three hours. She told us that she was one of the few people left who had known Misia eighty years before. But she had never forgiven her for the fact that Misia's first husband had sold *her* first husband shares in that worthless mine in Hungary. And she felt impelled to add, in a whispered confidence that had the faded perfume of stale theatrical gossip, "Misia was never any good in bed."

Misia had made Boulos her principal heir, and he in turn had left everything to a painter friend now known as Paul Uldace. No one could tell us where he was, except that he had left Paris and was living in the country somewhere. We hoped that he might have letters, documents, or photographs that had belonged to Misia, but he was nowhere to be found. Through an elaborate chain of circumstances we met Lilian Grumbach, who had been Chanel's assistant. With great sensitivity she told us her impressions of Chanel and Misia, and she also found a snapshot of them together. A week before we were to return to New York at the end of the third winter of our Parisian research, she telephoned for our advice about a collection of Chanel clothes she had inherited that she felt belonged in a museum. As Diana Vreeland, the special consultant to the Costume Institute of the Metropolitan Museum of New York, had just arrived in Paris, we took her to see the collection. It was fascinating to see Mrs. Vreeland's expert inspection of clothes that Chanel had designed and sewn herself for her own wear. Lilian Grumbach's brother, the actor Christian Marquand, was there that afternoon, and on hearing that we had not been able to locate Misia's heir said that Paul Uldace was his close friend and would be arriving in Paris that evening. Even so, there were difficulties in reaching Uldace, and we missed a hard-won appointment by our own carelessness. He granted us a second appointment, however, at the studio of his friend Mara Rucki, and we were determined not to keep them waiting. We decided to leave half an hour before it was necessary and sit in a café till the time of our rendezvous. We did not know that the President of Syria was expected to arrive in Paris during the afternoon or that there had been threats to assassinate him. Well ahead of time, we set out for the cab stand in the Place St.

Michel which usually had a line of taxis waiting. To our horror, there were a hundred people waiting for cabs and none in sight. The police were putting up roadblocks at the intersections. Then the woman at the head of the queue, a piano teacher who had heard our concerts, introduced herself and offered to share the first taxi with us. "It's not exactly in the same direction," she said when we told her where we were going, "but if you drop me first at least you'll have a cab. If you go to the end of the line you'll never get anywhere." We accepted gratefully and a few minutes later we were in a taxi, slowly creeping along in the wrong direction. The police barricades had produced a traffic jam that was historic, even for Paris. We arrived at Madame Rucki's exactly one hour late, convinced that Uldace would no longer be waiting. When we apologized he cut us short. He too had been out in the traffic. We spent a pleasant hour with them. Uldace had never known Misia, but he was able to tell us about Boulos. When we thanked him for his kindness and prepared to leave, he said, "But don't you want to see what I've brought?" He disappeared for a moment, then produced a large carton. "Take this. It's for you." He opened the box to show us what was in it: a copy of Misia's chapter on Chanel; Boulos' wartime diary of 1940–1941; old photographs of Misia and her circle; and letters— letters to Misia (and some to Sert) from Colette and Marie Laurencin, Gide and Stravinsky, Ravel and Valéry, Vuillard and Bonnard, Alexis Léger, Jean Cocteau, and Marcel Proust—a treasury of letters. To our question, "What can we do to thank you?" Monsieur Uldace replied, "Nothing. Just try to write a good book."

If this biography can in any way be called a good book, we can only say that it is owing to the extraordinary generosity, not only of Paul Uldace and of Boulos' sister Marie-Louise Ristelhueber, but of the many, many friends of Misia who gave us their time, their thought, and their confidence.

Bibliography

Fictional Accounts of Episodes in Misia's Life

BRISSON, PIERRE. *Le Lierre* (Paris: Gallimard, 1935).

COCTEAU, JEAN. *Thomas l'Imposteur* (Paris: Gallimard, 1923).

———. *Les Monstres Sacrés* in *Théâtre*, Volume II (Paris: Gallimard, 1948).

MIRBEAU, OCTAVE, WITH THADÉE NATANSON. *Le Foyer* (Paris: Fasquelle, 1909).

SAVOIR, ALFRED. *Maria* in *Comédies de Notre Temps* (Paris: Gallimard, 1938).

Other Works

ACTON, HAROLD. *Memoirs of an Aesthete, 1939–1969* (London: Methuen, 1948).

AGHION, MAX. *Hier à Paris* (Paris: Marchot, 1947).

ANTONA-TRAVERSI, CAMILLO. *Réjane* (Paris: Le Calame, 1930).

ARNAUD, NOËL. *Alfred Jarry d'Ubu Roi au Docteur Faustroll* (Paris: Table Ronde, 1974).

ARWAS, VICTOR. *Félicien Rops* (London: Academy Editions, 1972; New York: St. Martin's Press, 1973).

BARBIER, CARL PAUL. *Documents Stéphane Mallarmé*, Volume IV (Paris: Librairie Nizet, 1973).

BAUDELAIRE, CHARLES. *Le Peintre de la Vie Moderne* in *Oeuvres Complètes* (Paris: Gallimard, 1954).

BERTIN, PIERRE. *Le Théâtre et (Est) Ma Vie* (Paris: Le Belier, 1971).

BILLY, ANDRÉ. *L'Epoque 1900* (Paris: Tallandier, 1951).

BLANCHE, JACQUES-EMILE. *Cahiers d'un Artiste: Deuxième Série, Novembre 1914–Juin 1915* (Paris: Gallimard, 1916).

———. *La Pêche aux Souvenirs* (Paris: Flammarion, 1949).

BUCKLE, RICHARD. Catalogue, *The Diaghilev Exhibition* (Edinburgh: McLagan and Cumming, 1954).

———. *Nijinsky* (London: Weidenfeld and Nicolson, 1971).

———. *Diaghilev* (New York: Atheneum, 1979).

BUGUET, HENRY, WITH EDMOND BENJAMIN. *L'Univers dans Paris* (Paris: Marpon and Flammarion, 1889).

BURNAND, ROBERT. *La Vie Quotidienne en France de 1870 à 1900* (Paris: Hachette, 1947).

———. *Paris 1900* (Paris: Hachette, 1951).

CABANNE, PIERRE. *Pablo Picasso: His Life and Times*, translated by Harold J. Salemson (New York: Morrow, 1977).

CASTELLANE, BONI DE. *L'Art d'Etre Pauvre* (Paris: Crès, 1925).

CASTILLO, ALBERTO DEL, WITH A. CIRICI PELLICER. *José Maria Sert: Su Vida y Su Obra* (Barcelona: Editorial Argos, 1949).

CHANEL, PIERRE. *Album Cocteau* (Paris: Tchou, 1970).

CHARLES-ROUX, EDMONDE. *Chanel* (New York: Knopf, 1975). Originally published as *L'Irrégulière* (Paris: Grasset, 1974).

CHASTENET, JACQUES. *La Belle Epoque* (Paris: Fayard, 1949).

CLAUDEL, PAUL. *Journal*, Volume I: 1904–1932; Volume II: 1933–1955 (Paris: Gallimard, 1968, 1969).

COLETTE [SIDONIE GABRIELLE CLAUDINE COLETTE]. *Journal Intermittent* (Paris: Hachette, 1950).

———. *Earthly Paradise*, compiled from autobiographical writings by Robert Phelps, translated by Herma Briffault and others (New York: Farrar, Straus and Giroux, 1966).

COSSART, MICHAEL DE. *The Food of Love: Princess Edmond de Polignac and Her Circle* (London: Hamish Hamilton, 1978).

EMMANUEL, MARTHE. *Charcot: Navigateur Polaire* (Paris: Editions des Loisirs, 1943).

FOUQUIÈRES, ANDRÉ DE. *Mon Paris et Ses Parisiens*, Volumes I–V (Paris: Pierre Horay, 1953, 1954, 1955, 1956, 1959).

GERMAIN, ANDRÉ. *Les Fous de 1900* (Geneva and Paris: La Palatine, 1954).

GHEUSI, P.-B. *Cinquante Ans de Paris* (Paris: Plon, 1939).

GIDE, ANDRÉ. *Journal*, Volume I: 1889–1939; Volume II: 1939–1942 (Paris: Gallimard, 1948, 1946).

GODEBSKA-BLACQUE-BELAIR, MARIE. "Quelques Souvenirs Intimes sur Ravel," *La Revue Musicale*, December 1938.

GONCOURT, EDMOND, AND JULES DE. *Journal*, Volume III: 1879–1890; Volume IV: 1891–1896 (Paris: Fasquelle and Flammarion, 1956).

GOUDEKET, MAURICE. *Close to Colette*, translated by Enid McLeod (New York: Farrar, Straus and Cudahy, 1957).

———. *The Delights of Growing Old*, translated by Patrick O'Brian (New York: Farrar, Straus and Giroux, 1966).

GREGH, FERNAND. *L'Age d'Or* (Paris: Grasset, 1947).

GRIGORIEV, SERGE L. *The Diaghilev Ballet* (London: Constable, 1953; Harmondsworth, Essex: Penguin, 1960).

GUILBERT, YVETTE. *La Chanson de Ma Vie* (Paris: Grasset, 1927).

GUISAN, GILBERT, AND DORIS JAKUBEC. *Félix Vallotton: Lettres et Documents*, Volumes I and II (Lausanne and Paris: Bibliothèque des Arts, 1973–1974).

————. *Félix Vallotton, Edouard Vuillard, et Leurs Amis de la Revue Blanche* (*Etude de Lettres*) (Lausanne and Paris: Bibliothèque des Arts, 1975).

HAEDRICH, MARCEL. *Coco Chanel: Her Life, Her Secrets* (Boston: Little, Brown, 1972).

HARDING, JAMES. *The Ox on the Roof* (London: Macdonald, 1972).

HAUSSER, ELISABETH. *Paris au Jour le Jour* (Paris: Editions de Minuit, 1968).

HELL, HENRI. *Poulenc* (Paris: Plon, 1958).

HUGO, JEAN. *Avant d'Oublier* (Paris: Fayard, 1976).

HUISMAN, PHILIPPE, AND M. G. DORTU. *Lautrec by Lautrec* (New York: Viking Press, 1964).

JACKSON, A. B. *La Revue Blanche* (Paris: Minard, 1960).

JANKÉLÉVITCH, VLADIMIR. *Ravel* (Paris: Editions du Seuil, 1956).

JOURDAN-MORHANGE, HÉLÈNE. *Ravel et Nous* (Paris: Editions du Milieu du Monde, 1945).

JULLIAN, PHILIPPE. "Reine de Paris Pendant 40 Ans: Misia," *Le Crapouillot,* Winter 1973.

KARSAVINA, TAMARA. *Theatre Street* (New York: Dutton, 1931; reprinted 1950).

KESSLER, COUNT HARRY. *The Diaries of a Cosmopolitan, Count Harry Kessler, 1918–1937* (London: Weidenfeld and Nicolson, 1971). Published in the United States as *In the Twenties: The Diaries of Harry Kessler* (New York: Holt, Rinehart and Winston, 1971).

KIHM, JEAN JACQUES, WITH ELIZABETH SPRIGGE AND HENRI C. BÉHAR. *Jean Cocteau: L'Homme et les Miroirs* (Paris: Table Ronde, 1968).

KOCHNO, BORIS. *Diaghilev and the Ballets Russes* (New York: Harper & Row, 1970).

LARIONOV, MICHEL. *Diaghilev et les Ballets Russes* (Paris: Bibliothèque des Arts, 1970).

LECLERCQ, PAUL. *Autour de Toulouse-Lautrec* (Paris: Floury, 1921).

LE GALLIENNE, RICHARD. *The Romantic Nineties* (London: Putnam, 1925, new edition 1951).

LEMONNIER, CAMILLE. *Félicien Rops* (Paris: Floury, 1908).

LÉVESQUE, JACQUES-HENRY. *Alfred Jarry* (Paris: Seghers, 1963).

LIFAR, SERGE. *Chez Diaghilev* (Paris: Albin Michel, 1949).

————. *Ma Vie* (Paris: Julliard, 1965).

————. *Ma Vie* (Cleveland: World Publishing, 1970).

————. "Misia," *La Nouvelle Revue des Deux Mondes,* March 1975).

LUGNÉ-POË, AURÉLIEN. *La Parade: Souvenirs et Impressions de Théâtre,* Volume I: *Le Sot du Tremplin*; Volume II: *Acrobaties*; Volume III: *Sous les Etoiles* (Paris: Gallimard, 1930, 1931, 1933).

MALLARMÉ, STÉPHANE. *Oeuvres Complètes* (Paris: Gallimard, 1945).

MAYEN, MAURICE. *Le Yacht Mystérieux: La Mort de Lantelme* (Paris: Editions Astéria, 1911).

MEYER, MICHAEL. *Ibsen* (Garden City, N.Y.: Doubleday, 1971).

MILHAUD, DARIUS. *Notes Without Music* (New York: Knopf, 1953). Originally published as *Notes sans Musique* (Paris: Julliard, 1949).

MITCHELL, YVONNE. *Colette: A Taste for Life* (New York: Harcourt Brace Jovanovich, 1975).

MONDOR, HENRI. *Vie de Mallarmé* (Paris: Gallimard, 1941).

MORAND, PAUL. *1900* (Paris: Flammarion, 1931).

———. *Journal d'un Attaché d'Ambassade* (Paris: Gallimard, 1963).

———. *Venises* (Paris: Gallimard, 1971).

———. *L'Allure de Chanel* (Paris: Hermann, 1976).

MYERS, ROLLO H. *Erik Satie* (London: Dennis Dobson, 1948; New York: Dover, 1968).

———. *Ravel* (London: Duckworth, 1960).

NATANSON, THADÉE. *Peints à Leur Tour* (Paris: Albin Michel, 1948).

NATTIER-NATANSON, EVELYN. *Les Amitiés de la Revue Blanche et Quelques Autres* (Vincennes: Editions du Donjon, 1959).

NIJINSKY, VASLAV. *Journal* (Paris: Gallimard, 1953).

PAINTER, GEORGE D. *Marcel Proust*, Volumes I and II (New York: Random House, 1978).

PENROSE, ROLAND. *Picasso: His Life and Work* (London: Gollancz, 1958).

POLIGNAC, COMTESSE JEAN DE. "Edouard Vuillard," in *Hommage à Marie-Blanche, Comtesse Jean de Polignac* (Monaco: Jaspard, Polus et Cie., 1965).

PONIATOWSKI, PRINCE ANDRÉ. *D'un Siècle à l'Autre* (Paris: Presses de la Cité, 1948).

POREL, JACQUES. *Fils de Réjane: Souvenirs*, Volume I: 1895–1920; Volume II: 1920–1950 (Paris: Plon, 1951, 1952).

POUGY, LIANE DE. *Mes Cahiers Bleus* (Paris: Plon, 1977).

POULENC, FRANCIS. *Entretiens avec Claude Rostand* (Paris: Julliard, 1954).

———. *Moi et Mes Amis: Confidences Recueillies par Stéphane Audel* (Geneva and Paris: La Palatine, 1963).

———. *Journal de Mes Mélodies* (Paris: Grasset, 1964).

———. *Correspondance*, collected and edited by Hélène de Wendel (Paris: Editions du Seuil, 1967).

PROUST, MARCEL. *Remembrance of Things Past: Cities of the Plain, The Captive* (New York: Random House, 1927; Vintage Books, 1970).

———. *Lettres à Reynaldo Hahn* (Paris: Gallimard, 1956).

RACHILDE [MARGUERITE VALLETTE]. *Alfred Jarry ou Le Surmâle de Lettres* (Paris: Grasset, 1928).

RADIGUET, RAYMOND. *Le Bal du Comte d'Orgel* (Paris: Gallimard, 1924). Published in the United States as *Count d'Orgel*, translated by Violet Schiff (New York: Grove Press, 1953).

RAYNAUD, ERNEST. *En Marge de La Mêlée Symboliste* (Paris: Mercure de France, 1936).

RENARD, JULES. *Journal, 1887–1910* (Paris: Gallimard, 1965).

RENOIR, JEAN. *Renoir, My Father*, translated by Randolph and Dorothy Weaver (Boston: Little, Brown, 1962).

Revue Blanche, La, 1891–1903.

ROGER-MARX, CLAUDE. *Vuillard: His Life and Work* (London: Paul Elek, 1946).

RUSSELL, JOHN. *Edouard Vuillard: 1868–1940* (London: Thames and Hudson, 1971).

RZEWUSKI, ALEX CESLAS. *A Travers l'Invisible Cristal* (Paris: Plon, 1976).

SALOMON, JACQUES, WITH ANNETTE VAILLANT. "Vuillard et Son Kodak," *Vuillard Exhibition Catalogue* (Paris: L'Oeil, 1963).

———. *Vuillard* (Paris: Gallimard, 1968).

SEROFF, VICTOR I. *Debussy: Musician of France* (New York: Putnam, 1956; Milan: Nuova Accademia, 1960).

SERT, MISIA. *Misia par Misia* (Paris: Gallimard, 1952).

SHATTUCK, ROGER. *The Banquet Years* (Garden City, N.Y.: Doubleday/Anchor, 1961).

SOKOLOVA, LYDIA. *Dancing for Diaghilev*, edited by Richard Buckle (London: John Murray, 1960).

STEEGMULLER, FRANCIS. *Cocteau* (Boston: Little, Brown, 1970).

STRAVINSKY, IGOR, AND ROBERT CRAFT. *Memories and Commentaries* (Garden City, N.Y.: Doubleday, 1960).

———. *Expositions and Developments* (Garden City, N.Y.: Doubleday, 1962).

STRAVINSKY, VERA, AND ROBERT CRAFT. *Stravinsky in Pictures and Documents* (New York: Simon and Schuster, 1978).

STUCKENSCHMIDT, H. H. *Maurice Ravel: Variations on His Life and Work*, translated by Samuel R. Rosenbaum (Philadelphia: Chilton, 1968).

TERRASSE, ANTOINE. *Pierre Bonnard* (Paris: Gallimard, 1967).

VAILLANT, ANNETTE. *Bonnard*, translated by David Britt (Greenwich, Conn.: New York Graphic Society, 1965).

———. "*Les Amitiés de la Revue Blanche*," in *La Revue Blanche Exhibition Catalogue* (Paris: Maeght, 1966).

———. *Le Pain Polka* (Paris: Mercure de France, 1974).

VEBER, PIERRE. "Une Génération: Souvenirs," *La Revue de France*, Numbers 15–17, July, August, September, 1936.

WALEFFE, MAURICE DE. *Quand Paris Etait un Paradis* (Paris: Denoël, 1947).

Acknowledgments

WE THANK THE FOLLOWING publishers and individuals for permission to quote from the works listed below:

BIBLIOTHÈQUE DES ARTS: Gilbert Guisan and Doris Jakubec, *Félix Vallotton: Lettres et Documents*, and *Félix Vallotton, Edouard Vuillard, et Leurs Amis de la Revue Blanche*.

FARRAR, STRAUS & GIROUX, INC., AND PETER OWEN LTD.: Selections from *The Imposter* by Jean Cocteau. Translation by Dorothy Williams. Copyright © 1957 by The Noonday Press, Inc., now a division of Farrar, Straus & Giroux, Inc. Also published by Peter Owen Ltd., London. Reprinted by permission of Farrar, Straus & Giroux, Inc., and Peter Owen Ltd.

FAYARD: Jean Hugo, *Avant d'Oublier*.

FLAMMARION: Jacques-Emile Blanche, *La Pêche aux Souvenirs*.

GALLIMARD: Charles Baudelaire, *Le Peintre de la Vie Moderne*; Pierre Brisson, *Le Lierre*; Paul Claudel, *Journal*; Jean Cocteau, *Thomas l'Imposteur*, © Editions Gallimard 1923, and *Les Monstres Sacrés*, © Editions Gallimard 1949; André Gide, *Journal*, © Editions Gallimard 1939; Aurélien Lugné-Poë, *La Parade: Souvenirs et Impressions de Théâtre*; Stéphane Mallarmé, *Oeuvres Complètes*; Henri Mondor, *Vie de Mallarmé*; Paul Morand, *Journal d'un Attaché d'Ambassade*, and *Venises*; Vaslav Nijinsky, *Journal*; St. John Perse, *Oeuvres Complètes*, © Editions Gallimard 1973; Marcel Proust, *A la Recherche du Temps Perdu* and *Lettres à Reynaldo Hahn*, © Editions Gallimard 1956; Jules Renard, *Journal*; Alfred Savoir, *Maria*; Misia Sert, *Misia par Misia*.

HERMANN: Paul Morand, *L'Allure de Chanel*.

JOHN MURRAY: Lydia Sokolova, *Dancing for Diaghilev* (edited by Richard Buckle).

LIBRAIRIE NIZET: Carl Paul Barbier, *Documents Stéphane Mallarmé*.

PLON: Jacques Porel, *Fils de Réjane*; Liane de Pougy, *Mes Cahiers Bleus*.

Index

ABOUT THE AUTHORS

Arthur Gold died in 1990, shortly before the completion of
The Divine Sarah: A Life of Sarah Bernhardt. With his partner,
Robert Fizdale, he formed the celebrated piano duo that gave
concerts throughout the world for nearly forty years.